Justice, Memory and Redress in Romania

Justice, Memory and Redress in Romania:

New Insights

Edited by

Lavinia Stan and Lucian Turcescu

Cambridge Scholars Publishing

Justice, Memory and Redress in Romania: New Insights

Edited by Lavinia Stan and Lucian Turcescu

This book first published 2017

Cambridge Scholars Publishing

Lady Stephenson Library, Newcastle upon Tyne, NE6 2PA, UK

British Library Cataloguing in Publication Data
A catalogue record for this book is available from the British Library

ISBN (10): 1-4438-3152-2
ISBN (13): 978-1-4438-3152-9

TABLE OF CONTENTS

LIST OF ILLUSTRATIONS

LIST OF TABLES

INTRODUCTION

LAVINIA STAN

Transitional justice has attracted increased attention since the term first described state and society efforts to come to terms with past human rights abuses. In 1989, Central and Eastern Europe joined the growing number of regions interested in reckoning with their recent past with the help of a wide range of practices, programs, and methods. Whereas the practical experience of post-communist countries with transitional justice has been extremely rich, the academic literature has paid attention primarily to selected reckoning methods, countries and themes. Indeed, methods like the vetting, screening or lustration of governmental structures, court trials against former communist officials, and access to secret archives compiled on ordinary citizens by the secret police forces have attracted significantly more attention than commemorations, truth commissions, property restitution, or compensation packages. Similarly, the states that have engaged in sustained reckoning with the recent past (in particular, Germany, the Czech Republic, and Poland) have come under closer scrutiny than countries which have adopted only limited post-communist transitional justice (Albania, Bulgaria or Romania) or have done almost nothing to rectify past human rights abuses (Belarus or the former Soviet republics of Central Asia). At the same time, the literature that examines truth and justice greatly outpaces studies on reconciliation, a transitional justice goal which remains poorly understood in terms of its role and limitations in post-dictatorial contexts. The outcome of this preferential selection of cases has been the uneven mapping of reckoning efforts in post-communist Central and Eastern Europe, with important theoretically driven questions remaining largely unanswered and some empirically rich cases being systematically overlooked.

To address some of these gaps, the proposed volume looks closely at Romania, a country that has remained under-studied, although the communist regime of Nicolae Ceausescu retained a Stalinist flavour until the very end, the December 1989 Revolution was the only bloody regime change in the region, the Romanian courts organized a large number of trials to deal with the crimes perpetrated by state agents in 1989, and the country was among the few in the region to create a history (truth) commission. Rather than analyzing in-depth the most important transitional justice methods adopted to date – and thus echoing several recently published works – this volume identifies and discusses new insights that could open venues for future research in the field of post-communist transitional justice. Bringing together a group of researchers who are working inside and outside Romania, the volume weaves together novel themes and fresh theoretical perspectives engendered by the study of a country that has moderately engaged in efforts designed to address the human rights violations of communist times. Indeed, Romania stands somewhere in between Central Europe, where reckoning programs were implemented soon after the communist regime collapsed, and the former Soviet Union, where post-communist governments have blocked more than have promoted an honest assessment of the communist past. This "muddling through the past" – by neither fully reckoning with its legacies of rights abuse, nor fully rejecting their reconsideration – has characterized not only post-communist Romania as a whole, but also its society and civil society, as well as the main political formations that have taken turns to form successive governments. By studying a middle-of-the-pack case, we can appreciate a variety of reckoning methods, understand the interaction between judicial and non-judicial programs, and distinguish the reasons that led to delayed or abandoned initiatives. This volume's choice of Romania was, thus, determined not only by the still scarce academic literature devoted to that country but also by solid theoretical considerations.

The volume is divided into three parts, each of which is gathering chapters that deal with inter-connected themes relevant to the study of transitional justice. In what follows, transitional justice is understood as consisting of the judicial and non-judicial measures and programs implemented by state and non-state actors in post-communist Romania in view of redressing the human rights abuses perpetrated by the communist regime.[1] These include attempts to "come to terms with a legacy of large-scale past abuses, in order to ensure accountability, serve justice and achieve reconciliation."[2] In line with other recent studies, this volume

---

[1] This definition is adapted from International Center for Transitional Justice, "What Is Transitional Justice?," 2016, available at: https://www.ictj.org/about/transitional-justice, accessed 23 September 2016.

[2] UN Security Council, "The Rule of Law and Transitional Justice in Conflict and Post-Conflict Societies: Report of the Secretary-General," UN Doc. S/2004/616, New York: United Nations, 2004, available at: http://www.ipu.org/splz-e/unga07/law.pdf, accessed 24 September 2016.

defines transitional justice broadly to encompass a range of responses to past rights violations – from court trials (discussed in Chapter 5), lustration (Chapter 4), public identifications (Chapter 6), and access to (secret) archives (Chapter 4) to commemorations and memorialization (Chapter 7), truth commission (Chapters 4 and 11), and artistic projects (Chapters 8 and 12). Initiatives promoted by both government officials and civil society actors, including theater and movie directors as well as painters, are closely considered in the following chapters. To be sure, in December 1989 the self-declared incipient democracy was for the first time in decades in a position to reckon honestly and openly with the legacy of three different recent pasts – the more distant fascist dictatorship of World War II, the communist regimes of 1945-1989, and the brief but bloody December 1989 Revolution. In their unique ways, all three recent pasts necessitated a vigorous response from the society and considerable political will to seek redress, since each one of these pasts had led to significant loss of human lives. Future projects could look comparatively into these reckoning efforts, identify the reasons why some recent pasts have elicited more attention than others, and examine the consequences of addressing some pasts while neglecting others. Here, by contrast, the focus remains restricted exclusively to the crimes of the communist regime for reasons related to both space limitations and theoretical consistency.

The more theoretically oriented Part I includes four chapters that delve into key conceptual and theoretical issues relevant to any post-communist transitional justice program. The theoretical lens is directed toward some of the key concepts and terms we rely on when studying post-communist reckoning: how memory, historical redress, collaboration and resistance are understood and reflected in the literature, where does Romania stand vis-à-vis its neighbors with respect to the adoption and implementation of specific programs, and what do prompt and delayed transitional justice measures entail in a post-communist setting. Part II is more empirical in focus, examining a number of factors and actors that have determined the presence, pace and breadth of selected methods of post-communist redress. The four chapters included here contribute to both the literature that documents the many forms taken by reckoning during post-communist times and the literature that identifies the determinants and effects of transitional justice, highlighting the contribution of selected program aspects and of explanations neglected to date. Finally, Part III is dedicated to the examination of the victims and the victimizers of communist rights violations, that is, the individuals and organizations that were most directly affected by and involved with or against the feared repressive organ of the communist regime, the Securitate. Four chapters examine this theme by giving special attention to the bystanders, a social category that has been particularly overlooked by transitional justice experts and practitioners, the majority Romanian Orthodox Church, as well as the (un)repentant former Securitate torturers and Communist Party decision-makers. The ways in which the victims, the victimizers and the bystanders relate to the recent past, reconstruct and deconstruct it, and consider it in comparison to post-communist realities are investigated here from different viewpoints that build on the literature about transitional justice and memory.

More than half of the contributions included in this book were presented at the international congress organized by the Society for Romanian Studies in June 2015 at the Faculty of Political Science of the University of Bucharest. That congress allowed Turcescu, Stan, Ciobanu, Dragos and Cristina Petrescu, Tileaga, Vasile, Gussi, and Preda to present their work. The lively discussions we engaged in during the ten panels on transitional justice included in the conference program allowed us to exchange ideas and refine our arguments. These conference presentations were then turned into chapters by deepening their analyses, aligning their theoretical and conceptual frameworks, updating the concrete examples they refer to, and in some cases rethinking the conference talk almost in its entirety. Other scholars known for their work on transitional justice, but who unfortunately could not attend the Bucharest conference due to some other obligations (Horne, Grosescu and Fijalkowski, as well as Light and Young), were then invited to join this book project, so that the volume's theoretical scope and contribution would gain in significance.

The contributors to the volume are recognized for their considerable expertise in the area of transitional justice, especially as it has unfolded in post-communist Romania. All of them have published extensively on various aspects of post-dictatorial reckoning and de-communization, their studies having been presented at numerous international conferences or having been disseminated as scholarly articles, book chapters, or authored and edited books. Some of them (Stan and Turcescu, Grosescu and Fijalkowski, Dragos and Cristina Petrescu, as well as Light and Young) have already collaborated jointly in a number of research and writing projects. Several of them have acquired practical experience by becoming involved in various transition justice projects and programs in Romania and other countries – Stan, Vasile, and Grosescu were involved with the Institute for the Investigation of Communist Crimes in Romania, Vasile as well as Dragos and Cristina Petrescu worked for the Presidential Commission for the Study of the Communist Regime in Romania, while Gussi was a presidential adviser at the time when the Commission's final report was presented to the Romanian Parliament. This experience informs their contributions to this volume.

At the same time, we want to acknowledge the significant financial support offered by the Social Sciences and Humanities Research Council of Canada through its Insight Grant programs, which has allowed the co-editors to pursue work in the general areas of transitional justice, and religion and politics.

PART 1.

MEMORY, RECKONING, LEGITIMACY, AND JUSTICE: THEORETICAL CONSIDERATIONS

CHAPTER ONE

CONCEPTIONS OF MEMORY AND HISTORICAL REDRESS

CRISTIAN TILEAGA

In this chapter I start from the premise that the formal (official) condemnation of communism in Romania, primarily based on researching the physical archives of the communist regime, has offered only a limited framework for driving historical redress and social justice forward. I argue that the relatively limited impact of this official condemnation of communism is partly due to it being predominantly based on a narrow archival understanding of memory, and insufficient elaboration of alternative forms and conceptions of memory. Although the analysis of the dynamics of individual and social memory plays an important part in grounding transitional justice approaches, discussions and debates about the nature of different conceptualizations of memory that drive, and underpin, these approaches are conspicuously absent. It is acknowledged that different forms and conceptions of memory may underpin the relationship between official and unofficial processes of historical redress, but there is less focus on theorizing these different forms and conceptions of memory.

The various theoretical and practical concerns with lustration, decommunization, restitution of property, retroactive justice and, more generally, with the new political vocabulary of transition, can be said to have arisen out of, and received their significance from, the struggles of institutional and individual memory against the background of living with troubled, painful, and difficult, pasts.[1] Active, positive, revealing acts of remembering are usually seen as key means through which injustices can be redressed, victimization and responsibilities recognized, and suffering

---

[1] Lavinia Stan, "The Vanishing Truth: Politics and Memory in Post-Communist Europe," *East European Quarterly*, 40:4 (2006): 383-408.

acknowledged.[2] However, a series of socio-structural and political factors (see, for instance, Chapter 5 in this volume for the influence of legal culture, and Chapter 4 for the role of timing of transitional justice measures) have hindered or limited the reach and significance of these acts of remembering.

One, less-considered, aspect is the idea that troubled, painful, and difficult pasts can also be so "disruptive or disorientating that they become disconnected from the present, unamenable to narrative form and so off limits as a resource for making sense of experience."[3] The memories (especially, personal memories) that provided the impetus, and the substance, of transitional justice might be described as "vital memories,"[4] that is, memories that were articulated out of living with a difficult and sometimes contested past.[5] What defines "vital memories," Brown and Reavey argue, is that they are simultaneously *problematic* and *essential* in "terms of what is being recollected and its significance for ongoing identification with self and others."[6]

This chapter focuses particularly on some conceptual issues around individual and social memory that can contribute to a deeper, and more meaningful attempt at understanding the nature of personal and societal discourses around transitional justice and how to represent the communist era into public consciousness. I contend that broadening the scope of historical redress and social justice might entail a fuller appreciation of alternatives that place more emphasis on different forms and conceptions of memory which, in turn, might allow us to delve deeper into vital memories of troubled, difficult and painful pasts. Here, I distinguish between "archival," "relational" and "psychosocial" (or "psychodynamic") conceptions of memory, and explore their points of contact and tension. I start by exploring the differences between "archival" and "relational"

---

[2] Vladimir Tismăneanu, "Democracy and Memory: Romania Confronts Its Communist Past," *The Annals of the American Academy of Political and Social Science*, 617:1 (2008): 166-180.

[3] Emily Keightley and Michael Pickering, "Painful Pasts," in *Research Methods for Memory Studies*, eds. Emily Keightley and Michael Pickering (Edinburgh: Edinburgh University Press, 2013), 151.

[4] Steven D. Brown and Paula Reavey, *Vital Memory and Affect: Living with a Difficult Past* (London: Routledge, 2015).

[5] Jovan Byford and Cristian Tileagă, "Accounts of a Troubled Past: Psychology, History, and Texts of Experience," *Qualitative Psychology*, in press, forthcoming in 2016.

[6] Steven D. Brown and Paula Reavey, "Experience and Memory," in *Research Methods for Memory Studies*, eds. Emily Keightley and Michael Pickering (Edinburgh: Edinburgh University Press, 2013), 55.

understandings of memory. I then introduce and explore the relevance of a "psychosocial" understanding of memory by using the example of what I call "practices of avoidance" based on repression and resistance, and I show what might be gained from it. Finally, I argue that researchers of transitional justice ought to consider these three understandings of memory as complementary, mutually informing, positions. A deeper appreciation of the role of different conceptions of memory for the understanding of contextual conditions of acts of remembering and forgetting, preservation and loss, expression and repression will hopefully lead to a more meaningful appreciation of both official (formal) and vernacular (ordinary) mnemonic stances and activities.

The official condemnation of communism and archival memory

In the majority of former communist states reckoning with a troubled and painful communist past has presupposed a strong dimension of recuperation and reassessment of communist memory and history through empowering the victims, identifying the victimizers, and revealing the nature and the extent of crimes and abuses perpetrated by the defunct communist regime.[7] The official condemnation of the communist regime in Romania in the so-called "Tismăneanu Report," that is, the final report of the Presidential Commission for the Analysis of the Communist Dictatorship in Romania chaired by Professor Vladimir Tismăneanu, was a peculiar case in point. As an initiative unmatched by any other Central and Eastern European country except Germany, which constituted two history commissions in 1992 and 1994, the Presidential Commission set out to give a definitive account of the crimes and abuses of communism in that country (1945-1989).[8] The avowed ambition of the Tismăneanu Report

[7] Lavinia Stan, "Comisia Tismăneanu: Repere Internaţionale," *Sfera Politicii*, 126-127 (2007): 7-13; and Tismăneanu, "Democracy and Memory."

[8] For more details on the structure, scope and reactions to the Tismaneanu Report, see Monica Ciobanu, "Criminalising the Past and Reconstructing Collective Memory: The Romanian Truth Commission," *Europe-Asia Studies*, 61:2 (2009): 313-336, Ruxandra Cesereanu, "The Final Report on the Holocaust and the Final Report on the Communist Dictatorship in Romania," *East European Politics and Societies*, 22:2 (2008): 270-281, Cosmina Tănăsoiu, "The Tismăneanu Report: Romania Revisits Its Past," *Problems of Post-Communism*, 54:4 (2007): 60-69, Vladimir Tismăneanu, "Confronting Romania's Past: A Response to Charles King," *Slavic Review*, 66:4 (2007): 724-727, and Tismăneanu, "Democracy and Memory."

was to provide a synthetic and rational account of the history of communism and, in doing so, to facilitate the creation of a unified collective memory of communism capable of overriding lay, individual experiences or perspectives.[9]

The leading author of the Report was Vladimir Tismăneanu, an internationally renowned expert (political scientist and historian) of communism. The Report consisted largely of an account of communism's political methods and institutions. It aimed at documenting the repressive and criminal nature of the totalitarian society and giving an exhaustive account of communism as a self-perpetuating political system. In December 2006, in front of the Romanian Parliament, President Traian Băsescu, officially condemned the crimes and abuses of the communist regime, declaring communism as "illegitimate" and "criminal." This is demonstrated by the following three excerpts from the Report:

> *Excerpt 1*
> "Condemning communism is today, more than ever, a moral, intellectual, political, and social duty/obligation. The democratic and pluralist Romanian state can and ought to do it. Also, knowing these dark and saddening pages of 20th century Romanian history is indispensable for the younger generations who have the right to know the world their parents lived in."
>
> *Excerpt 2*
> "Against the facts presented in this report, it is certain that genocide acts have been committed during 1945–1989, and thus the communist regime can be qualified as criminal against its own people."
>
> *Excerpt 3*
> "Taking act of this Report, the President can say with his hand on the heart: the Communist regime in Romania was illegitimate and criminal."[10]

As I showed elsewhere, by emphasizing the criminality and illegitimacy of the communist regime, the Report creates, affirms, and legitimates a narrative for a normative ethics of memory that transmits responsibilities to new generations.[11] The key implication that can be derived from the

---

[9] Tismăneanu, "Confronting Romania's Past."

[10] Vladimir Tismaneanu, Dorin Dobrincu and Cristian Vasile, *Comisia Prezidentiala pentru Analiza Dictaturii Comuniste din Romania. Raport Final* (Bucharest: Humanitas, 2007), 35-36, 211, and 776, respectively.

[11] Cristian Tileagă, "The Social Organization of Representations of History: The Textual Accomplishment of Coming to Terms with the Past," *British Journal of*

Report is that the political category of "communism" belongs to an exceptional class of political categories. As such, one must wonder whether communism must be viewed "as manifesting only one story, as being emplottable in one way only, and as signifying only one kind of meaning?"[12]

The Report is nonetheless careful to openly announce the conception of memory that it uses in framing the criminality and illegitimacy of communism. Gleaning the "incontestable facts that demonstrate the systematic, methodical, antihuman, and utterly repressive nature of the communist regime," as the Report puts it, presupposes working with raw historical materials and repositories – "testimonies, recollections, reports, information notes, meetings of the Political Bureau."[13] These statements reflect an archival conception of memory based on the notion that the collective memory of communism is purportedly inscribed in documents, and documentary traces, and mediated by personal and institutional archives. This way, the historian of communism is akin to the ethnographer of institutions, as DeVault and McCoy suggest: "to find out how things work and how they happen the way they do, a researcher needs to find the texts and text-based knowledge forms in operation."[14] The emerging collective memory of communism is therefore inextricably tied to "text-based knowledge forms"[15] provided by personal and institutional archives. In this context, what matters primarily for the historian of communism is the *correspondence* between experience and its representation in documents. Moreover, this process is perceived as a "a necessary step in the development of the group's ability to speak in one voice or be a political actor in the process of its mobilization,"[16] as Misztal argued.

The archival conception of memory reflected in the Report is based on one of the most entrenched and enduring ways of thinking about memory: the idea of memory as storage of information, encoding and retrieval - the

---

Social Psychology, 48:2 (2009): 337-355, and Ross Poole, "Memory, History and the Claims of the Past," *Memory Studies*, 1:2 (2008): 149-166.

[12] Hayden White, "Historical Emplotment and the Problem of Truth," in *Probing the Limits of Representation: Nazism and the Final Solution*, ed. Saul Friedlander (Cambridge, MA: Harvard University Press, 1992), 38.

[13] Tismaneanu, Dobrincu and Vasile, *Raport Final*, 35.

[14] Marjorie DeVault and Liza McCoy, "Institutional Ethnography: Using Interviews to Investigate Ruling Relations," in *Institutional Ethnography as Practice*, ed. Dorothy Smith (Lanham: Rowman & Littlefield, 2006), 33.

[15] Ibidem.

[16] Barbara Misztal, "Memory and Democracy," *American Behavioral Scientist*, 48:10 (2005): 1329.

idea of memory as archive. The 'archive' metaphor is constitutive of everyday and scientific meanings of memory around the permanence and solidity of memory. According to Brockmeier, "Western common sense, both in everyday life and in science, assumes that there *is* a specific material, biological, neurological, and spatial reality to memory—something manifest—in the world."[17] Institutional and personal archives are the place for historical encoding and storage of information, and they are followed by contemporary retrieval based on the principles of accessibility and activation. In the process of reckoning with a troubled past, texts, documents, etc. are activated by the gaze of the historian, and made to speak of, and stand for, the vital memories of millions of people who lived under communism. Their accessibility is also crucial to this entire process. Although accessibility does not guarantee truthfulness, accessibility is a key criterion for judging their inclusion in the encoding-storage-retrieval sequence.

The model of encoding-storage-retrieval of information proposes a nomothetic, normative, version for writing about a specific collective memory of communism. The hallmark of creating and reproducing social memory in the public sphere is represented by a "dogmatic commitment to one – and only one account of the past."[18]

The communal memory of communism that is centered on the notions of criminality and illegitimacy, and is reflected in the Tismăneanu Report, is produced by probing the social organization of textual archives that reproduce a closed, self-perpetuating, system of inquiry. The archive model is firmly grounded in an individualistic and positivist outlook of human nature. As Brockmeier argues, what is lacking from the archive model of memory is a perspective on "human beings as persons who remember and forget, embedded in material, cultural, and historical contexts of action and interaction."[19] The archive model of memory limits our vision of how individual and collective memories are formed, how they are affirmed, how they are resisted against, or transformed.[20]

In the case of the official condemnation of communism that took place in Romania at the end of 2006, the archives of the communist secret political police, the notorious and much-feared Securitate, become a

---

[17] Jens Brockmeier, "After the Archive: Remapping Memory," *Culture & Psychology*, 16:1 (2010): 6, emphasis in original.

[18] James Wertsch, *Voices of Collective Remembering* (Cambridge: Cambridge University Press, 2002), 125.

[19] Brockmeier, "After the Archive," 9.

[20] Cristian Tileagă, *Political Psychology: Critical Perspectives* (Cambridge: Cambridge University Press, 2013).

"privileged space,"[21] a space of discovery, from where carefully selected details are used to support the perspective offered. The key (self-assigned) task of the historian or political scientist is to construct a representation of the recent past by uncovering "the facts about the past" and recounting them "as objectively as possible."[22] Archives, and texts, documents, contained therein, "universalize or objectify, create forms of consciousness that override the 'naturally' occurring diversity of perspectives and experiences."[23] Yet, the communist regime was not only "an administratively constituted knowledge,"[24] but also knowledge incorporated into various types and kinds of witnessing and testimonies, and various other public sources of memory. In order to appreciate the multitude of public sources of memory one needs to be able to reject a naïve notion of the past as a repository of social meaning, and of memory, as solidly preserved permanently in a material (or mental) archive.

Relational or sociocultural memory

The discursive,[25] narrative,[26] and sociocultural[27] turns have pushed the study of memory as both fashioned by and fashioning social and cultural frameworks. The realization that memory is not reducible to an archival model can be traced back to one of the classic formulations in the psychology of memory: "I have never regarded memory as a faculty," Frederic Bartlett argued, "narrowed and ringed round, containing all its peculiarities and all their explanations within itself. I have regarded it rather as one achievement in the line of the ceaseless struggle to master and enjoy a world full of variety and rapid change."[28] Bartlett's exegesis is

---

[21] Michael Lynch, "Archives in Formation: Privileged Spaces, Popular Archives and Paper Trails," *History of the Human Sciences*, 12:2 (1999): 65-87.

[22] Quentin Skinner, *Visions of Politics: Regarding Method*, vol. I (Cambridge: Cambridge University Press, 2002), 8.

[23] Dorothy Smith, *Writing the Social: Critique, Theory and Investigations* (Toronto, ON: University of Toronto Press, 2004), 195-196.

[24] Dorothy E. Smith, "The Social Construction of Documentary Reality," *Sociological Inquiry*, 44:4 (1974): 261.

[25] Rom Harré and Grant Gillett, *The Discursive Mind* (London: Sage, 1994).

[26] Jerome S. Bruner, *Actual Minds, Possible Worlds* (Cambridge, MA: Harvard University Press, 1986).

[27] Jaan Valsiner and Rene van der Veer, *The Social Mind: The Construction of an Idea* (Cambridge: Cambridge University Press, 2000).

[28] Frederic Bartlett, *Remembering: A Study in Experimental and Social Psychology* (Cambridge: Cambridge University Press, 1932/1995), 314.

showing how cultural (and community) meanings are not fixed, and how social conventions, social representations, as well as social institutions play a pivotal role in the process of remembering.[29]

The realization that memory is not reducible to the encoding-storage-retrieval model can also be traced to the work of French philosopher and sociologist Maurice Halbwachs on how people acquire their memories. Halbwachs famously argued that "it is in society that people normally acquire memories. It is also in society that they recall, recognize, and localize their memories."[30] Both Bartlett and Halbwachs believed that one needed to move away from individualistic, closed, nomothetic understandings of memory, and to research social life in and through the way in which individuals create life-worlds and actively use language-games that are "saturated" by the implicit or explicit presence of others, by relational, discursive and dialogical resources, by narrative tools, and ultimately by wider social frameworks of meaning-making.

The crux of a relational or sociocultural approach to memory that derives from the classic works of Bartlett and Halbwachs can be described along three lines. First, social memory is a social/cultural product. The task of researchers is to describe and understand the circumstances (for example, political, sociocultural, discursive) under which social memory becomes a public affair: how does "memory" actually "matter" to people.[31] This entails treating social (collective) memory as a "relational process at the intersection of different durations of living."[32] Social factors, social frameworks, and social relations make social remembering possible. For instance, Rowe, Wertsch and Kosyaeva have shown how history museums mediate the public memory of events and people by linking vernacular, everyday stories with official ones, linking personal lives to collective narrations in the public sphere.[33] By making official

[29] David Middleton and Steve D. Brown, *The Social Psychology of Experience: Studies in Remembering and Forgetting* (London: Sage, 2005).

[30] Maurice Halbwachs, *On Collective Memory* (Chicago, IL: Chicago University Press, 1952/1992), 38.

[31] Steven D. Brown, "The Quotation Marks Have a Certain Importance: Prospects for a 'Memory Studies'," *Memory Studies*, 1:3 (2008): 261-271; Sue Campbell, "The Second Voice," *Memory Studies*, 1:1 (2008): 41-48; as well as David Middleton and Steven D. Brown, "Issues in the Socio-Cultural Study of Memory: Making Memory Matter," in *The Cambridge Handbook of Sociocultural Psychology*, eds. Jaan Valsiner and Alberto Rosa (Cambridge: Cambridge University Press, 2007), 661-677.

[32] Middleton and Brown, *The Social Psychology of Experience*, vii.

[33] Shawn Rowe, James Wertsch and Tatyana Y. Kosyaeva, "Linking Little Narratives to Big Ones: Narrative and Public Memory in History Museums,"

narratives more accessible, and by bringing vernacular narratives to the surface, museums become sites where both consensus, as well as contestation, resistance around national and local history can take shape. A similar example is given by the recent “terror sites” and national museums dedicated to the legacy of communist totalitarianism in Eastern Europe (for example, the famous House of Terror in Budapest). They are designed as tools for the political socialization of younger generations through mnemonic socialization, that is, socialization into particular images (of genocide), memories (of victimhood), and narratives (of redemption) about the past, present and future of the nation.[34]

Second, interpretations and understandings of the recent past are a concern for professional academics as much as they are for ordinary people.[35] Professional academics and lay people may make use of and apply various (general and particular, universalist and individualist) interpretive schemes to understanding and interpreting a troubled and difficult recent past. The key task of the sociocultural approach to memory is to describe the variety of interpretative practices and to study the dilemmatic, and often contradictory, nature of social and political stance taking.[36] For instance, Bucur shows how both the communist and post-communist “official commemorative calendar” of the Romanian state has attempted to create national commemorative rituals (around a “heroes cult” and commemorative sites such as the Tomb of the Unknown Soldier and the Mărăşeşti Mausoleum) that implicitly or explicitly clash with local communities' own way of remembering and constructing social memories.[37]

Third, social memory neither simply reflects nor expresses “a closed system for talking about the world,” but rather “contrary themes, which continually give rise to discussion, argumentation and dilemmas.”[38] Social memory is distributed beyond one’s head, and as such it “involves active

---

Culture & Psychology, 8:1 (2002): 97–113.

[34] James Mark, *The Unfinished Revolution: Making Sense of the Communist Past in Central and Central-Eastern Europe* (New Haven: Yale University Press, 2010).

[35] Cristian Tileagă, “Communism in Retrospect: The Rhetoric of Historical Representation and Writing the Collective Memory of Recent Past,” *Memory Studies*, 5:4 (2012): 462-478.

[36] Michael Billig, *Arguing and Thinking: A Rhetorical Approach to Social Psychology*, 2nd ed. (Cambridge: Cambridge University Press, 1996).

[37] Maria Bucur, *Heroes and Victims: Remembering War in Twentieth-Century Romania* (Bloomington, IN: Indiana University Press, 2009).

[38] Michael Billig, Susan Condor, Derek Edwards, Mike Gane, David Middleton and Alan Radley, *Ideological Dilemmas: A Social Psychology of Everyday Thinking* (London: Sage, 1988), 6.

agents, on the one hand, and cultural tools such as calendars, written records, computers, and narratives, on the other."[39] The contingency, context-related and context-dependent emergence of social memory is contrasted with the presumed stability and permanence of archival memory. The troubled history of reconciliation in South Africa is a relevant example here. Andrews shows how in the context of testimonies and responses to the Truth and Reconciliation Commission (TRC) there was no unique or collective narrative model that was used by all of the social actors.[40] Although citizens recounting tales of suffering represented a unique (and successful) model of rebuilding a "broken" nation, it was far from being a uniform one, with different stories being told, sometimes as the result of pressures on victims to tell certain kinds of stories while testifying, or as the outcome of different experiences and perspectives of victims and perpetrators, and various other individuals and groups challenging official versions of the past and demanding redress. As Andrews argues, the concern of the TRC focused on the creation of acceptable, believable, pragmatic versions of memory more than on the truthful collective memory, and therefore on developing realistic and usable images of the past history of race relations rather than truthful ones.

Moreover, social/collective memory is also multidirectional memory.[41] It points in different directions, and operates on many fronts, at both conscious and unconscious levels. It was Rothberg who argued that "collective memory is not simply an archive awaiting political instrumentalization; the haunting of the past cannot be harnessed in the present without unforeseen consequences."[42] A telling example comes from Gallinat whose work focuses on the narrative work of a group of former political prisoners in their attempt to communicate their experiences of a painful past. She notes that, in most of the cases, participants could not move their stories beyond general phrases like "horrible," "awful," or "unbearable."[43] In a similar way very particular episodes of abuse in Stasi prisons were not mentioned, although other

---

[39] James V. Wertsch, "Collective Memory," in *The Cambridge Handbook of Sociocultural Psychology*, eds. Jaan Valsiner and Alberto Rosa (Cambridge: Cambridge University Press, 2007), 646.

[40] Molly Andrews, *Shaping History: Narratives of Political Change* (Cambridge: Cambridge University Press, 2007).

[41] Michael Rothberg, *Multidirectional Memory: Remembering the Holocaust in the Age of Decolonization* (Stanford: Stanford University Press, 2009).

[42] Rothberg, *Multidirectional Memory*, 223.

[43] Anselma Gallinat, "Difficult Stories: Public Discourse and Narrative Identity in Eastern Germany," *Ethnos*, 71:3 (2006): 343-366.

aspects were mentioned (lack of hygiene, privacy, sleep deprivation, etc.). The narratives of the inmates were also punctuated by heavy silences and difficulties of finding the right words. For Gallinat, all this shows the "tension between wanting to transmit the extraordinariness of the episode and a feeling of failing to do so."[44] Gallinat's interviewees were not finding it easy to be themselves; they were struggling to find both social and individual acceptable (rational and moral) identities that would satisfactorily capture their vital memories of pain, abuse, and marginalisation. In my own work,[45] I have shown how one might go about applying the idiographic principles and ethos of a sociocultural conception of memory to researching apologia for past wrongdoings (in the Romanian case, the informal collaboration with the Securitate) as a way of managing moral identity and moral accountability.

What discursive analyses show is that public apologies are culturally mediated experiences. They are not simple rhetorical exercises of image restoration nor do they reflect the hidden psychology of the person. Making "moral amends" presupposes a cultural orientation to an operative cultural norm of remedial work on social relationships through the use of language. In this context, remembering is a social practice that "enables the production of subjectivity,"[46] and the mobilisation of self-protective and self-affirming cultural repertoires. Analyses of public apologies reveal that social actors inhabit, enact, defend, or suppress multiple social identities, and they construct their accounts out of a carefully choreographed patchwork of material/cultural tools (narratives, written records, and social technologies). Public apologies express socio-cultural meanings (including the sociocultural meaning of what it means to be "sorry") about memory, people, identities, events, social relations, and institutions.

Social memory and social practices of avoidance

An analytic focus on relational or sociocultural memory shows how memory manifests itself and takes various forms at different levels of

---

[44] Gallinat, "Difficult Stories, 354.

[45] Tileagă, "The Social Organization of Representations of History," Cristian Tileagă, "(Re)writing Biography: Memory, Identity, and Textually Mediated Reality in Coming to Terms with the Past," *Culture & Psychology*, 17:2 (2011): 197-215, and Cristian Tileagă, "Apologia," in *Research Methods for Memory Studies*, eds. Emily Keightley and Michael Pickering (Edinburgh: Edinburgh University Press, 2013), 185-199.

[46] Steven D. Brown, "Two Minutes of Silence: Social Technologies of Public Commemoration," *Theory & Psychology*, 22:2 (2012): 239.

social and political organization, in public and in private, in elite discourse and in lay meanings, in the guise of personal as well as societal remembering. Researchers working within and across disciplines research memory for the social functions it fulfills, and for how it assumes collective relevance in the cultural, social, as well as political web in which it is entangled.

The struggle to find socially and individually acceptable stories, the mediation of vital memories by personal and social relationships, and material environments is typically portrayed as a contingent, active and conscious social activity. Yet, I want to argue that the unconscious also plays a part in the mediation of these vital memories. A closer inspection of narratives and accounts reveals gaps, silences, avoidances, ambivalence and, more generally, a tension between wanting to express the uniqueness of painful, shameful experiences and wanting to repress unwanted, shameful experiences. This tension arguably points to deeper difficulties that people (and collectives) experience when encountering, and facing, a painful, troubled past. "One wants to get free of the past," Adorno admitted, "one cannot live in its shadow," but the "past one wishes to evade is still so intensely alive."[47] In this section, I introduce what I would like to call a psychosocial or psychodynamic conception of memory that I see as a complement to a relational or sociocultural conception of memory. I focus on one set of social practices that are relevant to understanding the official appraisal of communism in public consciousness. I call these practices "social practices of avoidance."

One of my main concerns here is with understanding the role of what Billig calls "social repression" and what Frosh describes as "resistance."[48] Billig's account of repression stresses the importance of social practices of "avoidance" that are part and parcel of conversational practices of society around topics or feelings that are too "difficult" to discuss.[49] Resistance refers to "something to be overcome"; analysis is a process of understanding the mind that is "at war with itself, blocking the path to its

[47] Theodor Adorno, "What Does Coming to Terms with the Past Mean?," in *Bitburg in moral and political perspective*, ed. Geoffrey Hartman, trans. T. Bahti and G. Hartman (Bloomington, IN: Indiana University Press, 1986), 115.

[48] Michael Billig, *Freudian Repression* (Cambridge: Cambridge University Press, 1999), and Stephen Frosh, *Psychoanalysis Outside the Clinic: Interventions in Psychosocial Studies* (Basingstoke: Palgrave Macmillan, 2010).

[49] In a different, yet related, context see for the relevance of "social repression" in the analysis of extreme prejudice against ethnic minorities Cristian Tileagă, *The Nature of Prejudice: Society, Discrimination and Moral Exclusion* (London: Routledge, 2015).

own freedom."[50] Also, I am guided here by LaCapra's insights on the foundational problem that is facing historians and concerns "how to articulate the relation between the requirements of scientific expertise and the less easily definable demands placed on the use of language by the difficult attempt to work through transferential relations in a dialogue with the past having implications for the present and future."[51]

In his work on the Holocaust, LaCapra distinguishes between "constative" historical reconstruction and "performative" dialogic exchange with the past.[52] As he argues, this latter "performative" dialogic exchange relies on certain unconscious memory activities. The process of canonization of a single collective narrative around the nature of communism in Romania has been, predominantly, a constative historical reconstruction based on the factual reconstruction of experiences and an archival conception of memory. In contrast, according to a psychosocial conception, whatever comes out of the past, whatever is "discovered" in dusty, previously unexplored corners of mental and physical archives, can trigger resistance, repression and avoidance, and can activate unconscious fears, phantasies, unexpected identifications, as well as unresolved conflicts.

In the remainder of this chapter, I focus on describing the performative dialogic exchange with the past in the Tismăneanu Report. I follow LaCapra in the assumption that the basis of a performative dialogic exchange with the past is rooted in the notion of "working-through" taken-for-granted ethical and political considerations. As LaCapra argues, "working-through implies the possibility of judgment that is not apodictic or ad hominem but argumentative, self-questioning, and related in mediated ways to action."[53]

Perhaps the most striking aspect of the representation of communism in the Tismăneanu Report is the image of communism as the Other.[54] Throughout the Report, communism is described in general terms as a "regime" and an "ideology," a "utopian conception," an "enemy of the human race" that instituted "the physical and moral assassinate," and survived "through repression." However, communism is also described in national terms: a "(foreign) occupation regime," "criminal towards its own

---

[50] See Jacqueline Rose, *The Last Resistance* (London: Verso, 2007), 21, cited in Frosh, *Psychoanalysis Outside the Clinic*, 166.

[51] Dominick LaCapra, *Representing the Holocaust: History, Theory, Trauma* (Ithaca: Cornell University Press, 1994), 66.

[52] Ibidem, 4.

[53] Ibidem, 210.

[54] Tileagă, "Communism in Retrospect."

people," and "antinational," among others.[55] It is very clear in the Report that to write of communism means to narrate the (Romanian) nation, its past, present and future. In doing so, the Report is proposing a specific method of reasoning about Romanian history and memory that constitutes communism as the Other, not quite "us." Interestingly, the narrative of communism is not self-condemnatory or self-blaming, but rather communism is distanced from (the national) self. This is demonstrated by the following excerpts:

> *Excerpt 4*
> "The total Sovietisation, through force, of Romania, especially during the period 1948-1956, and the imposition under the name 'dictatorship of the proletariat' of a despotic political system ruled by a profiteering caste (nomenklatura), tightly united around its supreme leader."
>
> *Excerpt 5*
> "Pretending to fulfill the goals of Marxism, the regime has treated an entire population as a mass of lab mice part of a nightmarish social engineering experiment."
>
> *Excerpt 6*
> "…the imposition of a dictatorial regime totally surrendered to Moscow and hostile to national political and cultural values"
>
> *Excerpt 7*
> "The Romanian Popular Republic, who has come into being through diktat, or more exactly, through a coup d'état, symbolizes a triple imposture: it wasn't even a Republic (in the full sense of the phrase), it wasn't popular, and, most certainly, it wasn't Romanian."[56]

In the Tismăneanu Report the communist regime is also found "responsible" of crimes "against the biological makeup of the nation." Through references to physical and psychological effects (for example, "psychological weakening and disheartenment of the population," and "decreased capacity for physical and intellectual effort")[57] communism is externalized and objectivized as a sui generis political ideology designed to undermine the Romanian ethos.[58] The Report describes communism as

---

[55] Tileagă, "The Social Organization of Representations of History."

[56] Tismaneanu, Dobrincu and Vasile, *Raport Final*, 774, 775, 774, 765, respectively.

[57] Ibidem, 461-462.

[58] Theo van Leeuwen, "Representing Social Action," *Discourse & Society*, 6:1 (1995): 81-106.

"antipatriotic," whereas the Romanian communist leaders are portrayed as lacking "patriotic sentiments," and Romanian communist politics are described as not representing the affirmation of a "patriotic spirit/will."[59]

Paradoxically, the basic premise for the condemnation of Romanian communism is to construe communism as the Other, in other words as not reflecting Romanian values and national interests. This is not only in stark contrast with how ordinary people have experienced communism in both its positive and negative consequences,[60] but this also encapsulates an active avoidance of the implication that communism may have been in any way a "criminal" ideology that reflected, and furthered, national interests. This position can be seen as an example of how a progressive, social justice repertoire masks and represses an insufficiently worked-through transferential relation with a controversial past. The textual construction of the negative qualities of communism in the Tismăneanu Report ("enemy of human rights," "illegitimate," and "criminal") opens the way for the operation of social repression, the suppression of the socially inappropriate thought that communism may have been historically part and parcel of national identity. In this context, what is not said is even more significant than what is said. The negative attributes of communism are distanced from the (national) self. One can see how the writings of the professional historians of communism, who are adhering strictly to the conventions of their field, actively resist alternative ideological implications, especially those that closely reflect nationalist representations of communism in popular culture. As Frosh notes, resistance is a useful notion to understanding the subtleties of ambivalence. "Resistance," Frosh points out, "has general significance as a way of indicating how a person might want something but not want it at the same time."[61]

The topics of repression and resistance in the Romanian context will vary from those of other Central and Eastern European countries. Any thorough analysis of social repression and resistance will need to identify and explore general, but also specific, topics subject to repression and resistance. Post-communist transition has developed its own complex social conventions and discursive codes that resist and repress the topic of collective involvement in the perpetuation of the communist system. By constructing communism as the Other, paradoxically, even progressive texts such as the Tismaneanu Report are engaging in collective avoidance of this very sensitive topic. As new generations of young people participate

---

[59] Tismaneanu, Dobrincu and Vasile, *Raport Final*, 765, 773, 30, respectively. Cf. Tileagă, "The Social Organization of Representations of History."
[60] Bucur, *Heroes and Victims.*
[61] Frosh, *Psychoanalysis Outside the Clinic*, 167.

in the public debate on the nature of communism, they acquire specific routines of thought, and in addition they learn the accepted and acceptable social conventions and discursive codes that present communism, and its legacy, as the Other (not "us"!). Building a mnemonic community implies a process of formal mnemonic socialization (through museums and history textbooks, for example), as well as less formal mnemonic socialization (families) into what must be remembered or forgotten, what must be expressed or repressed.[62] According to the Report, the idea the "we" (Romanians) may have had anything to do with the perpetuation of the communist regime must be suppressed from national consciousness.

There is an inherent conflict present in any attempt to constitute a unitary and coherent version of the communist past. For the general public, communism is constructed as oppressive, persecutory, destructive, and aggressive. There are various powerful reminders of individual and collective powerlessness and suffering mentioned in the Tismaneanu Report. Yet, from the individual, professional perspective of the historian of the communist regime, communism does not seem so; it is rather something tamed, something already understood, as Tismaneanu himself acknowledges:

> *Excerpt 8*
> "For me, as historian and political scientist, the verdict of such a commission was not needed in order to argue that 'communism has been an aberrant system, criminal, inhuman'."[63]

The double self-categorization as "historian" and "political scientist" indexes and legitimizes Tismăneanu's scientific, academic credentials and prepares the ground for the public expression of a moral judgment.[64] It is interesting to note how any affective and relational aspects are subordinated to knowing rationally, intentionally, as well as scientifically (cognitively) the *true* characteristics of communism. For the professional historian, communism is both an object of loathing and desire. A process of "canonization" of a unique representation of recent history requires that alternative experiences, perspectives, and interpretations are actively suppressed. "Self-sufficient" professional research endeavors, to use

---

[62] Andrews, *Shaping History*.
[63] Vladimir Tismăneanu, *Refuzul de a uita: articole şi comentarii politice (2006-2007)* (Bucharest: Curtea Veche, 2007).
[64] Tileagă, "Communism in Retrospect."

LaCapra's term, are most effective in shielding official ideologies and images from the impact, contradictions, and paradoxes of memory.[65]

Conclusion

The vagaries and difficulties of a clean and ultimate break with the recent communist past in Central and Eastern Europe have been extensively documented.[66] One key insight coming out of the majority of studies is that the question of how to take communism into public consciousness arguably remains the greatest political, epistemological, and ethical challenge facing the post-communist states.

The conventional historical attitude is that "telling the truth" about the past and making it public will enlighten people and change perceptions. If one can only find the "right" words to describe the past, its nature (essence) will "reveal" itself to everyone. "Telling the truth" about the past is also seen as a progressive attempt to stifle and "control" returns of "negative currents" (for example, revisionist accounts and nostalgia), to bring the "repressed" oppressive ideology and effects of communism into public consciousness, and thus to banish the risk (and fear) of repetition. Yet, at the same time, the same progressive conventional historical attitude can obscure, mask, and suppress, as much as it reveals, key ideological aspects of the appraisal of communism in public consciousness.

This position should not be seen as denying the significance and overall social value of the conventional ways in which historians, political scientists, and sociologists approach the issue of coming to terms with the recent communist past. Historical knowledge of the objective (ideological) makeup of political regimes and other social formations should be continually sought as a remedy for half-truths, political manipulation, or simply ignorance. Yet, such knowledge, when used and reproduced as a "matter of fact," is arguably inadequate with regard to the handling of

---

[65] Dominick LaCapra, *Writing History, Writing Trauma* (Baltimore, MD: Johns Hopkins University Press, 2001).

[66] Stan, "The Vanishing Truth"; Andrzej Waśkiewicz, "The Polish Home Army and the Politics of Memory," *East European Politics and Society*, 24:1 (2010): 44-58; Aleksandra Galasińska and Dariusz Galasiński, eds., *The Post-Communist Condition: Public and Private Discourses of Transformation* (Amsterdam/ Philadelphia, PA: John Benjamins, 2010); Cristina Petrescu and Dragos Petrescu, "Mastering vs. Coming to Terms with the Past: A Critical Analysis of Post-Communist Romanian Historiography," in *Narratives Unbound: Historical Studies in Post-Communist Europe*, eds., Sorin Antohi, Balasz Trencsenyi and Peter Apor (Budapest: Central European University Press, 2007), 311-408.

dilemmas and ambiguities of collective memory or to the development of broader social scientific frameworks of analysis. One needs to strive to find the meaning of the collective memory of communism in the sometimes contradictory, paradoxical attitudes and meanings that members of society uphold and negotiate, and not only in and through official representations of recent history "compressed into generalities."[67]

A parallel can be perhaps drawn between psychological therapy and historical enquiry. In "Analysis Terminable and Interminable," Freud contemplated an answer to the question: "is there such a thing as a natural end to an analysis?"[68] The conditions that must be fulfilled for a "terminated" analysis are extremely complex, but they involve three key aspects: "that so much of repressed material has been made conscious, so much that was unintelligible has been explained, and so much of internal resistance conquered, that there is no need to fear a repetition of the pathological processes concerned."[69] Freud was skeptical of the idea that "it were possible by means of analysis to attain to a level of absolute psychical normality – a level, moreover, which we could feel confident would be able to remain stable, as though, perhaps, we had succeeded in resolving every one of the patient's repressions and in filling in all the gaps in his memory."[70]

It is resistance that "reveals the existence of an unconscious wish that gives glimpses of a subject's desire."[71] It is the *wish* for an all-encompassing narrative of communism that has led some historians and political scientists to believe that one could attain to a level of absolute certainty that would resolve, once for all, the concurrent societal dilemmas, and societal struggles with consensus. A process of "canonization" of cultural/collective memory of recent history "is a matter of interpretation and (to put it bluntly) politics."[72] In this context, it is not surprising that the Report was perceived as more a "spin-off of spin" than a genuine attempt at reconciliation with the past.[73]

---

[67] Paul Veyne, *Writing History: Essay on Epistemology*, translated by Mina Moore-Rinvolucri (Middletown, Connecticut: Wesleyan University Press, 1984), 63.

[68] Sigmund Freud, "Analysis Terminable and Interminable," *Standard Edition*, 23 (1937): 219.

[69] Ibidem, 219.

[70] Ibidem, 219-220.

[71] Frosh, *Psychoanalysis Outside the Clinic*, 167.

[72] Poole, "Memory, History and the Claims of the Past," 151.

[73] James Wertsch and Zurab Karumidze, "Spinning the Past: Russian and Georgian Accounts of the War of August 2008," *Memory Studies*, 2:3 (2009): 388.

There is no "natural end" to understanding the recent past; there is no ultimate story. The imperative of a "shared memory" entails the "integration" and "calibration" of different perspectives and stances.[74] This means, primarily, the integration and calibration of what is not yet worked-through, of ambivalent and suppressed meanings. Furthermore, this *wish* for an all-encompassing narrative of communism can be seen as a claim of (explanatory) ownership of its (negative) after-effects. Yet, as LaCapra rightly argues, "the after effects … of traumatic events are not fully owned by anyone and, in various ways, affect everyone."[75] That is indeed the case of the Romanian official appraisal of communism. Any attempt at a definitive description of its after effects has been met with fierce, direct, and/or passive/aggressive resistance. The fixation on a single, unique, all-or-nothing description of the nature of (Romanian) communism has led to resistance. Resistance is puzzling to historians and political scientists; it is misunderstood by being attributed to and explained with reference to the internal psychology of the person and democratic "competence" of individuals:

> the population lacks a sophisticated understanding of 'suffering' during the communist regime. One needs to explain, in order to make one's own, the criminal nature of dictatorship … Perceiving yourself as a victim of a totalitarian regime entails a full understanding of the inner workings of the regime … there is a danger of creating a selective memory of communism, based primarily on personal experience and which disregards the repressive nature of the regime.[76]

The core assumption here is that the ordinary person is "ideologically innocent"[77] and lacks political sophistication.[78] The commentator's views express an entrenched attitude that actively downplays the value of the everyday morality of (social and political) experiences.[79] Yet, as Todorov

---

[74] Avishai Margalit, *The Ethics of Memory* (Cambridge, MA: Harvard University Press, 2002).
[75] LaCapra, *Writing History, Writing Trauma*, xi.
[76] Bogdan Iacob, "Avem nevoie de o pedagogie a memoriei colective a trecutului communist," *Evenimentul Zilei*, 23 September 2010, available at: http://www.evz.ro/bogdan-cristian-iacob-avem-nevoie-de-o-pedagogie-a-memoriei-colective-a-trecutului-comunist-90689.html, accessed 25 May 2016.
[77] Donald R. Kinder and Cindy D. Kam, *Us against Them: Ethnocentric Foundations of American Opinion* (Chicago: Chicago University Press, 2009), 232.
[78] Philip E. Converse, "The Nature of Belief Systems in Mass Publics," in *Ideology and discontent*, ed. David Apter (New York: Free Press, 1964), 206-261.
[79] See Tileagă, *Political Psychology*, for an extended critique of this position.

has argued, "if historians are going to further their understanding, to collect as many facts as possible and formulate the most accurate interpretations, then they must not decide ahead of time what morality they want to see in the end. History comprises very few pages written in black and white only."[80] It also downplays the multiplicity of social sources of memory, and it treats people as "memory consumers."[81] Individual and collective memories are neither fixed nor given once and for all, but can be shaped and transformed into specific forms by cultural, societal and political/ideological constraints.

Can issues of retrospective justice really be "fixed for all time," to use Teitel's words?[82] The analysis of social practices of avoidance is largely absent from the agenda of historians and political scientists working on transitional justice. By taking social practices of avoidance seriously historians and political scientists of transitional justice may be in a better position to appreciate the fluidity of collective (psychic) life that turns the "real" into "fantasy," the "unsettledness of psychic life, in which the tendency to rest at ease with oneself is undermined by the appalling capacity of unconscious elements to introduce something fantastic and full of desire."[83] By analyzing the sociocultural workings of social repression and resistance, the analyst engages in ideological analysis and social critique of what it means to *come to terms with* the past. As Billig argues, when one engages in ideological analysis one shifts the focus from the individual unconscious to the social and collective constitution of the unconscious.[84] Frosh also reminds us that "psychoanalysis has an intrinsic link to radical social critique, because its concern is with unconscious impulses understood as destabilizing and subversive of social as well as personal norms."[85]

A psychosocial conception of memory is not sufficient, on its own, in addressing the challenges of conceptualizing historical redress in historical/political science analysis. As LaCapra has shown in his wide-

---

80 Tzvetan Todorov, *In Defense of the Enlightenment* (London: Atlantic Books, 2009), 89-90.

81 Wulf Kansteiner, "Finding Meaning in Memory: A Methodological Critique of Collective Memory Studies," *History & Theory*, 41:2 (2002): 180.

82 Ruti Teitel, *Transitional Justice* (New York: Oxford University Press, 2000), 104.

83 Frosh, *Psychoanalysis Outside the Clinic*, 6.

84 Michael Billig, "Discursive, Rhetorical and Ideological Messages," in *The Message of Social Psychology*, eds. Craig McGarty and S. Alexander Haslam (Oxford: Blackwell, 1997), 210-221.

85 Frosh, *Psychoanalysis Outside the Clinic*, 12.

ranging studies of the Holocaust, adapting psychoanalytic concepts to historical analysis can present advantages as well disadvantages. On one hand, they can help support "sociocultural and political critique in elucidating trauma and its aftereffects in culture and in people."[86] On the other hand, concepts derived from psychoanalysis should not "become a pretext for avoiding economic, social and political issues."[87]

Researchers of transitional justice ought to consider archival, relational and psychosocial understandings of memory as complementary, mutually informing positions. A deeper appreciation of the role of different conceptions of memory for memorialization and historical redress will hopefully lead to dispelling the illusion of a linear relationship between the accumulation of "positive" knowledge and the creation of "shared" collective narratives. In doing so, researchers of communism and transitional justice should be able to more clearly theorize and take into account the cross-cutting possibilities and challenges of researching vital memories. Any hope of full mastery of historical events, of the "last word" is a regressive step. Historians of communism should perhaps appreciate more the subtle consequences of the psychic operations of "definitive closure … and radically positive transcendence."[88] They must not make the mistake "to use consensus to cure the diseases of consensus."[89]

The task of the historian of communism is to produce an integrated view of coming to terms with the recent past, to introject or incorporate into the (master) narrative both aspects of an idealized, virtuous, (national) self as well as aspects projected outward, and perceived as uncharacteristic of the (national) self. As a nation, a liberal polity that "aspires to justice,"[90] Romania has sustained a strong, unfailing commitment to meaningful, official and unofficial memory and identity projects of coming to terms with the communist past. It has overcome numerous barriers and, over the years, it has created a "vigilant critical culture"[91] that has supported

---

[86] LaCapra, *Writing History, Writing Trauma*, ix. On the implications of drawing upon psychoanalysis "outside the clinic," see Frosh, *Psychoanalysis Outside the Clinic*. On the role of psychoanalytic vocabulary for working through the socio-historical trauma of apartheid racism, see Garth Stevens, Norman Duncan and Derek Hook, eds., *Race, Memory and the Apartheid Archive: Towards a Transformative Psychosocial Praxis* (Basingstoke: Palgrave Macmillan, 2013).
[87] Ibidem, ix.
[88] Ibidem, 71.
[89] Jacques Rancière, *On the Shores of Politics* (London: Verso, 2007), 106.
[90] Martha Nussbaum, *Political Emotions: Why Love Matters for Justice* (Cambridge, MA: Harvard University Press, 2013), 3.
[91] Ibidem, 124.

transitional justice, and the continuation of liberal and democratic values. This vigilant critical culture, however, is not devoid of ambivalence; it is not immune to the operations of repression and resistance. There is a need to excavate the nature of this ambivalence, to unearth more of the nature of repression and resistance that may stand in the way of a full understanding of a myriad of vital memories of communism.

CHAPTER TWO

COLLABORATION AND RESISTANCE: SOME DEFINITIONAL DIFFICULTIES

LUCIAN TURCESCU AND LAVINIA STAN

Post-communist debates on transitional justice have often made extensive use of concepts such as collaboration, compromise, resistance, opposition, defiance, dissent, and consent to explain the wrongdoings of the communist regime, to define the groups that have benefited under that regime and the groups that have been persecuted by it, and to formulate the legislative pieces and policies designed to reckon with the legacy of the communist past. A very large number of individual examples have been invoked during these debates, and many of them have been documented in painstaking detail by former victims, historians, anthropologists, and even politicians. Nevertheless, it is evident that not all of the interlocutors have shared the same understanding of these words, and a thorough review shows that very few transitional justice scholars and practitioners have tried to elucidate these concepts. As such, for the past twenty-five years we have conducted vigorous debates on possibly misconstrued foundations.

Definitions, some more precise than others, were included in the transitional justice legislation of the region. For example, the lustration laws identified secret collaborators, whereas the rehabilitation and compensation laws defined victims and made reference to individuals engaged in (armed) resistance and opposition. Perhaps not surprisingly, given the vast number of cases they had to be applicable to, these laws tended to depict communist reality in dichotomous terms. They left the impression that the communist society consisted only of evil collaborators whose compromises placed them at an undeserved advantage, and of virtuous objectors who were at the receiving end of a repressive system. In addition, the laws saw very little need to acknowledge overlap between the two categories (that is, cases in which an individual had engaged in actions that could simultaneously denote resistance and collaboration) or changes over the course of a lifetime (since an individual could have dissented during one decade and consented at some other time). In almost all Central and Eastern Europe, including Romania, legal definitions were set in stone in the absence of vigorous scholarly examinations of empirical examples of collaboration and resistance or theoretical conceptualizations of these terms.

This chapter summarizes the scholarly literature that has pondered over the meaning of collaboration with and resistance against dictatorial regimes in Romania in particular, and Europe, more generally. As stated above, not much reflection on the meaning of these terms has taken place since 1989. Make no mistake: collaboration and resistance have been seen as self-evident terms by many historians and transitional justice scholars, and a lot of ink has flown to document relevant examples in various dictatorial contexts. To gain a fuller picture of the meaning of these terms, we consider not only the communist regime but also the Nazi regime, which have elicited much greater interest much earlier. Definitions are discussed below mostly chronologically, both in order to separate those applicable to the Nazi cases from those proposed for the communist regime and to recognize that some of the most recent work has occasionally built on its predecessors.

Resistance and collaboration under the Nazi regime

The first modern definition of collaboration was proposed in relation to Vichy France. Through his work, American scholar Robert O. Paxton changed forever the historians' and French people's understanding of the way in which the French society related to that regime. Whereas the French scholars claimed that the Vichy regime had engaged in passive resistance against the Nazis, Paxton presented the French as hungry for collaboration with the Nazis occupation forces. His argument, which was instantly vilified in France, rested on a close scrutiny of previously unavailable German archives, not French archives and scholarship.[1] As Martin Evans noted, "Paxton's basic argument – that Vichy was not merely a shield to protect France against Nazi victors, but a regime that begged Hitler to accept its collaboration – was shocking to large numbers of French people."[2] Paxton's scholarship showed that the Vichy regime's claims of having valiantly resisted the occupier concealed a deep predisposition toward collaboration, since the occupied supported many of

[1] Robert O. Paxton, *Vichy France: Old Guard and New Order, 1940-1944* (New York: Knopf, 1972).
[2] Martin Evans, "Robert Paxton: The Outsider," *History Today* 51:9 (2001): 26.

the same values as the occupier. Now a classic analysis of the Vichy regime, Paxton's book identified, without systematically categorizing, several types of collaboration and resistance. Among the types of collaboration that the Vichy regime members invoked as necessary for their country's survival, Paxton mentioned: 1) "loyal service to the state," which later became a frequent Vichy defense at the court trials organized after World War II; 2) defending the continued existence of the French regime, but not its policies; 3) fleeing the country, a decision that was seen as lacking in heroism; 4) and any other acts that helped to preserve national sovereignty.

Collaboration already featured in the armistice document that France was forced to sign with Nazi Germany in June 1940. Article 3 of that document called on the French government to assist the German Reich in exercising "all rights of an occupying power" in the territories taken over by the Nazis, "to comply with the regulations of the German military commanders and to cooperate with them in a correct manner."[3] As Paxton noted, that is the moment when the word "collaboration" underwent a dramatic change in its meaning. From a positive, "banal term for working together" it transmogrified into a negative "synonym for high treason after the occupation had run on for four years. The most elementary promptings of normalcy in the summer of 1940, the urge to return to home and job, started many Frenchmen down a path of everyday complicity that led gradually and eventually to active assistance to German measures undreamed of in 1940."[4] Given the extent of collaboration, Paxton further noted, "Vichy was not a Band-Aid. It was deep surgery. To an extent unique among the occupied nations of Western Europe, France went beyond mere administration during the occupation to carry out a domestic revolution in institutions and values"[5] that only benefited the occupation forces. When turning his lens to resistance, Paxton mentioned several types of resistance such as desertions from the Vichy territory, support for resistance leader Charles de Gaulle and his political views, assassinations of members of the occupying administration, encampments of young men who fled to the mountains or forests in order to avoid working for the German war factories, organized armed resistance, as well as sabotage.

---

[3] "Armistice Agreement between the German High Command of the Armed Forces and the French Plenipotentiaries, Compiagne, June 22, 1940," Lillian Goldman Law Library, Yale Law School, 2008, available at: http://avalon.law.yale.edu/wwii/frgearm.asp, accessed October 29, 2016.

[4] Paxton, *Vichy France: Old Guard and New Order, 1940-1944*, 19. For the concept's transformation, see Bertram M. Gordon, "The Morphology of the Collaborator: The French Case," *Journal of European Studies* 23:89-90 (1993): 1.

[5] Paxton, *Vichy France*, 20.

At the same time as Paxton published his groundbreaking study, another scholar of Nazi Europe, David Littlejohn labeled the members of Nazi parties in six European countries that were conquered by Germany in 1940 (Norway, Denmark, the Netherlands, Belgium, France, and the Soviet Union) as simply "patriotic traitors" who fully supported the Nazi ideals, and thus behaved as unconditional collaborators. [6] Littlejohn suggested that the boundaries between *collaborateur* and *collaborationniste* remained unclear, a point later reinforced by other historians. On the one hand, the *collaborationnistes* were motivated by ideological reasons to join pro-Nazi parties either because they embraced totalitarian ideals or because they were anti-communists. The French term was used only to refer to those supportive of collaboration with the German occupiers. On the other hand, the *collaborateurs* (and the related German verb *kollaborieren*) were motivated by more mundane concerns, related to personal interests or broader national goals.[7] The fact that both groups had similar positions towards the Nazi occupation did not mean they did not resort to violence against each other. The busy *collaborateurs* in the Vichy regime arrested hundreds of *collaborationnistes* who passed information to the Germans out of greed, denunciation or Germanophilia. Through these arrests the regime sought to centralize collaboration in order to enjoy a monopoly in Franco-German relations and thus to negotiate with the occupation forces from a position of strength that would ultimately maintain France's privileged status in the new Nazi Europe.[8]

In 1982, journalist Werner Rings published a volume that was written in a more journalistic tone for a general public, and repeated some of the themes previously examined by Paxton and Littlejohn.[9] Nevertheless, his definitions of collaboration and resistance have been praised as major strengths of the book. Rings distinguished four types of collaboration and five types of resistance that often represented the two sides of the same coin.[10] The collaboration spectrum, according to him, included: neutral

[6] David Littlejohn, *Patriotic Traitors: History of Collaboration in German Occupied Europe, 1940-1945* (London: W. Heinemann, 1972).

[7] Philippe Burrin, *France under the Germans: Collaboration and Compromise* (New York: The New Press, 1998), and Gerhard Hirschfeld and Patrick Marsh, eds., *Collaboration in France: Politics and Culture During the Nazi Occupation 1940-1944* (New York: Berg, 1989).

[8] Simon Kitson, *The Hunt for Nazi Spies: Fighting Espionage in Vichy France*, translated by Catherine Tihanyi (Chicago: University of Chicago Press, 2008).

[9] Werner Rings, *Life with the Enemy: Collaboration and Resistance in Hitler's Europe, 1939-1945*, translated by J. M. Brownjohn (New York: Doubleday, 1982).

[10] Idem, 129.

collaboration (or "I conform"), unconditional collaboration (or "our enemy is my friend"), conditional collaboration (or "I collaborate up to a point"), and tactical collaboration (or "I do but I don't"). For Rings, the neutral collaborator found in the Netherland and Belgium reasoned in these terms:

> I accept that life must go on. Knowingly and from self-interest, I directly or indirectly work for the occupying power without professing the political and ideological principles of National Socialism. My attitude is dictated by circumstances beyond my control. The sole alternative appears to be bankruptcy, unemployment, starvation, chaos, and destruction. I am determined to survive the war and my country's defeat as best as I can.[11]

This logic differed from that of an unconditional collaborator, who argued that: "I join forces with the occupying power because I endorse its principles and ideals. My attitude is dictated not by circumstances, but by allegiance to National Socialism. I am prepared to do anything and make any sacrifice for the occupying power as long as I can thereby serve our common cause." [12] For Rings, the unconditional collaborator was a "miniature Hitler" who could be found in Norway, the Netherlands, Denmark, and France, among other Western European countries.[13]

The conditional collaborator cooperated but at the same time endorsed only some, not all the Nazi doctrines: "I am ready and eager to collaborate faithfully because I wish to change the circumstances that dictate my attitude."[14] Conditional collaboration became the official policy of the Vichy regime, having been introduced by Marshal Philippe Pétain, the Chief of State of Vichy France in 1940-1944. Last, the tactical collaborators agreed to collaborate despite their hostility to National Socialism and the Third Reich. They told themselves: "I may do so for a variety of reasons: to throw off the foreign yoke and regain my freedom; to prevent the mass murder of innocent people whenever possible; or to consummate a political idea whose fulfillment is obstructed by National Socialism."[15] In every case, tactical collaboration disguised resistance and was part of the fight against the occupation forces. The highly controversial Jewish Councils (Judenräte), the agencies set up in many Nazi occupied countries to ensure that Nazi orders and regulations were implemented, represented examples of such tactical collaboration that backfired when the Council members themselves were deported to

[11] Idem, 73.
[12] Idem, 86.
[13] Idem, 94.
[14] Idem, 106.
[15] Ibidem.

concentration camps. The "hazardous and contradictory business" of tactical collaboration made Dutch historian Louis de Jong to lament the fact that "almost everyone practiced resistance and collaboration at one and the same time."[16]

Resistance, according to Rings, took the following five forms: symbolic resistance (or "I remain what I was"), polemic resistance (or "I tell the truth"), defensive resistance ("I aid and protect"), offensive resistance (or "I fight to the death"), and enchained resistance (of the freedom fighters in camp and ghetto). The symbolic resister rationalized his position in this way: "I signalize my inviolate self-respect by means of personal gestures or actions expressing allegiance to my country, its individuality and right to exist. I do not shrink from conveying to the forces of occupation that they are dealing with a proud and confident people."[17] The polemic resister was defending his position by arguing that: "I oppose the occupying power by protesting or organizing protests, even at risk to myself. I say or do things calculated to persuade my fellow countrymen of the need to fight on."[18] This type of resistance included the June 1941 refusal of the Church of Norway to answer Berlin's call to join a "crusade against Bolshevism," and was often supported by the activity of clandestine newspapers. Other churches "carried nonviolent resistance to the limit" with dire consequences, as hundreds of clergy members were arrested or killed.[19]

The defensive resister contended that "I take the side of those in danger or on the run; I rally to those who protect them; I defend, by force if need be, the human beings and human values endangered by the occupying power."[20] For Rings, this type of resistance (and the one described below) animated some segments of the underground resistance, which got organized in Western Europe during the second year of Nazi occupation. The offensive resister was prepared to "combat the forces of occupation by every available means. I attack or prepare to attack them whenever the opportunity arises. I regard myself as a soldier – a volunteer member of the Underground."[21] This form of resistance made use of armed raiders and murder squads, punitive assassinations, and even secret armies. Last, the enchained resister was a freedom fighter living in the concentration and labor camp or in the ghetto. One such example was Polish officer

[16] Idem, 139-141.
[17] Idem, 153,
[18] Idem, 162.
[19] Idem, 163-164.
[20] Idem, 172.
[21] Idem, 189.

Witold Pilecki, who volunteered to be sent to Auschwitz in order to organize the resistance within the concentration camp. Pilecki was also the first to report to the world the existence of the mass gassings carried out in the camp beginning in mid-May 1942.[22]

In another book of some relevance to our topic, Detlev Peukert distinguished three realms of conflict within the Third Reich. These included "external conflicts between the Nazi government and its opponents or those defined as the enemy, whether from outside or from within; horizontal internal conflicts between powerful factions in the government; and vertical internal conflicts between the Nazi government and the masses or between the Nazi elite and specific groups in the population under Nazi rule."[23] Each conflict realm generated a different form of resistance, ranging from non-conformist behaviour (which included telling jokes), refusal, and protest to armed resistance. These forms in turn depended on whether the scope of anti-regime criticism was partial or general, and whether the sphere within which the dissident behaviour took place was private or public.

Not surprisingly, some of the richest literature that documented cases of resistance and collaboration focused on the Holocaust. In his analysis of Jewish resistance, Dan Michman noted that scholars distinguished "steadfastness" from "subversion or armed resistance."[24] He pointed to Nahman Blumental, for whom resistance meant "not only physical acts, but also the spiritual and moral stand which Jews displayed under Nazi occupation," and to Marc Dworzecki, for whom "the concept of 'stand' is comprehensive, embracing all expressions of Jewish non-conforming and all forms of resistance and all acts by Jews aimed at thwarting the evil design of the Nazis."[25] Michman recognized that the revised approach that included too many activities under resistance had been criticised by renowned Holocaust historians Raul Hilberg and Lucy Dawidowicz. Hilberg wrote that "food smuggling, escapes and even elemental struggle for life under starvation conditions" did not constitute resistance because

---

[22] Idem, 229-230.

[23] Detley Peukert, *Inside Nazi Germany: Conformity, Opposition, and Racism in Everyday Life*, translated by R. Deveson (New Haven, CT: Yale University Press, 1987), 81-84.

[24] Dan Michman, "Jewish Resistance during the Holocaust and Its Significance: Theoretical Observations" in *Holocaust Historiography: A Jewish Perspective – Conceptualizations, Terminology, Approaches and Fundamental Issues*, ed. Dan Michman (London: Vallentine Mitchell, 2003), 217-250. The two terms correspond to amidah and hitnagdut in Hebrew.

[25] Idem, 218.

they "did not stem the Nazi advance [and] did not divert or delay the assailants in any measurable degree."[26] Hilberg preference for reserving the word "resistance" for only a subset of cases was not embraced by the vocal Dawidowicz. Dawidowicz thought that an all-inclusive definition of resistance did not necessarily make a disservice to the historians who tried to assess the possibilities, costs, and effectiveness of Jewish resistance. She insisted that the most widely accepted definition of resistance, formulated at the 1971 Yad Vashem conference on Jewish resistance, did not see resistance "as an auxiliary form of warfare, but rather as a process familiar in medicine or physics: resistance as the ability of an organism to withstand disease or as an opposing or retarding force to motion or energy."[27] From her point of view, the most "strained" definition of the term claimed that telling jokes against Hitler was a form of resistance, but she still considered those who had starved in the Jewish ghettos as resisters to the Nazi regime.

For a variety of reasons, Michman disagreed with these critics and instead considered Roger Gottlieb's approach, who argued that resistance was an act of free will, with the resisters intently acknowledging their self-identity and intent to resist the oppressor.[28] Moreover, resistance was not just physical (as Hilberg and Dawidowicz implied), but also spiritual, having religious, national or other dimensions. Gottlieb considered the temporal and spatial contexts as important for classifying resistance types, since different actions could be seen as resistance before and after the Final Solution was implemented in 1942. While armed resistance was possible before the concentration camps, a conscious choice to stay alive represented resistance at a time when the Nazis sought death for the Jews. Gottlieb further looked at "the relationship between the intent to resist and

---

[26] Idem, 219-220. Raul Hilberg, *Perpetrators, Victims, Bystanders: The Jewish Catastrophe, 1933-1945* (New York: Aaron Asher Books, 1992).

[27] Hilberg, *Perpetrators, Victims, Bystanders*, 220. Meir Grubsztein, ed., *Jewish Resistance during the Holocaust: Proceedings of the Conference on Manifestations of Jewish Resistance, Jerusalem, April 7-11, 1968* (Jerusalem: Yad Vashem, 1971). For the 1971 Yad Vashem conference on Jewish resistance, see Union of American Hebrew Congregations, *Spiritual Resistance: Art from Concentration Camps, 1940-1945: A Selection of Drawings and Paintings from the Collection of Kibbutz Lohamei Haghetaot, Israel* (Philadelphia: The Jewish Publication Society of America, 1981).

[28] Roger S. Gottlieb, "The Concept of Resistance: Jewish Resistance during the Holocaust," *Social Theory and Practice*, 9:1 (1983): 31-49.

the effectiveness of such resistance."[29] Michman summarized Gottlieb's ideas in this way:

> The element of intent is central to the concept of resistance because, by its very nature, resistance involves moral, political, and theoretical aspects (that is, the state of oppression and the attempt to fight or limit it). If we take only effectiveness into account, acts that were expressly geared to oppose but failed to do so would not be categorized as resistance.... By considering intent, we may claim that, because the oppressed did not fully understand the situation or the machinations of their oppressor, their resistance was ineffective – but they did, nevertheless, try to resist.[30]

During the 1970s and the 1980s, other studies supported the amidah approach, whereby numerous activities were seen as forms of resistance. These included "counterfeiting identity cards, assisting family members of prisoners, and hiding fugitives from forced labour," and were considered as examples of "non-violent self-defence," "charitable acts of resistance," or "cultural," "passive" or "symbolic" resistance.[31] Louis de Jung also preferred a wider definition of resistance that extended to "every action performed to inhibit [the enemy] from realizing the aims it had set itself."[32] The German terminology describing resistance also reflected this wide spectrum of behavior: Widerstand (resistance), Resistenz (ability to withstand), Teilwiderstand (partial resistance), Verweigerung (opposition), Dissens (veering from the accepted path because of a fight, disagreement or ideological conflict), Verhinderung (disturbance), innere Immigration (internal immigration in the sense of philosophical departure), alternative Politik (alternative policy), and Selbstbehauptung (self-preservation, acts of survival, in the sense of amidah).[33]

European resistance to the Nazis may have had other motivations than Jewish resistance, Michman rightfully acknowledged. While these forms of resistance sometimes overlapped, they could also be very different in nature due to their different motivations. These theoretical concerns were taken up by Richard Löwenthal, who distinguished three forms of resistance (Widerstand) to Nazi totalitarianism: "conscious political struggle; social protest; and ideological dissidence (weltanschauliche

[29] Michman, "Jewish Resistance during the Holocaust and Its Significance," 222.
[30] Ibidem.
[31] Ibidem.
[32] Idem, 223-224.
[33] Michman, "Jewish Resistance during the Holocaust and Its Significance," 224.

Dissidenz)."[34] These forms frequently overlapped. At the same time, they were "all fundamentally directed against three [different] institutionalized monopolies of the ruling party: political power; social organization; and information."[35]

These conceptualizations of resistance and collaboration have been largely ignored in post-communist Central and Eastern Europe, and even more so in Romania. That was partly because they had been developed on the basis of short-lived war-time regimes and therefore their applicability to decades long peace-time communist contexts was thought to be limited. The lack of information in communist times prevented Central and Eastern European supporters of transitional justice to fully understand the similarities between the European right-wing and left-wing totalitarian regimes. In addition, the region had already developed its own way of thinking about relations between communist authorities and the nascent civil society. Concepts like dissent and consent were more widely employed than resistance and collaboration. In Romania, it was only with the opening of the Securitate archives that collaboration, mostly in its secret, undeclared form, took center stage in public debates. Resistance, by contrast, was a term whose use was restricted to the armed resistance of the early years of communist rule.

This does not mean that Central and Eastern European scholars have ignored the Nazi occupation of their own countries. Czech scholars, for example, have reflected extensively on resistance and collaboration in the Protectorate of Bohemia and Moravia of 1939-1945. Some historians argued that the majority of the population neither collaborated with nor resisted the Nazi occupation, and that those who collaborated were mostly the politicians. During the Protectorate, "forced collaboration" was the dominant type of interaction with the occupation forces. Such collaboration did not stem from ideological identification with the Nazi regime, embraced only by the small group of Czech fascists grouped in the Vlajka (Flag) organization. Forced collaboration, historian Stanislav Kokoška contended, stemmed from the brutality of the occupation regime, which imposed exemplary punishments, as well as arbitrary and disproportionate violence in order to spread "a mortal fear, paralyzing the

---

[34] Richard Löwenthal, "Widerstand in totalen Staat," in Richard Löwenthal and Patrik von zur Mühlen, *Widerstand und Verweigerung in Deutschland 1933 bis 1945* (Berlin: Dietz, 1982) 13-14. Cited in Michman, "Jewish Resistance during the Holocaust and Its Significance," 225.

[35] Löwenthal, "Widerstand in totalen Staat," 14.

Czech society."[36] Within the framework of "forced collaboration," two strands could be distinguished: collaboration as a temporary accommodation until the end of the war, and active systemic collaboration that was viewed by some politicians as part and parcel of a more fundamental strategy of individual and national survival.

Kokoška further noted that the Czechoslovak government's strategy to "defend national interests by making only absolutely unavoidable concessions" turned out to be simply "nonviable" by late 1939. As such, in 1940 it was succeeded by a policy of "opportunistic adaptation to the occupying power."[37] Depending on their attitude toward collaboration, various actors rejected or accepted resistance. Those who embraced active collaboration rejected any form of resistance, but others viewed resistance, especially resistance in exile, as significant. The Czech language had no words for collaboration (*kolaborace*) and collaborator (*kolaborant*) until after World War II, when the words were imported from French with the pejorative meanings associated to the Vichy regime. This importation of terms is evident in Decree no. 33/1945 of the Slovak National Council, which stipulated the punishment of former criminals, occupiers, traitors and collaborators. The Decree defined a collaborator as:

> anyone who helped the occupiers or domestic traitors in waging war, in damaging the war efforts of the USSR and Allies or in the struggle of the Slovak people for liberation, who ordered or carried out persecution for racial, national, religious or political reasons or for anti-fascist convictions, who took part in the deportation of Slovak citizens to other countries or holding camps, who by exploiting wartime conditions made themselves unduly reach, or who in public functions helped to maintain the occupying regime or publicly approved it.[38]

After the war, the emphasis on personal motivation became increasingly important in ascertaining collaboration and determining whether a person wittingly supported the occupying power. Another decree spoke of whether "the special eagerness [for collaboration] has gone beyond the normal framework of [a person's] duties."[39] While noting that the word's "shameful connotations" continued to be evoked by the Czech media in post-communist times, Kokoška argued that a distinction

---

[36] Stanislav Kokoška, "Resistance, Collaboration, Adaptation: Some Notes on the Research of the Czech Society in the Protectorate," *Czech Journal of Contemporary History* 1 (2013): 60.
[37] Ibidem.
[38] Cited in Kokoška, "Resistance, Collaboration, Adaptation," 62-63.
[39] Idem, 63.

must be introduced between voluntary and forced collaboration, since one behavior was less morally defensible than the other.

Kokoška further argued in favor of replacing the term collaboration with a range of more nuanced "forms of behavior" adopted by individuals and groups under the occupation regime. His article included a chart that considered the level of Adaptation/Non-Adaptation and the level of Identification/Non-Identification with the regime, which determined a person's Attitude toward the regime that in turn translated into his/her Form of Behavior. He came up with four different situations; two of them described individuals who sought to adapt to the regime, while the two other categories included individuals who refused to do so. First, an individual could exhibit adaptation to the regime and identify with it; in that case the person was loyal. Second, individuals who strive to adapt to but do not identify with the regime ended up engaging in delinquency. Individuals who did not seek to adapt to the occupation fell into two different categories. They either identified with the regime, in which case they were opportunistic, or they had a hostile attitude toward the regime, in which case they engaged in resistance. Note that none of the four categories led to collaboration, a term Kokoška wanted to move away from.

Positions toward the communist regimes

Attempts to conceptualize relations between the society and the communist state have been fewer. Some definitions were formulated under the communist regime, often to justify the behavior of antigovernment individuals and social groups, or provide a working framework for the repressive state organs. Other conceptualizations were proposed only after 1989, often to recast communist-era behavior in a new register that would defend specific actors' lack of open public opposition to the regime.

Polish writer Czeslaw Milosz, Czech dissident Vaclav Havel, and activists who departed from the official doctrine and policy of the Communist Party have presented a nuanced picture of collaboration and resistance under communism. Studies on European communism, especially after the 1970s, mainly employed terms like "dissent" and "opposition."[40] By that time the armed resistance mounted during the first decades of communist rule had almost completely died down. Terms like "dissent" and "dissidence,"

[40] We acknowledge Michael Kraus's oral presentation given at the Centre for German and European Studies (Université de Montreal) workshop that Lucian Turcescu and Barbara Thériault organized on 28 February 2015.

which denoted an opposition against the communist regimes that placed respect for human rights at its core, made their way into modern languages from the Latin "dissidentia" (diversity, contrariety). By contrast, the Russian word *inakomyslia* indicated "a disagreement, rejection of the official ideology and politics, opposition to the dominant opinions and convictions."[41]

Before Russian dissidents manifested themselves publicly beginning in the 1960s and 1970s and before Havel proposed his own definition of dissidence, Milosz used a term borrowed from Islamic jurisprudence, the *kitman*, which refers to a doctrine that supported the "prudential concealment" of one's allegiance to a minority (religious) group that risked persecution.[42] In his *The Captive Mind*, Milosz attacked the intellectuals' accommodation to the communist regimes and depicted the Ketman [sic] as the persons who "can live with the contradictions of saying one thing and believing another, adapting freely to each new requirement of their rulers while believing that they have preserved somewhere within themselves the autonomy of a free thinker—or at any rate a thinker who has freely chosen to subordinate himself to the ideas and dictates of others."[43] Milosz's framework recognized the value of the passive opposition that allowed some Central and Eastern Europeans to practice criticism while also avoiding the public exposure that would have turned them into targets of persecution. This kind of behavior was also examined by Kenneth Jowitt who used the word "dissimulation" to describe resistance strategies that crossed the boundary between the public and private spheres. However, Jowitt warned that such strategy amounted to "a strong anti-political privatism in which family and personal interests are emphasized at the expense of regime and societal interests,"[44] not opposition.

---

[41] Ana Maria Cătănuș, "Disidență," in *Romania 1945-1989. Enciclopedia Regimului Comunist: Represiunea*, ed. Octavian Roske (Bucharest: Institutul National pentru Studiul Totalitarismului, 2011), vol. 1: 567.

[42] James W. Morris, "Taqīyah," in *Encyclopedia of Religion*, ed. Lindsay Jones (Detroit: Macmillan Reference, 2005), available at: http://www.encyclopedia.com/environment/encyclopedias-almanacs-transcripts-and-maps/taqiyah, accessed on 11 June 2015.

[43] Tony Judt, "Captive Minds, Then and Now," *The New York Review of Books* (13 July 2010), available at: http://www.nybooks.com/blogs/nyrblog/2010/jul/13/captive-minds-then-and-now, accessed on 11 June 2015.

[44] Kenneth Jowitt, *New World Disorder: The Leninist Extinction* (Berkeley: University of California Press, 1992), 80.

During the protest of 5 December 1965 in the Pushkin Place in Moscow, dissenters displayed slogans that asked the authorities to respect the constitution and to allow for "transparency in the court trial against Andrei Sinyavsky and Yuli Daniel, writers who had published books in the West and were accused of anti-Soviet propaganda."[45] A similar protest took place in the Red Square on 25 August 1968, but that time it was directed against the invasion of Czechoslovakia by the Warsaw Pact armies. During the 1970s and the 1980s, dissent movements multiplied throughout the Soviet bloc. Many intellectuals took the lead, but workers and churches were also involved. These protests varied widely in terms of their demands, making it difficult to put together a definition to describe all of them. However, Ana Maria Cătănuş defined dissidence as "the totality of movements, groups, texts and individual actions, varied in their aims (as they envisaged religious, ethnic or other forms of freedoms), performed in close connection with fundamental principles like transparency, achieving fundamental rights and freedoms, as well as respect for the law."[46] The dissidents' opposition to communism, Cătănuş proposed, came in the form of the "uncensored texts, public actions – demonstrations, spreading leaflets, declaring hunger strikes – or other types of actions, such as [producing and distributing] literary texts, texts defending human rights, scientific texts, informing the public through samizdat [literature] and informing the western mass-media, writing petitions to official institutions, or sending open letters."[47] Dissidents found themselves "in disagreement with the ideological, political, economic or moral bases of society, proclaimed their disagreement openly and publicly in front of their compatriots and state institutions, and demonstrated consistency in their discourse and action."[48]

Havel's writings on the topic gained a much broader audience and prominence. In 1978, Havel famously warned that "a specter is haunting Eastern Europe: the specter of what in the West is called 'dissent'."[49] This specter, he continued, was "a natural and inevitable consequence of the present historical phase of the system it is haunting" because the communist system "can no longer base itself on the unadulterated, brutal, and arbitrary application of power, eliminating all expressions of

---

[45] Cătănuş, "Disidenţă," 567.
[46] Idem, 568.
[47] Ibidem.
[48] Ibidem.
[49] Vaclav Havel, "The Power of the Powerless," October 1978, available at: http://vaclavhavel.cz/showtrans.php?cat=clanky&val=72_aj_clanky.html&typ=HTML, accessed on 13 June 2015.

nonconformity" and "has become so ossified politically that there is practically no way for such nonconformity to be implemented within its official structures."[50] For Havel, dissent occurred when individuals started to live within the truth. His example of the greengrocer, a reference to any ordinary person, who refused to live within the lie was telling. Barbara Falk noticed that "the moment Havel's greengrocer reflects on his own phenomenological universe and becomes susceptible to truth, he discovers both responsibility and power. By locating power in the powerless and in such a personal decision, Havel democratizes the nature and possibility of such responsibility."[51]

Western historians proposed their own typologies of dissent and opposition under communist regimes. In his *A Carnival of Revolution*, Padraic Kenney preferred the term "opposition" to "dissent," since the latter had been criticized even by the very individuals who practiced it.[52] For Kenney, opposition in communist Central Europe took five different forms. First, reformist dissent within the hegemonic Communist Party was practiced by activists who departed from the official ideological line while retaining their party membership and privileges. Second, the best known type of opposition was the "civil society" dissent described by Havel, the anti-political concrete actions mounted by groups organized outside the reach of the communist government. Third, the churches amounted to a powerful critic of communism in countries like Poland, where Pope John Paul II had an unrivaled influence, and also in Slovakia, Slovenia, Germany, where underground churches enjoyed great moral authority. Fourth, opposition also came from the counterculture which allowed musicians and artists to drift from alternative culture to alternative politics by playing rock-and-roll and jazz music. Last, "nationalist opposition" focused on the preservation of sovereignty and the protection of cultural values. In Romania, this type of opposition ceased to challenge the regime, once Ceausescu enforced his own brand of national-communism.

Having worked extensively on Central and Eastern European intellectual dissenters, Barbara Falk also reflected on the meaning of these basic terms. As other authors before her, Falk found that the collaboration-resistance and consent-dissent dichotomies could not capture the full range of behavior and attitudes toward the regime. Instead she proposed a

---

[50] Idem.

[51] Barbara Falk, *The Dilemmas of Dissidence in East-Central Europe: Citizen Intellectuals and Philosopher Kings* (Budapest: Central European University Press, 2003), 8.

[52] Padraic Kenney, *A Carnival of Revolution: Central Europe 1989* (Princeton: Princeton University Press, 2002), 10-11.

"continuum model" that placed activities on a spectrum stretching from "benign activities" at one end to "dissent" at the other end.[53] Benign activities were activities other than official events sponsored by the party: personal travel, sport exercises. Dissent referred to activities that risked regime persecution and imprisonment: public protests, active involvement in groups independent from the state, or the production and distribution of samizdat. An activity that came close to dissent was signing a petition or discussing with friends and workmates news obtained from independent media channels like Voice of America or Radio Free Europe. The middle of the spectrum was represented by the "grey zone" of activities such as reading samizdat, publicly telling jokes, listening to a banned radio broadcast, or writing an essay without distributing it further.[54]

Two additional definitions were peculiar to Romania: resistance through culture, and resistance through spirituality. Given the brutality of the Romanian communist regime in 1945-1965 (when physical and psychological violence as well as killings were directed against political prisoners) and 1965-1989 (when dictator Nicolae Ceausescu replaced the Securitate's physical violence with psychological terror), very few people dared to oppose the regime. One thus must question whether resistance through culture and resistance through spirituality really constituted resistance or were merely normal activities allowed by the Securitate in order to give the impression that a space free of state control existed even under a heavy-handed and vigilant regime.

Resistance through culture was connected with a group of intellectuals (including Gabriel Liiceanu, Andrei Plesu, and Andrei Cornea) who gathered around philosopher Constantin Noica (1909-1987).[55] They described their pursuit of philosophical knowledge not related to modern ideologies through the Paltinis school, their translation into Romanian of the works of Plato, Kant, Hegel, and Heidegger, and their refusal to

[53] Barbara J. Falk, "Resistance and Dissent in Central and Eastern Europe, An Emerging Historiography," *East European Politics and Societies,* 25:2 (May 2011) 318-360.

[54] Idem, 321-322.

[55] Irina Culic, "The Strategies of Intellectuals: Romania under Communist Rule in Comparative Perspective," in *Intellectuals and Politics in Central Europe,* ed. Andras Bozóki (Budapest: Central European University Press, 1999), 50-53; Irina Livezeanu, "Romania's Cultural Wars: Intellectual Debates about the Recent Past," *Working Papers Series of the National Council for Eurasian and East European Research*, March 27, 2003 (available at https://www.ucis.pitt.edu/nceeer/2003-816-08-Livezeanu.pdf, accessed on November 4, 2016).

engage in communist politics as "resistance through culture," a project that sought nothing short of ensuring the survival "through spirit" of "a nation historically under threat."[56] Kenney also recognized this type of opposition as legitimate.[57] Little did they know that Noica, a one-time political prisoner, had signed a pledge of collaboration with the Securitate to allow for such "resistance."[58] After 1989, these intellectuals, in particular Liiceanu, self-appointed as gatekeepers of the Romanian cultural scene and tried to define resistance and collaboration on their own terms. In his capacity as gatekeeper, Liiceanu tried to discredit the recipient of the 2009 Nobel Prize for literature, Romanian-born German writer Herta Müller, and to belittle her opposition to the communist regime.[59]

The religious equivalent of "resistance through culture" was "resistance through spirituality." This type of resistance, proposed as a phrase by George Enache and Adrian Petcu, was manifested when members of the clergy celebrated the liturgy, said the Jesus prayer ("Jesus Christ, Son of God, have mercy on me a sinner") or preached religious teachings, while not officially and openly taking a stand against the regime and its ideology.[60] The two authors found in Securitate files several "self-denunciations" written by former members of the Burning Bush (Rugul Aprins), a spirituality group active in the 1940s and the 1950s in Romania. Group members self-denounced for having repeated the Jesus prayer as "an activity contrary to the communist regime," and through it allegedly gaining the ability to detach themselves from the harsh daily communist reality. These activities resembled Milosz's *kitman* more than resistance. One secret file described the preaching of Orthodox spirituality as an act of opposition against the communist regime. According to one of the denunciations, Daniil Sandu Tudor and Benedict Ghius, two of the Burning Bush group's leaders, encouraged members to practice the Jesus

---

[56] Gabriel Liiceanu, "Adsum? Modelul cultural Noica si urgentele istoriei / Noica's Cultural Model and the Emergencies of History," *22* (November 23, 1990), 6-7.

[57] Kenney, *A Carnival of Revolution*, 10.

[58] Gabriel Andreescu, *Carturari, opozanti si documente: Manipularea Arhivelor Securitatii* (Iasi: Polirom, 2013), and Stelian Tanase, *Anatomia mistificarii* (Bucharest: Humanitas, 2000).

[59] Lavinia Stan, "Women as Anti-communist Dissidents and Collaborators of the Secret Police," in *Genre and the (Post)Communist Woman. Analyzing Transformations of the Central and Eastern European Female Ideal*, eds. Florentina Andreescu and Michael Shapiro (New York: Routledge, 2014), 80-97.

[60] George Enache and Adrian Nicolae Petcu, "Biserica Ortodoxă Română şi Securitatea: Note de Lectură," in *Totalitarism şi rezistenţă, teroare şi represiune în România comunistă* (Bucureşti: CNSAS, 2001), 108-137.

prayer, which became a mind game that allowed them to survive the vicissitudes of communism. Eventually, most group members were arrested also because many of them had once belonged to the fascist Iron Guard.

Other activities have been thought to demonstrate willingness to defy the communist regime and its prohibitions. In a way, these peculiar instances of opposition, if this was what they amounted to, reflected Romania's particular situation in the 1980s when the society was deprived of basic necessities. After championing "resistance through culture" as a legitimate way to defy the regime without openly challenging it, writer Andrei Plesu proposed "the samizdat of clandestine food" as one strategy in which millions of Romanians engaged during the 1980s to survive the chronic food shortages imposed by the authorities. For him, the very act of eating amounted to opposition.[61] In a similar vein, historian Maria Bucur asked whether abortion, the refusal to birth children in a country where abortion was illegal and monthly gynecological exams compulsory, amounted to anti-government defiance.[62] While not having the Romanian example in mind, Barbara Falk also listed productivity kept deliberately low, absenteeism from work, and retreat into the personal/private sphere as forms of resistance, but not dissent.[63]

Other definitions considered the need to ascertain an individual's collaboration with the communist regime on the basis of the extant secret archives. Written after the relevant legislation was adopted, these definitions merely echoed the legal provisions. Constantin Buchet and Cristian Troncotă, for example, defined collaborator as "a person possessing a limited capacity to inform within a professional milieu or about a problem of operational interest,"[64] and noted that collaborators had a "network file," which usually included the pledge they signed after being recruited as secret informers by the Securitate. Collaborators were also considered those persons who "provided occasionally and in an uninterested way information that was useful for the Securitate and who were not registered as such [in the Securitate archives], that is, they did not have a written pledge nor a 'network file'."[65]

---

[61] Andrei Plesu, *Obscenitatea publică* (Bucharest: Humanitas, 2004), 103-104.

[62] Maria Bucur "Gendering Dissent: Of Bodies and Minds, Survival and Opposition under Communism," *Oxford Slavonic Papers*, 7 (2008): 9-26.

[63] Falk, "Resistance and Dissent in Central and Eastern Europe."

[64] Constantin Buchet and Cristian Troncotă, "Colaborator," in *Romania 1945-1989. Enciclopedia Regimului Comunist: Represiunea*, ed. Octavian Roske (Bucharest: Institutul National pentru Studiul Totalitarismului, 2011), vol. 1: 335.

[65] Ibidem.

Legal definitions

The first relevant legally defined term in post-communist Romania was "the persecuted," a category that had overlapped with dissenters, opponents and resisters until 1989. Decree-Law 118 of 1990 listed among those who benefited from compensation packages several categories of individuals persecuted by the communists. Its provisions extended to those who: a) were imprisoned for political reasons as a result of a definitive court order or as a result of an arrest order; b) were imprisoned as a result of administrative orders or for being investigated by the repressive organs; c) were placed in psychiatric wards; d) had a forced residence; e) were deported to another locality; f) were deported abroad [mostly in the Former Soviet Union] after 23 August 1944; b) were taken prisoners by the Soviet troops after 23 August 1944.[66] These legal provisions were meant to be all-inclusive, allowing most of those persecuted by the communist authorities, often because they openly acted against it, to seek reparations.

By the late 1990s it was clear that many politicians and ordinary Romanians rejected radical lustration programs that would have led to the dismissal from the public life of former collaborators with the communist regime. In this context, attention was turned to the secret collaborators, who had occasionally given information to the Securitate. As such, the vast majority of those deemed collaborators in post-war France or Germany – the party activists, the civil servants, the propaganda chiefs in the press, radio and television – were excluded from the definition of the collaborator. Article 5 of Law 187 of 1999, which allowed for access to the secret archives for ordinary citizens and screening of a variety of post-communist public office holders, defined a Securitate collaborator as:

> the person who a) was remunerated or otherwise compensated for his activity in this capacity; b) held a conspiratorial house or a meeting house; c) was a resident of the Securitate; d) any other person who gave information to the Securitate, through which were affected, directly or through other organs, the fundamental human rights and liberties.[67]

---

[66] Consiliul Provizoriu de Uniune Nationala, "Decret-Lege nr. 118 din 30 martie 1990 privind acordarea unor drepturi persoanelor persecutate din motive politice de dictatura instaurată cu începere de la 6 martie 1945, precum şi celor deportate în străinătate ori constituite în prizonieri," *Monitorul Oficial al României, partea I* (9 April 1990).

[67] "Law no. 187 on the Access to the Personal File and the Disclosure of the Securitate as a Political Police," *Monitorul Oficial*, part I, no. 603 (9 December

The same article further branded as collaborators the persons who "passed on or facilitated the passing on of information, notes, reports or other documents, by which the activity or attitudes against the totalitarian communist regime were denounced, liable to affect the fundamental rights and liberties," and the persons who "had decision, legal or political competence or who, by abuse of political power, took decisions at central or local level, regarding the activity of the Securitate, or of other repressive structures of the totalitarian communist regime."[68] Note that the Romanian legislation stresses that punishment is reserved for those individuals who collaborated with the Securitate "as a political police," a term implying direct involvement with human rights abuses.

Other screening, vetting and lustration laws adopted in Eastern Europe did not necessarily mention the word "collaborator," but provided similar lists of individuals considered to have been instruments of communist repression. The list of such positions differed from country to country, but the terminology was similar. The term "collaborator" was reserved for the informers who agreed to provide the secret police with information on others. These individuals were identified as "unofficial collaborators" in Germany, "conscious collaborators" in Czechoslovakia, and "collaborators" or "informers" elsewhere. The full-time secret agents were referred to as "employees" or "officers."[69] Tellingly enough, members of the state

---

1999), available at: http://www.cdep.ro/legislatie/eng/vol44eng.pdf, accessed on 5 June 2015. The law was amended by the Government Emergency Ordinance 24 of 2008, and Law 293/14 November 2008. See also Dragos Petrescu's chapter in this book.

[68] Idem.

[69] See Law for Banks and Credit of March 4, 1992 and Law for Temporary Introduction of Additional Requirements for Members of the Executive Bodies of the Scientific Organizations and the Higher Certifying Commission of December 9, 1992 (Panev Law), both cited in Human Rights Watch, "Decommunization in Bulgaria," 5:14 (August 1993): 5, available at: https://www.hrw.org/sites/default/files/reports/BULGARIA938.PDF, "Act Regarding the Records of the State Security Service of the former German Democratic Republic of December 20, 1991 (Stasi Records Act)," Berlin, 2013, available at: http://www.bstu.bund.de/DE/BundesbeauftragterUndBehoerde/Rechtsgrundlagen/StUG/StUG_englisch/StUG_englisch_pdf.pdf?__blob=publicationFile; as well as Act No 451/1991 in Czechoslovakia, cited in Pavel Zacek, "Lustration Laws in the Czech Republic. The application of Act No 451/1991 Coll. and Act No 279/1992 Coll.," no date, available at: http://etickakomisecr.cz/data/pdf/clanky/zacek-lustrace.pdf, all of them accessed on October 30, 2016.

apparatus at all levels (including the army and the border guards), the Communist Party leadership structures (including the political officers), and party affiliated (youth, antifascist, peasant) organizations that were listed in these legislative pieces were never referred to as "collaborators," since they were considered as principal decision-making agents.

Conclusions

The Romanian transitional justice legislation was formulated in a way that ignored shared academic wisdom about the citizens' various types of involvement with the previous dictatorial regime. As the chapter suggests, on the one hand, the academic literature on Nazism and communism has increasingly accepted the vast plurality and diversity of behavior that placed individuals on the side of the dictatorship or on the side of those critical of it. Shades of collaboration and consent have been juxtaposed to as many shades of resistance, dissent, and defiance. On the other hand, the legislation passed in Romania (and other post-communist countries) has tended to reserve the term "collaborator" primarily for the secret informers who surreptitiously aided the repressive apparatus. In these countries most areas of life had been controlled by the communist regime, and therefore factory managers, newspaper editors, university professors, heads of agricultural cooperatives, and other decision-makers had all collaborated with the hegemonic Communist Party. However, in legal terms these categories were mostly excluded from the de-communization process, although individuals who occupied similar positions in German-occupied countries had been targeted by the much earlier denazification process.

Note that in Romania no serious academic or intellectual debate took place during the early 1990s, that is, before the legislation was passed, to ponder on the meaning of these basic terms. This paucity could have stemmed from the repressiveness of the communist regime, which stifled debates of all sorts; the insistence of former communist leaders like Ion Iliescu that they had been the true dissenters, overshadowing the claims of other dissenters and sufferers; the vicious campaigns waged by the "revolutionary" leaders to discredit communist-era anticommunists such as Doina Cornea, whose anticommunist crusade and claims of victimhood were ridiculed; the emphasis with which independent associations like the Group for Social Dialogue championed concepts like "resistance through culture," downplaying the plight of the former political victims; as well as the weakness of other civil society groups. Whatever the reason for overlooking previous efforts to conceptualize basic terms of the debate, the Romanian public would greatly benefit from greater familiarity with it.

CHAPTER THREE

EVALUATING MEASURES AND THEIR OUTCOMES

CYNTHIA M. HORNE

Romania's efforts to confront its communist past using transitional justice measures have often been highly politicized, thwarted by entrenched interests, overridden by various political actors, including the President and the Constitutional Court, and circumvented by former members of the communist political elite.[1] In this chapter, the term transitional justice describes a broad set of measures by which society confronts the wrongdoings in its past with the goal of obtaining some combination of truth, justice, rule of law, and durable peace for the future.[2] Even with such a broad definition, if a consensus exists, it might agree that Romania missed many opportunities to authentically engage with possibly beneficial measures. Taking as a starting point the well documented problems with Romania's transitional justice efforts, this chapter is motivated by two questions: first, how did Romania's transitional justice measures compare to other regionally proximate post-communist cases,

---

[1] Adrian Cioflanca, "Politics of Oblivion in Post-Communist Romania," *Romanian Journal of Political Science*, 2:2 (2002): 85-93; Bogdan Iancu, "Post-Accession Constitutionalism with a Human Face: Judicial Reform and Lustration in Romania," *European Constitutional Law Review*, 6:1 (2010): 28-58; Ed Maxfield, "Romania," in *Encyclopedia of Transitional Justice*, eds. Lavinia Stan and Nadya Nedelsky (Cambridge: Cambridge University Press, 2013), 2:7-14; Lavinia Stan, *Transitional Justice in Post-Communist Romania: The Politics of Memory* (New York: Cambridge University Press, 2013); Lavinia Stan and Diane Vancea, "Old Wine in New Bottles: The Romanian Elections of 2008," *Problems of Post-Communism*, 56:5 (2009): 47-61.

[2] Neil Kritz, "Policy Implications of Empirical Research on Transitional Justice," in *Assessing the Impact of Transitional Justice*, eds. Hugo Van der Merwe, Victoria Baxter and Audrey Chapman (Washington, D.C.: U.S. Institute of Peace, 2009), 14.

and second, have Romania's (extremely) flawed efforts to address the past produced any positive results? To address these questions, the chapter focuses on the use and misuse of lustration laws, secret police file access procedures, and public disclosures of previous regime collaboration as a triumvirate of related transitional justice processes. By lustration measures, I mean specialized forms of employment screening, which could include the "banning of communist officials and secret political police officers and informers from post-communist politics and positions of influence in society" and/or the naming of individuals without formal employment removal penalties.[3] Lustration measures, public disclosures of regime collaboration for individuals in positions of public trust, and general citizen access to information in secret police files are related transitional justice measures due to the focus on the secret police files and potential formal or informal consequences associated with revelations of the past. Since these measures are allegedly used to support transition goals like building trust in public institutions, promoting democracy and curbing corruption, this chapter also examines Romania's progress in meeting some of these stated goals over the past twenty-five years.

This chapter takes a comparative perspective on Romania's transitional justice measures and transition outcomes. If one were to look only at Romania, it would be relatively easy to point out all the ways Romania deviated from a transitional justice ideal. In order to contextualize Romania's experience, it needs to be considered with respect to what has actually been achieved in other comparable post-communist cases. However, the transitional justice comparison must be appropriate if it is to be illustrative. Comparing Romania to a transition trajectory which was not a viable possibility in 1989, like the Czech Republic's, will yield few valuable insights.[4] To that end, first this chapter reviews the measures passed and implemented in Romania in comparison with the other Balkan countries that were considered regionally comparable in 1989, namely Bulgaria and Albania. The comparison spotlights the implementation of measures, the timing of measures, and the politicization of measures. Second, this chapter examines three transition goals linked to transitional justice measures, namely the building of trustworthy public institutions, support for democracy, and anti-corruption progress across several post-communist countries. Romania's performance on these three outcomes will be considered with respect to the Balkan experience as well as cases

---

[3] Lavinia Stan, ed., *Transitional Justice in Eastern Europe and the Former Soviet Union: Reckoning with the Communist Past* (London: Routledge Press, 2009), 11.
[4] Eva-Clarita Pettai and Vello Pettai, *Transitional and Retrospective Justice in the Baltic States* (Cambridge: Cambridge University Press, 2014).

considered to have had more effective lustration and transitional justice programs, like Poland and Hungary. To preview the findings, Romania finds itself stuck in the middle—the middle of regional reforms and the middle of regional progress. The conclusion speaks to what the presence or absence of transitional justice measures in Romania says about its larger post-communist transition.

Transitional justice measures

Timing and implementation

Balkans countries are considered regional laggards in terms of transitional justice, but measures were both proposed and adopted in the region early in the transition. This section considers the timing, passage and implementation of measures in the Balkans as a way to draw parallels between Romania and its neighbors. The focus is not only on measures that were passed, but also on measures that were passed over or failed to be implemented. Albania and Bulgaria passed lustration-style laws before Romania, and therefore their efforts will be considered before Romania's in keeping with temporal considerations of the range of possible and concurrent measures available to Romania in the immediate transition environment. Table 3.1 lays out the measures in the three countries for ease of comparison.

Table 3.1: Lustration, Public Disclosure and File Access Laws and Policies

Country	Transitional justice measures (both passed and rejected)
Albania	1991—Ruli Report—first trials of former regime on economic grounds. Law 7541 of 18 December on Advocacy in the Republic of Albania becomes first attempt at lustration, with narrow focus on lawyers. 1992—Purges of political opposition in public sector--no file access. 1993 – Law 7666 of 26 January 1993 On the Creation of a Commission to Re-assess Licenses for the Exercise of Advocacy and for an Amendment to Law 7541/1991 facilitated the implementation of the 1991 Law on Advocacy. 1995—Law 8001 of 22 September On Genocide and Crimes Against Humanity Committed in Albania during the Communist Regime for Political, Ideological and Religious Reasons (The Genocide Law). No real implementation of this lustration measure.

	1995—Law 8043 of 30 November On the Control of the Moral Figure of Officials and Other Persons Connected with the Protection of the Democratic State (The Verification Law). No real implementation of this lustration measure. 1997—Government reduces scope of Verification Law and both the Genocide and the Verification Laws expire without implementation in 2001. 2008—Law 10034 of 22 December On the cleanliness of the figure of High Functionaries of the Public Administration and Elected Persons (Clean Hands Bill) 2009—Clean Hands bill declared unconstitutional and not implemented.
Bulgaria	1990—Publication of unconfirmed list of collaborators. 1992—Law 25 of 18 March on Banks and Credit Activity, passed as lustration of banking sector, but declared unconstitutional. 1992—Law of 9 December for Temporary Introduction of Some Additional Requirements for the Members of the Executive Bodies of Scientific Organizations and the Higher Certifying Commission (Panev Law) — narrow focus of lustration on science and academics. 1993-4—several trials of former leadership, limited scope. 1997—Access to the Former State Security Files Act of 30 July, and creation of Committee for Access to the Former State Security Files (Bonev Committee). Limited effect: 23 public disclosures of collaboration. 1998—Law on Public Radio and Television. 1999—Constitutional Court limits publication of informers. 2001-2—Access to the Former State Security and the General Staff Intelligence Directorate Files Act of 28 February 2001; and creation of Commission Determining Connections to the Former State Security (Andreev Committee). 7000 individuals investigated, 517 collaborators disclosed. 2002—Classified Information Protection Act repeals access to files. 2006—Declassification of secret police archives. 2006—Law for Access and Disclosure of the Documents and Announcing Affiliations of Bulgarian Citizens to the State Security and the Intelligence Services of the Bulgarian National Army, December. 2007—Committee for Disclosing the Documents and Announcing Affiliation of Bulgarian Citizens to the State Security and the Intelligence Services of the Bulgarian National Army (Kostadinov

	Committee)—to implement the new law, April 2007. 2007-present—Dossier Commission engages in file review and public disclosures. During 2011-4 extensive public revelations of collaboration of academics, media, clergy, Foreign Service, cabinet positions, and "credit millionaires" with secret police backgrounds.
Romania	1990—Proclamation of Timişoara's call for lustration are not implemented. Long period of no activity—President declares lustration over in 1997. 1999—Law 187 of 9 December on Access to the Personal File and Disclosure of the Securitate as Political Police (Ticu Law). Created Council for the Study of the Securitate Archives (CNSAS) to oversee the secret police files and control public access to this information. CNSAS functions as a de facto vetting institution, issuing symbolic rulings, but implementation limited (70 collaborators revealed, 38 candidates resign). 2005—Emergency Ordinance 149 of 10 November extends the CNSAS's activities. 2006—Emergency Ordinance 16 of 22 February modifies Law 187/1999 to facilitate the work of the CNSAS. Renewed lustration—270 collaborators revealed through informal disclosures. 2008—Constitutional Court Decision 51 of 31 January declares Law 187/1999 unconstitutional. 2008—Parliament passes Law 293 of 14 November to modify Emergency Ordinance 16 and change the activities of the CNSAS. 2012—New Lustration Law, passed by Parliament in February 2012, is declared unconstitutional. 2012-present—public disclosures continue through CNSAS.

Albania purged its public sectors in 1992, replacing an estimated 250,000 bureaucrats with party loyalists.[5] The non-transparent forced personnel change constituted a purge, not a transitional justice act, and affected subsequent interest in other more legally constrained bureaucratic change measures. The 1991 Law On Advocacy and its 1993 amendment (Law 7666) constituted a type of lustration measure, but it narrowly targeted lawyers, preventing certain categories of collaborators or officers

[5] Robert Austin and Jonathan Ellison, "Post-Communist Transitional Justice in Albania," *East European Politics and Societies,* 22:2 (2008): 373-401.

with the State Security agency, and members of the Albania Labor Party (the Communist Party), from legal work for a period of five years. The Constitutional Court struck down this limited lustration law, resulting in no implementation.[6] Of note is the extremely narrow scope of the measures—lawyers—which would have resulted in a nominal, limited lustration effort at best. The Genocide Law 8001/1995 and the Verification Law 8043/1995 were wider in scope, providing screening provisions across a range of government positions, the educational system, and the media. The Verification Committee created to implement the measures immediately barred 139 people from participating in elections. However, the Committee was largely made up of Democratic Party members, whereas those barred were from opposition parties, thus rendering lustration a tool of political vendetta against opposition parties.[7] In 1997, the Socialist Party came to power after a scandal involving the Democratic Party, and they reduced the scope of the Verification Law. The Genocide Law was also rolled back, and the Supreme Court acquitted all those accused. Despite several lustration laws, there was little implementation in practice, and the Verification and the Genocide Laws expired in 2001.[8] The overt political manipulation of the laws, smear campaigns against opposition parties, and informal allegations published in newspapers, combined with a lack of citizen access to the files, resulted in the delegitimization of the measures. In 2008 a new lustration law was passed popularly called The Clean Hands Bill, but it was declared unconstitutional and annulled by the Constitutional Court, thereby foreclosing lustration in Albania.[9] Issues were raised with the objectivity of the Court's decision, since judges and prosecutors might have been personally affected by lustration. Nevertheless, the decision stood.[10] In sum, Albania forced politicized bureaucratic change through the use of purges and several lustration laws, but looking at the implementation one cannot say Albania engaged in authentic transitional justice.

---

[6] Kathleen Imholz, "A Landmark Constitutional Court Decision in Albania," *East European Constitutional Review* 2:3 (1993): 22-25.

[7] Austin and Ellison, "Transitional Justice in Albania," 388.

[8] Robert Austin, "Albania," in *Encyclopedia of Transitional Justice*, eds. Lavinia Stan and Nadya Nedelsky (Cambridge University Press, 2013), 2:7-14.

[9] Venice Commission, "Law on the Cleanliness of the Figure of High Functionaries of the Public Administration and Elected Persons of the Republic of Albania, Opinion No 524/2009" (Strasbourg, 13 August 2009); and Austin, "Albania."

[10] "Albanian High Court Annuls Lustration Law," *BalkanInsight*, 2 February 2010.

In the case of Bulgaria, the 1992 Law on Banks and Credit Activity focused very narrowly on individuals in bank management positions but was declared unconstitutional in 1992, never implemented, and abolished by Parliament in 1997.[11] The 1992 Panev Law narrowly targeted academics and scientific institutions, and was in force until 1995.[12] Again, the narrow focus on academics did not suggest a lustration process with substantial bureaucratic change potential. Finally, the 1998 Law on Public Radio and Television prohibited state security officers and informers from being elected as members of the Council for Electronic Media, and in practice the Council did remove one member for being a former informer.[13] As with the early Albanian lustration laws, the very narrow focus of the laws suggested an attempt to deflect transitional justice attention away from public office holders, rather than engage with an authentic lustration of public institutions and governance. It was not until 2001 that public disclosures of previous collaboration began across public sectors in a manner that could be considered a fledgling and extremely limited attempt at real lustration. In practice, the implementation of lustration and public disclosure processes in Bulgaria started in earnest only in 2006 with the passage of the Law for Access and Disclosure of the Documents and Announcing Affiliations of Bulgarian Citizens to the State Security and the Intelligence Services of the Bulgarian National Army, suggesting significantly delayed accountability mechanisms in Bulgaria in practice.[14] As such, despite passing three lustration style laws, Bulgaria had no real accountability or bureaucratic change before 2006.

---

[11] "Bulgaria: Law on Banks and Credit Activity, No. 25 of March 18, 1992," in *Transitional Justice: How Emerging Democracies Reckon with Former Regimes*, ed. Neil Kritz (Washington, DC: United States Institute of Peace Studies, 1995), 3:293; and Momchil Metodiev, "Bulgaria," in Stan and Nedelsky, eds., *Encyclopedia of Transitional Justice*, 73-79.

[12] "Bulgaria: Law for Temporary Introduction of Some Additional Requirements for the Members of the Executive Bodies of Scientific Organizations and the Higher Certifying Commission ("Panev Law"). December 9, 1992," in Kritz, ed., *Transitional Justice*, 296-299, and "Bulgaria: Constitutional Court Decision on the Panev Law, Constitutional Court Case No. 32, Decision No. 1 (February 11, 1993)," in Kritz, ed., *Transitional Justice*, 300-302.

[13] Metodiev, "Bulgaria."

[14] "Law for Access and Disclosure of the Documents and Announcing Affiliations of Bulgarian Citizens to the State Security and the Intelligence Services of the Bulgarian National Army," December 2006, available at: http://lex.bg/bg/laws/ldoc/2135540283, and Bulgarian Dossier Commission, "The Curtain Is Raised," no date, available at: http://www.comdos.bg/, both accessed on 26 August 2016.

Taking a closer look at both the timing and implementation of regional measures puts Romania's transitional justice in comparative perspective (Table 3.1). Although Romania was late to pass a lustration law, it was early to start discussing lustration as a transitional justice possibility. In March 1990, the Proclamation of Timişoara called for lustration through the adoption of electoral law amendments that would have in effect screened and banned Communist Party leaders and Securitate agents from running in presidential elections and from being included on party lists.[15] As Stan explained, although it stands as only a missed opportunity, since lustration would fail to materialize in Romania for almost another decade, it set the parameters of the lustration debate in the country. In 1993 Senator Constantin Ticu Dumitrescu introduced a lustration type proposal that would have prevented part-time Securitate informers from being blackmailed based on their previous collaboration, but the proposal was rendered inert by a lack of general access to the secret police files. Dumitrescu pushed forward another lustration proposal, which was more expansive, highly contentious, hotly debated, rewritten and stripped of lustration provisions. It finally narrowly passed to become Law 187/1999 on Access to the Personal File and Disclosure of the Securitate as the Political Police (Ticu Law).[16] In practice, Consiliul Național pentru Studierea Arhivelor Securității (CNSAS or National Council for the Study of the Securitate Archives), the agency charged with administering the process, lacked independent file access privileges. Institutional constraints on CNSAS and a review process based on voluntary confessions and self-resignations resulted in the overall politicization of the process and no real implementation.[17] It was not until 2005-2006, when President Traian Băsescu intervened and had some 1.3 million files transferred from the Romanian Information Service (SRI) to the CNSAS, that public disclosures became a real possibility.

The timing of the actually implemented measures puts Romania on par with Bulgaria and ahead of Albania. To put the timing of Romania's reforms in regional context, Poland also engaged with late lustration measures, passing its first measure in 1997, as compared to Romania's 1999 law. Poland also expanded its lustration provisions significantly in 2006, about the same time that Romania engaged in its expanded public

[15] Lavinia Stan, "Civil Society and Post-communist Transitional Justice in Romania," in *Transitional Justice and Civil Society in the Balkans*, eds. Olivera Simić and Zala Volčič (London: Springer, 2013), 22.

[16] Stan, *Transitional Justice in Romania.*

[17] Author's interviews with members of the Collegium, CNSAS, Bucharest, Romania, October 2012.

disclosure program.[18] Lithuania passed a lustration law in 1999, and Hungary expanded and extended lustration in 2000. Even the Czech Republic did not grant public file access until 2002.[19] In essence, placing Romania within a regional context illustrates the many late lustration measures in the post-communist region. Moreover, the most expansive period of public disclosures in Romania corresponded with a similar late, expansive public disclosure program in Bulgaria.

Public Disclosures

There was temporal and procedural continuity between the public disclosure programs adopted in Romania and Bulgaria in terms of the implementation of late transition accountability measures. The CNSAS in Romania and the Dossier Commission in Bulgaria are both file repository agencies and members of the European Network of Official Authorities in Charge of the Secret Police Files.[20] The Bulgarian Constitution officially prohibits lustration and the Romanian Constitutional Court has ruled many times on the unconstitutionality of similar lustration measures.[21] Thus, these file repository agencies play a pseudo-lustration role using the secret

---

[18] Lustration Act of 11 April 1997, Law on Disclosing Work for or Service in the State's Security Services or Collaboration with Them between 1944 and 1990 by Persons Exercising Public Functions; and Act of 18 October 2006, On the Disclosure of Information on Documents of State Security in 1944-1990 and the Content of These Documents. For a comparison of the Polish and Romanian cases of late lustration, see Cynthia M. Horne, "Late Lustration Programs in Romania and Poland: Supporting or Undermining Democratic Transitions?," *Democratization* 16:2 (2009): 344-376.

[19] Lithuania's Lustration Law is Law VIII-1436 of 23 November 1999 On the Registration and Acknowledgment ("Confession") of Those Who Secretly Collaborated with the Soviet Special Services. In Hungary Act 93/2000 extended lustration for four years, and increased the number of people to be screened, and Act 3/2003 created the Historical Archives and amended the lustration law to include all secret service divisions. In the Czech Republic Act 422/2000 indefinitely extended lustration law.

[20] Rafał Leśkiewicz and Pavel Žáček, eds., *Handbook of the European Network of Official Authorities in Charge of the Secret Police Files* (Prague: The Institute for the Study of Totalitarian Regimes and the Institute of National Remembrance, 2013).

[21] Romanian Constitutional Court, "Decision no. 820/2010," *Monitorul Oficial al Romaniei*, 420, 23 June 2010; and Bulgarian Dossier Commission website, available at: http://www.comdos.bg/, accessed on 2 May 2014.

police files to disclose the background of individuals in a variety of positions of public trust.

The Romanian CNSAS's active role in unmasking collaborators and agents did not start until after the file transfer of 2006, and commenced in earnest in 2008. The Bulgarian Dossier Commission was empowered in December 2006, but really began to expand the scope of its work in 2007-2008. At that time, the Dossier Commission and the CNSAS began to review the files of political candidates and individuals in positions of public trust, and publicly disclose any former collaboration found in the secret archives. This information could not result in formal employment penalties, as there were no punitive lustration laws in place, but they had an important disclosure purpose with potential bureaucratic change elements. The scope of positions screened was broad, covering elected officials and public bureaucrats at the national and regional levels, as well as semi-public positions, such as cultural directors, or clergy members in the case of Bulgaria. While both the Dossier Commission and the CNSAS have limitations on the degree to which they can engage with formal lustration, they used their capacity as public disclosure agencies with access to the secret archives to pursue informal lustration.[22]

The public disclosures of former secret police agents and collaborators in positions of power were and are published openly on the agency websites, as forms of symbolic public accountability.[23] Both agencies reported that fear of public disclosure caused political parties to self-lustrate potential candidates before placing them on electoral tickets, thereby demonstrating an institutional change function to disclosures.[24] The agencies also reported that some individuals resigned positions to avoid media attention or public backlash. Therefore, a self-selection mechanism is associated with public disclosures as well, much like the non-punitive employment change components of lustration measures used in Hungary and Poland.

---

[22] For more extensive comparisons between the programs and an elaboration of limitations on the activities of CNSAS, see Cynthia M. Horne, "Silent Lustration: Public Disclosures as Informal Lustration Mechanisms in Bulgaria and Romania," *Problems of Post-Communism* 63:2 (2015): 131-144.

[23] The Bulgarian Registrar, available at: at http://agentibg.com/index.php/bg/, accessed on 13 September 2016. The Romanian archives and publications can be found at: http://www.cnsas.ro/, accessed on 26 August 2016.

[24] Author's interviews with Chairman Evtim Kostadinov, Dossier Commission, Sofia, Bulgaria, 12 July 2012 and his counterpart in Romania, Dr. Dragoş Petrescu, Chairman of the Board, CNSAS, Bucharest, Romania, 12 October 2012.

In sum, the Romanian and Bulgarian public disclosure programs currently operate as transitional justice mechanisms, albeit late and informal mechanisms. In both cases, file revelations are the primary symbolic efforts to come to terms with the past, and catalyze potential bureaucratic change. This is less than the bureaucratic change effected in other post-communist states with more formal and exclusionary lustration laws. By contrast, Albania largely terminated any remaining efforts to deal with the past. The next section compares the politicization of transitional justice in several post-communist countries to elucidate some of the delays in and misuse of measures.

Political parties and manipulation

Lustration and file disclosure policies are politically sensitive, with potential political blowback from the disclosure of complicity with the previous regime. Nalepa documented how fear of public disclosure affected the attitudes of political parties at the Round Table talks in Poland in 1989, and post-communist attitudes toward transitional justice in Czechoslovakia and Hungary.[25] There is evidence that the political orientation of the dominant party affected the initiation and content of lustration laws, with parties dominated by former communist elites and secret police informants disinclined toward lustration and public disclosure. In many post-communist countries, lustration laws have been wielded by parties in an attempt to potentially discredit opponent parties in the eyes of voters.[26] This was true in the case of Romania, where vacillations in support for transitional justice and accountability made for a politicized, and at times questionable, transitional justice experience.[27] No one party was to blame for stymieing lustration, for as Stan noted, opposition to lustration came from parties across the political spectrum.[28] The instrumental manipulation of measures in Romania affected implementation and perceived legitimacy.

---

[25] Monika Nalepa, *Skeletons in the Closet: Transitional Justice in Post-Communist Europe* (New York: Cambridge University Press, 2010).

[26] Cynthia Horne and Margaret Levi, "Does Lustration Promote Trustworthy Governance? An Exploration of the Experience of Central and Eastern Europe," in *Building a Trustworthy State in Post-Socialist Transition*, eds. János Kornai and Susan Rose-Ackerman (New York: Palgrave/Macmillan Press, 2004).

[27] Lavinia Stan, "Witch-Hunt or Moral Rebirth? Romanian Parliamentary Debates on Lustration," *East European Politics and Societies*, 26:2 (2012): 274-295.

[28] Stan, *Transitional Justice in Romania,* 92.

For example, Senator Ticu Dumitrescu originally proposed a lustration type measure in 1993, but it was rejected by the left-dominated parliament, and then reconsidered in 1996 under the center-right government.[29] A significantly modified version finally passed in 1999, surviving attempts to block the measure by members of Dumitrescu's own National Peasant Party.[30] Parliament modified the standing lustration law in 2006, but two years later the Constitutional Court struck down the modifications and the original 1999 law. Renewed and highly contested lustration efforts in 2010 resurrected elements of the 2006 law, but they were also struck down by the Court in 2010.[31] In 2012 another lustration law was passed despite opposition from parties across the political spectrum, but prior to implementation the Court struck it down as well. A legislatively active Constitutional Court significantly shaped transitional justice in Romania.[32]

Constitutional Courts have been active in lustration and transitional justice issues across the post-communist region in Bulgaria, Poland, Hungary and Albania. The Hungarian Court struck down the retroactive justice components of lustration, significantly limiting the lustration implemented in Hungary, at the same time the Czechoslovak Constitutional Court ruled in favor of similar measures.[33] The highly activist Polish Constitutional Court ruled on the admissibility or lack of constitutionality of lustration-type measures on more than one occasion. The communist appointees in the Bulgarian Constitutional Court ruled on the unconstitutionality of the first lustration provisions, the Law on Banking and Credit (1992) and the Panev bill, soon after their passage.[34] Albania's Constitutional Court struck down the last effort at passing lustration: the

---

[29] Maxfield, "Romania."

[30] Stan, *Transitional Justice in Romania*, 92.

[31] Romanian Constitutional Court, "Decision No. 820/2010."

[32] Iancu, "Post-Accession Constitutionalism."

[33] Neil Kritz, ed. "Czech Republic: Constitutional Court Decision on the Screening Law (November 26, 1992)," in *Transitional Justice*: *How Emerging Democracies Reckon with Former Regimes*, ed. Neil Kritz (Washington, DC: United States Institute of Peace Studies, 1995), 3:369-374, and "Hungary: Constitutional Court Decision on the Statute of Limitations, No. 2086/A/1991/14 (March 5, 1992)," in *Transitional Justice*: *How Emerging Democracies Reckon with Former Regimes*, ed. Neil Kritz (Washington, DC: United States Institute of Peace Studies, 1995), 3:351.

[34] Helsinki Watch, "Decommunization in Bulgaria," *Human Rights Watch*, 5:14 (August 1993), available at: https://www.hrw.org/sites/default/files/reports/BULGARIA938.PDF, accessed on 14 September 2016.

Clean Hands Bill.[35] In a word, while Romania's Constitutional Court has been politically interventionist on the topic of lustration, it was not regionally anomalous.

Political parties also played a heavy hand influencing both the passage and the blockage of transitional justice measures in Romania. Table 3.2 pairs some transitional justice measures alongside the dominant political party in Parliament. Between 1990 and 1996 both the ruling government and the opposition blocked lustration efforts. As Table 3.2 illustrates, support for or rejection of lustration cannot be simplistically explained as a function of the political orientation of the party in power. Center-left and center-right party coalitions have been in power and neither has adopted a single approach—either for or against—transitional justice measures. The 2006 law in particular was highly contentious and largely opposed by parties comprised of many former Communist Party members. However, it was backed by the National Liberal Party, which would have been negatively affected by lustration due to the known collaborators in their ranks, including the popular minister of culture Mona Musca.[36] While there is clear evidence of political gaming of transitional justice measures in Romania, party affiliations or communist legacies cannot explain neatly the presence or absence of transitional justice measures over time.

To put Romania's experience in regional context, in Poland there is also evidence of significant party involvement in lustration debates. Although the first parliamentary motion on lustration was adopted in 1989, it was not until 1996 that a draft lustration law passed the Polish Parliament and it took effect only in 1997. After final passage, the Polish Constitutional Court, political parties and even the president weighed in both positively and negatively on aspects of lustration, resulting in what some described as "no lustration at all" up until the passage of the 2006 expanded lustration provisions.[37] Even that version of the law was politically contentious, with the Constitutional Court striking down some elements of that law.[38]

---

[35] Austin, "Albania."

[36] For a discussion of the parliamentary debates surrounding the 2006 lustration efforts see Stan, "Witch Hunt or Moral Rebirth."

[37] Lavinia Stan, "The Politics of Memory in Poland: Lustration, File Access and Court Proceedings," *Studies in Post-Communism Occasional Paper*, No. 10, St. Francis Xavier University, Centre for Post-Communist Studies (2006): 46; and Cynthia M. Horne, "Late Lustration."

[38] Polish Constitutional Tribunal, Judgment of 11th May 2007, file Ref. No. K 2/07 LUSTRATION.

Table 3.2: Timing of Transitional Justice Compared with Dominant Political Parties

Year	Transitional Justice Measure	Political Parties Dominant in Parliamentary Elections (% votes)	Year	Transitional Justice Measure	Political Parties Dominant in Parliamentary Elections (% votes)
1990	*Proclamation of Timişoara's* calls for lustration are not implemented	66.31% National Salvation Front (FSN)—*left/center-left, made up of former communists*	**2004**		36.61% National Union PSD+PUR—*center-left* 31.33% Justice and Truth Alliance (DA)—*center-right*
1992		27.72% Democratic National Salvation Front (FDSN)—*center-left* 20% Democratic Convention of Romania (CDR)—*center-right* electoral alliance of parties against National Salvation Front (FSN, former communists)	**2005**	Emergency Ordinance No. 149, extending the CNSAS's activities. 1 million files transferred to CNSAS from Romanian Intelligence Service	
1996		30% Democratic Convention of Romania (CDR)—*center-right liberal electoral alliance* 21.52% Social Democracy Party of Romania (PDSR)—*center-left*	**2006**	Emergency Ordinance No. 16 modifies Law 187/1999 to facilitate the work of the CNSAS. Renewed lustration—270 collaborators revealed.	

1997	President declares lustration over.		**2008**	Constitutional Court Decision No. 51 declares Law 187/1999 unconstitutional (31 January).	33.10% Alliance Social Democratic Party + Conservative Party (PSD+PC)—*center-left political alliance* 32.36% Democratic Liberal Party (PDL)-*center*
1999	Law 187/1999 On Access to the Personal File and Disclosure of the Securitate as Political Police (Ticu Law) Created CNSAS to oversee the files.		**2009**	CNSAS's power to issue collaboration verdicts taken away	
2000		36.61% Social Democracy Party of Romania (PDSR)—*center-left* 19.48% Greater Romania Party (PRM)—*nationalist*	**2012**	2012 lustration law initiative declared unconstitutional	58.63% Social Liberal Union (US)—*coalition of center-right and center-left parties*
2001	Limited CNSAS activity. 70 collaborators revealed, 38 candidates resign.		**2016**	CNSAS continues public disclosures	Elections organized in Fall

Sources: For party information, European Elections Database, available at: http://www.nsd.uib.no/european_election_database/country/romania/parties.html, accessed on 15 September 2016

Table 3.3 compares the immediate post-transition political environment in Hungary, Poland and Czechoslovakia, helping to contextualize the Romanian experience. As it shows, support for transitional justice fluctuated in Hungary and Poland, depending on the orientation of the dominant party, but remained relatively constant in the Czech Republic. Lustration measures were both rejected and expanded in Hungary under the socialist/former communist led government in 1994. The very polarized elections of 2002 yielding a slim socialist majority, and corresponded with an expansion of file access information. At one point the radical populist Hungarian Justice and Life Party (MIEP) proposed an expansion of screening measures, and at other times the Socialist-Free Democrat coalition and the opposition parties FIDESZ and the Hungarian Democratic Forum (MDF) proposed expansion of lustration and citizen access.[39] In places with strong hold over communist legacy parties, there has been both rejection of and support for lustration and file access at different times. For example, the Bulgarian Socialist Party (BSP) led government passed the 2006 public disclosure/lustration law and appointed Chairman Evtim Kostadinov as head of the Dossier Commission.[40] Under his leadership, Bulgaria embarked on a wide and deep public disclosure program. Political orientation affected attitudes toward lustration but was not deterministic, even in countries considered more forward thinking with respect to transitional justice than Romania. In many ways the absence of overt politicization of the Czech laws looks like the regional outlier rather than Romania.

In sum, the first section of this chapter considered the timing, passage, implementation, and politicization of measures in three Balkan countries in order to contextualize Romania's experience with transitional justice. If one were to assess transitional justice measures in the region simply based on whether a lustration law was in place and according to which country passed a law first, then Romania would look like the Balkan laggard. However, on closer inspection both the timing and the implementation of measures in Romania mirrored those in Bulgaria and significantly outpaced the lack of measures in Albania. Moreover, the political manipulation of transitional justice was not a Romanian phenomenon; the same could also be said of Bulgaria, Poland and Hungary. Although Romania has not been as successful with its transitional justice measures as it could have been, it is neither a regional outlier nor extraordinary. Unfortunately, Romania's missed opportunities with transitional justice,

[39] Horne and Levi, "Trustworthy Governance."
[40] Metodiev, "Bulgaria."

Table 3.3: Political Fractionalization and Lustration Measures

CZECH REPUBLIC								
Elections # parties in election party fractioning[1]	**1990** 12 0.55		**1992** 20 0.79	**1996** 20 0.76	**1998** 18 0.73			
Dominant Party in Parl elections	***Civic Forum***		***conservative rightwing***	***Czech Dem Party slim lead no clearwinners***	***Czech Social Democratic Party***			
Lustration Law	**1990** candidates request screening	**1991** lustration law enacted	**1992** citizens get access to files extend statute of limitations	**1996** extend time of law		**2000** extend law indefinitely		
HUNGARY								
Elections # parties in election party fractioning		**1990** 59 0.71		**1994** 43 0.65			**1998** 33 0.74	**2002**
Dominant Pol Party in Parl elections		***center-right govt***		***socialist-former Comm govt***			***center-right returns to power***	***very polarized elections Socialist slim majority***
Lustration Law	**1989 (Nov)** Zetenyi-Takacs Law	**1990** lustration law enacted	**1991** extend statute of limitations	**1994** rejects extension of screening lists	**1995** citizens granted access	**1996** all individuals taking parl positions		**2002** change citizen access change scope of
POLAND								
Elections # parties in election party fractioning		**1991** 111 0.9		**1993** 35 0.75		**1997** 21 0.67	**2001**	
Dominant Pol Party in Parl elections				***Democratic Left Alliance socialist***		***Center-Right parties reelected after 1993 defeat AWS Solidarity Election Action***	***Democratic Left Alliance socialist***	
Lustration Law			**1992** no lustration law but leaked list timed w/elections		**1996** lustration law drafted	**1997** lustration law adopted		

[1] The higher the number (scale 0-1) the more dispersed the seats, and the less strong is any one party in Parliament. Calculated by Grzymala-Busse (2002: 304-Table C.1).

Sources: European Forum for Democracy and Cooperation, http://www.europeanforum.net/; RFE/RL Reports, various years;
Anna Grzymala-Busse, *Redeeming the Communist Past: The Regeneration of Communist Parties in East Central Europe.* Cambridge University Press (2002).
Neil Kritz, ed. *Transitional Justice.* Washington DC: United States Institute of Peace Studies(1995).

politicization of measures, and implementation delays were echoed in other post-communist experiences as well. The next section turns to an evaluation of transition goals in Romania, again placing its progress in regional context.

Evaluating transition outcomes

This section considers Romania's progress on several transition goals linked to transitional justice measures like lustration, public disclosures and file access procedures, namely building trust in public institutions, tackling corruption, and promoting democratization. As with the previous section, Romania is compared to the regionally proximate cases of Albania and Bulgaria, as well as the cases of Poland and Hungary, in order to evaluate possible relationships between transition goals and transitional justice.

Trust in Public Institutions

Public institutions like the judiciary, the courts, and the police are important for the effective functioning of a state. It is not just the staffing of those institutions that matters, but also public perception that those institutions are trustworthy. Effective and trustworthy public institutions are linked to good governance and democratization in the comparative politics literature.[41] As such, building trustworthy public institutions was a transition goal for post-communist countries.[42] Transitional justice measures like lustration and public disclosures were first and foremost designed to expose the collaborator backgrounds of individuals in these very public institutions. Lustration started out as a means of screening individuals in public positions, to assess their integrity and capacity to do their job based on evidence of previous collaboration or employment with the secret police and/or communist regime.[43] As such, lustration and its

[41] Matthew Cleary and Susan Stokes, *Democracy and the Culture of Skepticism: Political Trust in Argentina and Mexico* (New York: Russell Sage, 2006); Mark Warren, ed., *Democracy and Trust* (New York: Cambridge University Press, 1999).

[42] János Kornai and Susan Rose-Ackerman, eds., *Building a Trustworthy State in Post-Socialist Transition* (New York: Palgrave/Macmillan Press, 2004).

[43] Roman David, *Lustration and Transitional Justice: Personnel Systems in the Czech Republic, Hungary, and Poland* (Philadelphia: University of Pennsylvania Press, 2011).

employment vetting aspects were intimately linked to efforts to improve the functionality and trustworthiness of targeted public institutions.

In Romania, most of the public institutions were heavily staffed by loyalists to the Communist Party. Securitate networks of agents and informers infiltrated public institutions as a means of maintaining control over the population and ensuring that those institutions enforced policies consistent with the regime goals. Because Romania had limited lustration and did not engage in compulsory employment sanctions for individuals with known collaborator backgrounds, there was more limited employment turnover in public positions than experienced in other places with more direct bureaucratic change provisions. There is a perception that Romania's trust in public institution levels are below regional standards due to a lack of effective transitional justice. To see whether this intuition is correct, this section compares Romania and five regional countries in terms of trust in the judiciary, the police, the press, and the parliament over 2001-2015 (data limitations for trust in the press truncated this comparison to 2013). Using annual Eurobarometer Public Opinion surveys of trust in public institutions, I plot the percentage of people who said they could trust a certain public institution. These institutions were included in most lustration, public disclosure and file access provisions in the region. There is a strong argument to be made that transitional justice measures targeting these institutions might make them appear more trustworthy to citizens.[44]

Figure 3.1 compares trust in the judiciary across six countries. Trust in the judiciary in Romania has generally improved after 2006, and as of 2015 Romania scored relatively well compared to other countries in the region. In fact, citizens in Romania cited more trust in the judiciary than citizens in Hungary and the Czech Republic. In terms of trust in the press, Figure 3.2 illustrates that Romania was in the middle of this group of comparative cases as of 2013. Although Romania enjoyed more trust in the press than most regional cases prior to 2008, its levels still declined over time. As of 2013, Romania's trust levels were on par with Hungary's, above Bulgaria's, but below the Czech Republic and Poland. In other words, Romania's trust in the press was in the middle of the comparative set. Figure 3.3 shows that trust in parliament fluctuated in Romania, declining from 2001 to 2010 but then slowly rising over time. In terms of trust in parliament, Romania again scored in the middle of this comparative set, having neither very high nor very low trust levels. Finally, Figure 3.4 shows that trust in the police improved over time in

[44] David, *Lustration*; and Cynthia M. Horne, "Assessing the Impact of Lustration on Trust in Public Institutions and National Government in Central and Eastern Europe," *Comparative Political Studies* 45:4 (2012): 412-446.

Romania. In 2001 Romania ranked toward the bottom of the trust index, but has slowly seen an increase in trust in the police over time. As of 2015, Romania's level of trust in the police was on par with Poland, setting Romania in the upper half of countries in this grouping.

Figure 3.1: Trust in the Judiciary

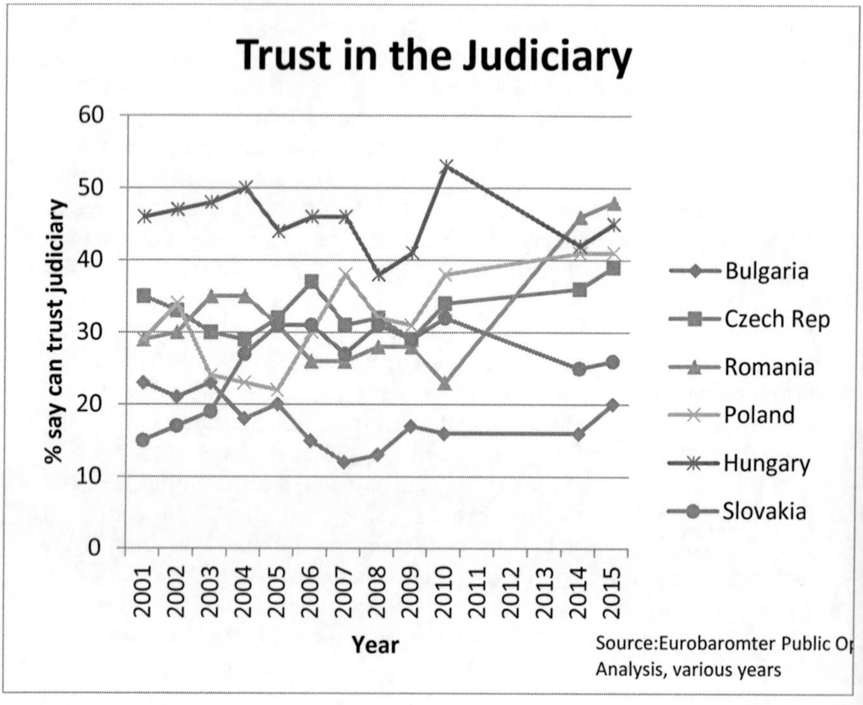

Figure 3.2: Trust in the Press

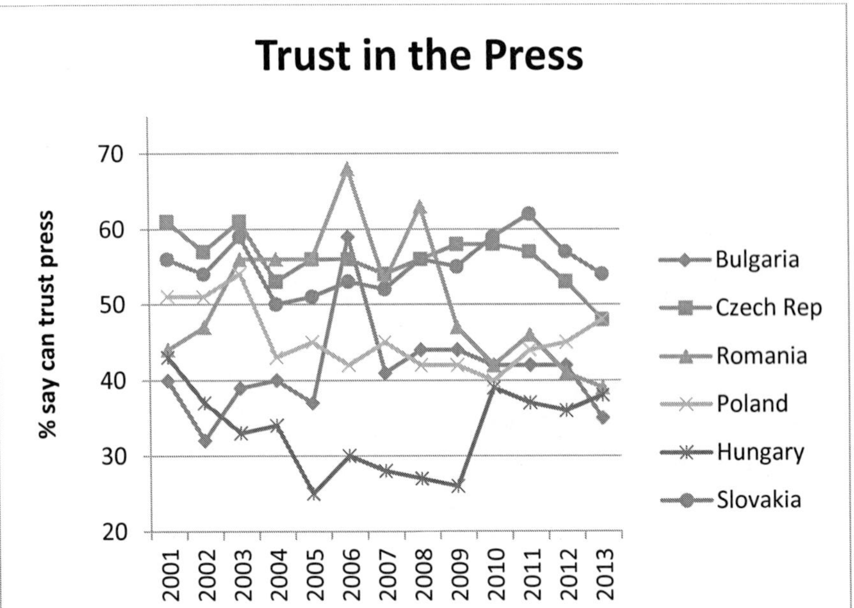

Source: Eurobarometer Public C
Analysis, various years

Table 3.4 presents data on trust in public institutions from the New Democracies Barometer project, a different dataset with survey questions corresponding to Eurobarometer. The data represent the average of citizen responses to questions about how much they trusted different public institutions on a scale from 1 to 7, with 7 being the highest level of trust. Information on trust in the parliament, the courts, the police, the army, political parties and the press is presented here for the two time periods for which data was available, 1993 and 2004. These time periods captured citizen trust assessments early in the transition and almost a decade later, providing sufficient data to compare changes within Romania, and assess how Romania compared to other post-communist countries. As Table 3.4 illustrates, trust in all of the public institutions appeared to decline between 1993 and 2004 in Romania. This is the period prior to any real transitional justice measures and, as such, is a slightly different temporal slice of trust data than the national level charts previously presented. This snapshot presents a gloomy picture of trust in public institutions a decade after the transition.

Figure 3.3: Trust in Parliament

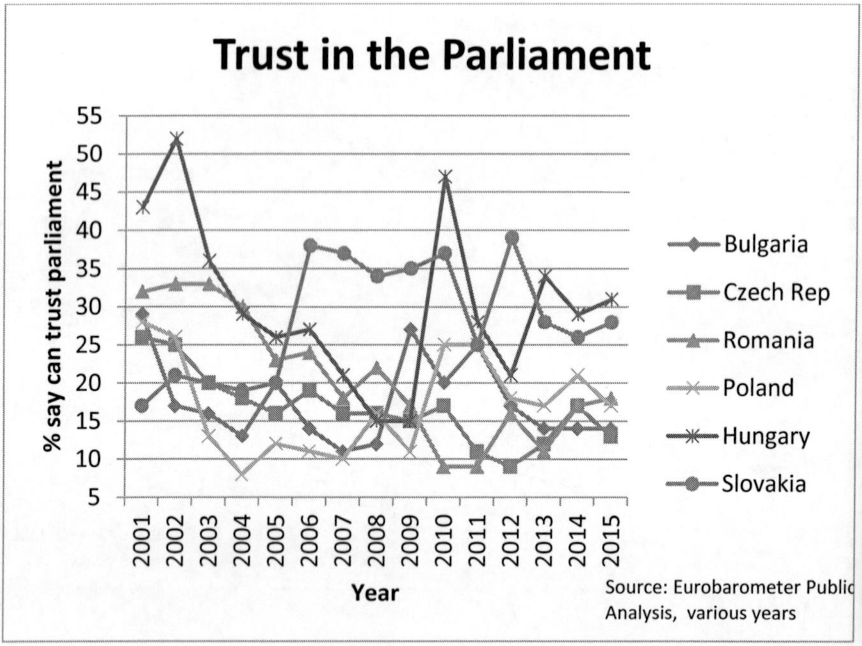

Figure 3.4: Trust in the Police

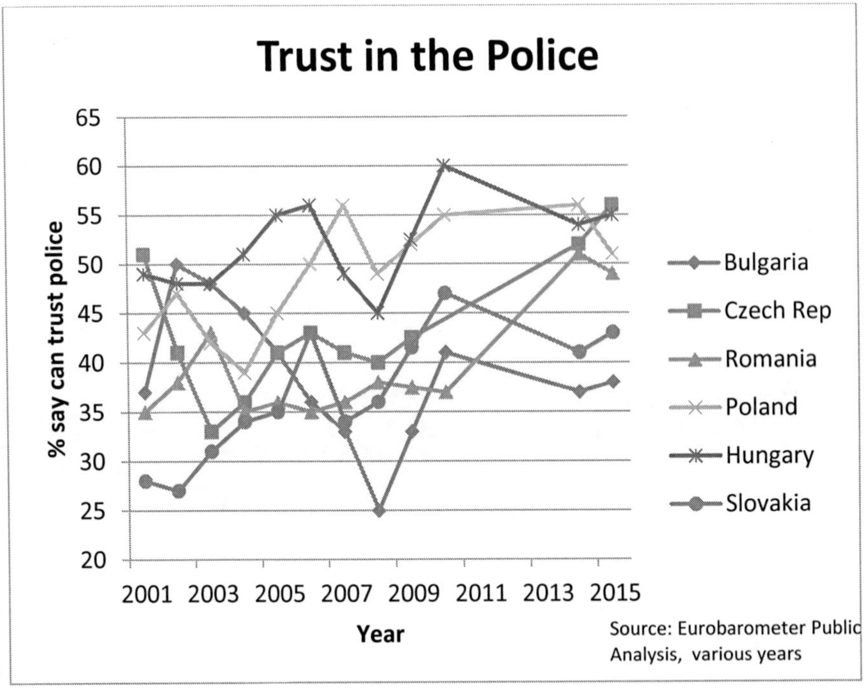

Table 3.4: Trust in Public Institutions: Individual Level Survey Results

Mean of Trust in Institution: Years 1993/2004

To what extent do you trust the following public institutions? (Scale 1-7, 7 most trust)

	Parliament 1993/2004	Courts 1993/2004	Police 1993/2004	Army 1993/2004	Political Parties 1993/2004	Press 1993/2004
Bulgaria	2.16/ 2.22	2.75/ 2.63	2.85/ 3.69	4.61/ 3.75	2.52/ 2.14	3.99/ 4.18
Czech Republic	3.65/ 2.93	4.02/ 3.60	3.88/ 3.64	4.06/ 3.72	3.69/ 2.89	5.13/ 4.41
Estonia	4.1/ 3.18	4.31/ 4.21	3.85/ 4.18	4.39/ 4.57	3.13/ 2.66	4.45/ 5.10
Hungary	3.18/ 3.42	4.3/ 4.22	4.17/ 4.17	4.31/ 3.98	2.77/ 3.10	5.04/ 4.54
Latvia	3.94/ 2.95	4.23/ 3.81	3.67/ 3.90	4.26/ 3.95	3.17/ 2.63	4.79/ 4.32
Lithuania	3.99/ 3.13	3.99/ 3.58	3.83/ 3.72	4.16/ 4.89	3.3/ 2.83	4.71/ 4.94
Poland	3.48/ 2.41	3.85/ 3.20	4.12/ 3.74	4.78/ 4.73	2.63/ 2.03	3.1/ 3.92
Romania	3.22/ 2.74	4.06/ 3.29	3.83/ 3.57	5.5/ 4.76	3.02/ 2.44	4.11/ 4.05
Slovakia[1]	3.43/ 2.78	3.78/ 3.36	3.66/ 3.48	4.46/ 4.32	3.1/ 2.63	3.54/ 4.13

[1] Slovakia is 1995/2004 comparison

Author calculations of *New Democracies Barometer I-XV Trend Dataset, 1991-2007.*

Source: Richard Rose. *New Europe Barometer I-XV Trend Dataset, 1991-2007.* [computer file].

2nd Edition. Colchester, Essex: UK Data Archive [distributor], July 2010.

Comparing Romania's trust levels to regional counterparts allows us to contextualize these levels. Romania's trust in the army was higher than any of the other countries, and its levels of trust in the press were higher than in Poland and Slovakia and on par with Bulgaria. Levels of trust in the police were above Slovakia's and on par with Lithuania, Latvia and Bulgaria. Trust in the courts was higher in Romania than Poland in 2004, and significantly better than in Bulgaria. Levels of trust in parliament and trust in parties were relatively low across all of the countries, with Romania's levels looking on par with Poland and Latvia, as well as just below the Czech Republic. The regional comparisons of trust levels both immediately after the transition and a decade later showed that trust levels declined over this time period in many of the post-communist states, not just Romania. This hints that a larger regional phenomenon might have affected trust levels, such as the fading of post-transition euphoria, the sobering realization of the challenges of reform, and particular national level factors related to domestic economic, social or political circumstances. In short, Romania's trends were experienced by other post-communist countries, suggesting Romania was not such a trust outlier. This is not an endorsement of Romania's transitional justice program, so much as an acknowledgment that in terms of trust building, Romania ranks in the middle of regional comparisons.

Corruption

Directly tied to the narrative about corruption in the post-communist space is a suggested corrective in the form of transitional justice. No other transitional justice mechanism has been so explicitly framed as a corruption corrective as lustration.[45] Informal networks of former secret police officials continued to dominate economic activities in many post-communist countries after the transition. In some countries, like Bulgaria and Poland, the disbanding of the security services created a pool of unemployed, or unemployable, well connected, former security personnel who could use their privileged networks for personal gain in post-communism.[46] Many late lustration programs were explicitly framed as

[45] Alexander Mayer-Rieckh and Pablo de Greiff, eds., *Justice as Prevention: Vetting Public Employees in Transitional Societies* (New York: Social Science Research Council, 2007); Natalia Letki, "Lustration and Democratisation in East-Central Europe," *Europe-Asia Studies* 54:4 (2002): 529-552.

[46] Author's interview with Dimitar Markov, Senior Analyst/Project Director Anti-corruption and Judicial Reform Unit, Center for the Study of Democracy, Sofia,

methods to address the widespread economic and political corruption linked to the continued prevalence of former *nomenklatura* networks in positions of power.[47]

Romania's problems with lingering corruption have been tied to the political class, for which there was little turnover after the transition.[48] The Securitate network maintained powerful ties to business elites in the post-communist regime, facilitating an extension of their political access into economic networks. The renewed and expanded Romanian lustration law of 2006-2007 was proposed and circulated in Parliament at the same time as an anti-corruption law. When politicians argued for "the moral cleansing of society," they were clearly framing lustration as a corruption corrective.[49] The CNSAS's public disclosures directive allowed them to reveal the backgrounds of individuals in current positions of economic and political power, including related private sector fields, as part of the broader, national anti-corruption goals.[50] That said, it was not until late in the transition that Romania began its expansive public disclosure measures. Thus, possible anti-corruption effects from transitional justice would also be late in the transition, if they were discernible at all. One would predict Romania's corruption levels would be regionally high, given its relatively limited and late lustration measures.

Figure 3.5 compares the corruption levels in Romania with several other post-communist countries. Romania remained in the middle of the five countries as of 2015. Poland and Hungary had the lowest corruption levels, Albania the highest. Romania tracked closely with Bulgaria, with corruption levels declining in both countries after 2006, when the more expansive public disclosure programs began. Romania was not an extreme outlier, and showed improvement over time. It remained situated firmly in the middle of the countries considered here.

Bulgaria, 2 July 2012, and author's interview with Alexander Stoyanov, Director Research Vitosha, Sofia, Bulgaria, 5 July 2012.

47 Lavinia Stan, "The Romanian Anticorruption Bill," *Studies in Post-Communism*, Centre for Post- Communist Studies, St. Francis Xavier University, Occasional Paper no. 6 (2004).

48 Stan, "Witch Hunt or Moral Rebirth?," 276.

49 Ibid., 283.

50 Author's interviews with members of the CNSAS Collegium, Bucharest, Romania, October 2012.

Figure 3.5: Comparative Corruption Measures

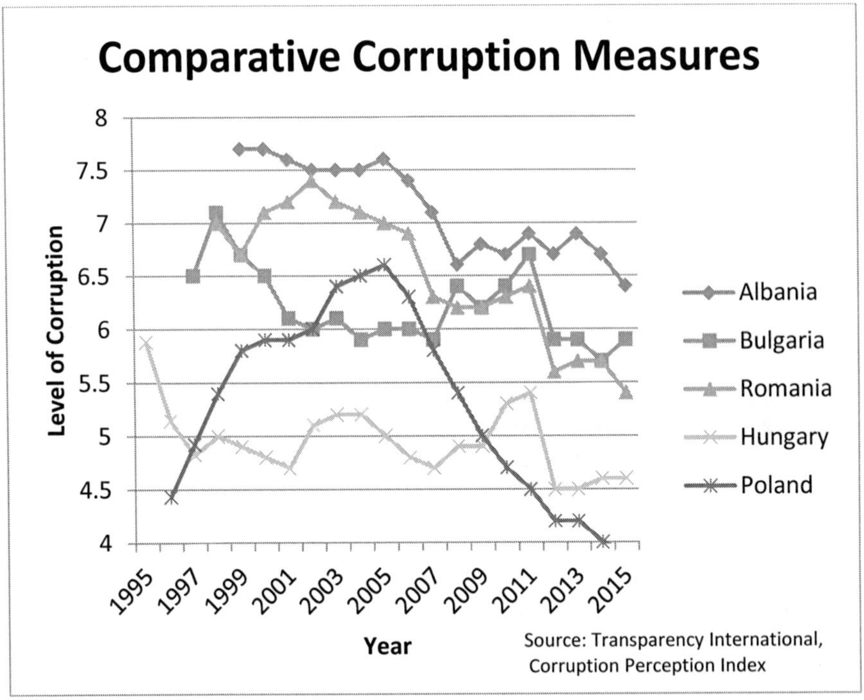

The change in Romania's corruption levels over time is curious, and suggests a possible role for transitional justice in this narrative. In particular, Romania's corruption levels were significantly higher than Bulgaria's in 2000-2006, but started a marked decline and even fell slightly below Bulgaria's after 2006. This is the period that corresponded with the start of Romania's significant file revelations and public disclosures program. Of note, Bulgaria's also declined over this time period, corresponding with public disclosures under the Dossier Commission. Poland's corruption levels slowly rose until 2006 with a noticeable and sharp decline around the same time as the country launched its late and expansive lustration program. Again, no causal claims can be made about the corruption fighting power of lustration and public disclosures, and lustration measures might simply be part of larger governmental reforms. What we can assert is that Romania's corruption levels improved over time, corresponding with its late transition public disclosure program. Moreover, compared to other countries in the region, after 2006 Romania's corruption levels were in the middle of similar post-communist experiences.

Democracy

Scholars and policy practitioners have linked lustration to democratization, citing both bureaucratic changes and moral value realignments as possible causal mechanisms.[51] For Elster, holding individuals accountable for their past actions could prevent future abuses under the new system.[52] This way, lustration as a punitive consequence could support democracy by creating an environment in which individuals were accountable for their actions. Other scholars suggested that democratization was indirectly promoted by combating corruption and preventing the continued abuse of power by officials associated with the old regime.[53] Given these connections, one would predict that countries with limited transitional justice would make less progress in democratization.

Figure 3.6 compares Romania's democratization levels over time to its post-communist counterparts. Romania once again was in the middle of the group, ranking above Albania, for which there was limited reform and very limited transitional justice, and on par with Bulgaria and Hungary. Only Poland had significantly higher democracy scores. Romania's democracy levels remained largely stable over time, showing no significant improvement during the wave of late transitional justice and public disclosures after 2006. However, Romania did not regress, something unfortunately visible in the case of Hungary. While Romanian democracy has not benefited from late transitional justice measures, Figure 6 once again placed Romania's reform outcomes in the middle of similarly situated post-communist countries.

In sum, Romania would surely rank below the Czech Republic in terms of corruption and democratization levels. However, comparing Romania to the regional vanguard case, or the slightly exceptional cases of the Baltics, would not tell us much about Romania's transition. The point was to

---

[51] Guillermo O'Donnell and Philippe Schmitter. *Transitions from Authoritarian Rule: Tentative Conclusions about Uncertain Democracies* (Baltimore: The Johns Hopkins University Press, 1986); and Samuel Huntington, *The Third Wave: Democratization in the Late Twentieth Century* (Norman: University of Oklahoma Press, 1991).

[52] Jon Elster, ed., *Retribution and Reparation in the Transition to Democracy* (New York: Cambridge University Press, 2006).

[53] Letki, "Lustration and Democratisation"; Mayer-Rieckh and de Greiff, "Justice as Prevention."

review Romania's progress compared to its regional compatriots (Albania and Bulgaria) and countries considered one step higher up the ladder of regional transitional justice reforms (Hungary and Poland). When Romania was viewed from this contextualized perspective, it appeared in the middle of the pack, higher in terms of trust in public institutions than some, and lower in terms of democracy than others. Overall, Romania's reform measures and reform outcomes placed it within the middle of other post-communist experiences.

Figure 3.6: Comparative Democracy Measures

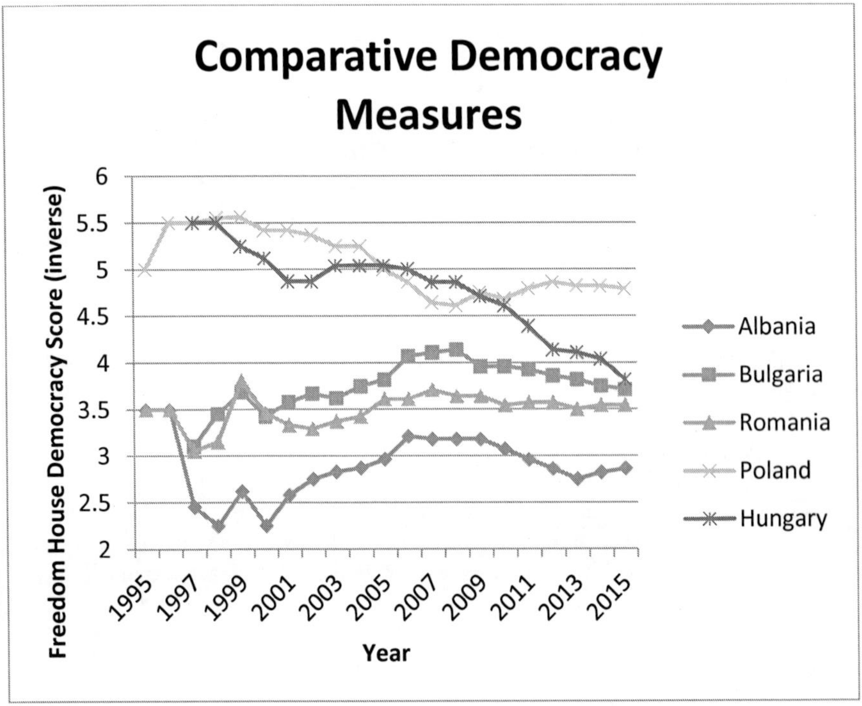

Conclusion

This chapter provided a short retrospective on Romania's experience with lustration and public disclosure, putting both its transitional justice and progress on several transition goals within a regional context. Both the lustration measures and the informal public disclosures overseen by the CNSAS have suffered from delays, problematic implementation, political instrumentalization, and information bias. Although this chapter did not engage with other forms of transitional justice in Romania, like the Tismăneanu Commission or property restitution, there were similar problems with their implementation. The Commission produced a rushed report on communist repression that was largely academic and without real impact.[54] The final results were somewhat tainted by the inclusion of two Securitate members on the Commission.[55] Legislation was passed in 1990, 1992 and 2001 to allow some property restitution, but in practice many of the court-approved property restitution cases were rejected by Romanian authorities, with very few properties returned to the original owners, in a familiar cycle of failed reforms.[56] When considered altogether, Romania's record of transitional justice was tainted.

Putting this record in context, Romania looks similar to other post-communist countries. Most of the post-communist states, including Poland, Hungary and Lithuania, experienced politicized, delayed, and/or narrowed or truncated measures over the course of their transitional justice efforts. Romania's late public disclosure program was temporally and structurally similar to Bulgaria's, and a significant improvement compared to Albania's. In a word, Romania's flawed transitional justice program was unfortunately not regionally anomalous. Romania's missed opportunities were post-communist missed opportunities, with all of the countries in the region struggling to implement measures that could authentically and fairly engage with the past. Romania is neither the regional laggard nor the regional vanguard, but finds itself at an uncomfortable spot in the middle.

Given Romania's poor performance with transitional justice, one might predict that the country would be a regional laggard in terms of meeting transition goals. Countries with significantly more transitional justice did have higher democratization measures and lower corruption levels, suggesting that Romania missed opportunities to leverage transitional justice measures and facilitate various transition goals. Be that as it may, when evaluating changes in Romania's levels of trust in public institutions, corruption and democratization over time, Romania once

---

[54] Vladimir Tismăneanu, "Democracy and Memory: Romania Confronts Its Communist Past," *The Annals of the American Academy of Political and Social Science*, 617 (2008): 166-180; and author's interview with Mircea Stanescu, historian at the National Archives and formerly with the CNSAS, Bucharest, Romania, October 2012.

[55] Maxfield, "Romania," 403.

[56] Lavinia Stan, "The Roof over Our Head: Property Restitution in Romania," *Journal of Communist Studies and Transition Politics*, 22:2 (2006): 180-205.

again appeared in the middle of post-communist comparison countries. Romania's trust in public institutions rose, corresponding with the post-2006 period of more transparency about the past. Corruption levels also declined commensurate with public disclosure programs. While Romania missed opportunities for meaningful reform early in the transition, and repeatedly thwarted its own transitional justice efforts, it still remained in the middle of countries on a number of transition goal metrics after 2006. While Romania is not at the vanguard of regional reforms, it outpaced its Balkan compatriots on many metrics. Its transitional justice measures were in the middle of other regional efforts, and its transition outcomes remained in the middle as well. While this is not a glowing endorsement of Romania's post-transition democratization efforts, it is also not an across the board condemnation, perhaps hinting at limitations in transitional justice measures more generally.

In conclusion, the temporal window for using transitional justice might be closed (or rapidly closing) more than 25 years after the fall of communism. There was no evidence that the post-2006 measures affected democracy levels in Romania, and corruption levels were plateauing. This means that it is unlikely that more transitional justice will solidify democracy or change perceptions of trust in government or public institutions so late in the transition. Transitional justice does not have a built-in expiration date, and accountability, transparency, and acknowledgment of the past are goals in and of themselves. However, at this point in the transition, real progress on democracy, corruption, rule of law, and civil society might require more than transitional justice measures.

CHAPTER FOUR

PARADOXES OF DELAYED TRANSITIONAL JUSTICE

ALEXANDRU GUSSI

At a time when democratic backlashes are more topical than ever in Central and Eastern Europe, the case of Romania remains highly suggestive for the role the communist past can play in the emergence of undemocratic slips. Does this past remain relevant for post-communist democratic processes? This chapter focuses on the delegitimizing effects of late and incoherent transitional justice policies, and also analyzes the way in which politically driven interpretations of the communist past undermine the credibility of the post-communist state and its ability to reckon with the legacy of past human rights abuses.

The question of the legitimacy of the state occupied the center stage of political life at the beginning of the post-communist transition,[1] mainly because the revolutionary regime change of December 1989 contradicted the underlying continuity of the Romanian state precisely because revolutions have been usually associated with discontinuity in the state structure.[2] Twenty-five years after those revolutionary events, this contradiction is still remarkably present in public debates, thus confirming that the question of political legitimacy is as important in post-communism

---

[1] Monica Ciobanu, "Communist Regimes, Legitimacy and the Transition to Democracy in Eastern Europe," *Nationalities Papers: The Journal of Nationalism and Ethnicity*, 38:1 (2010): 3-21.

[2] Vladimir Tismăneanu, *Fantasies of Salvation. Democracy, Nationalism and Myth in Post-Communist Europe* (Princeton: Princeton University Press, 1998), Ed Maxfield, "Romania," in *Encyclopedia of Transitional Justice*, eds. Lavinia Stan and Nadya Nedelsky (New York: Cambridge University Press, 2013), 3:398-403, and Lavinia Stan, "Reckoning with the Communist Past in Romania: A Scorecard," *Europe-Asia Studies*, 65:1 (2013): 127-146.

as it was after World War II when, as Seymour M. Lipset pointed out, "The extent to which contemporary democratic political systems are legitimate depends in a large measure upon the ways in which the key issues which have historically divided a society have been resolved."[3]

Revolutionary legitimacy and state continuity

Compared to the fervor of the 1989 Revolution and the lavish celebrations organized throughout the 1990s, its anemic 20th and 25th commemorations in 2009 and 2014 signaled a paradigm shift in the assessment of the birth moment of the post-communist regime. Criticism of the Romanian "revolutionary miracle" was voiced as early as 1990. By 2009 the initial discourse of the National Salvation Front, which praised the Revolution for radically changing the country by putting the repressive communist regime behind, enjoyed no public support except from former President Ion Iliescu, a former communist nomenklatura member, and his close associates. The legitimizing potential of the 1989 Revolution faded away, but the public discourse remained dominated by positions countering Iliescu's narrative.[4] Without reflecting nostalgia for communism, perceptions of the 1989 Revolution still reflect the public's general attitudes towards the political regime that emerged from it. Negative assessments of the Revolution result not from a positive appraisal of the communist past, but from dissatisfaction with the post-communist present and the economic hardships it brought along. A combination of major institutional failures and endemic high-level political corruption has undermined both the functioning of the rule of law and the credibility of the post-communist political elite.[5]

How is something new possible? When applied to post-communism, this classical philosophical question calls for leniency towards the many institutional and cultural continuities that are linking the pre-1989 and the post-1989 regimes. The collapse of communism and the beginning of democratization created an unavoidable gap between the legitimizing

---

[3] Seymour M. Lipset, *Political Man: The Social Basis of Politics* (New York: Doubleday, 1960): 78.

[4] Ruxandra Cesereanu, *Decembrie 89. Deconstructia unei revolutii* (Iasi: Polirom, 2009).

[5] Ronald King and Paul Sum, eds., *Romania Under Băsescu: Aspirations, Achievements, and Frustrations During His First Presidential Term* (Lanham, MD: Rowan & Littlefield, 2011), and Cynthia Horne, "Late Lustration Programmes in Romania and Poland: Supporting or Undermining Democratic Transitions?," *Democratization*, 16:2 (2009): 344-376.

discourse of the new power and the pre-existing institutional order.[6] The shift from street protests to political stability was made possible by re-setting the legitimacy of the Romanian state. A legal and institutional construct, post-communism has also been a rhetorical tool that simultaneously proclaimed the end of the one-party regime and the beginning of the democratization process. The shift from the communist to a new post-communist legitimizing discourse drew credibility from the official proclamation of the end of the old regime.

Romania's revolutionary change, unique in the Central and Eastern European context, made this process all the more remarkable. The civilian victims of the December 1989 Revolution, the urban guerrillas, and the execution of dictator Nicolae Ceausescu led to what Guy Hermet called "transition without transition."[7] Both the legitimizing discourse of the political leaders and the entire state structure changed radically within hours of the National Salvation Front Council assuming power in December 1989. A vicious circle emerged: street protests led to revolutionary change in the political regime, whereas the country's new leaders gained the right to rule by raising the protesters' demands to the rank of official discourse.[8] The protesters could then go home, since those who replaced Ceausescu stayed in power without the support of the street.

The frailty of the post-communist regime thus originated in its birth, which allowed the then political and state elite (overwhelmingly represented by members of the communist nomenklatura, the Securitate secret agents, and the army generals) to re-legitimize itself.[9] The Revolution permitted the continuity (or reproduction, to use a more

---

[6] Alexandru Gussi, "Political Uses of Memory and the State in Post-Communism," *Studia Politica. Romanian Political Science Review*, XIII:4 (2013): 721-732.

[7] Guy Hermet, *L'hiver de la democratie ou le nouveau regime* (Paris: Armand Colin, 2007): 135.

[8] Peter Siani-Davies, "Revoluția în societățile comuniste și postcomuniste," in *Revoluția Română din decembrie 1989. Istorie și memorie*, ed. Bogdan Murgescu (Iasi: Polirom, 2007), 122-126; Raluca Grosescu, "Conversia elitelor comuniste în perioada de tranziție: 1989-2000," in *Mobilitatea elitelor în România secolului XX*, eds. Mihai Dinu Ghorghiu and Mihăiță Lupu (Pitesti: Paralela 45, 2008), 310-321; Dragoș Petrescu, *Explaining the Romanian Revolution of 1989. Culture, Structure and Contingecy* (Bucharest: Editura Enciclopedică, 2010), 400.

[9] Raluca Grosescu, "Fizionomia nomenclaturii," in *Anuarul Institutului de Investigare a Crimelor Comunismului*, vol. I (2006): 109-140; and Anna Grzymala-Busse, *Rebuilding Leviathan. Party Competition and State Exploitation in Post-communist Democracies* (New York: Cambridge University Press, 2007), 8-10.

consecrated scholarly term[10]) of the communist elite, which many Romanians believed had hijacked the revolutionary discourse and the state itself. The Front Council, which included nomenklatura members sidelined sometimes during the 1970s and the 1980s, used and abused the revolutionary discourse to assume political power in the name of the protesters. After its sudden disappearance, the Communist Party concealed itself within a state apparatus re-legitimized through revolutionary discourse. Continuity was paradoxically made possible by the discourse of discontinuity and democratization. The sudden change, which set the old communist and the new post-communist regimes apart, occurred on 22 December 1989, an important temporal milestone that legitimized the new state rulers.[11] The "transition without transition" meant that the change affected the discourse more than the substance and functioning style of state institutions. The proclaimed regime change in fact re-legitimized the personnel and institutional structures of the old communist regime.

The Romanian communist regime was ousted at the price of many innocent lives. Those who announced its death used the revolutionary pro-democratic discourse as a concession made to the people. Revolutionary legitimacy alone supported the Salvation Front's claim to power. This legitimizing discourse centered on the relationship between the past and the future. Thus, the framework for coming to terms with the communist past in post-1989 Romania was largely set in December 1989 by the nomenklatura members who formed the National Salvation Front. The Front replaced the old Communist Party, its first statements concomitantly alluding to its identity as a new political formation and as the new political regime. The confusion between the two lasted well into 1990, hampering an official debate about the communist past as distinct from that of the Front leaders. The self-legitimizing discourse of the Front leaders touched on the communist past only implicitly, by recognizing the revolutionary nature of the regime change. Its official discourse about the communist past revolved solely around the idea of "revolution." Although reluctant to remember the communist regime, party or republic, and their numerous human rights abuses, the Front leaders still emphasized revolutionary legitimacy as an implicit condemnation of the repressive past.

---

[10] The scholarly literature distinguishes elite reproduction (continuity) from elite circulation (renewal) as two distinct outcomes of the 1989 regime changes in Central and Eastern Europe. Ivan Szelenyi and Szonja Szelenyi, "Circulation or Reproduction of Elites during Post-Communist Transformation in Russia and Eastern Europe," *Theory & Society*, 24:5 (1995): 615-638.

[11] Peter Siani-Davies, *The Romanian Revolution of December 1989* (Ithaca, NY: Cornell University Press, 2005).

The break with the past led to limited institutional changes and some freedoms, but because it was not part of their legitimizing discourse the new rulers showed no political will to talk about communist crimes or to recognize communist victims. Before the 1990 general elections, the Salvation Front verbally attacked former political prisoners, blaming them for trying to turn back history, and for seeking revenge and restoration. President Iliescu applauded the Front for its efforts to facilitate "the destruction of the structures of the former [communist] regime," but claimed that the regime change was over, and a constructive period had to start because "the cadres who know the situation cannot be blamed for the simple fact that they were part of the old structures" and "there were communists among those who sacrificed themselves to bring about the fall of the dictatorship."[12] In response, the civic Bucharest-based Group for Social Dialogue reminded Iliescu that "until 20 May [the country's first general elections] the state apparatus owed its survival to you, afterwards you owed your legitimacy to the state."[13]

Except for a handful of court trials and some meager compensation packages for time spent in communist prisons, the early 1990s were marked by continuity and oblivion as the main transitional justice strategies.[14] The anti-communist opposition contested oblivion as a policy that sought to save the political careers of those involved in the abuses perpetrated by the Communist Party, the Securitate, the justice system, and the police before 1989. These individuals had retained their positions in the post-communist state institutions. Not only transitional justice, but also democratization writ large was thus sacrificed by turning the state against de-communization demands. The new state structures assured the continuity of the bureaucratic and military staff, and its quasi-impunity in relation to pre-1989 crimes. This, in turn, negatively affected the credibility of the new regime and democratic order.

After 22 December, the continuity of state institutions assured a measure of political stability. Institutional continuity was hard to accomplish in the case of the feared Securitate, which therefore was formally placed under the authority of the Army. The difference between its invoked revolutionary legitimacy and the reality of institutional

---

[12] Ion Iliescu, "Keynote Speech at the National Salvation Front Conference," *Dimineața*, 8 April 1990, Ion Iliescu, "Discourse at the Romanian Public Radio and Television," *Monitorul Oficial al României*, 8 January 1990:1, Ion Iliescu, *Momente de istorie* (Bucharest: Editura Enciclopedică, 1996): 1: 270-284 and 278.

[13] "Official statement of the Group for Social Dialogue," *22*, 1 June 1990, 1.

[14] Alexandru Gussi, "The Ex-communists' Policy of Forgetting in Romania after 1990," *Studia Politica. Romanian Political Science Review*, IX:2 (2009): 273-290.

continuity was too great for the Securitate not to become the Achilles' heel of the new regime. The Front's undisputed control of the mass media somewhat limited this vulnerability.[15]

Newly formed civic organizations, an independent press, and public protests challenged this continuity. The opposition revolved around former political prisoners who assumed the leadership of the newly reborn historic parties, most prominent of which were the National Liberal Party and the National Peasant Party. The anti-communism of the civic and political opponents of the Salvation Front remained the main political identity alternative to the Front and its selective interpretation of the communist past until 1996, when the anticommunist democratic opposition formed the government for the first time. Until 1996 the rift between the Front-led government and the anticommunist opposition centered on the legitimacy of the new regime, accused of having hijacked the Revolution for its own selfish purposes and of rejecting transitional justice policies.[16] The opposition questioned the 1989 Revolution, the controversial installation of the communist regime in 1946, and the imposition of a republican system by the 1991 Constitution.[17] As such, this discourse about the communist past was also a discourse about the legitimacy of the new regime and its constitutional institutions.

In Romania, the transition to post-communism permitted continuity of the elites, of most state institutions, including the repressive apparatus, and even of the former Communist Party turned into the Salvation Front. Contested by the anticommunist opposition, this continuity undermined the legitimacy of the new leaders and regime. In June 1990, Romania's nascent civil society openly protested against the new leaders in downtown Bucharest. The Front-led government used openly undemocratic means to quash public demonstrations, and called on the Valea Jiului miners to descend on the capital in its defense.[18]

The continuity of the elite echoed the continuity in political culture and

---

[15] Henry F. Carey, "From Big Lie to Small Lies: State Mass Media Dominance in Post-Communist Romania," *East European Politics and Societies*, 10:1 (1996): 16-45.

[16] Alexandru Gussi, "L'anticommunisme en Roumanie (1996-2000)," *Studia Politica. Romanian Political Science Review*, VII:1 (2007): 117-132.

[17] Dan Pavel and Iulia Huiu, *Nu putem reuşi decît împreună. O istorie analitică a Convenţiei Democratice, 1989-2000* (Iasi: Polirom, 2003).

[18] Mihnea Berindei, Adriana Colombes and Anne Planche, *Roumanie: le livre blanc. La réalité d'un mouvement néocommuniste* (Paris: La Découverte, 1990), and Alin Rus, *Mineriadele. Între manipulare politică şi solidaritate muncitorească* (Bucharest: Curtea Veche, 2007).

the systematic politicization of state institutions. As such, the opposition's calls for transitional justice, including lustration, were less about the past and more about contesting the hold on power of the Front, which was denounced for its strong ties to the former Communist Party.[19] Calls for reckoning with the communist past primarily attempted to show that the new regime enjoyed none of the revolutionary legitimacy it invoked in December 1989. From this perspective, the lustration proposal included in the Timisoara Declaration of March 1990 sought to "continue the revolution" by renewing the public administration.[20] The Revolution was initially the sole source of political legitimacy for the Salvation Front, and the founding myth of the new regime. Over time, Iliescu and his Front promoted a memory centered on other symbolic moments, but the Revolution remained a source of legitimacy for the anti-communist opposition, which wanted to keep it alive until the replacement of the communist elite with a new, untainted one was complete.

In 1992-1996, the Front, re-named the Social Democrat Party, co-opted into the government the apologists of the Ceausescu regime, the Greater Romania Party and the Socialist Party. During this time, the Romanian Information Service and the Army questioned the Revolution and its legitimacy.[21] Their radical views gained respectability and recognition when they were echoed by the Information Service in its report on December 1989, although the main government partner remained the product of the Revolution. During the same period, continuity became less shameful for the Social Democrats. When speaking about the Revolution, Iliescu insisted that the Social Democrat Party was "the legitimate continuator of the Revolution,"[22] whose goals had been satisfied by the 1991 Constitution.[23] As such, the anti-communist claim that the communist nomenklatura hijacked the Revolution lost its value. The Revolution could be neither anti-communist, since its leader was the former communist Iliescu, nor unfinished, since its demands had been

[19] Alexandru Gussi, "Construction et usages politiques d'un lieu de mémoire. La Place de l'Université de Bucarest," *Studia Politica. Romanian Political Science Review*, II:4 (2002): 1058-1091.

[20] Emil Constantinescu, *Timpul dărâmării, timpul zidirii* (Bucarest: Universalia, 2002), 3:725-726.

[21] Serviciul de Informatii Roman, "Evenimentele din decembrie 1989 vazute de SRI," *Ordinea, Supliment special*, 1994.

[22] Mesajul lui Ion Iliescu la Conferinta Nationala a PDSR, *Adevărul*, 25 November 1995.

[23] Ion Iliescu, "Cred in schimbarea in bine a Romaniei," in Ion Iliescu, *Momente de istorie* (Bucharest: Editura Enciclopedică, 1996), 3: 313-331.

fulfilled by the new Constitution. The mass-media frequently presented conspiracy theories whose popularity increased when they criticized the Front and indirectly disconfirmed the anti-communist nature of the Revolution.

This trend gained strength after the 1996 political change, which failed to produce the "truth" about the Revolution, President Emil Constantinescu's main campaign promise.[24] The Revolution ceased to be idealized when the public started to refer to it as simply "the December 1989 events." The phrase, coined jointly by the Greater Romania Party and the Information Service report, became established by the mid-2000s. Commemorations of the revolutionary moment were gradually abandoned or dramatically scaled down. Nevertheless, the Revolution has retained its public relevance because "the truth" remains unknown more than twenty-five years after. The judiciary has yet to hear all cases related to the Revolution, although in 2006 the Presidential Commission for the Analysis of the Communist Dictatorship called for the abuses perpetrated by state agents in January-June 1990 to be prosecuted alongside communist crimes.[25] Only historians have acknowledged these two sets of crimes.[26]

As such, the regime change of December 1989 and the political debate on the communist past partly lost their relevance. The Revolution no longer creates historical meaning or bestows legitimacy on politicians. This was the price paid by those who benefited from the continuity discussed above and supported the Front's politics of oblivion after they no longer needed continuity to gain legitimacy. It was also the price paid by the anti-communist camp after its main political formations, the Democratic Convention and the National Peasant Party, disappeared from the political scene. By the general elections of 2000, the Revolution had become a symbol of continuity more than one of discontinuity, and as such

[24] Emil Constantinescu, *Timpul dărâmării, timpul zidirii* (Bucharest: Universalia, 2002), 2: 36.

[25] Vladimir Tismăneanu, Dorin Dobrincu and Cristian Vasile, eds., *Comisia Prezidențială pentru Analiza Dictaturii Communiste din România. Raport Final* (Bucharest: Humanitas, 2007), 454-456 and 776-777.

[26] Constantin C. Giurescu, "Postfață," in *Adevaruri incomde. Decembrie 1989*, ed. ACMRRSRI (Bucharest: Semne, 2013), 385-388; Apostol Stan, *România, București 1989. Enigmele Revoluției?* (Bucharest: Saeculum I.O, 2013); Alina Mungiu Pippidi, "Cât de revoluționară a fost revoluția română?," 22, 23-29 January 2007; and Horia-Roman Patapievici, "Revoluția română și anul 1989," *Idei in dialog*, 12:63 (December 2009): 45-47.

the post-communist regime lost its (re)founding myth.[27]

The condemnation of communism, the defensive anticommunism and the vicious circle

The 2006 official condemnation of the communist regime by President Traian Basescu could have reduced the delegitimizing effect of the Revolution's loss of public importance, and in turn produce a plausible narrative to justify continuity.[28] In post-communist Central and Eastern Europe, democratization generally required transitional justice, but in Romania significant segments of the political elite opposed reckoning. The Front's refusal to embrace de-communization betrayed its ambiguity about democratization and preference for an "original democracy" distinct from its Western liberal variant.

In Romania, the regime change determined the way in which transitional justice unfolded. The policy of oblivion was part of a larger political model under which the elite that regained legitimacy in 1989 retained its domination over the political game, and preserved the continuity of the state. The 1996 alternation in power did not de-block transitional justice, and after the anticommunist forces lost the 2000 elections de-communization almost disappeared from the political discourse simply because no other political forces took up that cause. Anti-communism no longer informed party platforms, but remained important in public discourse.[29] In the 2004 elections, it was used by the new governing coalition that united the Democrats and the Liberals to attack the Social Democrats. During the following four years, the civil society raised transitional justice demands that led to an ever-increasing number of relevant policies proposed by various government partners. This policy competition facilitated the opening of the secret archives, the official condemnation of the communist regime, and a lustration bill, among

---

[27] Sergiu Gherghina, "Attitudes towards the Communist Past in Five Central and East European Countries," *History of Communism in Europe*, I (2010): 167-181.

[28] Alexandru Gussi, *La Roumanie face à son passé communiste. Mémoires et cultures politiques* (Paris : l'Harmattan, 2011).

[29] Cristina Petrescu, "Cum ne-am recuperat trecutul recent. Interpretarea comunismului în sfera publică postcomunistă," in *Mobilitatea elitelor în România secolului XX*, eds. Mihai Dinu Ghorghiu and Mihăiță Lupu (Pitești: Paralela 45, 2008), 362-365; as well as Cosmina Tănăsoiu, "Intellectuals and Post-Communist Politics in Romania. An Analysis of Public Discourse, 1990-2000," *East European Politics and Societies*, 22:1 (2008): 80-113.

others.[30] All major political forces, except for the Social Democrats, used anticommunism to boost their legitimacy and popularity.

After 2004, both the Democrats and the Liberals assumed an anti-communist discourse, but neither wholeheartedly. Their anticommunism catered to civil society demands only to the extent to which such demands did not challenge the two parties, their leaders, the head of state, or the prime minister. This meant that the most radical reckoning gestures were made by President Băsescu, whose Democrat allies were, together with the Social Democrats, the successors to the Salvation Front and therefore the most vulnerable to anticommunist challenges. Their anticommunism sought to overcome the legacies of the 1990s more than to effect meaningful transitional justice. The anticommunist discourse weakened not only some political forces, but also some state institutions. As in the 1990s, the continuity of the state undermined the legitimacy of the government. Romania was a NATO member and a European Union candidate, but transitional justice was off the agenda of the political elite. The policy of silence and amnesia concealed vulnerability because former Salvation Front members dominated the political elite, which in turn dominated key state institutions. In 1989 the regime change was very sudden, and so was the shift in the regime of memory in 2006.

In 2001, the nomination of the National Council for the Study of the Securitate Archives (Consiliul National pentru Studierea Arhivelor Securitatii, CNSAS) leaders rekindled court trials for redress. In the coming years, an exceptional political context made possible the transfer of the secret archives from the Securitate's successors to the CNSAS, the opening of the archives of the Communist Party's Central Committee, the creation of the Institute for the Investigation of Communist Crimes (Institutul pentru Investigarea Crimelor Comunismului, IICC), and the Presidential Commission, the official condemnation of communism by President Basescu, and several bills. To understand this development, one should emphasize not specific political calculations, but the larger context in which state institutions and the political elite were so vulnerable to the delegitimizing anti-communist discourse of the civil society that they had no choice but to engage in what I call defensive anti-communist policies.

This defensive anti-communism is illustrated by the creation of the Presidential Commission, the report it prepared, and the ensuing official condemnation of the communist regime. President Basescu never claimed to be an anticommunist, a fact that made more credible his condemnation

---

[30] Lavinia Stan, *Transitional Justice in Post-Communist Romania: The Politics of Memory* (New York: Cambridge University Press, 2013).

of the communist regime on behalf of the Romanian state. His unequivocal condemnation in truth concealed the ambiguities of the Romanian post-communist state structures, political parties, political elites, and even Băsescu himself. The condemnation represented a fracture in the official treatment of the communist past and a concession to the civil society.[31] It was also the first official statement to legitimize the post-communist state by univocally condemning its communist predecessor. It redefined the relationship of the state with its totalitarian past, opening it up to new reckoning demands.[32] Let me show why the condemnation concealed the past and prevented the state from assuming guilt, and comment on the extent to which the expectations of the civil society were satisfied by the president's radical condemnation.

Basescu's statement that the communist state was "illegitimate and criminal" was the first to transform anticommunism into an official discourse, and thus to reaffirm the legitimacy of the post-communist regime.[33] The final report of the Presidential Commission represented the foundation for such condemnation, which acknowledged the illegitimate and criminal nature of the communist regime, and the legitimacy of the post-communist state in terms of national historical traditions, observance of human rights and democracy. As such, the post-communist state could no longer be challenged on anticommunist grounds. The condemnation reflected defensive anticommunism because it preempted anticommunist attacks, and granted renewed legitimacy to state institutions. However, this re-legitimization was short lived partly because the promises included in the condemnation speech were never fulfilled and partly because the emphasis on condemnation obscured the state's need to take responsibility

---

[31] "The Tismaneanu Commission undoubtedly marked a significant milestone in Romanian transitional justice by reviving the public debate on the need to come to terms with a dictatorship whose legacies have deeply divided the Romanian society even after its demise." Stan, *Transitional Justice in Post-Communist Romania*, 134.

[32] Stan, *Transitional Justice in Post-Communist Romania*, 127; Cosmina Tănăsoiu, "The Tismăneanu Report: Romania Revisits Its Past," *Problems of Post-Communism*, 54:4 (2007): 60-69; Monica Ciobanu, "Criminalising the Past and Reconstructing Collective Memory: The Romanian Truth Commission," *Europe-Asia Studies*, 61:2 (2009): 313-336; James Mark, *The Unfinished Revolution. Making Sense of the Communist Past in Central-Eastern Europe* (New Haven: Yale University Press, 2010); and Cristian Vasile, "CPACCR, Tismăneanu Comission," in Lavinia Stan and Nadya Nedelsky, eds., *Encyclopedia of Transitional Justice*, 366-371.

[33] James Mark, *The Unfinished Revolution. Making Sense of the Communist Past in Central-Eastern Europe* (New Haven: Yale University Press, 2010), 38.

for past crimes and its post-1989 continuity.

The most important accomplishment of the condemnation was that the president assumed responsibility for communist crimes on behalf of the state. True, the speech downplayed the state's responsibility to make room for a condemnation that was important in the Romanian context precisely because it came late, at a time when most Romanians no longer expected any redress.[34] But that is the very reason why assuming responsibility and apologizing to the victims were all the more important. The act of taking responsibility brought the victims once again to the forefront of public debates, a place they deserved but from which the Front banished them in 1990. But in December 2006 the need for the state to assume responsibility was almost ignored. The focus on condemnation might have been explained by its effects, which were much anticipated but never materialized: lustration, court trials, and other transitional justice initiatives. An anticommunist rhetoric dominated the civil society's demands for condemnation, the selection of the members of the Presidential Commission, the writing of the report, the structure of the presidential speech, and even its initial reception. However, the entire process was designed by anticommunists for the benefit of anticommunists for whom the condemnation was the first step towards belated transitional justice.

To see why the state's responsibility and the apology to the victims took a back seat to the official condemnation we must see the presidential speech as a political statement. To the extent that it sought to legitimize and neutralize the anticommunist discourse, Basescu saw the emphasis on assuming responsibility and delivering the apology as counterproductive because, as Ruti Teitel suggested, "apology implies a certain continuity of the state."[35] The apology was quickly brushed over because acknowledging the continuity between the communist and post-communist states was precisely what the official discourse aimed at avoiding. The apology and the need to assume responsibility feature in the speech only to legitimize the condemnation. Whereas taking responsibility and apologizing implied continuity, the condemnation proclaimed a radical break with the past by condemning the communist regime as "illegitimate and criminal." This implicitly downplayed the need to assume responsibility, and the state continuity. The imbalance between condemnation, on one side, and the responsibility and apology, on the other, echoes the policy of oblivion by

---

[34] "Mesajul Președintelui României, 18 December 2006" in *Comisia prezidențială pentru analiza dictaturii communiste din România. Raport Final*, eds. Vladimir Tismăneanu, Dorin Dobrincu, Cristian Vasile (Bucharest: Humanitas, 2007): 15-16.

[35] Ruti Teitel, *Transitional Justice* (New York: Oxford University Press, 2000): 84.

neglecting victims, forgetting state continuity, and ignoring the need for redress.

Thus, in 2006 the demands of the anticommunist civil society groups met the defensive anti-communism of the key state officials, but their goals were different. For the anticommunists, condemnation was a first step toward re-launching transitional justice programs, especially radical lustration with job loss. For the officials engaged in defensive anticommunism, the emphasis lay on radical condemnation as the end of de-communization, and a re-legitimization of state continuity.

Some anticommunists denounced this latter position, but the credibility of their claims was negatively affected by some of their political options. By contrast, the supporters of the presidential undertaking wished for the adoption of the transitional justice measures promised in the presidential speech. This political cleavage between these anticommunist groups diminished their influence. Let me summarize the positions of three of the most active anti-communist civil society groups: the Association of Former Political Prisoners, the Civic Academy, and the 21 December 1989 Association. Initially they supported the presidential initiative, but soon thereafter expressed discontent with the insufficiency of follow-up measures. Their criticisms rendered Basescu's condemnation moot.

The Association of Former Political Prisoners' chairman, Octav Bjoza, denounced the laws that "made us point fingers at each other, not at the ones who are guilty,"[36] that is, the communist officials and secret agents. In 2009, Bjoza became a vocal critic of President Basescu, whom he accused of ignoring the plight of the victims of the communist regime. A similar but less radical position was expressed by Ana Blandiana, the Civic Academy leader. For her, reckoning with the communist past was important because "memory helps us understand what is happening to us today" in a country like Romania, "dominated by [elites that are] originating before 1989."[37] For the 21 December 1989 Association chairman, Teodor Mărieş, in post-communist Romania "no one has managed to put in jail one's own torturer."[38] Thus, all three believed that transitional justice failed, although some steps forward had been made by opening court cases related to the December 1989 Revolution.[39] Mistrust in state institutions resulted from what was seen as the unjustified

[36] Octav Bjoja, intervention at Scoala Memoriei, Sighet, July 2013. Document with the author.

[37] Idem.

[38] Author's personal interview with Teodor Mărieş, Bucharest, 15 September 2013.

[39] See the Attorney General's decision of 5 April 2016 on the reopening of the prosecution regarding the December 1989 events. Document with the author.

inconsistency between guilty sentences handed down by the civil courts and the military courts' refusal to sentence those guilty of rights abuses.

These criticisms were subjective, reflecting exclusively the expectations of the victims, but no less significant. They diminished the credibility of the official condemnation, and reflected both the conflict between civic and defensive anticommunism and the fact that the post-communist state was not credible in the eyes of the anticommunists as long as transitional justice remained incomplete. Therefore, the condemnation was to gain weight only if followed by additional transitional justice programs. Any delay or step backward increased frustrations and fuelled public resentment toward the elite continuity demonstrated by the wealth and influence of the former nomenklatura members. Although some transition justice measures followed, the results were deemed below expectations and each new measure created ever-higher expectations. For instance, if a former perpetrator was put on trial, the expectation was for him to be found guilty and sentenced, and for other indictments to follow suit. Often these expectations remained unfulfilled.

In the absence of meaningful transitional justice, the defensive anticommunism of state actors was unable to limit the de-legitimizing effect of the anticommunist discourse of the civil society. Over time, this trend was enhanced by the frustration of the anticommunists, whose expectations were thwarted. The de-legitimizing effect also affected the condemnation of the communist regime, because subsequent transitional justice efforts revealed increased institutional resistance.

Marginalized memory institutions

Students of transitional justice in Romania err when they see the report of the Presidential Commission as amounting to the country's official narrative on communism. Even if the report and the presidential speech had an official dimension, they failed to change the way in which state institutions relate to the communist past. The Commission's very existence and its report marked a break with the past, but they were only a belated victory of the civil society, which had long pressed for transitional justice. The report was an official narrative on the past initially proposed by the anticommunist intellectuals in the 1990s, but never fully accepted by state institutions. Indeed, the state institutions that were called to fulfill the promises of the presidential speech did nothing in that respect. The Ministry of Education never introduced as obligatory the textbook on the history of communism, which remained an optional subject in schools until 2012, when a Social Democrat minister removed it altogether.[40] The Ministry of Culture never created a museum of communism. The Ministry of Interior never re-wrote its own history, and kept on its website in 2012-2014 a portrait of communist minister Tudor Postelnicu, who has since been prosecuted for his involvement in the bloodshed of the 1989 Revolution. The Ministry is still in charge of the National Archives, an institution discussed below. Last but not least, since 2015 the Presidential Commission's report has disappeared, for no discernible reason, from the website of the Romanian Presidency. President Klaus Iohannis declared himself an anticommunist in a book published ahead of the 2014 elections,[41] and his first act as president was to bestow a medal on Bjoza. At the same time, his indifference towards the report echoes the position of the current Liberal-dominated government.

The creation of the CNSAS in 2000 and of the IICC in 2005-2006 breached the policy of oblivion, as did the National Archives, which under the supervision of the Ministry of Interior offered only preferential access to the documents that detailed the abuses of the Communist Party. When the CNSAS started its activity in 2000, the Securitate archives were still in the hands of the Romanian Information Service, the heir to the Securitate. Until 2000 access to the archives was granted on a privileged basis to the apologists of the Service. This resulted in a Service-controlled history of the Securitate, exemplified by the *White Book of the Securitate*.[42] After 2000, the CNSAS only lent more credibility to the Service-controlled narrative of the past, although respectable intellectuals led the Council. The transfer of the archives from the Service repositories to the CNSAS repository in 2006 amounted to a revolutionary step for access to the archives, one that came seventeen years after the collapse of the communist regime. However, the empowerment of the CNSAS following the transfer was so important that it prompted a reaction from the Constitutional Court, which at the time was dominated by former Social Democrat justices who tried to dismantle the CNSAS or at least render it ineffective as a transitional justice institution.[43] Preventing this institutional

---

[40] Daniel Colceru, "L'entrée du totalitarisme dans les manuels roumains," *Histoire et Liberté. Les cahiers d'histoire sociale*, 42 (2010): 45-53.

[41] Klaus Iohannis, *Pas cu pas* (Bucharest: Curtea Veche, 2015).

[42] Serviciul Roman de Informatii, *Cartea albă a Securității. Istorii literare și artistice (1969-1989)* (Bucharest: Presa Românească, 1996).

[43] The Romanian Constitutional Court Decision 51 of 31 January 2008 tried to dismantle the National Council for the Study of Securitate Archives. For more on the history and activities of the CNSAS, see the chapter by Dragos Petrescu in this volume.

annihilation became an important quest for the thousands of Romanians who were interested in looking at their secret files and in the limited "moral lustration" represented by the posting on the institution's website of materials exposing the relationship with the Securitate of public officials. The Constitutional Court decision 51/2008 drastically curtailed the CNSAS attributions and rendered it even more marginalized once the Social Democrats returned to the government in 2008, but a new law passed by parliament the same year made it possible for the CNSAS to continue its work (see the Chapter by Dragos Petrescu in this volume for details on the trials and tribulations of the CNSAS). For different reasons, the same marginalization affected the IICC, which answered directly to the Prime Minister. The Institute's leadership was changed in 2010, 2012, and also 2014, after each major cabinet reshuffling. Its close relationship with the executive branch of the government has sparked criticism.

The lack of independence from the government and the main political parties of these two transitional justice institutions did not render their activities political in nature, perhaps because none of the parties that could exert control over the Council and the Institute claimed to be anticommunist. These two institutions' dependences on the government or political parties seemingly limited their activity and public influence, instead of turning it advantageous for this or that governing party. Both institutions have appropriated the anticommunist perspectives championed by the civil society, and showed that successive governments have co-opted anticommunists within their ranks, and thus have limited their criticism about the past and the continuity of the state.

In short, during the past decade these two institutions, as well as the National Archives, conducted their activity in a context in which the policy of oblivion made way to limited transparency. The archives have been partly opened, but it is unclear to what extent they have been pruned; a number of memory institutions have been created, but it is unclear to what extent they are effective. This observation confirms the existence of a "cat and mouse game"[44] played by these institutions, the state, and the political parties that have formed successive governments. The lack of consistent memory policies on the part of the main political parties leaves memory institutions marginalized among state institutions. They can barely survive, and therefore cannot influence other institutions' relationship with their own past, the general public, or the communist abuses. Similarly, the Wiesel Institute for the study of Romania's fascist past has only minimally impacted public awareness of the country's involvement in the

[44] Stan, *Transitional Justice in Post-Communist Romania*, 53-54.

Holocaust.[45] Thus, from a transitional justice viewpoint, the state context is as important as the political context. Note that in post-communist Romania bureaucratic continuity numerically surpassed the reproduction of the political elite.[46] The state bureaucracy has counterbalanced, even annulled, the influence of the elected politicians.[47] For example, in 1996-2000 the Information Service publicly opposed in Parliament the legislative initiative to turn the Securitate archives over to the CNSAS.

In 1996-2000, when the self-declared anticommunists represented a majority in Parliament, the pressure for transitional justice from within state institutions almost always trumped the pressure from society. In this context, the sentencing of the Army officers who had been involved in the loss of lives during the 1989 Revolution, but who then occupied ministerial positions during early post-communism, seemed like the only exception, but was not free of political influence.[48] This sentencing was an exceptional compensation offered by the judiciary to the anticommunist civil society groups that supported the Democratic Convention's electoral success in 1996. Another exception was the 2016 verdict in the case of Alexandru Vişinescu, the first communist-era prison guard to be sentenced for crimes against humanity that had taken place some fifty years earlier.

Today, the expectations triggered by Basescu's 2006 condemnation remain unsatisfied for two main reasons. First, because state institutions have not embraced the anticommunist view that the communist regime was "illegitimate and criminal." The second reason is the dearth of comprehensive memory policies and of political parties willing to promote such policies. The only actor with an unwavering position has been the Social Democrat Party, which never assumed responsibility for the communist past, and always supported the policy of oblivion. Its return to government in 2012 ended the "window of opportunity" opened for transitional justice by the 2006 condemnation. State institutions like the

---

[45] Jean Ancel, *The History of Holocaust in Romania* (Jerusalem: Lincoln University of Nebraska Press and Yad Vashem, 2011), Alexandru Florian, "The perception of the Holocaust in Historiography and the Romanian Media," in *Local History, Transnational Memory in the Romanian Holocaust*, eds. Valentin Glajas and Jeanninne Teodorescu (New York: Palgrave Macmillan, 2011), 19-45.

[46] Raluca Grosescu,"Fizionomia nomenclaturii," *Anuarul Institutului de Investigare a Crimelor Comunismului*, I (2006):109-140.

[47] Institutions of the state worked as forms of counter-power, a role noticed, in another context, by Jean Louis Quermonne, *L'appareil administratif de l'Etat* (Paris: Seuil, 1991), 10.

[48] Raluca Grosescu and Raluca Ursachi, *Justiţia penală de tranziţie. De la Nurnberg la postcomunismul românesc* (Iaşi: Polirom, 2009), 168-181.

Constitutional Court rendered de-communization irrelevant.[49]

Eighteen years had to pass for Romania to create the legislative framework needed to open the communist archives. The length of this time period was directly proportional to the desire of successive governments to control access to, and implicitly the writing of, the history of the communist regime. This was not simply a policy of oblivion, but rather a policy of control over the writing of history by selecting the documents that became public, and by granting privileged access to the archives of the Communist Party and of the Securitate to selected historians.[50]

Here the transferring of the Securitate archives from the Information Service to the CNSAS is less of a focus than the access to all of the pre-1989 archives. Significantly, access to the archives of the Securitate and the Communist Party was granted simultaneously. The opening was contested by the Constitutional Court in the case of the Securitate archives,[51] and by the Ministry of Interior in the case of the Communist Party archives. In both cases, resistance to opening the archives was counteracted successfully, at least initially. The CNSAS could be deprived by its custody over the Securitate archives only by an executive order of Prime Minister Calin Popescu Tariceanu, whereas changes in the National Archives leadership were blocked for a long time by President Băsescu.[52] The political will that allowed for access underlined the fragility of the institutional changes that affected the CNSAS and the National Archives, as the Law 16/1996 on Archives remains unchanged, allowing for only controlled access. The law was bypassed by a series of executive decisions that led to the opening of the archives of the Communist Party and the Union of Communist Youth. First, the president, as head of the Higher Defense Council, allowed the Presidential Commission to enjoy unlimited access to the archives of the Communist Party. The vast majority of the Securitate files was transferred to the CNSAS by December 2006.

---

[49] Lavinia Stan, "Which-hunt or Moral Rebirth? Romanian Parlamentary Debates on Lustration," *East European Politics and Societies*, 26:2 (2012): 274-295.

[50] The best example here is the White Book of the Securitate, see above, or how close the 1990s director of the archives, Ioan Scurtu, was to President Ion Iliescu. See also Alina Pavelescu,"Reconcilierea posttotalitară cu trecutul pe tărâmul istoriei publice-relaţia între arhivişti şi istorici în românia" in *Fără termen de prescriptie. Aspecte ale investigării comunismului în Europa*, eds. Sergiu Mustaţă and Igor Caşu (Chişinău: Cartier, 2011), 190-200.

[51] The Constitutional Court Decision 51 of 31 January 2008 dismantled the CNSAS. Only the last-minute intervention of the government, which issued an executive order, prevented this, but the fragility of the CNSAS was proven right at the moment they gained custody of the Securitate archives.

[52] Author's personal interview with Dorin Dobrincu, Bucharest, 10 July 2013.

The National Archives leadership changed in June 2007, in part because the Presidential Commission accused the former Archives leaders of trying to conceal key documents.[53] In this context, Prime Minister Popescu Tariceanu appointed young historian Dorin Dobrincu as head of the National Archives. Dobrincu used the precedent of the opening of the archives to the Presidential Commission in 2006, under his predecessor, to turn the exception into a rule for all researchers. Note, however, that the opening of the archives became reality because of several personal decisions, not of any coherent policy, prepared ahead of time and assumed by political parties represented in Parliament.

Appointed in June 2007 at the helm of the National Archives, Dobrincu was a researcher with the Romanian Academy. Because his appointment was supported by the IICC, Dobrincu's tenure seemed to show the wish of the Liberal government to open the Communist Party archives, and thus promote reckoning at a time when Prime Minister Popescu Tariceanu was engaged in a public competition with President Basescu to demonstrate political will to promote transitional justice. Dobrincu's appointment did not give the executive branch any privileged access to the National Archives, but neither did it signal its resolve to completely reform this institution or to take the custody of the Archives away from the Ministry of Interior, which inherited the personnel and institutional culture of its communist predecessor. In addition, although formally the Ministry became de-militarized before Romania joined the European Union in January 2007, that same year Dobrincu took over an institution where the portraits of the communist generals were prominently displayed.[54] The Archives' subordination to it allowed the Ministry of Interior to control the access to documents by researchers and members of the general public. Until 2007, even the Archives' personnel was recruited exclusively from among graduates of a branch of the Police Academy in Bucharest.

In July 2007, the archives of the Communist Party and of the Communist Youth Union were opened when Dobrincu re-interpreted the provisions of Law 16/1996 and invoked the precedent created by the Higher Defense Council Decision 61/2006, which granted the Presidential Commission access to previously inaccessible documents. The opening might not have been possible without the spoken mandate given to

[53] Cristian Vasile, "Comisia Prezidenţială pentru Analiza Dictaturii Comuniste şi accesul la arhivele comunismului românesc," in *Fără termen de prescriptie. Aspecte ale investigării comunismului în Europa*, eds. Sergiu Mustaţă and Igor Caşu (Chişinău: Cartier, 2011): 201-215.

[54] Author's interview with Dorin Dobrincu, Bucharest, 10 July 2013.

Dobrincu by the higher government echelons: "Open up the archives!"[55] Under Dobrincu, the archives started to be catalogued and digitized, and the centralization of the former Central Committee archives was accelerated. The opening of the archives became a priority so much so that by 2012 as many as 2,000 collections, including 700,000 files produced by various communist institutions, were opened for research. Thus, the number of researchers who consulted files increased from 8,000 in 2006 to 13,500 in 2011.[56]

Dobrincu's most significant and controversial decision was to give researchers access to the archives of the Cadre Section of the Communist Party and to those produced by the Party and the Communist Youth Union in the 1980s. He did so by re-interpreting Article 20 of Law 16/1996, which stipulated that documents produced during the past thirty years could be accessed only with the approval of the head of the unit that created or held them. By invoking the EU Recommendation R(2000)13, which stated that once a researcher viewed a document other researchers could not be refused access to that document, and by arguing that the archives had been created by institutions that no longer existed and had no clear successor, Dobrincu claimed that it was up to the National Archives, as archive custodian, to decide access.[57] His interpretation significantly departed from the spirit of the 1996 Law, which sought to limit access to the documents, especially the most recent ones, left behind by the communist regime. Unprotected by the law, this sudden access ultimately remained temporary.

After the 2008 parliamentary elections, a new government was formed. The new Social Democrat Minister of Interior launched an internal investigation into Dobrincu's actions. The investigation showed the Social Democrats' displeasure with the newly liberalized access to the communist archives.[58] In July 2009, the investigation concluded that the head of the National Archives should not have opened the Central Committee archives

---

[55] Dorin Dobrincu, "Miza destainuirii: Accesul la documentele comunismului," *22*, 3 July 2012, available at: http://revista22.ro/16045/.html, accessed on 16 September 2016.
[56] Idem.
[57] Dorin Dobrincu, "A Brief History of Romanian Arhive Acces Since 1989," *Euxeinos*, 3 (2012): 18-25.
[58] Iulius Cezar and Răzvan Popa, "Directorul Arhivelor Naţionale a desecretizat fără drept informaţii," *Adevărul,* 21 July 2009, and Dorin Dobrincu, "Neadevăruri despre Arhivele Naţionale," *22*, 28 April 2009, available at: http://revista22.ro/6005/.html, accessed on 16 September 2016.

because by doing so he violated citizens' rights and freedoms.[59] Those accusations led to Dobrincu's removal in June 2012. In his reply, Dobrincu argued that after the Presidential Commission report was released and President Basescu condemned the communist rule. Thus,

> all structures of the former Communist Party became automatically illegitimate. As such, the documents produced by them could no longer remain classified. The Romanian state, which has distanced itself from the communist regime, cannot consider secret the crimes and abuses perpetrated by that regime against the citizens...The Romanian state's new commitment [for archive transparency] cannot be overlooked by the Ministry of Interior.[60]

The conflict between the Ministry and Dobrincu revealed the existence of two divergent "memories" of the totalitarian regime, which resulted in policies of access to the communist archives that called for either continuity or a break with past practices. Resistance to access rules change was felt by Dobrincu throughout his tenure.[61] Significantly, Dobrincu remained an interim director throughout his five-year term. That status placed him in a precarious position, as his appointment was periodically reviewed by Ministry of Interior decision makers who were not always sympathetic to his cause. Dobrincu's dismissal in 2012 was not seriously opposed by the Liberals, who had appointed him in 2007, had included transitional justice in their electoral platform, and were junior partners in the government in 2012. Not only did the Social Democrats and the Liberals turn against him, but Dobrincu was also unpopular with Basescu's Democrat Liberals who in January 2009 voted for his removal. The political support of the Liberals and the Democrat Liberals was essential for opening the archives, but their unwillingness to enact institutional and legislative reforms showed their resistance to change the status of the archives and promote transitional justice. Dobrincu faced intimidation even after his dismissal,[62] when the Ministry of Interior asked the National

---

[59] Control Corps of the Ministry of Interior, Report 2015.796, 20 July 2009, document with the author.

[60] Dorin Dobrincu, "Către Corpul de Control din cadrul Ministerului Administraţiei şi Internelor," 24 July 2009, unpublished document available with Dobrincu.

[61] For Dorin Dobrincu "The harassment was especially due to opening for researchers the 1980s archives". Quoted in Dorin Dobrincu, "Miza destainuirii: Accesul la documentele comunismului," *22*, July 3, 2012, available at: http://revista22.ro/16045/.html, accessed on 16 September 2016, and author's personal interview with Dorin Dobrincu, Bucharest, 10 July 2013.

[62] Author's personal interview with Dorin Dobrincu, Bucharest, 10 July 2013.

Anti-Corruption Directorate to investigate his decision to open for research the Romanian Communist Party cadres' files of local luminaries, most notably that of the Orthodox Patriarch Teoctist. The Directorate ruled that such an investigation was unjustified.

Conclusion

In the unconsolidated Romanian democracy, where parties do not really represent the electorate and have no credible ideological identities, transitional justice programs can shake the very legitimacy of the state. Post-communist Romanian political actors first instituted a culture of oblivion and embraced a policy of denial, and only much later assumed a belated form of responsibility for the crimes perpetrated by the communist regime. Even after responsibility was assumed, the post-communist state resisted comprehensive transitional justice.

A short review of the most active period in transitional justice (2006-2012) and of the subsequent period of ignoring the communist past (2012-2016) reveals four aspects. First, almost all state institutions were exempted from transitional justice. De-communization was not achieved, and in addition the responsibility for coming to terms with the past is recognized only for memory institutions. Second, the executive branch retained control over the discourse about the past, and many pro-transitional justice civil society representatives and academics became members of the CNSAS and the IICC, thus having to face all the institutional limitations these nominations entailed. Third, the anticommunist camp became divided, being concerned about the communist past less than about the activity of these memory institutions and their independence from the main political parties. These new concerns overshadowed the debate on the past, affected the credibility of the transitional justice supporters, and weakened the public influence of the anticommunists. Fourth, especially after 2012, memory institutions lost some of their relevance for the general public, the mass-media, and the conflicts within the political elite.

The Romanian transitional justice model entailed first a shameful institutional continuity and then some shameful initiatives. The state officials' refusal to engage in de-communization during the 1990s made way to memory institutions that legitimized state-led transitional justice but were marginalized by and disconnected from other state agencies and therefore unable to impact their institutional culture. If these memory institutions were created to protect the credibility of state institutions from anticommunist criticism, this objective was only partially reached.

Reaching this objective seems more the result of the diversification of anti-communist voices (what I would call the emergence of an "anti-communist galaxy" of voices) than the consequences of these institutions' actions after 2006. In Romania during the 1990s, the lack of transitional justice became a barometer of democratization, since the political elite, the ruling parties, and the state leaders marginalized memory institutions that risked to hide a belated and shallow de-communization.

The incomplete transitional justice policies relate to Romania's incomplete democratization, dysfunctional state-civil society relations, parties that do not represent the interests of the electorate, and state institutions that lack transparency. In addition, many of the anticommunist parties of the 1990s disappeared by merging with the successors of the Salvation Front, which today almost completely dominate the political spectrum. The marginalization of the memory institutions was also facilitated by the local mass media, which includes few quality, politically independent outlets. Many important media owners have ties to the former Securitate, which the CNSAS proved by consulting the secret archives. As the anticommunist camp weakened, it lost its influence with the political and economic elites, the mass media, and key state institutions.

The study of memory policies must therefore consider not only the political context and the place of the past in competing political agendas, but also the conflicting "memories" prevalent in key state institutions that are called to implement transitional justice. Even when the political will to deal with the past is present, it can face inimical institutional cultures and state bureaucrats can render it null. At the same time, the misuse of the communist past for post-communist political ends diminishes the credibility of transitional justice policies, as was the case with the official condemnation. Without the support of political actors, transitional justice could not take place, but political will could trigger mistrust in the political elite members and the state institutions that uphold the policies of oblivion. The Romanian case illustrates the vicious circle of de-legitimization caused by transitional justice expectations that grow faster than the elites' political will and the state's ability to fulfill such expectations. The issue of timing is fundamental, as some transitional justice programs came too late to boost trust in the government and rather showed the country's ambiguous position toward its undemocratic communist past.

PART 2.

TRANSITIONAL JUSTICE IN PRACTICE: SUCCESSES, FAILURES, AND CHALLENGES

CHAPTER FIVE

RETROSPECTIVE JUSTICE AND LEGAL CULTURE

RALUCA GROSESCU AND AGATA FIJALKOWSKI

As other Central and Eastern European countries, post-communist Romania faced legal constraints in prosecuting political crimes committed under communist rule.[1] Until 2014, the statutes of limitation provided by the Criminal Code and the absence of the international category of "crimes against humanity" in the national legislation were the main legal obstacles for trials. Given that no special laws regulated these difficulties, the Romanian judiciary played an important role in mediating the conflict between the duty to prosecute severe violations of human rights and the duty to respect the basic principle of non-retroactivity of law.

The literature to date has identified the nature of the communist regime, the exit from communism, or the post-communist party struggle for political power as factors determining a country's preference for enacting or opposing transitional justice measures in post-communist Central and Eastern Europe.[2] This chapter discusses another possible

[1] Raluca Grosescu's work was supported by the Romanian National Authority for Scientific Research and Innovation, CNCS – UEFISCDI, project PN-II-RU-TE-2014-4-0335.

[2] John Moran, "The Communist Torturers of Eastern Europe: Prosecute and Punish or Forgive and Forget?," *Communist and Post-Communist Studies*, 27:1 (1994), 95-109; Eva Jaskovska and John Moran, "Justice or Politics? Criminal, Civil and Political Adjudication in the Newly Independent Baltic States," *Journal of Communist Studies and Transition Politics*, 22:4 (2006), 485-506; Nadya Nedelsky, "Divergent Responses to a Common Past: Transitional Justice in the Czech Republic and Slovakia," *Theory and Society*, 33:1 (2004), 65-115; Lavinia Stan, ed., *Transitional Justice in Eastern Europe and the Former Soviet Union* (London: Routledge, 2009); Samuel Huntington, *The Third Wave: Democratization in the Late Twentieth Century* (London: University of Oklahoma Press, 1991), especially 211-231; Helga Welsh, "Dealing With the Communist Past: Central And East European Experiences After 1990," *Europe Asia Studies*,

explanation: a country's legal culture, in particular the judiciary's understanding of legal formalism, international human rights law and international criminal law. We assume that this determinant is crucial in cases of criminal justice that entail a conflict between the prosecution of heinous crimes and the prohibition of ex-post facto punishment.

The discussion below focuses on the Romanian trials concerning political crimes perpetrated during the 1950s, with references to two other post-communist cases: the Bulgarian Lovech camp trial and the German Border Guards trials. All these cases involved strategies to overcome retroactivity in order to indict perpetrators, and mirrored debates about retrospective justice that emerged at the beginning of the 1990s and have continued ever since. Here, retrospective justice refers to criminal prosecutions conducted by a legal order other than the one in effect at the time and place of the actions in question. Contrary to the Czech Republic, Poland, or Hungary, where special laws lifted the statute of limitations or prolonged it for certain categories of crimes, in Romania, Bulgaria and Germany the conflict between the duty to prosecute and the duty to respect the principle of non-retroactivity of law remained a dilemma to be solved directly by the judiciary. In this context, legal experts' education and approaches to constitutionalism, international human rights law, and international criminal law became essential.

Friedman defined legal culture as a set of ideas, values and discourses about law, as well as a pattern of behaviour and practices deployed by both legal professionals ("internal legal culture") and non-legal actors ("external legal culture") that are shaped by, and in return influence, the legal systems and their ideological underpinnings.[3] In this chapter, we discuss only the "internal legal culture," that is, the way in which legal experts understand and apply law. Since we are interested in how courts adjudicate retrospective justice, we do not discuss "external legal culture," namely the public's attitude towards the law, the legal mobilization, or the legal consciousness of the citizens.[4] According to the literature, the

48:3 (1996), 413-428; Kieran Williams, Aleks Szczerbiak and Brigid Fowler, "Explaining Lustration in Eastern Europe: A Post-communist politics approach," *SEI Working Paper* 62 (2003), University of Sussex; Monika Nalepa, *Skeletons in the Closet: Transitional Justice in Post-Communist Europe* (New York: Cambridge University Press, 2010).

[3] Lawrence M. Friedman, "The Concept of Legal Culture: A Reply," in *Comparing Legal Cultures,* ed. David Nelken (Aldershot: Darmouth, 1997), 34.

[4] Sally Engle Merry, "What is legal culture? An anthropological Perspective," in *Using Legal Culture*, ed. David Nelken (London: Wildy, Simmonds & Hill Publishing, 2012), 56-57.

practices and ideologies that characterize legal systems can be identified through (1) organizational analysis and ethnographic study of legal institutions and proceedings, and (2) examination of law textbooks and legal scholarship.[5]

The concept of legal culture has been criticised for being vague, over-generalising, and hard to operationalize,[6] but it can be useful in empirical research if specifically delineated.[7] In this chapter, we examine how the judiciary's exposure to a set of values and patterns of behaviour concerning (a) the relationship between law and politics, (b) legal formalism, and (c) approaches to international human rights law and international criminal law has impacted the judicial discourse on transitional justice. We use law university syllabi and textbooks, and the works of various legal scholars who shaped the dominant understanding of the role of law in society. Where the post-communist discourses on retrospective justice are concerned, we examine the trial documents and the legal debates occasioned by court proceedings. We have also conducted interviews with jurists involved in transitional justice to correlate their legal ideas and approaches with the judicial solutions adopted in post-communist trials.

Our chapter first discusses the dilemma of retrospective justice in transition, where after World War II the general tendency was to abandon legal positivism in the case of mass atrocity and political repression. We then consider the legal culture of the Romanian communist judiciary, analyse the legal debates on the application of retrospective accountability, and conclude that the approach to retrospective justice was strongly influenced by the dominant judicial culture. Focusing on Romania, we bring comparative elements from Bulgaria and Germany in order to underline the broader implications of legal culture on transitional justice. Judiciaries in Romania and Bulgaria shared the common experience of

---

[5] Ibidem, 62, also Javier A. Couso, "The Transformation of Constitutional Discourse and the Judicialization of Politics in Latin America," in *Cultures of Legality. Judicialization and Political Activism in Latin America*, eds. Javier A. Couso, Alexandra Huneeus and Rachel Sieder (Cambridge: Cambridge University Press, 2010), 142-144.

[6] Roger Cotterrell, "The Concept of Legal Culture," in *Comparing Legal Cultures*, ed. David Nelken (Aldershot: Darmouth, 1997), 13-31, as well as David Nelken, "Using Legal Culture: Purposes and Problems," in *Using Legal Culture*, ed. David Nelken (London: Wildy, Simmonds & Hill Publishing, 2012), 1-51.

[7] John Bell, *French Legal Cultures* (London: Butterworths, 2001); David Nelken, "Using the Concept of Legal Culture," *Australian Journal of Legal Philosophy,* 29:1 (2004): 1-26; Engle Merry, "What Is Legal Culture?," 52-75.

Soviet legal culture, and its post-communist transformation. In contrast, transitional trials were adjudicated in post-1990 Germany by West German jurists, according to Western legal standards. This comparison sheds light on the role of different legal cultures (West German and Soviet) in transitional justice, the significance of legal culture, and its relationship with political and historical factors.

Dilemmas of retrospective justice in transition

At the international level, the principle of non-retroactivity was established by the 1948 Universal Declaration of Human Rights, and Article 15(1) of the International Covenant on Civil and Political Rights (ICCPR). Article 7(1) of the European Convention on Human Rights (ECHR) enforces the same principle. However, transitions from dictatorial regimes invoke a different narrative. The 1945 "Nuremberg principles" allowed for prosecutions of crimes against humanity, even if these acts had not been criminal under the Nazi legislation. The 1968 UN Convention on the Non-Applicability of Statutory Limitations for War Crimes and Crimes against Humanity provides punishment of such crimes "irrespective of the date of their commission." Article 15(2) of the ICCPR and Article 7(2) of the ECHR also assert that non-retroactivity should not prejudice the punishment of any act which, "at the time when it was committed, was criminal according the general principles of law recognised by civilised nations." These provisions seek to guard against the use of the non-retroactivity principle for preventing retribution for heinous crimes, and to allow prosecution on the basis of customary international law.[8]

Since 1945, many countries chose to forsake, in part, the principle of non-retroactivity for penalising state-crimes committed under dictatorial rule.[9] After World War II, various legal philosophers addressed the conflict between the duty to prosecute and the duty to respect the principle of non-retroactivity. In a formulation still associated with his name, Gustav Radbruch argued that when an intolerable conflict exists between the written law and a higher conception of justice, the written law must be declared "unjust" and subordinated to the cause of morality. He also advanced the idea that non-retroactivity should be transcended where Nazi

---

[8] Eva Brems, "Transitional Justice in the Case Law of the European Court of Human Rights," *The International Journal of Transitional Justice*, 5:2 (2011): 299.
[9] Jon Elster, "Preference Formations in Transitional Justice," in *Preferences and Situations. Points of Intersection between Historical and Rational Choice Institutionalism*, eds. Ira Katznelson and Barry R. Weingast (New York: Russell Sage Foundation, 2005), 268.

crimes were concerned, because the contradiction between Nazi legislation and the sense of justice had become unbearable.[10] Herbert Hart, a scholar steeped in legal positivism, criticised the Radbruch formula in the name of the predictability of law. Although Nazi law was immoral, fidelity to the written law must prevail, he said, because it constitutes the only unambiguous principle that assures the predictability of law.[11] In opposition to Hart, Lon Fuller considered, like Radbruch, that norms must contain an internal morality to be valid. Therefore, when applied to heinous crimes, retrospective justice does not endanger, but rather supports the rule of law.[12] Radbruch's and Fuller's theories are currently accepted worldwide and represent the "escape clause" for jurists who exercise "legal imagination" in order to reclaim the "original social function of the law."[13]

Aspects of legal culture

The Romanian legal experts involved in the trials of former communist leaders have been socialised in the Soviet model of legal culture. While this model has been gradually transformed after 1990, it continued to influence the attitudes and practices of jurists.[14] This section analyses the state socialist legal culture and its post-communist adaptation, with reference to the West German model. We focus on (a) the relationship between ideology, law and politics, (b) the approaches to legal formalism, and (c) the attitudes toward international human rights law and international criminal law.

Ideology, law and politics

Communist ideology held that the "will of the working people" was the source of power. The Communist Party, representing the "ideals and aspirations of the proletariat," was elevated above all state structures,

---

[10] Gustav Radbruch, "Injustice légale et droit supralégal," *Archives de l'Association Française de Philosophie du Droit*, 39:1 (1994) : 309.

[11] Herbert L.A. Hart, "Positivism and the Separation of Law and Morals," *Harvard Law Review*, 71:4 (1958), 593-629.

[12] Lon L. Fuller, "Positivism and Fidelity to Law – A Replay to Professor Hart," *Harvard Law Review*, 71:4 (1958), 630-672.

[13] Jiří Přibáň, *Legal Symbolism: On Law, Time and European Identity* (London: Ashgate, 2007), 151.

[14] Ramona Coman, *Réformer la justice dans un pays post-communiste. Le cas de la Roumanie* (Brussels: Université de Libre Bruxelles, 2009), 228-229.

including the judiciary.[15] The 1952 Romanian Constitution underlined the role of the judiciary in defending the socialist order. The Party was declared the "leading force" of the society, while all other bodies, including the judiciary, served as "transmission belts of the Party."[16]

Nikita Khrushchev's rise to power in the Soviet Union marked a turning point for Soviet legal thought with the development of a new concept of socialist legality, entailing due process and more protection of citizens' individual rights.[17] The party's pressure and control over judges continued to undermine the judiciary's independence. Judges enjoyed autonomy in deciding most of the cases, but political interference persisted in courts, particularly when political issues were at stake.[18] Whenever a conflict appeared between the constitution and the regular laws, judges had to apply the regular laws until parliament solved the controversies. Moreover, the judicial impunity granted to the communist political leadership remained part of the justice system and culture throughout the communist period.

In contrast, in the context of the Cold War and the division of Germany, the 1949 constitution of the Federal Republic of Germany, the Basic Law, declared the state a welfare democracy, based on the rule of law (*Rechtsstaat*) as opposed to the East German "dictatorship of the proletariat."[19] The judiciary was granted independence and irremovability, and, through the creation of the Federal Constitutional Court, the power to analyse and decide on the constitutionality of laws.[20] As the Basic Law was not politically neutral but prioritised democratic values, "aggressive attitudes towards the free democratic order" were prohibited. This approach was exacerbated by the competition between East and West, leading to prosecutions of communist sympathizers in the 1950s.[21] These

---

[15] Andrei Vyshinsky, *The Law of the Soviet State* (Westport, CT: Greenwood Press, 1948), 503.

[16] The Romanian Constitution of 1952, art. 65, available at http://legislatie.resurse-pentru-democratie.org/constitutie/constitutia-republicii-populare-romane-1952.php, accessed 9 May 2016.

[17] Maria Łoś, *Communist Ideology, Law and Crime. A Comparative View of the USSR and Poland* (New York: St. Martin's Press, 1988), 16.

[18] Inga Markovits, "Justice in Lüritz," *The American Journal of Comparative Law*, 50:4 (2002): 829.

[19] Anke Freckmann and Thomas Wegerich, *The German Legal System* (London: Sweet and Maxwell, 1999), 282.

[20] Ibidem, 125-126.

[21] Patrick Major, *The Death of the KPD: Communism and Anti-Communism in West Germany, 1945-1956* (Oxford: Oxford University Press, 1997), 282.

trials involved, however, due process and were found constitutional by the Constitutional Court.

Approaches to legal formalism

In the first decade after World War II, legal practice in the new popular democracies was left to the "revolutionary consciousness" of law enforcers, who were called to defend the new order by all available means. Laws and procedures had no value *per se*, and could be applied differently from case to case, according to the consciousness and the interests of the working class.[22]

In the 1960s and 1970s, improved rules and procedures were introduced into the relevant statutes. By the 1970s the Romanian legal community saw a new wave of graduates from courses that were of better quality and less ideologized. An important shift occurred from a "flexible and open-ended approach to the law" to respect for the "basic legal structures closely resembling the disapproved 'bourgeois law'."[23] Due process was introduced and respected in most cases.[24] Legal interpretations tended to be formalist in nature and adopt a position whereby the judge would simply apply "what the Party puts into laws; I am not passing any value judgments of my own," a survival strategy that continued after 1989.[25] Furthermore, constitutional provisions remained marginal in the communist legal systems.

Positivism and formalism marked also the West German legal culture until the mid-1960s. Most German legal scholars considered the Nuremberg trials a form of "victors' justice" and denounced the London Charter as *ex post facto law*. Consequently, they asked prosecutions of Nazi criminals only on the basis of the national law in force at the time when crimes were committed.[26] Between 1946 and 1951, natural law,

---

[22] Hans Kelsen, *The Communist Theory of Law* (London: Stevens & Sons, 1955), 119.

[23] Łoś, *Communist Ideology*, 57.

[24] Markovits, "Justice in Lüritz."

[25] Michal Bobek, "Judicial Transformations in Post-Communist Societies: A Study in Institutions, Administration and Interpretation," *CAS Working Paper Series*, no. 4 (2011), 39, available at http://www.cas.bg/uploads/files/Shaken%20Order/M.%20Bobek.pdf, accessed on 10 May 2016.

[26] Ronen Steinke, *The Politics of International Criminal Justice. German Perspective from Nuremberg to The Hague* (Oxford: Hart Publishing, 2012), 50-51.

according to Radbruch's formula, and the Nuremberg criminal categories were also used in several court cases (both criminal and civil) to annul the exculpatory effect of the Nazi legislation. In 1968, the Constitutional Court approved this line of argument.[27] Another legal strategy in the 1950s was to declare invalid various repressive laws adopted under the Third Reich because they contradicted the provisions of the Weimar Constitution (still in force under Hitler's rule). In such cases, the judges applied the 1871 German criminal code, not the Nazi one.[28] Finally, in 1979, the Bundestag lifted the statute of limitations for murder (committed in the past or in the present), in order to permit the continuation of prosecutions of Nazi crimes.[29]

The 1960s and the 1970s also witnessed the emergence of a new generation of German lawyers, who restarted the debates on the importance of applying the Nuremberg criminal categories, especially crimes against humanity.[30] This school of thought and related debates concerning Radbruch, Hart and Fuller began to play an important role in the discussions regarding the post-World War II German transition.[31]

International human rights and criminal law

Socialist legal frameworks did not clearly specify the relationship between municipal and international law.[32] If contradictions appeared between national and international norms, the legal hierarchy was not stipulated in the constitutions. The Romanian law textbooks criticised any form of monist approach to international law. States were free to create their own domestic legislation in accordance with ratified international treaties, and their national ideological goals.[33] International law could thus not be applied directly by courts.

---

[27] Guillaume Mouralis, *Une épuration allemande. La RDA en procès 1949-2004* (Paris: Fayard, 2008), 296-297.

[28] Ibidem, 297.

[29] Robert A. Monson, "The West German Statute of Limitations on Murder: A Political, Legal, and Historical Exposition," *American Journal of Comparative Law*, 30:4 (1982): 605-625.

[30] Mouralis, *Une épuration*, 309.

[31] Interview with Christian Tomuschat, Berlin, 24 April 2014.

[32] William Butler, *Soviet Law* (London: Butterworths, 1988), 41-63.

[33] Gheorghe Moca, *Dreptul International* (Bucharest: Editura Politica, 1983), 308; Nicolae Ecobescu, ed., *Drepturile Omului in Lumea Contemporana. Culegere Selectiva de Documente* (Bucharest: Editura Politica, 1983), 10.

Until 1990, international law was taught only during one semester during the four-year law curriculum and it did not include human rights or international criminal law. International instruments such as the 1948 UN Convention on Genocide, the 1968 UN Convention on crimes against humanity, or the 1966 ICCPR were not studied in universities, although Romania had ratified them. Legal practitioners who graduated during the communist regime recall that concepts like "genocide" or "crimes against humanity" represented "exotic crimes mentioned only exceptionally."[34] The 1945 London Charter, the Nuremberg trials or post-World War II transitional justice remained unknown to most law students.[35]

In contrast, the West German constitution situated international customary law (human rights, humanitarian and criminal law) above ordinary laws, although below the constitutional level.[36] From the early 1980s, the curriculum of West German law universities incorporated human rights, European law, and international law. Germany gradually came to adhere to European developments in judicial interpretation that were marked by more open, substantive approaches and argumentative judicial opinion. Eventually legal formalism was overcome. International law also started to play an important role in legal practice.[37] This would prove important for a unified Germany and its decision to adopt the West German legal framework and to use it as a basis for reinterpreting East German law.

After 1990, Romanian legal culture gradually changed. The 1992 constitution granted the separation of powers and the independence of the judiciary. It also elevated international human rights law above national norms. With the adherence to the ECHR, individuals became subjects of international law. Yet, the legacy of the communist regime continued to influence the judiciary after 1989. Legal formalism, "the myth of moral-free judging by technocratic judicial officials,"[38] and the de facto subordination of the judiciary to the executive persisted in the first twenty years of transition.[39] So did most of the communist corpus of criminal law,

---

[34] Interview with Adriana Stamatescu, judge at the Romanian Supreme Court of Justice (graduated law in 1990), Bucharest, 8 April 2013.

[35] Interview with Dan Voinea, military prosecutor in 1982-2009 (graduated law in 1980), Bucharest, 20 November 2006.

[36] Helmut Satzeger, "German Criminal Law and the Rome Statute - A Critical Analysis of the New German Code of Crimes against International Law," *International Criminal Law Review*, 2:3 (2002): 264.

[37] Interview with Christian Tomuschat, Berlin, 24 April 2014.

[38] Bobek, "Judicial Transformations," 7.

[39] Coman, *Réformer la justice*, 220-229.

which remained almost intact until 1997. Legal positivism and formalism continued to dominate as a method of interpretation. Judges and prosecutors rarely used constitutional provisions or international law in court cases, relying only on regular laws.[40]

Judging the communist past: negotiating between procedural and substantive justice

After 1990, Romania faced legal constraints in prosecuting political crimes committed in the 1950s, the harshest repressive period of the communist regime.[41] The socialist Criminal Code - in force until 2014, with amendments – provided for a 15-year statute of limitation for homicide.[42] This provision meant that in 1990, it was no longer possible to investigate homicides committed before 1975. Also, until 2014 the Code contained no provisions for crimes against humanity,[43] a category which could have been applied to the communist political felonies. As such, most of criminal investigations into communist crimes were closed. Prosecutors argued that indicting would violate the principle of non-retroactivity.

Until 2014, two trials dealt with crimes committed by former communist officials during the 1950s. In 1993, Alexandru Drăghici, former Minister of Interior in 1953-1965, was charged with ordering, in 1954, the murder of an individual who had crossed him in private life. Three other Securitate officers were accused of executing this person, without judicial mandate.[44] The allegations did not involve political crimes, but the case was important because of the role Draghici had played in the communist repression.[45] In the second trial, initiated in 2000,

---

[40] Interview with Dan Voinea, Bucharest, 20 November 2006.

[41] For the trials of former communist officials in Romania see: Raluca Grosescu and Raluca Ursachi, *Justitia Penala de Transitie de la Nuremberg la Post-comunismul Romanesc* (Iasi: Polirom, 2009); Lavinia Stan, *Transitional Justice in Post-Communist Romania: The Politics of Memory* (New York: Cambridge University Press, 2013).

[42] The Romanian Criminal Code of 1968, art. 122, available at http://lege5.ro/Gratuit/he2demzw/codul-penal-din-1968, accessed 9 May 2016.

[43] Of the international crimes not subject to statute of limitations, only crimes against peace, war crimes, and genocide were included (Art. 356-359).

[44] The Archives of the Bucharest Military Court of Appeal (ABMCA), File no. 15/P/1999, "Indictment from 8 of April 1993."

[45] As Minister of the State Security (1952-1953) and Minister of Interior (1953-1965), Draghici coordinated the political repression during the harshest period of the communist regime.

Colonel Gheorghe Crăciun, former director of the largest political prison in Transylvania (Aiud) in 1958-1964, was accused of the murder of 216 political prisoners, who had been executed, tortured or starved to death during detention.[46]

To resolve the statute of limitations issue, prosecutors invoked an article in the communist Criminal Code,[47] which states that the prescribed terms can be suspended if a "legal disposition or an irremovable circumstance" is hindering the criminal investigations and trials. Both indictments stated that the statute of limitations for crimes committed by communist leaders had to be suspended for the entire communist period (1945-1989), because the political interference in the justice process, and the secret character of information relating to nomenklatura members rendered impossible the investigation of such cases before 1989.[48] Prosecutors invoked a 1968 secret report of the Communist Party, which brought to light crimes and abuses perpetrated during the 1950s by communist leaders, Draghici included. The investigations deemed criminal prosecutions to be necessary, but the communist authorities decided to avoid criminal justice and take only administrative measures against those involved.[49] In the Craciun case, prosecutors stated that under communist rule, mistreatment of political opponents was a state policy, and all documents concerning political repression were classified. This context made impossible any investigation into such cases until 1989.[50] In both cases, the defence argued that suspending the statute of limitations would violate the rules of due process, as "there was not enough evidence to demonstrate the Communist Party's interference in the justice process before 1989." But the judges allowed the trials to continue, concluding that the political context of the communist period was an "irremovable circumstance" that hindered criminal action against those in power.[51]

In 1992, when the investigations started, Draghici fled to Hungary. The following year, the Romanian state called for his extradition, but the Hungarian authorities rejected the request, arguing that the statute of limitations for the alleged crime had expired in 1969 and that the defendant risked an unfair trial. In 1993, Draghici died in Budapest, before

[46] ABMCA, File no. 15/P/1999, "Indictment from 7 September 2000."
[47] The Romanian Criminal Code of 1968, art. 128.
[48] ABMCA, File no. 15/P/1999, 230.
[49] Ibidem, 228-230.
[50] Ibidem, 230.
[51] Ibidem, 244.

any sentence could be pronounced. In 2001, Craciun's trial ended similarly, when the defendant passed away.[52]

Although no conviction was pronounced, these trials are important because they illustrate a compromise between procedural and substantive justice. The courts regarded the lack of judicial independence during the communist regime as an "irremovable circumstance" that blocked criminal investigations. This vision reflects the judiciary's concern to interpret law in a historical context. The judges' choice to suspend the statute of limitations reflects an inclination for substantive justice over procedural justice. However, this decision relied exclusively on article 128 of the Criminal Code, without any interpretation of constitutional provisions or international law. Also, these two cases were an exception. Prosecutors closed most criminal investigations for violating the principle of non-retroactivity.

The introduction of crimes against humanity in the Criminal Code

In 2006, the Romanian government established the Institute for the Investigation of Communist Crimes in Romania, with the purpose to lodge criminal complaints against those responsible for political crimes perpetrated before 1989. But the legal framework was, once again, unfavourable to prosecutions. Even if considered to begin with 1990, the 15-year statute of limitations for murder expired once again in 2005. As such, the strategy of the Institute was to document deeds that could be considered crimes against humanity and militate for the synchronisation of the national legislation with the international law concerning this category of crimes. In 2008, the Institute petitioned the Ministry of Justice to introduce crimes against humanity in the criminal code and include the provision of the 1968 UN Convention: "punishable no matter when committed." The Institute argued that the principle of non-retroactivity would not be violated, as Romania had ratified the 1968 UN Convention under communism. The request also underlined similar European experiences, especially the modification of the French Criminal Code in 1964, or of the

---

[52] Raluca Grosescu and Raluca Ursachi, "Transitional Criminal Justice in Post-Communist Romania," in *Kilometer Null. Politische Transformation und gesellschaftiche Entwicklungen in Rumanienseit 1989,* eds. Thede Kahl and Larisa Schippel (Berlin: Frank & Timme, 2011), 405-422.

Estonian statute in 1994.[53] This initiative belonged to a new generation of lawyers and political scientists specialised in international law and transitional justice. By the nature of their studies, they were aware of the evolution of international human rights law after World War II and of the resolutions of the European Court of Human Rights with respect to retrospective justice after dictatorship.[54]

The Ministry of Justice rejected the proposal, invoking the principle of non-retroactivity of laws. It rejected not only the idea of considering crimes against humanity punishable no matter when they were committed, but also the idea of punishing them starting with 1969, when Romania ratified the 1968 UN Convention. The Ministry avoided discussing the relationship between national and international law and referred only to the fact that the Institute's request was implying *ex-post facto* consequences, violating thus the rules of a due process.[55] This interpretation reflects lack of engagement and awareness toward international human rights law and international criminal law. The special concern for the principle of non-retroactivity indicates in this case not only attention to the principle of due process, but also disregard for international treaties. The Ministry's approach reveals a restrictive positivist vision on the spirit of the law, with very little concern for both substantive justice and international norms.

In 2011, when parliament was discussing a new Criminal Code, the Institute approached several representatives of the political elite to obtain backing for its project. It found support in Monica Macovei, member of the European Parliament and former Minister of Justice in 2004-2007. A civil prosecutor during the late 1980s, Macovei became an important civic activist in the field of human rights and justice reform after 1990. From 2001 to 2004, she served as president of the Helsinki Committee in Romania. In 2012 she proposed an amendment to the Criminal Code that echoed the Institute's request. Since the adoption of the Code in 2014, the crimes against humanity are sanctioned in Romania "irrespective of the

---

[53] The Archive of the Institute for the Investigation of Communist Crimes in Romania, "Proposal regarding the modification of the Title XI of the Criminal Code, 22 February 2008," 1-2.

[54] Personal correspondence with Oana Axinia, legal representative of Institute for the Investigation of Communist Crimes in Romania between 2008 and 2013, 18 April 2013.

[55] The Archive of the Institute for the Investigation of Communist Crimes in Romania, "Answer of the Ministry of Justice regarding the Proposal of the Institute for the Investigation of Communist Crimes in Romania with respect to the modification of the Title XI of the Criminal Code 20 April 2008," 1-3.

date of their commission."[56] In 2014, two former directors of political prisons during the 1950s were charged with crimes against humanity, upon this new provision of the Criminal Code. One defendant, Alexandru Visinescu, was sentenced in 2016, and the other, Ion Ficior, is still facing trial.

Macovei's amendment to the Criminal Code was thus crucial for the debates regarding retrospective justice in Romania. First, the proposal of synchronising national legislation to the 1968 UN Convention came from a new generation of scholars educated in Western Europe, who did not perceive non-retroactivity as immutable. Second, owing to her personal experience as a human rights legal activist, Macovei was also sensitive to these issues. As a member of the European Parliament, she was keenly aware of the ECHR practices in this matter. While the Institute and Macovei were attentive to substantive justice and decided to use international law to break impunity, the experts of the Ministry of Justice preferred a formalist approach on law, where the importance of non-retroactivity outweighed international law and obligations, or any arguments put forward on the grounds of natural justice.

Bulgaria: no escape from legal formalism

In January 1990, in response to public pressure, the Bulgarian judiciary launched investigations into the killings perpetrated in Lovech, the last communist forced labour camp, where 151 persons had been killed and around 1,500 people had been imprisoned in appalling conditions in 1959-1962.[57] The inquiry documented 14 murders and indicated five alleged perpetrators, including former Deputy Minister of Interior Mirtcho Spasov. In March 1990, they were all taken into police custody as a preliminary detention measure. Three of them were placed under house arrest, because of health problems, and two were kept in prison for three years, although no indictment was formulated against them until 1993.[58]

---

[56] The Romanian Criminal Code of 2014, art. 121.

[57] Hristo Hristov, "The Bulgarian Gulag," available at http://www.vagabond.bg/politics/item/1390-the-bulgarian-gulag.html, accessed on 11 October 2015.

[58] Hristo Hristov and Alexander Kashumov, "Justice and Accountability Mechanisms in Bulgaria in the Transition Period (1989 – 2008)," in *After Oppression. Transitional Justice in Latin America and Eastern Europe*, eds. VesselinPopovski and Monica Serrano (New York: United Nations University Press, 2012), 279.

As in Romania, prosecutors faced problems concerning the statute of limitations. The Bulgarian communist Criminal Code – adopted in 1951, amended in 1968 and 1998 - provided for a 20-year statute of limitation for homicide.[59] This provision meant that after 1982 it was no longer possible to judge the murders committed in the Lovech camp in 1962. Also, the Criminal Code did not contain provisions for crimes against humanity. The communist Bulgarian Constitutions of 1947 and 1971 provided no ban on retroactivity, but article 2 of the 1968 Criminal Code stated that a crime should be judged upon the law in force at the moment of its commission. Since 1991, the Bulgarian Constitution has forbidden retroactivity, but elevated international law above national norms (art. 5(3) and art. 5(4)).

In 1990, prosecutors ruled that the Criminal Code provided no legal solution for prosecuting the crimes committed at Lovech. Their interpretation relied on the national Criminal Code alone, without reference to constitutional provisions or international law. They stated that the only solution was for Parliament to adopt a retroactive law that would specifically sanction the political abuses of the communist period.[60] In March 1990, in the context of the negotiated transition, the last communist Parliament, dominated by reformist elements, amended the Criminal Code to extend the statute of limitation for "murder of two or more persons" from 20 to 35 years. The avowed purpose of this change was to allow prosecutions of crimes that violated international human rights law, even if the statute of limitations had expired. But Parliament did not clearly specify if the amendment had retroactive effect or if it referred only to homicides committed after March 1990.[61] In 1991, the prosecutor in charge of the Lovech case called on the Parliament and the Supreme Court to give an explicit ruling on this matter. Parliament did not reply, while the Supreme Court refused to issue a decision, indicating that no ongoing trial required it.[62]

In 1993, the new general prosecutor appointed by the anti-communist Union of Democratic Forces reopened the case and drafted an indictment. The defendants were accused of murder and mistreatment of political

[59] The Bulgarian Criminal Code, chapter 9.

[60] Hristov and Kashumov, "Justice and Accountability," 279.

[61] Bulgarian Parliamentary debates, available at http://www.parliament.bg/pub/StenD/2012121210500530031990_4.pdf, accessed on 26 March 2013.

[62] Hristov and Kashumov, "Justice and Accountability," 280.

opponents detained in Lovech.[63] To resolve the statute of limitations issue, the prosecutor argued that it had been impossible to judge such crimes under communist rule, since they had been ordered by state officials. Consequently, the prescribed terms for such offences should start in 1990, once the transition to democracy had been accomplished.[64] He claimed that law should be interpreted in its historical context, especially in cases of state criminality and of political hegemony over the justice system. But the indictment did not refer to any legal basis in the national criminal law or international law that would have allowed for the suspension of the statute of limitations. The prosecutor simply relied on his historical interpretation of the judiciary's status under communism.

For more than nine years any decision was postponed because of procedural matters. Finally, in 2002, the Supreme Court dropped all charges. On the one hand, the Court stated that the accused undoubtedly had committed the crimes, and were guilty from a moral viewpoint. "Murder and mistreatment of innocent people arrested and placed in the Lovech camp are reprehensible acts, which contradict any form of moral understanding of justice."[65] On the other hand, the Court declared that according to the 1951 Criminal Code (in force at the time when the killings had been committed), it was no longer possible to prosecute the crimes because the statute of limitations had expired. The Court also argued that a conviction in the Lovech case would violate Article 15(1) of the ICCPR, by ignoring the statute of limitations embedded in the national criminal codes. Nevertheless, the Court considered that the ICCPR would allow the Bulgarian Parliament to extend the statute of limitations for acts considered criminal according to the general principles of law recognised by civilised nations. In the absence of specific provisions on the matter, the Court decided to close the trial.[66]

The Lovech trial manifests continuities with the former socialist legal culture in two respects. First, the defendants were imprisoned or placed under home arrest for almost three years before the trial started. The communist Criminal Code allowed such extensive preliminary arrests, but in a democratic context the measure was arguably a violation of due process. Also, the indictment did not rely on specific national or international legal provisions, but only upon the prosecutor's historical

[63] Meanwhile two defendants had passed away. The Archives of the Bulgarian Supreme Court of Justice (ABSCJ), "Accusation Act No. 2 / 1994", 1-5.
[64] Hristov and Kashumov, "Justice and Accountability," 280.
[65] The Archives of the Bulgarian Supreme Court of Justice, "Decision No. 3/2002 of the Bulgarian Supreme Court of Justice," 5.
[66] Ibidem, 4-5 and 7.

considerations. Second, the Supreme Court's decision was unable to dispense with the technocratic and formalistic approach manifested in the communist legal framework. This is evident in the Court's application of the 1951 Criminal Code without any corroboration from the constitution or from international law, such that a special status for retroactivity might be permitted in the case of heinous crimes. The Court employed Article 15(1) ICCPR to close the trial, but did not make any reference to Article 15(2) or the 1968 UN Convention that would have allowed prosecutions for political crimes.

Germany: the creative power of judges

Dilemmas of retrospective justice also arose in reunified Germany, in cases regarding the killings perpetrated at the inter-German border. The East German government did its utmost to stop its citizens from fleeing to the West. Various regulations required the border guards to prevent, by deadly force if necessary, any attempts to illegally cross the frontier. At least 246 people were killed while trying to cross the border.[67]

In 1990, the Unification Treaty did not specify anything about how the reunified Germany should address cases of so-called "government criminality" that had been lawful in East Germany, but were considered serious crimes in the Federal Republic. The Treaty stated that criminal acts committed in the East German territory prior to unification were to be judged on East German legislation, unless the criminal law of the Federal Republic was more favourable to the defendant. Accordingly, homicides should have been judged under provisions of West German law, which involved lesser penalties for such crime.[68] But applying the federal law to the manslaughters at the frontier would have involved retroactivity, since preventing escape to the West, even by deadly force, had been legal under East German law. Prosecuting acts that were lawful at the time of commission would have violated the Basic Law.[69]

In the absence of explicit legislation, this dilemma had to be solved directly by the courts. Between 1990 and 1999, over 100 people were prosecuted for the killings committed at the borders. Most of them were

---

[67] John Borneman, *Settling Accounts. Violence, Justice and Accountability in Postsocialist Europe* (Princeton: Princeton University Press, 1997), 74.

[68] Peter E. Quint, "Judging the Past: The Prosecution of East German Border Guards and the GDR Chain of Command," *The Review of Politics*, 61 (2) (1999): 305.

[69] Manfred J. Gabriel, "Coming to Terms with the East German Border Guards Cases," *Columbia Journal of Transnational Law*, 38:2 (1999): 380-385.

young soldiers, who had opened fire on fugitives, but members of the Politburo of the communist party and members of the National Defence Council (in charge of the East German border regime) were also held responsible as the guards' superiors.[70]

The courts were generally composed of West German jurists, Eastern judges being excluded from these trials.[71] This point is important, given that the legal culture of the judiciary adjudicating such cases was based on the Western German legal tradition. From the outset, the courts refused to consider the conviction of the border guards retroactive. This was in fact the main argument of the defence, which invoked the 1982 Border Law supplying the statutory justification for the use of deadly force at the border. The defence asked for the application of East German legislation to respect the principle of non-retroactivity of laws. It argued that the guards should be acquitted, as they had done nothing else but abide by the East German border regime. But the courts rejected these arguments, and adopted two different approaches in order to overcome retroactivity.[72]

The first approach was the reinterpretation of the East German border legislation within the larger scope of the East German law. Various courts, the Supreme Court included, stated that the border law might have authorised shootings at the frontier, but the East German Constitution contained an implicit "right to life," while the Criminal Code "required that the means employed to prevent a crime be proportioned to the crime being committed." Within this wider interpretation of the East German law, the guards should not go unpunished, as "the flight of a single, unarmed person (...) could not be considered a violation serious enough to justify the use of deadly force." Consequently, the guards were to be convicted, since they had violated the East German constitutional principle of the "right to life."[73] Certain jurists criticised this interpretation, arguing that it evaluated the East German law according to the standards of the Federal approach to constitutional rights. The East German Constitution formally endorsed individual rights, but these rights were always curtailed by the overriding commitment to the communist regime. This approach

---

[70] James McAdams, "Communism on Trial: The East German Past and the German Future," in *Transitional Justice and the Rule of Law in New Democracies,* ed. James McAdams (Notre Dame: University of Notre Dame Press, 1997), 239-265.

[71] Quint, "Judging the Past," 310.

[72] McAdams, "Communism on Trial."

[73] Ibidem, 248. In most of the cases, the guards' sentences were suspended on the grounds that the East German political context was curtailing their independent action and decision-making.

can be also seen as a creative legal interpretation whereby constitutional provisions corroborate specific criminal regulations to permit a broader understanding of the meaning of law. Although they might have chosen to apply Western human rights standards, the judges allowed prosecutions within the East German legal framework and avoided application of retroactive law.

The second approach was to reject the exculpatory effect of the East German legislation and seek justifications for applying retroactive law. In various guards' trials, the judges explicitly cited the Radbruch formula and emphasised that the East German legal standards stood in blatant contradiction to the generally recognised foundations of the rule of law. To prove the non-legitimacy of the East German border policy, the tribunals evoked international human rights law, such as the 1948 Universal Declaration and the 1966 ICCPR, which protected the "inherent right to life" and the "right to leave any country, including [one's] own."[74] This approach was criticised from two points of view. First, although East Germany ratified it in 1976, the ICCPR was never incorporated into domestic law. The courts rejected such arguments, holding that states, by dint of ratifying international conventions, agreed to be bound by them and fulfil the resulting international obligations. Second, the courts did not enquire whether the 1948 Universal Declaration, invoked with regard to the killings committed before 1976, met the requirements on international legal obligation. The courts' purpose was not so much to find the proof of "hard" international law, but to invoke international conventions to delegitimise East German domestic law.[75]

In 1996, three National Defence Council members convicted by the Supreme Court lodged a complaint with the Federal Constitutional Court, denouncing violation of the constitutional principle of non-retroactivity. The court dismissed the complaint, explicitly citing the Radbruch formula. The constitutional provision of non-retroactivity could thus not allow the exculpatory effect of a legal system that was undemocratic and that systematically disregarded basic human rights principles.[76]

These verdicts suggest strong affinities with principles of natural law and the gradual shift in the Western German legal culture after World War

[74] Rudolf Geiger, "The German Border Guard Cases and International Human Rights," *European Journal of International Law*, 9: 3 (1998): 543-544.
[75] Streletz, Kesseler and Krentz v. Germany (2001), App. 34044/96, 35532/97 and 22801/98, Judgement 22 March, available at file:///C:/Users/raluca/Downloads/CASE%20OF%20STRELETZ,%20KESSLER%20AND%20KRENZ%20v.%20GERMANY.pdf, accessed on 30 July 2013, 9.
[76] Ibidem, 11-13.

II. The explicit citing of the Radbruch formula and the questioning of the moral legitimacy of the East German laws point towards the abandonment of the positivist approach to the validity of written laws, irrespective of their content. In addition, the solutions of the courts emphasise a judicial culture where international law plays an important role in the legal system. International conventions on human rights became the legal basis that allowed prosecutions and invalidated the legitimacy of the East German border regime.

Conclusion

Our analysis draws attention to an overlooked factor that shapes transitional justice outcomes: legal culture. This determinant is particularly important when legal dilemmas of retrospective justice are not regulated by special laws (in other words, by politics), and have to be solved directly by the judiciary. In such contexts, the creative power of judges, their approaches to legal positivism and international law exert a profound influence. The following table summarises the main characteristics of the legal culture and the approaches to retrospective justice after 1989 in the three settings.

After 1945, communist law operated upon the notion of unity of state power, not the separation of powers. Consequently, the judiciary functioned under political control. Also, there was no sense of a robust constitutionality or of questioning the constitutionality of statutes. Communist judiciaries were constructed "on a myth that judging and deciding cases is a clear-cut analytical exercise of a mechanical matching of facts with the applicable law."[77] In contrast, West German legal culture was characterized by the independence of the judiciary, a strong respect for civil and political rights, and a gradual withdrawal from legal positivism and legal formalism. International law became a feature of legal practices and education. These aspects were reflected after 1989 in cases of retrospective justice regarding crimes committed under communist rule.

---

[77] Bobek, "Judicial Transformations," 6.

Table 5.1: Legal Culture and Retrospective Justice in Romania, Bulgaria and Germany

Country and Type of Judiciary	Ideology, Law, and Politics	Legal formalism	International human rights and criminal law	Judicial decisions and legal discourses after 1989
Romania 1990-2010: judiciary educated during communist times In the late 2000s, with the creation of IICCR, a new generation of scholars trained in international law and transitional justice rises	▪ Subordination of the judiciary to political power ▪ Forms of independence only in non-political cases	▪ Weak constitutionalism ▪ Strong legal formalism as an escape from political authority	▪ Ambiguous relationship between international and municipal law ▪ Absence of courses on international human rights and criminal law ▪ Little regard for international law in domestic legal proceedings	▪ Exclusive use of the domestic written law, which allowed for the suspension of the statute of limitations in certain cases (Art. 128 of the Criminal Code) ▪ No application of international human rights law by courts ▪ In the late 2000s, reception of international human rights into the domestic approach to the non-applicability of statutory limitation for crimes against humanity
Bulgaria: judiciary educated during communist times	▪ Subordination of the judiciary to political power ▪ Forms of independence only in non-political cases	▪ Weak constitutionalism ▪ Legal formalism as an escape from political authority	▪ Ambiguous relationship between international and municipal law ▪ Absence of courses on international human rights and criminal law	▪ Exclusive use of the domestic written law (the 1951 Criminal Law) ▪ Use of international law (Article 15(1) ICCPR) to defend application of the positive law in force, but dismissal of other

			▪ Little regard for international law in domestic legal proceedings	international law provisions (Article 15(2) ICCPR, 1968 UN Convention) that would permit overcoming retroactivity ▪ The permanent turn of the judiciary to the political authority to resolve legal dilemmas
Germany: civilian West German judiciary	▪ Strong independence of the judiciary	▪ Strong constitutionalism ▪ 1946-1951: Radbruch formula overcomes retroactivity ▪ 1951-1970: A particular form of legal positivism ▪ 1970-1980: Reception of natural law doctrines	▪ Primacy of international law over domestic law ▪ Courses on international human rights and international criminal law at the end of the 1970s ▪ Rigorous use and importance of international law	▪ Re-interpretation of the East German border regime in connection with the East German constitutional provision concerning the "inherent right to life" ▪ Overcoming retroactivity through application of international human right law and use of the Radbruch formula

First, the German judiciary engaged in the interpretation of a problematic legal framework without turning to political authorities for solving legal dilemmas of retrospective justice. In contrast, in the Bulgarian Lovech case, the judiciary turned to Parliament to furnish the legal solution for lifting the statute of limitations for heinous crimes (both in 1991 and in 2002). In Romania, judges and prosecutors found a solution in the positive law (the communist Criminal Code) for suspending the statute of limitations for the entire communist period. However, the two indictments drafted between 1990 and 2002 were an exception. The debates concerning crimes against humanity showed that both the judiciary and the legal experts of the Ministry of Justice lacked commitment towards, and awareness of, international law. The initiative to harmonize domestic legislation with the UN 1968 Convention was in the end taken by a new generation of scholars with transnational experience and it was finally regulated by politics, through Macovei's efforts to change the Criminal Code.

Second, the robust constitutionalism of the West German legal culture was reflected in the courts' decision to interpret the East German border regulations in connection with the East German constitutional provision concerning the "inherent right to life." The reception of natural law doctrines in German legal culture was also reflected in the Federal Constitutional Court's decision concerning the National Defence Council case. The judges directly cited the Radbruch formula as an argument against the exculpatory effects of the "unjust" East German legal regime. In contrast, both Bulgaria and Romania demonstrate weak constitutionalism, since the Criminal Code was never interpreted in connection with the Constitution. Principles of natural law were never invoked by courts, which permanently adhered to the written law. The Bulgarian case proves just how reluctant the judiciary was to go "beyond the text." The reference to international legal instruments was made in view to defending the application of positive law. Romania reflected a partly anti-formalist stance through the interpretation of the Criminal Code in historical context.

Third, concerning international law, West Germany provided courses on human rights and international criminal law starting at the end of the 1970s. In legal practice there was the primacy of international law over domestic law, and the rigorous use and importance of international law, stemming from the jurisprudence of the European Court of Human Rights. These aspects of legal culture were reflected after 1989 in the National Defence Council trial. Importantly, international human rights obligations were used to invalidate the East German border regime. In Bulgaria and

Romania, in contrast, there was a notable lack of legal education on international human rights law. In practice, there was scant regard for the place of international law in domestic legal proceedings, and the Constitution did not provide for its primacy over domestic law. After 1989, the courts in both jurisdictions did not employ international law to overcome retroactivity.

From a broader theoretical perspective, our investigation underlines the importance of the judiciary's institutional ideology when addressing grave human rights violations. Since legal professionals do not operate in a vacuum, an exploration of a judiciary's particular history at a specific moment in time tells us about judicial power, its approaches to constitutionalism, and its understanding of international law. Our study shows that a judiciary will be more ready to look for solutions to legal dilemmas when there is a strong sense of judicial independence, and scope for judges to exercise their creative power. Where judicial independence is deficient, the tendency is towards a conservative and weak constitutionalist orientation among judges. In the final two decades of the communist regime, the Eastern European judiciaries learned that the best tactic to achieve professional success was to avoid independent or innovative interpretations in favour of conservative readings of the law that appeased the political authorities. This resulted in a strong legal formalism, where judges applied the letter of the law, ignoring the effect of their decisions and not questioning the law's content. In contrast, in Western continental Europe the end of World War II witnessed the empowerment of the judiciary. Another important aspect is the exposure of the judicial body to international law. The higher the level of education and the greater the intensity of transnational exchanges concerning international law, the greater the tendency to abandon legal formalism and to overcome impunity for heinous crimes.

CHAPTER SIX

PUBLIC EXPOSURE WITHOUT LUSTRATION

DRAGOS PETRESCU

On 31 January 2008, the Romanian Constitutional Court decided that Law 187/1999 on Access to the Personal File and the Disclosure of the Securitate as a Political Police was unconstitutional. As a result, Decision 51 of 31 January 2008 of the Constitutional Court pushed into a severe crisis the post-communist process of dealing with the files of the feared Securitate, the communist secret political police. A heated debate broke out, as many Romanian commentators were afraid that the process of dealing with the Securitate files, which had just gained momentum, would come to an abrupt end. In a rare display of responsibility and concern, however, the government ensured that the process would continue.

This chapter focuses on some less obvious aspects of the process of opening, administering and accessing the Securitate files in the aftermath of Decision 51/2008, which prompted a significant change of the legal framework that governed the opening of the Securitate files. Consequently, in the Romanian case that process has led primarily to the systematic public exposure of the misdeeds of the former communist regime. Such public exposure has prompted moral condemnation of the abuses of the *ancien régime*, which in turn enabled informal lustration. By "informal lustration" I understand as a process that induces institutional and moral changes somewhat similar to lustration, but only as a side effect of widespread access to the files of the former secret police agencies, systematic public exposure of the wrongdoings of the defunct communist regime, and moral condemnation of the very act of providing the communist secret police with information on fellow citizens. As Cynthia Horne observes, informal lustration prompts "preemptive employment of vetting by employers, selective voluntary resignations by individuals to avoid disclosure, as well as an increase in citizen engagement with the secret police files."[1]

The chapter is divided into three main parts. The first addresses the legal framework regarding the opening of the Securitate files, from the passing of Law 187 in December 1999 and the establishment of a new institution, the National Council for the Study of the Securitate Archives (Consiliul Național pentru Studierea Arhivelor Securității, CNSAS), the following year, and up until January 2008. The second part discusses the legal and institutional changes brought about by the Constitutional Court Decision 51/2008. Finally, the third part of this study focuses on two important issues: (1) the successive attempts at adopting a lustration law in post-1989 Romania, which, as shown below, ended in utter failure; and (2) the process of informal lustration, which resulted from the systematic public exposure of the wrongdoings of the Securitate and the moral condemnation of the abuses of the communist regime enabled by the 2008 change of the legal framework governing the activity of the CNSAS.

Belated access to the Securitate files, 1999–2008

The Central and Eastern European countries that experienced a regime change in 1989 generally followed the German model of opening and administering the files of the former communist secret police forces. As such, one can speak of an intra-regional diffusion of the German model of dealing with the files of the communist Ministry for State Security (known as Stasi) to the other countries. This diffusion had important legal as well as institutional dimensions.[2] As Valerie Bunce and Sharon Wolchik argue, diffusion can be defined as "a process wherein new ideas, institutions, policies, models or repertoires of behavior spread geographically from a core site to other sites, whether within a given state […] or across states."[3] In post-communist Romania, a law regarding the opening and administering

[1] Cynthia Horne, "'Silent Lustration:' Public Disclosures as Informal Lustration Mechanisms in Bulgaria and Romania," *Problems of Post-Communism*, 62:3 (2015): 131-144.

[2] For a discussion of diffusion of other transitional justice methods, programs and practices within Central and Eastern Europe, see Helga Welsh, "Beyond the National: Pathways of Diffusion," in *Post-Communist Transitional Justice: Lessons from Twenty-Five Years of Experience*, eds. Lavinia Stan and Nadya Nedelsky (New York: Cambridge University Press, 2015), 167-187.

[3] Valerie Bunce and Sharon L. Wolchik, "International Diffusion and Post-Communist Electoral Revolutions," *Communist and Post-Communist Studies*, 39:3 (2006): 286.

of the Securitate files, drawing on the German legislation on the matter, was passed in 1999.

Note that former political prisoners played a paramount role in pushing for a complex solution comprising "retribution," "disqualification," and "restitution" in dealing with the systematic violation of basic human rights perpetrated by the communist regime.[4] Former political prisoners became prominent leaders of the three so-called "historic" political parties that were active before 1945, were disbanded by the communist authorities, and were then again reestablished after 1989: the National Peasant Party (which after 1989 added a Christian Democrat dimension), the National Liberal Party, and the Romanian Social Democratic Party. However, former political prisoners lost ground in 2000, when the Social Democrat Party, the main successor to the Communist Party, returned to government, after the National Peasant Party lost its representation in Parliament. During the December 1989 Revolution former political prisoners also organized themselves in the Association of the Former Political Prisoners in Romania (Asociaţia Foştilor Deţinuţi Politici din România, AFDPR), which worked closely with the historic parties, especially with the National Peasant Party, and other civil society organizations to promote reparations for all those who had been politically persecuted under communism.[5] In 1990, the AFDPR numbered as many as 98,700 members, but its membership has dwindled ever since. For the former political prisoners, the process of coming to terms with the communist past meant not only bringing perpetrators to justice in the courts, but also restoring victims to their proper place in society by acknowledging the injustice made to them under the communist regime.

From a legal viewpoint, one of greatest victories registered by the AFDPR was the passing of Law 187 by Parliament in December 1999. The law has been widely known as the Ticu Law, after its main proponent, former National Peasant Party senator and AFDPR president Constantin Ticu Dumitrescu (1928–2008). The law was passed only after years of heated debates and numerous modifications aimed at changing its substance,

---

[4] All three terms are used by Claus Offe, *Varieties of Transition: The East European and East German Experience* (Cambridge, MA: MIT Press, 1996), 82-104.

[5] In 1990 former political prisoners received some special rights, including: medical care and local transport free of charge, subventions for medicines, limited free railroad transport, etc. See "Decret-Lege din 30 martie 1990 privind acordarea unor drepturi persoanelor persecutate din motive politice de dictatura instaurată cu începere de la 6 martie 1945, precum şi celor deportate în străinătate ori constituite în prizonieri," *Monitorul Oficial al României*, 118 (18 March 1998): 5–7.

which deeply frustrated Dumitrescu. As its title suggests, the law granted to the Romanian citizens, and former citizens established abroad, the right to read their Securitate files by creating the first legal framework that offered access to the Securitate archives to any citizen interested in assessing "the political police activities of the former secret police in order to offer to society as correct as possible a picture of the communist period."[6]

To offer access to secret files, a new institution was established to take over and administer the secret files, which had been housed with the post-communist intelligence services, the successors to the Securitate, after 1989. According to the law, an eleven-member College leads the CNSAS. Nine of the College members are nominated by the parties represented in Parliament, one by the President, and another one by the Prime Minister.[7] The major function of the CNSAS is to provide evidence for publicly identifying the former officers and informal collaborators of the secret police. Initially, it was thought that this official mandate would prompt lustration. The College is empowered to check holders of, and candidates for, post-communist public office and assess if they had been involved in the activities of the Securitate as a "political police." Law 187/1999 defined political police (*poliţie politică*) so as to enable lustration by making access to public office dependent on "certificates of morality" issued by the CNSAS on the basis of the Securitate archives. Thus, the Romanian law assigns individual responsibility based on individual deeds that constitute proof "beyond a reasonable doubt," not collective guilt assumed by an individual's mere association with the Securitate. In this respect, the Romanian law is similar to the German, but not to the Czechoslovak, legislation.

Looking retrospectively, it is evident that Law 187/1999 was drafted in such a way as to make it as consistent as possible to the rule-of-law principles. According to Article 3, people seeking, or occupying, public office must fill out a special form in which to state whether they were or not agents or collaborators of the communist secret police. Article 5 defined three fundamental terms: (1) political police, (2) agent of the Securitate, and (3) collaborator of the Securitate. Political police described "all those activities performed by the Securitate or by other repressive

---

[6] "Lege nr. 187 din 7 decembrie 1999 privind accesul la propriul dosar şi deconspirarea Securităţii ca poliţie politică," *Monitorul Oficial al Romaniei* 603 (9 December 1999): 1–5. For an electronic copy of the law, see "Legea nr. 187 din 1999 privind accesul la propriul dosar şi deconspirarea Securităţii ca poliţie politică," 9 December 1999, available at: http://legislatie.resurse-pentru-democratie.org/legea/187-1999.php, accessed on 25 May 2016.

[7] Idem.

structures or institutions, which envisaged the establishment and perpetuation of the communist totalitarian power, as well as the suppression or limitation of fundamental human rights and liberties." An agent (or officer) of the Securitate as a political police is an individual who was an operative, including undercover, during 1945–1989. A collaborator is "an individual who: (a) was remunerated or recompensed in any other way for their activity in that capacity; (b) possessed a safe house or a secret meeting place; (c) was a Securitate resident in the terms of the present law; (d) any other individual who provided information to the Securitate, which affected directly or indirectly fundamental human rights and liberties." In addition, a collaborator is also an individual who "transmitted or facilitated the transmission of information, notes, reports or other documents which denounced activity or attitudes against the totalitarian communist regime and which could affect fundamental human rights and liberties." Assimilated to the notion of collaborator were also "the individuals who were empowered to make judicial or political decisions or who, by abuse of political power, made decisions at central or local level regarding the activity of the Securitate or of other repressive bodies of the totalitarian communist regime."[8]

One should emphasize a confusion introduced by Articles 1, 5 and 16. Article 1.2 grants an individual placed under surveillance by the Securitate the right to know the real names of the officers and collaborators who contributed information to her file. Article 5 defines the term "collaborator." However, Article 16 states that verdicts of collaboration issued by the CNSAS College may be appealed in court within 30 days. Therefore, the process of establishing whether an individual was a Securitate collaborator implies that the CNSAS College issues a decision of collaboration and more often than not a court of appeal hands down a final verdict. Consequently, an individual who contributed information to a given Securitate file cannot be termed collaborator before this process is completed. In fact, Article 1.2 talks about sources, that is, individuals who contributed information to a file, but for whom no CNSAS decision or final appeal verdict were issued. There is, therefore, a major distinction between a source and a collaborator. A source is an individual who contributed information to the file, under her real or code names, but whose relationship with the Securitate is not yet confirmed by the CNSAS and the courts. By contrast, a collaborator is an individual for whom proof beyond a reasonable doubt was found in the Securitate archives and a CNSAS decision of collaboration, followed by its final confirmation in a court of law, were issued. Such a distinction is particularly important for

[8] Idem for all citations included in this paragraph.

the victims of the Securitate, who could face a libel suit if they label as collaborators individuals who were unveiled only as sources. It is also important because disqualification from public office applies only to collaborators and by no means to sources.

Disqualification of individuals proven to have acted as Securitate agents or collaborators from their elected or nominated public office was supposed to occur if such individuals did not acknowledge their position within, or their collaboration with, the Securitate apparatus when completing the mandatory special form required by the law. If collaboration was demonstrated by the CNSAS and the courts but not acknowledged by the individual, the individual could be charged with providing false statements in a public document. Thus, according to Romanian legislation, what is really punished with disqualification is not the act of spying on behalf of the Securitate, but its withholding or denial. Nonetheless, until 2006 the application of Law 187/1999 proved to be very difficult, because the government lacked the political will to physically transfer the Securitate archives from other public institutions to the CNSAS. Therefore, the CNSAS was the legal custodian of a Securitate archive it could access only at the whim of the heirs to the Securitate's departments. Moreover, verifications of individual past involvement with the Securitate turned out to be a difficult operation that required the work, and collaboration, of many people over a very long period of time. Whereas to the Federal Agency for the Administration of the Stasi Files (BStU) employed some 3,300 people over the first fifteen years of its existence, and the Polish Institute of National Remembrance (IPN) may employ a maximum of 2,100 people, the Romanian CNSAS can have only up to 300 posts, of which around 230 have been actually occupied only since 2010.[9]

Having examined the legal framework, let us analyze the 2000–2008 period. During 2000–2005, the CNSAS was confronted with major problems related to the transfer of the Securitate files, which at the time

---

[9] For additional details regarding the legal framework, structure and mission of each of the institutions established in Bulgaria, Czech Republic, Germany, Hungary, Poland, Romania, and Slovakia to administer the files of the former secret police agencies in those countries, see Bundesbehörde für die Stasi-Unterlagen (BStU), *The European Network of Official Authorities in Charge of the Secret Police Files: A Reader on their Legal Foundations, Structures and Activities*, 2nd revised edition (Berlin: BStU, 2013), and Lavinia Stan and Nadya Nedelsky, eds., *Encyclopedia of Transitional Justice*, 3 vols. (New York: Cambridge University Press, 2013). For more on the formation of the archives administered by these institutions, see Rafał Leśkiewicz and Pavel Žáček, eds., *Handbook of the European Network of Official Authorities in Charge of the Secret-Police Files* (Prague: ÚSTR & IPN, 2013).

were hosted mainly by the Romanian Intelligence Service (Serviciul Român de Informaţii, SRI), the Foreign Intelligence Service (Serviciul de Informaţii Externe, SIE), and the Ministry of National Defense (Ministerul Apărării Naţionale, MApN). Since its establishment in 2000, the CNSAS constantly fought with these three institutions over the custody of the documents produced by the Securitate. Because of these institutions' resistance, such documents were transferred to the CNSAS very selectively until March 2005. One should note that from March 2001 to February 2005 only 9,442 files comprising 19,064 volumes (some 700 m of archive) were transferred to the CNSAS. Afterwards, the situation improved tremendously mainly because of the political will to effect change showed by the new government and president elected in the general elections of 2004. From March to December 2005, the SRI transferred 1,298,960 files comprising 1,542,550 volumes (some 12.5 km of archive) to the CNSAS, which had to inaugurate a new, larger building for their preservation.[10] Government Ordinance 149 of 10 November 2005 extended the application of the Law 187/1999 for another six years under a newly elected College. Also, Government Ordinance 16 of 27 February 2006 and Government Decision 731 of 7 June 2006 improved the functioning of the CNSAS.[11] Furthermore, during April–August 2006 the Supreme Council of National Defense (Consiliul Suprem de Apărare a Ţării, CSAT) issued four decisions meant to ensure the continuation of the transfer to the CNSAS archive of documents produced by the former Securitate and housed with other institutions or public bodies. By the end of 2006, the CNSAS archive already contained as many as 1,555,905 files, comprising 1,894,076 volumes, which amounted to some 24 linear kilometers of archive. Thus, the activity of the CNSAS gained momentum. For instance, in 2006 the institution unmasked as many as 270 Securitate sources – more than the total number of sources unmasked during the entire period 2000–

[10] Consiliul Național pentru Studierea Arhivelor Securității, *Raport de Activitate privind anul 2005* (Bucharest, 2006), 3, 11 and 12; available at: http://www.cnsas.ro/documente/rapoarte/Raport%202005.pdf; accessed on 20 June 2016.

[11] Law 187/1999 underwent some modifications. See in this respect "Ordonanța de urgență a Guvernului României nr. 16 din 22 februarie 2006 pentru modificarea și completarea Legii nr. 187/1999 privind accesul la propriul dosar și deconspirarea Securității ca poliție politică," *Monitorul Oficial al Romaniei* 182 (27 February 2006): 1–8; for the extension of the activity of CNSAS, see "Ordonanța de urgență a Guvernului României nr. 149 din 10 noiembrie 2005 privind unele măsuri pentru asigurarea continuității activității Consiliului Național pentru Studierea Arhivelor Securității," *Monitorul Oficial al Romaniei* 1008 (14 November 2005): 7–8.

2005.[12] In 2007, the number of sources unmasked by CNSAS rose to 341.[13]

The activity of the CNSAS gained momentum after early 2006 and consequently more and more public figures – from all fields of activity, ranging from the judiciary to the academia – were gradually exposed as former sources, collaborators or agents of the Securitate. At the same time, the insufficient personnel working in the CNSAS could not do wonders with a huge archive that had to be simultaneously investigated and put in order. Time and again, the media raised questions about the destruction of relevant files after 1989. Indeed, the collaboration of prominent politicians was revealed not by their personal files, which in many cases were not preserved or were not transferred to the CNSAS, but by the files of their former victims, in which evidence of collaboration (usually in the form of copies of informative notes) was found. In other words, even though the files of some former collaborators are now missing, their information notes can still be found in the files of those on whom they provided information, so that the process of unmasking the act of collaboration is neither totally irrelevant nor useless.

CNSAS reborn: Emergency Ordinance 24/2008 and Law 293/2008

The second major period in the activity of the CNSAS was inaugurated in January 2008, when the Constitutional Court decided that Law 187/1999 was unconstitutional. The case was brought in front of the Constitutional Court by Dan Voiculescu, businessman and politician.[14] Previously, on 15 June 2006, the CNSAS College had issued the Decision

[12] Consiliul Naţional pentru Studierea Arhivelor Securităţii, *Raport de Activitate privind anul 2006* (Bucharest, 2007), 5; available at: http://www.cnsas.ro/documente/rapoarte/Raport%202006.pdf; accessed on 9 July 2016.

[13] Consiliul Naţional pentru Studierea Arhivelor Securităţii, *Raport de Activitate privind anul 2007* (Bucharest, 2008), 15; available at: http://www.cnsas.ro/documente/rapoarte/Raport%202007.pdf; accessed on 9 July 2016.

[14] See “Decizia nr. 51 din 31 ianuarie 2008 referitoare la excepţia de neconstituţionalitate a dispoziţiilor Legii nr. 187/1999 privind accesul la propriul dosar şi deconspirarea poliţiei politice comuniste,” *Monitorul Oficial al Romaniei* 95 (6 February 2008): 2–8. An electronic version of the Constitutional Court’s Decision no. 51 of 31 January 2008 is available at: http://www.cnsas.ro/documente/cadru_legal/DECIZIE%2051_2008.pdf; accessed on 9 July 2016.

no. 234, which stated that, in accordance with the provisions of the Law 187/1999, Voiculescu was a collaborator of the former Securitate.[15] The Court's Decision 51 of 31 January 2008 was highly contested and condemned as another attempt of the neo-communist forces (presumably the successors to the Romanian Communist Party) to stop a process that finally started to look promising.[16]

However, a genuine problem did exist and it concerned the status of CNSAS as a parallel judicial structure (*putere judecătorească paralelă*). Moreover, under the Law 187/1999 the CNSAS College performed simultaneously the functions of prosecutor and judge, since it was empowered under the law not only to search for proofs of collaboration with the Securitate as a "political police," but also to formulate a first judgment on the collaboration of the individuals undergoing verification. This aspect was emphasized by the Constitutional Court as *the* major fallacy of the Law 187/1999 from a constitutional point of view (*viciul constituțional principal al Legii nr. 187/1999*).

At the time, many observers believed that the Constitutional Court decision would actually terminate the functioning of the CNSAS. However, two Emergency Governmental Ordinances – no. 1 of 6 February 2008 and no. 24 of 5 March 2008 – were issued in due time and enabled the functioning of the institution until November 2008, when a new piece of legislation (Law 293/2008) was passed.[17] This most recent law solved the key issue which prompted the Constitutional Court's Decision 51 of 31

---

[15] After a long battle in court, a definitive verdict of collaboration in the Voiculescu case was issued in 2011. For the major court rulings concerning this case, see: Dosar nr. 22502/3/2008, Curtea de Apel București, Secția a VIII-a Contencios Administrativ și Fiscal, "Sentința civilă nr. 671, Ședința publică din data de 5 februarie 2010;" available at http://www.cnsas.ro/documente/monitoare/2013/Voiculescu%20Dan.pdf; and Înalta Curte de Casație și Justiție, Secția de Contencios Administrativ și Fiscal, "Decizia nr. 3678 din 23 iunie 2001: Respinge contestația în anulare formulată de V. D. ca inadmisibilă;" available at: http://legeaz.net/spete-contencios-inalta-curte-iccj-2011/decizia-3678-2011; both accessed on 8 July 2016.

[16] Corneliu-Liviu Popescu, "Uzurparea de putere comisă de Curtea Constituţională în cazul cenzurii dispoziţiilor legale privind deconspirarea poliţiei politice comuniste," *Noua Revistă de Drepturile Omului* 4:1 (2008): 3–14.

[17] "Ordonanța de urgență a Guvernului României nr. 1 din 6 februarie 2008 pentru asigurarea continuității unor activități ale Consiliului Național pentru Studierea Arhivelor Securității," *Monitorul Oficial al Romaniei* 95 (6 February 2008): 9–10; and "Ordonanța de urgență a Guvernului României nr. 24 din 5 martie 2008 privind accesul la propriul dosar și deconspirarea Securității (OUG 24/2008)," *Monitorul Oficial al Romaniei* 182 (10 March 2008): 2–10.

January 2008 and allowed the CNSAS to continue its activity. Under the new legislation, CNSAS definitely lost its status of parallel judicial structure and the CNSAS College was assigned exclusively the role of prosecutor with the task of bringing the cases of Securitate officers or collaborators that qualified according to the new law in front of the Administrative Court of Justice.

Although the new legislation is more restrictive than the previous one with regard to disqualification, it ultimately allows more transparency in the process of unmasking the officers and collaborators of the Securitate, and of publicly exposing the wrongdoings of the communist regime. As mentioned above, Law 187/1999 was based on the concept of "political police," according to which an act of collaboration meant any denunciation that implied an infringement of the rights guaranteed by the communist Constitution. The Emergency Governmental Ordinance 24/2008, which was modified and completed by Law 293/2008, abandoned the concept of "political police" and provided new definitions for the notions of officer and collaborator of the Securitate. Article 2(a) sets forth the notion of Securitate operative (*lucrător al Securității*) instead of Securitate agent (*agent al Securității*). Thus, a Securitate operative is "any individual who, in their capacity of officer or sub-officer of the Securitate or of the Militia with duties in the area of the Securitate activity, including that of undercover officer, performed during the period 1945–89 activities through which they suppressed or limited fundamental human rights and liberties."[18]

A key change occurred with regard to the notion of Securitate collaborator. In this respect, Article 2(b) reads: "Collaborator of the Securitate – an individual who provided information, no matter in what form, such as written notes and reports, verbal communication recorded in verbatim reports by Securitate operatives, through which one denounced activities or attitudes against the totalitarian communist regime *and* which were aimed at limiting fundamental human rights and liberties [emphasis added]." The same article further states that a collaborator of the Securitate is also an individual "who facilitated the gathering of information from other individuals, by putting their dwelling or other premises they possessed at the disposal of the Securitate, as well as those who, in their capacity of Securitate residents, coordinated the activity of the Securitate

[18] "Ordonanța de urgență a Guvernului României nr. 24 din 5 martie 2008 privind accesul la propriul dosar și deconspirarea Securității (OUG 24/2008)," *Monitorul Oficial al Romaniei* 182 (10 March 2008): 2–10.

informers."[19] Very similar to Law 187/1999, ambiguity persists with regard to the notions of source and collaborator of the Securitate, as one can easily see by reading of Article 1.7 and Article 2(b), which provides the definition of collaborator.

The Emergency Governmental Ordinance 24/2008 and the Law 293/2008 define collaboration with the Securitate as pertaining to those deeds that not only violated fundamental rights of individuals, but also "denounced activities or attitudes adverse to the communist state."[20] I contend that the new legislation introduced in 2008 defines collaboration on the basis of a principle of simultaneity, that is, infringement of fundamental rights *and* denunciation of anti-regime attitudes and activities. This definition obviously narrows down the range of cases that can be identified as acts of collaboration. Indeed, the introduction of this principle of simultaneity reduced the number of cases identified as acts of collaboration, all the more that another major modification was operated with regard to the way the very decision of collaboration with the Securitate is issued in accordance with the new legislation.

According to Article 11.1, when relevant information is found in the Securitate files, the CNSAS brings the case in front of the Administrative Court of Justice. Furthermore, Article 11.2 states that the losing party – that is, the CNSAS or the individual under investigation – has the right to appeal the verdict to a higher court. On the one hand, the new legislation passed in 2008 significantly limited the number of cases brought in front of the Administrative Court on the grounds of collaboration with the Securitate. On the other hand, the same legislation has unleashed a multifaceted process of unmasking and exposing the repressive actions of the Securitate. Thus, Article 10.2 states that the certificates of non-collaboration with the Securitate issued by the CNSAS (the so-called *adeverințe*) are published on the official website of the institution and the interested parties have the right to appeal these certificates to the Administrative Court within 30 days of their publication. Note that the CNSAS College issues two types of certificates of non-collaboration. The first type is a simple certificate, which applies to individuals for whom no information has been found in the secret files, and who were therefore

[19] Idem. Both citations in this paragraph refer to the same Emergency Governmental Ordinance.

[20] "Lege nr. 293 din 14 noiembrie 2008 pentru aprobarea Ordonanței de urgență a Guvernului nr. 24/2008 privind accesul la propriul dosar și deconspirarea Securității," *Monitorul Oficial al Romaniei* 800 (28 November 2008): 1–4.

"unknown" to the communist secret police.[21] The second type is a certificate with a preamble, which applies to individuals who transmitted information to the Securitate, but did not denounce activities or attitudes against the communist regime. In such cases, the preamble mentions, when appropriate, the existence of one or all of the following elements: (1) a network file (that is, a file showing that the person was recruited by the Securitate); (2) a pledge of collaboration (*angajament*) between the individual and the communist secret political police; as well as (3) a code name under which the individual provided information. In addition, the preamble summarizes the pieces of information transmitted to the Securitate by the individual. In some cases, such a preamble can exceed ten pages.[22] Obviously, the information provided in the preamble enables moral condemnation of the very act of passing information to the Securitate, although these cases cannot be brought in front of the Administrative Court of Justice. At the same time, the number of cases brought by individuals before the Administrative Court in order to officially assess the status of collaborator or officer of the former communist secret police is by no means negligible. For instance, during the period spanning from the change of legislation in March 2008 until the end of 2012, the total number of cases brought in front of the Administrative Court reached 1,932. Of these, 797 sought to assess the status of collaborator, and 1,135 to assess the status of operative (officer).[23]

Nevertheless, the functioning of the CNSAS should not cover only one dimension of the intricate process of dealing with the wrongdoings of the

---

[21] All certificates issued are posted on the official website of the CNSAS at http://www.cnsas.ro/adeverinte.html. A search engine permits users to search for a particular certificate by: (1) the name of the individual; (2) certificate number; (3) date of issue; (4) year of issue): (5) date of posting; and (6) year of posting. One can identify the following certificates on the CNSAS website by searching for the certificate number, date, and year of issue. See Certificate no. (*Adeverința nr.*): 1386 of 21 March 2013, 1388 of 21 March 2013, and 1390 of 21 March 2013; accessed on 9 July 2016.

[22] One can identify the following certificates on the CNSAS website by searching for the certificate number, date, and year of issue. See Certificate no. (*Adeverința nr.*): 479 of 21 May 2015, 480 of 21 May 2015, and 2512 of 14 July 2015; available at: http://www.cnsas.ro/adeverinte.html, accessed on 9 July 2016.

[23] Consiliul National pentru Studierea Arhivelor Securitatii, *Raport de Activitate privind anul 2012* (Bucharest, 2013), 27; available at: http://www.cnsas.ro/documente/rapoarte/Raport%20CNSAS%202012.pdf, accessed on 30 January 2016. The CNSAS's activity reports of 2009–2015 are posted on its website.

defunct communist regime. In the communist regimes, the secret police were always the "iron fist" of the hegemonic Communist Party. Therefore, the principles of public exposure and disqualification must be extended to the former nomenklatura members, many of whom gave direct orders to the secret police. In this respect, information brought to light after 1989 indicates that in order to recruit party members who occupied relatively important posts in the communist regime, Securitate officers were compelled to ask first for approval from party officials. Only after such approval was obtained could the recruitment procedures could be pursued. This is just one example of the need for a second dimension of the process of dealing with past wrongdoings, which should focus on the high-ranking officials of the former Communist Party. On 18 December 2006, President Traian Basescu read in front of the joint chambers of Parliament an official statement, which characterized the defunct communist regime in Romania as "illegitimate and criminal." The statement was based on the conclusions of a special Presidential Commission for the Analysis of the Communist Dictatorship in Romania (Comisia Prezidenţială pentru Analiza Dictaturii Comuniste din România, CPADCR), which functioned during April–December 2006.[24] At the time, many believed that the report devised by the Presidential Commission, followed by the official condemnation delivered by the President of Romania, would open the way for adopting a law allowing for the lustration of former nomenklatura members.

Failure to adopt a lustration law, 2005–2010

After the general elections of 2004, debates over the adoption of lustration legislation became even more intense in Romania. As shown above, Law 187/1999 created the legal framework for the public exposure of the former agents and collaborators of the infamous Securitate. The joint efforts of the newly elected president, government agencies, and civil society organizations led to a massive transfer of Securitate files to the CNSAS, as mentioned above. Simultaneously, in 2005 a group of members of Parliament belonging to the National Liberal Party formulated a bill meant to limit the access to public office of persons who held positions in the power structures of the communist regime. The four initiators were deputies Mona Muscă, Viorel Oancea and Eugen Nicolăescu, joined by senator Adrian Cioroianu. The initiative was based on the principles put forward by the "Proclamation of Timişoara" of 11

---

[24] Vladimir Tismăneanu, Dorin Dobrincu and Cristian Vasile, eds., *Comisia Prezidenţială pentru Analiza Dictaturii Comuniste din România, Raport final* (Bucharest: Humanitas, 2007).

March 1990 in its famous Article 8.[25] The draft law was entitled Lustration Law on the Temporary Limitation of Access to Public Office of Persons Who Held Official Positions in the Power Structures and Repressive Apparatus of the Communist Regime. One can observe that the bill's initiators put forward the principle of collective responsibility. In other words, lustration was meant to apply in relation to the positions the respective individuals occupied within the party or state structures of the communist regime, not in relation with the deeds in which they engaged under that regime. Basically, the bill defined as members of the power structures of the former communist regime the individuals who held top positions within the central and local organizations of the Communist Party and the Union of Communist Youth, as well as those who held top positions in the state administration (at both central and local levels), the judiciary, diplomacy, internal affairs (Militia), propaganda, foreign trade (heads of commercial offices abroad), and the banking system. In all the cases mentioned by Article 1, the bill proposed an interdiction of ten years for access to public offices such as: president of Romania, senator and deputy, mayor and deputy mayor, cabinet member, presidential counselor, director or deputy director of intelligence agencies, director or member of the board of state companies, judge or attorney at law, head of state-sponsored cultural institutions (at both central and local levels), or member of the diplomatic corps. The project was voted by the upper chamber of the Parliament (the Senate) on 10 April 2006, but subsequently the bill's discussion in the Chamber of Deputies was systematically postponed.

After years of oblivion and neglect, the debate on lustration was revived in the new Parliament that resulted from the general elections of 2008. The Lustration Law was finally adopted by the lower Chamber of Deputies on 19 May 2010, four years after Senate adopted it. The May 2010 vote in the Chamber of Deputies divided this way: 203 legislators voted for the adoption of the Lustration Law, 40 voted against, and 12 others abstained. Close to 80 percent of the deputies who participated in that vote supported the new law and the moral cleansing it entailed. The Lustration Law was based on the bill drafted in 2005. Thus, Article 1 provided a brief description of the positions within the power structures and repressive apparatus of the communist regime whose former holders are subject to lustration with job loss. These positions included individuals who held paid jobs within the leading structures of the Romanian Workers Party, the Romanian Communist Party, the Union of Working Youth, the

[25] For "Proclamaţia de la Timişoara," see Domniţa Ştefănescu, *Cinci ani din istoria României: O cronologie a evenimentelor decembrie 1989–decembrie 1995* (Bucharest: Maşina de Scris, 1995), 453–454.

Union of Communist Youth, the central and local state administration; institutions of political education; agents and collaborators of the Securitate; the judiciary; the Militia and the penitentiary system; heads of the Romanian diplomatic and consular missions abroad; political and propaganda officers within the Ministry of National Defense, Ministry of Internal Affairs, and the Department of State Security (that is, the Securitate). Article 2 enumerated the positions the individuals listed in Article 1 are temporarily not allowed to occupy. These included positions within the presidential administration; various legislative bodies; the central state administration; the local administration (from county to commune level); the judiciary; state-owned companies; state institutions (including the national television and the radio, as well as the CNSAS); diplomacy; armed forces; state-funded institutes for researching the communist period and the revolution of 1989; and the European institutions. The period of temporary limitation of access to public office was nevertheless reduced from ten to five consecutive years. Article 3 specified that the individuals applying for the posts covered by Article 2 had to fill out a declaration stating whether they occupied from 6 March 1945 to 22 December 1989 one of the positions specified in Article 1. Also according to Article 3, verifications were to be carried out by the CNSAS, which had to provide a formal written confirmation note (*notă de constatare*). Finally, Article 6 stipulated that the individuals elected to their posts were allowed to fulfill their mandate, while the mandate of individuals appointed to their positions was to be terminated 90 days after the law went into force.[26]

Ultimately, the law did not go into force. Not long after its adoption by the Chamber of Deputies on 25 and 28 May 2010, 87 legislators (29 senators and 58 deputies) raised the issue of its non-constitutionality before the Constitutional Court. On 7 June 2010, the Court issued Decision 820 on the unconstitutional character of the Lustration Law. The most powerful argument of the Constitutional Court related to the principle of collective responsibility on which the Lustration Law was based, because it prescribed lustration on the basis of an individual's association with the communist power structures and repressive apparatus,

---

[26] For the Lustration Law, see Parlamentul României, Camera Deputaților, *Legea lustrației privind limitarea temporară a accesului la unele funcții și demnități publice pentru persoanele care au făcut parte din structurile de putere și din aparatul represiv al regimului communist în perioada 6 martie 1945–22 decembrie 1989* (19 May 2010), available at:
http://www.cdep.ro/proiecte/2006/200/80/2/pr282_06.pdf: accessed on 10 April 2016.

not the individual's personal deeds. Thus, the Court argued against the law, which it saw as prescribing a "collective sanction based on collective responsibility and generic culpability."[27] In addition, the Court argued that the late adoption of the law, twenty-one years after the demise of the communist regime, meant that the punitive measures it stipulated were "disproportionate" in relation to the threat posed to the process of democratic consolidation by the individuals it targeted. That was because the vast majority of the communist officials and Securitate agents and collaborators had already withdrawn from public life by the mid-2000s. The Constitutional Court decision of June 2010 practically put an end to public debates on the adoption of a lustration law in post-communist Romania.

Systematic public exposure and informal lustration

In the absence of formal lustration, I contend that in Romania informal lustration has been primarily facilitated and encouraged by the constant interest of the general public in the Securitate files. Informal lustration is rooted in three major processes, which were set in motion after 2005, when the bulk of the Securitate files were transferred to the CNSAS. These processes consist of: (1) vetting individuals who are holding or seeking public office: (2) disclosing the real names of the Securitate sources who informed on their fellow citizens, at the request of the victims; and (3) engaging in research and education activities aimed at publicly exposing the wrongdoings of the Securitate.

The first two processes represent major objectives of the CNSAS, as defined by the law. Vetting individuals who are seeking or holding public office is a fundamental task of the institution. In virtue of the current legal framework (Article 3 of the Law 293/2008), vetting is performed ex officio – in accordance with Article 3, Points a) to h^1), or by request – according to Article 3, Points i) to z). When relevant information demonstrating an individual's involvement with the Securitate is found in the archives and the above-mentioned principle of simultaneity is fulfilled,

---

[27] See Curtea Constitutionala a Romaniei, "Decizia nr. 820 din 7 iunie 2010 referitoare la obiecția de neconstituționalitate a dispozițiilor Legii lustrației, privind limitarea temporară a accesului la unele funcții şi demnități publice pentru persoanele care au făcut parte din structurile de putere şi din aparatul represiv al regimului comunist în perioada 6 martie 1945–22 decembrie 1989," *Monitorul Oficial al Romaniei* 420 (23 June 2010); an electronic version of this decision is available at http://www.legex.ro/Decizia-820-2010-105400.aspx; accessed on 14 July 2016.

the cases are brought in front of the Administrative Court of Justice. In all other cases, the CNSAS College issues a certificate (*adeverință*) of non-collaboration. For the present discussion on informal lustration, the most interesting case is represented by the certificates with preamble. The mechanism of issuing these certificates has been described above in the section dedicated to the Emergency Governmental Ordinance 24/2008 and the Law 293/2008. Here, it is important to emphasize the role played by the preamble in informal lustration. As shown above, the preamble specifies the existence (or absence) of a network file, an agreement of collaboration, and a code name, and summarizes all relevant pieces of information transmitted to the Securitate by the individual. After being issued, the certificates are posted electronically on the CNSAS website. It may be argued that these certificates with preamble, which can be read by everyone without restriction, provide strong arguments for a moral condemnation of the very act of passing information to the Securitate.

Furthermore, as previously mentioned, individuals who are seeking or holding public office are requested to fill out a special form to specify if they collaborated or not with the Securitate. Since 2015, the CNSAS has filed over 130 legal cases against individuals who received a final verdict of collaboration, but who had stated in the special forms that they did not collaborate with the Securitate. In addition, citizens have the right to find out the real names of the individuals (sources) who informed on their fellow citizens during the communist period. Thus, the CNSAS communicates the real names of the sources directly to the victims, who in turn can decide if they want to make these names public.

As the number of cases brought before the Administrative Court of Justice multiplied, information related to these cases has constantly reached the public. The Romanian newspapers (*Evenimentul Zilei*, *Adevărul*, *Gândul*), online media portals (like Hotnews), or news agencies (such as Mediafax), to name only a few, have constantly kept the public informed about cases of collaboration with, or violation of fundamental human rights by, the Securitate as brought to light by the CNSAS. The local press, both in print and online, has also offered good coverage of the collaboration with the Securitate especially of local public figures, ranging from politicians to artists. Moreover, the process of disclosure of the real names of individuals who contributed information to the Securitate files helps to raise public awareness about the violation of basic human rights by the former communist regime.

Another dimension of informal lustration refers to its capacity to facilitate the transfer to the young generations of knowledge about the role of the secret police agencies in supporting the communist dictatorship, the dire consequences of non-democratic politics, as well as the healing of the fear and trauma associated with past dictatorial repression. Such a goal could be reached only by developing research and education programs in collaboration with universities and schools, and organizing traveling exhibitions, seminars, and workshops throughout the country. The CNSAS supports the research activities carried out by its own researchers, as well as by other researchers both from Romania and abroad. The number of outside researchers allowed to access material from the CNSAS archives has constantly grown. At the time this chapter goes into print, some 1,800 researchers not affiliated with the CNSAS work on scholarly articles, studies, monographs, collections of documents, as well as on their BA, MA and PhD dissertations.[28] In addition, numerous students (at the undergraduate and graduate levels) participate in the internship program offered by the CNSAS (110 students in 2014, and as many as 330 in 2015).[29] The CNSAS also publishes a biannual journal, *Caietele CNSAS*, which can be accessed free of charge on the CNSAS website. Since 2011, the CNSAS and the reputed Nicolae Iorga History Institute of the Romanian Academy have organized an annual conference on the Romanian communism every year in March, as a reminder of 6 March 1945, the date when the communists took control of Romania at the end of World War II. The conference, which is sponsored by the Konrad Adenauer Foundation, brings together academics, civic activists, students, and members of the public interested in the communist dictatorship in Romania and Central and Eastern Europe.

The Securitate files represent a key source of information necessary for understanding the repressive policies of the former communist regime. In order to reach a wider audience and make these sources available for all those interested in the Romanian communism, the CNSAS has engaged in a complex process of publishing on its website a great number of documents that can be downloaded free of charge. These documents can be roughly divided into the following categories: (1) over 8,500 secret

---

[28] The list of researchers not affiliated with the CNSAS who are allowed to access the secret archives, and their research topics, is available on the CNSAS website and is updated regularly.

[29] See Consiliul National pentru Studierea Arhivelor Securitatii, *Raport de Activitate privind anul 2014* (Bucharest, 2015), 39; available at: http://www.cnsas.ro/documente/rapoarte/Raport%20CNSAS%202014.pdf; accessed on 26 May 2016, and Consiliul National pentru Studierea Arhivelor Securitatii, *Raport de Activitate privind anul 2015* (Bucharest, 2016), 45; available at: http://www.cnsas.ro/documente/rapoarte/Raport%20CNSAS%202015.pdf; accessed on 8 July 2016.

orders, resolutions, decisions, and action plans issued by the Ministry of Internal Affairs from 1948 to 1989, as well as other thematically organized documents dealing with internments in labor camps, the communist takeover of 23 August 1944, the 1968 official party inquiry into the abuses of the Securitate during the Stalinist period of 1945 –1964; (2) the complete collection of 88 issues of the journal *Securitatea* (published during 1968–1989), which was dedicated solely to the activity of the Securitate apparatus and was labelled as "secret" by the communist regime and therefore was not distributed to the general public; (3) the complete collection of the nine issues of the Securitate publication *Studii şi documente* (Studies and documents), published during 1969–1971; (4) propaganda brochures, educational materials prepared for the Securitate personnel, and other similar publications; and (5) relevant official documents of the Romanian Workers Party and the Romanian Communist Party from 1945–1989. In terms of their relevance for the historic reconstruction of the past, the Securitate files reflect the viewpoint of the repressive apparatus of the former communist regime. In order to give voice to the victims of the Securitate, an Oral History Center has been established by the CNSAS. This center gathers the testimonies of the victims of the Securitate, who accessed their files and are willing to provide details on their surveillance by the communist secret political police.

Systematic public exposure of the wrongdoings of the former communist secret police through the publication in electronic format on the CNSAS website of documents, witness accounts, and scholarship enables informal lustration and prompts moral condemnation of the violation of basic human rights by the communist dictatorship. Such a process is facilitated by the adoption of a more proactive stance by the CNSAS. Rather than simply responding to public demand for disclosing the misdeeds of the former communist secret police, the institution has established a complex framework of reaching a wide public. These efforts seek to help especially the young generations, who have no personal memory of communism, to understand the nature of the dictatorial past and to develop a democratic political culture.

Conclusion

In Romania, the violent exit from communism was not followed by a rapid process of democratic consolidation. Until 1996, the political rulers allowed only limited criminal justice for the bloody repression of the 1989 protesters in Timişoara and Bucharest, but were by no means interested in introducing lustration legislation since they would have been among the first to be affected by it. Given the state officials' lack of political will to further transitional justice, civil society organizations advocated lustration as a means of consolidating democracy. Thus, in March 1990 the Timişoara Society issued in Timişoara, the city that sparked the 1989 revolution, the so-called Proclamation of Timişoara, whose Article 8 called for the adoption of lustration legislation.

After the power shift of 1996 from the successors of the Communist Party to the anti-communist opposition organized as the Democratic Convention of Romania, and primarily due to the efforts of the former political prisoners, Parliament adopted Law 187/1999 which created the legal framework to deal with the officers and collaborators of the former Securitate. Effectively enforced after 2000, the vetting process provided by the law gained momentum in late 2005, when the bulk of the Securitate files were transferred to the CNSAS. In January 2008, the CNSAS successfully survived a major institutional crisis, after the Romanian Constitutional Court declared the Law 187/1999 unconstitutional. That decision prompted a change in the legal framework on the activity of the CNSAS.

When the 2008 change in the legal framework occurred, few could predict that it would enable the systematic public exposure of the abuses committed under the communist dictatorship. Nevertheless, the new legislation opened three avenues of disseminating information about the human rights violations and misdeeds of the Securitate operatives, collaborators and sources: (1) the cases brought in front of the Administrative Court of Justice that seek to officially establish the status of Securitate collaborator or operative for an individual, cases which have received wide media coverage and have allowed for details about the misdeeds of the Securitate to reach the wider public; (2) the posting of the certificates of non-collaboration on the CNSAS website, especially of the certificates with preamble which specify the existence of a network file, an agreement of collaboration or a code name, and summarize all relevant pieces of information transmitted to the Securitate by the individual; and (3) the disclosure by the CNSAS to the victims of the real names of the Securitate sources, which can then be made public, if the victims so desire.

Furthermore, research and education represent key activities of the CNSAS, which permit a transfer of knowledge to the younger generations with no memories of their own about the communist period. As stated above, systematic public exposure of the wrongdoings of the Securitate through expositions, workshops, publications, witness accounts, and scholarship enables informal lustration and prompts moral condemnation of acts of violation of fundamental human rights and liberties under the communist dictatorship. This is all the more important since the many initiatives that aimed at adopting lustration legislation in post-communist Romania have utterly failed. The Lustration Law, adopted in May 2010 by Parliament, was not subsequently enforced since the Constitutional Court found it unconstitutional and put an abrupt end to prolonged and heated debates on the matter.

CHAPTER SEVEN

MEMORY, COMMEMORATIVE LANDSCAPES AND TRANSITIONAL JUSTICE

DUNCAN LIGHT AND CRAIG YOUNG

Transitional justice is usually addressed through institutional processes such as lustration, restitution, prosecution, and truth commissions, around which a comprehensive academic literature has developed.[1] However, this chapter explores a relatively neglected symbolic dimension of transitional justice,[2] namely practices of memorialization and commemoration that are represented, played out, and contested in urban space. There is widespread acknowledgment within the transitional justice literature that memorialization – in the form of monuments, statues and museums – has a key role to play in healing the wounds of the communist past. Such memorials "represent a critical terrain where the past is confronted and conflict can be addressed."[3] Memorialization is a means of giving recognition to those who suffered hardship, repression, exile, or death under communist regimes. The practice makes a visible statement about what (and who) a political order considers worthy of remembrance, and is a means of reaching large numbers of people over an extended time period.

---

[1] This chapter is a revised version of Duncan Light and Craig Young, "Public Memory, Commemoration and Transitional Justice: Reconfiguring the Past in Public Space," in *Post-Communist Transitional Justice: Lessons from 25 Years of Experience*, eds. Lavinia Stan and Nadya Nedelsky (New York: Cambridge University Press, 2015), 233-251. Reprinted with permission.

[2] Janine N. Clark, "Reconciliation through Remembrance? War Memorials and the Victims of Vukovar," *International Journal of Transitional Justice*, 7:1 (2013): 117.

[3] Brendon Hamber, Liz Ševčenko and Ereshnee Naidu, "Utopian Dreams or Practical Possibilities? The Challenges of Evaluating the Impact of Memorialization in Societies in Transition," *International Journal of Transitional Justice*, 4:3 (2010): 397.

This chapter focuses on the ways in which transitional justice for the victims of Romania's communist regime is expressed in the highly complex entanglement of urban cultural landscapes, public memory, and commemorative sites and practices. We contend that attempts to shape public memory through practices of commemoration and memorialization are important (if neglected) aspects of transitional justice, that have much to tell us about how post-communist societies choose to remember (and forget) the Communist Party rule of 1945-1989. Following a review of the relationships between public memory and urban space, we begin by examining efforts to erase the commemorative landscape produced by Romania's communist regime. We then look at the variety of initiatives (by diverse elites and publics) to commemorate the victims of communism, with particular reference to monuments, memorials and museums. We also highlight the importance of both domestic and international tourism to these sites of memory as central to the way in which they 'work'.

Public memory, commemoration and urban space

Public memory can be defined as "a body of beliefs and ideas about the past that help a public or society understand both its past, present, and by implication, its future."[4] It is a society's collective understanding of the past, but also the ways that this past is represented in the present.[5] Since memory is integral to the formation of identities, collective (or public) memory has long been important in the construction of collective identities.[6] In particular, nation-states construct and promote a particular understanding of the past within nation-building projects that are intended to foster social cohesion and allegiance to a particular "imagined community."[7] The formation of such a collective memory involves choices

---

[4] John Bodnar, *Remaking America: Public Memory, Commemoration, and Patriotism in the Twentieth Century* (Princeton: Princeton University Press, 1992), 15.

[5] Kenneth E. Foote and Maoz Azaryahu, "Towards a Geography of Memory: Geographical Dimensions of Public Memory and Commemoration," *Journal of Political and Military Sociology*, 35:1 (2007): 127.

[6] John R. Gillis, "Memory and Identity: The History of a Relationship," in *Commemorations: The Politics of National Identity*, ed. John R. Gillis (Princeton: Princeton University Press, 1994), 24; and Cristiane Wilke, "Remembering Complexity? Memorials for Nazi Victims in Berlin," *International Journal of Transitional Justice*, 7:1 (2013): 141.

[7] Benedict Anderson, *Imagined Communities: Reflections on the Origin and Spread of Nationalism*, 2nd edition (London: Verso, 2006).

about what a society wishes to remember. Nevertheless, while states may play a leading role in the construction of collective memory they do not enjoy a monopoly over this process. Instead various elites and publics both within and without the state (each of which may be fractured by competing and contesting agendas) participate in the process,[8] so that the formation of public memory is a fluid process of negotiation.[9] Public memory "emerges from the intersection of official and vernacular cultural expressions"[10] and, for this reason, it is best regarded as an activity or process, rather than an outcome.[11]

Public memory is a process that is worked out in the public arena. This is achieved through various practices of remembrance and commemoration intended to reify public memory by turning it into visual spectacle. In particular, human geographers argue that urban space – or landscape – is essential to the "working" of public memory.[12] All political orders seek to create an "official public landscape"[13] intended as a rhetorical statement of specific political values. Remembrance and commemoration are central aspects of such landscapes: Edensor has coined the term "memoryscape" for those parts of the urban landscape that are given over to collective remembrance.[14] The urban environment can be the setting for a range of temporary (if cyclical) commemorative practices including ceremonies, parades, festivals, and rituals. However, most forms of commemoration are permanent and include statues, monuments, memorials and other

---

[8] Benjamin Forest, Juliet Johnson and Karen Till, "Post-totalitarian National Identity: Public Memory in Germany and Russia," *Social and Cultural Geography*, 5:3 (2004): 358, 362.

[9] Karen Till, "Staging the Past: Landscape Designs, Cultural Identity and Erinnerungspolitik at Berlin's Neue Wache," *Ecumene*, 6:3 (1999): 254.

[10] John Bodnar, "Public Memory in an American City: Commemoration in Cleveland," in *Commemorations: The Politics of National Identity*, ed. John R. Gillis (Princeton: Princeton University Press, 1994), 75.

[11] Forest, Johnson and Till, "Post-totalitarian National Identity," 358.

[12] Derek H. Alderman, "Memory and Place: Geographies of a Critical Relationship," *Social and Cultural Geographies*, 5:3 (2004): 347-355; Nuala Johnson, "Public Memory" in *A Companion to Cultural Geography*, eds. James S. Duncan, Nuala C. Johnson and Richard H. Schein (Oxford: Blackwell, 2004), 316-327; Karen Till, *The New Berlin: Memory, Politics, Place* (Minneapolis: University of Minnesota Press, 2005).

[13] James Bell, "Redefining National Identity in Uzbekistan: Symbolic Tensions in Tashkent's Official Public Landscape," *Ecumene*, 6:2 (1999): 186.

[14] Tim Edensor, "National Identity and the Politics of Memory: Remembering Bruce and Wallace in Symbolic Space," *Environment and Planning D*, 15:2 (1997): 178.

public buildings, along with commemorative names attached to streets, buildings, and other urban landmarks. Such commemorative practices concretise "official" conceptions of public memory, rendering it immutable in the public arena. They can also be sites for the expression of opposition to, and contestation of, this official public memory.

Since public memory is produced in a particular political context it is vulnerable to political change. In particular, all shifts of political power "generate a reconfiguration of the 'known past'."[15] This issue is of particular relevance in post-communist societies which have sought to build political identities based on an emphatic rejection of communism (a strategy which generally enjoyed widespread popular support). Such societies faced the need for a new, appropriate and 'usable' past to replace now discredited communist-era constructions of the collective past. The most readily available exemplar was that of the period before communist rule.[16] Thus, Romania and other post-communist states have looked to their pre-communist past as the model for a post-communist future. As Katherine Verdery argued, this is about effectively excising the communist period from the historical time line and connecting the post-communist present with the period before World War II.[17] This enabled post-communist societies to 'resume' the historical trajectory that they would have followed had it not been for the 'aberration' of four decades of communist rule. Clearly in post-communist contexts, the past is fluid and flexible, with different state and non-state groups competing to establish a new historical narrative.

Similarly, public memory is also in a state of reformation.[18] Within the political transformation from totalitarianism to democracy, Romania (and other post-communist societies) face new choices about what (and who) they want to remember, and how (and where) this remembrance will be enacted. At the same time as seeking to forget communism, there is an imperative to memorialise the repression and violence of the communist regime, and to honour the victims of state persecution. There may also be a desire to remember the events that brought about the collapse of communist regimes (even if, in cases like Romania, these events did not in

---

[15] Gail Kligman and Katherine Verdery, *Peasants Under Siege: The Collectivization of Romanian Agriculture, 1949-1962* (Princeton: Princeton University Press, 2011), 9.

[16] Katherine Verdery, *What Was Socialism and What Comes Next?* (Princeton: Princeton University Press, 1996), 136.

[17] Katherine Verdery, *The Political Lives of Dead Bodies: Reburial and Postsocialist Change* (New York: Columbia University Press, 1999), 116, 124.

[18] Forest, Johnson, and Till, "Post-totalitarian National Identity," 358-363.

themselves bring about a clear break with those regimes). Moreover, given that the urban landscape is central to the expression of public memory these debates will, in some way, be worked out in urban space. In particular, there will be a significant remaking of the commemorative landscape. People and events honoured by the previous regime will be de-commemorated and their memorials removed from the public arena. New acts of commemoration will subsequently follow in a way that accords with the political values and public memory of the new regime.

In this way, practices of commemoration and memorialization within the urban landscape can be important (if often overlooked) elements of transitional justice projects in post-communist states. Indeed, memorialization and collective remembrance are fundamental processes in societies recovering from traumatic pasts.[19] Barsalou and Baxter argue that memorialization has a number of roles in such projects: it offers symbolic reparations to the victims of violence; it can promote reconciliation; it can encourage engagement with education programmes about the recent past; and it creates specific sites that can be the focus both of individual mourning and official ceremonies of remembrance.[20] Of particular relevance to this chapter is that memorialization makes a highly visible statement in the public arena about a post-communist society's commitment to a new set of political values. In fact, of all the forms of transitional justice, memorialisation is the most visible and can have an impact on the everyday lives of the greatest number of people. Yet, to date, there has been only sporadic attention in the transitional justice literature to the role of memorialization projects within the urban landscape. This reflects a broader context in which political scientists have paid relatively little attention to the role of monuments and memorials as political symbols.[21] In the following sections we explore changing practices of memorialization in post-communist Romania, focussing first on the removal of the commemorative landscapes created by the

[19] Hamber, Ševčenko, and Naidu, "Utopian Dreams or Practical Possibilities?," 398.

[20] Judy Barsalou and Victoria Baxter, *The Urge to Remember: The Role of Memorials in Social Reconstruction and Transitional Justice* (Washington DC: United States Institute of Peace, 2007), 4, available at: http://www.usip.org/publications/the-urge-remember-the-role-of-memorials-in-social-reconstruction-and-transitional, accessed on 3 October 2013.

[21] Benjamin Forest and Juliet Johnson, "Unravelling the Threads of History: Soviet-Era Monuments and Post-Soviet National Identity in Moscow," *Annals of the Association of American Geographers* 92:3 (2002): 271.

communist regime, and then on efforts to create new memorial sites and landscapes within transitional justice projects.

Erasing the commemorative landscape of communism

When communist regimes came to power in the late 1940s they immediately set about remaking public memory. This was principally achieved through a comprehensive rewriting of history and total control over the education system. It also included a comprehensive remaking of the urban landscape to decommemorate the historical narrative associated with the discredited former regime. Since communist regimes attached special importance to the transformative power of public space for creating a new socialist consciousness,[22] the public arena effectively became an instrument of state propaganda. An entirely new commemorative landscape was produced, which was saturated with a variety of symbols (including statues, memorials, monuments, plaques, murals, banners, and slogans) that were intended to shape the ways that people thought about their individual and collective pasts.[23]

As communist regimes collapsed in 1989 their official commemorative landscapes swiftly became the targets of protest, resulting in the familiar process of "landscape cleansing."[24] This activity was initiated by the populace during the euphoria that accompanied the collapse of communist rule, and was continued by the new post-communist administrations. This process satisfied the demand to see evidence of political change.[25] Czepczyński identifies a number of strategies for landscape cleansing: removal, renaming, rededication, and reuse.[26] The most visible strategy is removal, where monuments placed by the communist states were directly expunged from the urban arena. By far the most iconic images of the

---

[22] David Crowley and Susan E. Reid, "Socialist Spaces: Sites of Everyday Life in the Eastern Bloc," in *Socialist Spaces: Sites of Everyday Life in the Eastern Bloc*, eds. David Crowley and Susan E. Reid (Oxford: Berg, 2002), 11.

[23] Gordon Church, "Bucharest: Revolution in the Townscape Art," in *The Socialist City: Spatial Structure and Urban Policy*, eds. R.A. French and F.E.I. Hamilton (Chichester: Wiley, 1979), 502-503; as well as Robert Argenbright, "Remaking Moscow: New Places, New Selves," *The Geographical Review*, 89:1 (1999): 6.

[24] Marius Czepczyński, *Cultural Landscapes of Post-Socialist Cities: Representations of Powers and Needs* (Aldershot: Ashgate, 2008), 116-125.

[25] Deborah Schultz and Alina Serban, "Public Memory and National Identity under Construction: The Trajectory of Monuments in Romania in the Communist and Post-Communist Periods," *Centropa*, 10:1 (2010): 64.

[26] Czepczyński, *Cultural Landscapes,* 115.

collapse of communist regimes were the removal of statues of Soviet figures such as Lenin. These events required considerable organisation and resources, and so were usually orchestrated by the state.[27] They provided a dramatic and highly visible proclamation that political order was changing. However, in most cases the eradication of communist statuary was both less spectacular and less immediate, with most removals taking place quietly during the early years of post-communism.[28] For example, prominent statues of Lenin and Petru Groza which stood in Bucharest were removed in March 1990, more than two months after the overthrow of Nicolae Ceaușescu.[29]

A less dramatic strategy was the renaming of streets, buildings, and other urban landmarks to de-commemorate events and personalities from communist-era historiography. This practice has been termed "toponymic cleansing."[30] Such renaming is "an act of political propaganda with immense proclamative value and public resonance"[31]: it makes an immediate statement that public memory is changing, and is relatively quick and simple to implement. Renaming was intended to decommemorate the communist past, and 'place' a new narrative of national history and memory into public space. However, renaming urban streets and buildings was relatively limited in scale and was most prominent in the central areas of towns and cities. Since many toponyms allocated during the communist era had no ideological connotations, they did not need to be renamed. For example, in Bucharest only 6.6 percent of the city's streets were renamed after 1989.[32] In other post-communist cities the proportion was lower.

---

[27] Schultz and Serban, "Public Memory and National Identity under Construction," 63.

[28] Kenneth E. Foote, Atilla Tóth and Annet Árvay, "Hungary after 1989: Inscribing a New Past on Place," *Geographical Review*, 90:3 (2000): 310-311.

[29] Duncan Light and Craig Young, "Socialist Statuary as Post-Socialist Hybrids: Following the Statues of Dr Petru Groza in Romania," *Journal of Historical Geography*, 37:4 (2011), 497.

[30] Reuban Rose-Redwood, Derek Alderman and Maoz Azaryahu, "Geographies of Toponymic Inscription: New Directions in Critical Place-Name Studies," *Progress in Human Geography*, 34:4 (2010): 460.

[31] Maoz Azaryahu, "The Power of Commemorative Street Names," *Environment and Planning D: Society and Space*, 14:3 (1996): 318.

[32] Duncan Light, "Street Names in Bucharest, 1990–1997: Exploring the Modern Historical Geographies of Post-Socialist Change," *Journal of Historical Geography*, 30:1 (2004): 160.

Strategies of rededication and reuse were applied mostly to museums. Communist regimes attached considerable importance to museums[33] as a means of socialist propaganda, and therefore hundreds of new museums were established in communist Central and Eastern Europe. Most countries had at least one museum dedicated entirely to the history and activities of that country's Communist Party. These were complemented by a network of regional and local museums, all of which interpreted local history through the lens of Marxism-Leninism. With the fall of communism, the museums dedicated to Party history were swiftly closed. Some reopened as different museums (for example, in Bucharest the former History Museum of the Communist Party, of the Revolutionary and Democratic Movement of Romania reopened in 1990 as the Museum of the Romanian Peasant[34]). As Romania, in common with other formerly communist states, was gripped by 'collective amnesia' about the recent past,[35] museums simply closed any galleries which dealt with the communist period: the displays remained in place but in locked rooms with no public access. This approach was apparent with the National History Museum in Bucharest and in other museums in the country. Bădica describes this as the "black hole paradigm," where the historical narrative presented in museums simply ended in 1945 (or earlier).[36]

Overall, the efforts to neutralise the commemorative symbols of communism (and the public memory that they represented) was a crude first step in achieving redress for the abuses and hardship of the communist era. However, the process of landscape cleansing was always partial. It was applied most thoroughly to the central parts of cities (particularly Bucharest) and to a lesser extent (sometimes hardly at all) in more peripheral districts. Its target was the most visible and iconic symbols of the communist regime, while smaller or more inconspicuous symbols were often ignored or overlooked.[37] Removing or reconfiguring

---

[33] Zbynek Z. Stransky, "Museums in Post-Communist Countries," in *Museums and Europe 1992*, ed. Susan Pearce (London: Athlone Press, 1992): 174-6.

[34] Simina Bădica, "The Black Hole Paradigm: Exhibiting Communism in Post-Communist Romania," in *History of Communism in Europe: Volume 1 Politics of Memory in Post-Communist Europe* (Bucharest: Zeta Books, 2010), 88-89.

[35] Lavinia Stan, *Transitional Justice in Post-Communist Romania: The Politics of Memory* (New York: Cambridge University Press, 2013), 216; Duncan Light and Craig Young, "Local and Counter-Memories of Socialism in Post-Socialist Romania," in *Local Memories in a Nationalizing and Globalizing World*, eds. Marnix Beyen and Brecht Deseure (Basingstoke: Palgrave, 2015): 224-226.

[36] Bădica, "The Black Hole Paradigm."

[37] Duncan Light and Craig Young, "Public Space and the Material Legacies of Communism in Bucharest," in *Post-Communist Romania at Twenty-Five: Linking*

the commemorative landscape of communism effectively cleared space in the urban arena for an entirely new set of commemorative practices specifically intended to remember the victims and abuses of communism. These are discussed in the following section.

Commemorating the victims of, and resistance to, Romania's communist regime

Within strategies to redefine public memory there have been two broad strands to the remaking of commemorative landscapes. First, in the effort to (re)establish a 'normal' past, the post-communist societies have attempted to correct the distortions of communist-era historiography. In addition to de-commemorating key figures from the communist version of history, there has been a focus on reinstating and re-commemorating those people (politicians and monarchs) who were excised from public memory by communist historians. This, in turn, resulted in new practices of memorialisation in the public arena which, once the official public landscape had been de-communised, could be repopulated with new monuments, statues, memorials, and toponyms. The most straightforward way to do this was by returning streets to their pre-communist commemorative names. For example, in central Bucharest fourteen streets commemorating pre-communist politicians (such as Ion C. Brătianu and Lascar Catargiu) that had been renamed by the communist regime returned to their former names, as did four streets that commemorated the Romanian monarchy.[38] Over time, new statues and monuments were commissioned to commemorate those figures who had been disavowed during the communist period. For example, a statue of King Carol I (based on an earlier statue destroyed by the communist regime) was unveiled in Bucharest in 2010, while in 2014 plans were announced to erect a statue of Ion C. Brătianu to replace one removed in 1948.[39] Such practices represent a symbolic correction of a form of historical injustice, although they are not usually considered as part of transitional justice projects.

Past, Present and Future, eds. Lavinia Stan and Diana Vancea (Lanham, MD: Lexington Books 2015), 46-50.

[38] Light, "Street Names in Bucharest, 1990–1997," 163-164.

[39] Cristina Răduţă, "Statuia lui Ion C. Brătianu va fi reconstruită şi amplasată în Piaţa Universităţii," *Adevarul*, 31 January 2014, available at: http://adevarul.ro/news/bucuresti/statuia-ion-c-bratianu-reconstuita-amplasata-piata-universitatii-1_52eb7965c7b855ff56f4bd06/index.html, accessed on 12 February 2016.

Second, Romania, like other post-communist societies, faced the challenge of how to remember the communist period and how to commemorate its victims. Although there was an initial desire to forget the communist past completely, at a later stage there was a growing acceptance that the abuses of communism should be memorialised. The construction of memorials, monuments and museums is a means of acknowledging the abuses of the communist era, giving recognition to the victims, and promoting a sense of social cohesion and belonging that is rooted in a traumatic recent past.[40] A range of actors and elites has participated in such memorialisation. The state has played an important (but inconsistent) role, and some of Romania's post-communist governments have been active in promoting remembrance of the abuses of the communist regime as a form of transitional justice that compliments other legal and institutional measures. State sponsored practices of memorialization can be used to affirm and legitimate (to both domestic and international audiences) a commitment to political values that are the antithesis of communism.[41] However, in Romania, it is the non-state sector – civil society groups and nongovernmental-organisations – that has been most active in memorialising the communist past through what have been termed "unofficial truth projects."[42] This was particularly the case at times when the former communist elites – often unwilling to condemn the communist regime or engage in debates about the nature of the communist past[43] – were in power. In addition, ordinary individuals have been involved in the process of remembrance through creating and placing their own, informal memorials in the urban landscape. The commemorative landscape is therefore characterised by a bricolage of memorial forms, dedicated to different subjects and groups, in a wide range of locations, and with a wide range of sponsors. In what follows, we focus on two broad categories of memorialization: 1) monuments and memorials, and 2) museums (with associated practices of tourism).

[40] Elizabeth Jelin, "Public Memorialization in Perspective: Truth, Justice and the Memory of Past Repression in the Southern Cone of South America," *International Journal of Transitional Justice*, 1:1 (2007): 147.
[41] Forest and Johnson, "Unravelling the Threads," 270.
[42] Stan, *Transitional Justice in Post-Communist Romania*, 208.
[43] Lavinia Stan, "Reckoning with the Communist Past in Romania: A Scorecard," *Europe-Asia Studies*, 65:1 (2013): 142.

Monuments and Memorials

The erection of monuments and statues in the public arena has provided an important means for recognising communist-era injustices. As a result, there are many examples of such commemoration, although it is by no means a thorough, consistent, and comprehensive practice. Indeed, what is perhaps surprising is the relative paucity of such memorials combined with the controversy that they sometimes generate. Representing the condemnation of the communist past and its injustices through memorialisation is not, therefore, a straightforward process.

Many commemorative monuments have been erected in Romania since 1989 and they differ widely in terms of their form, the subject that they commemorate, and the sponsoring organisation behind them. Some memorials commemorate the actions and death of a specific individual. While they focus on the sacrifice of the individual, they implicitly draw attention to the broader injustices of the regimes responsible. Examples here include the pre-communist politicians Iuliu Maniu and Corneliu Coposu, who were both imprisoned by the communist regime (Maniu died in prison and was buried in an unmarked grave). Both were commemorated through memorials in Revolution Square in central Bucharest that were erected in 1998 and 1996, respectively. Other memorials are dedicated to groups of individuals who died in specific sites such as the memorial erected at the site of the former Piteşti prison, which commemorates those who suffered during the infamous 'experiments' that took place there during the early years of the communist regime.

Other monuments have been erected to commemorate a range of other aspects of communist-era repression, a process that has been led by non-governmental organizations. For example, the Association of Former Political Prisoners has erected hundreds of monuments and memorials at the sites of communist-era prisons and labour camps throughout Romania.[44] Other monuments commemorate specific aspects of communist repression, such as the monument erected in Timisoara in 1996 to commemorate the forced deportation of the non-Romanian population of the Banat to the Bărăgan plain in the west of Romania during the early 1950s. In various towns and cities local groups and individuals have erected monuments to the victims of communism but, despite numerous proposals, no such monument has been erected in the capital. Clearly such a memorialization process becomes significantly more complex when trying to represent the suffering of all the victims of communism, compared to the memory of a single individual.

---

[44] Stan, *Transitional Justice in Post-Communist Romania,* 218.

There are also many monuments which commemorate resistance to communism. From the late 1940s until the early 1960s there was an informal, but active resistance movement (comprising over a thousand different groups) to the communist regime. These were progressively infiltrated and defeated by the communist security forces, and many of the participants were executed. The existence of the resistance movement was largely unknown to the Romanian population (since the communist regime was silent on the issue) until their activities came to light after 1989. Subsequently, many monuments (of varying forms and sizes) have been erected throughout Romania to commemorate particular local groups.[45] Furthermore, in December 2015, one of the largest monuments in the country was erected in Bucharest to commemorate those who fought against the communist regime. Its location on the site of the former statue of Lenin in front of Casa Scînteii/Casa Presei Libere finally resolved the problematic and prolonged dilemma of how to reconfigure a space inseparably associated with communism in a way that was appropriate to a post-communist democracy.

In addition to memorialising the abuses of the communist regime, many monuments have been raised throughout the country to commemorate the events of December 1989, which brought about the downfall of Romania's communist regime.[46] Once again, a wide range of state and non-state actors have participated. The central state authorities have led the way in memorialising the 1989 Revolution by constructing two memorials in Revolution Square, Bucharest. The first, inaugurated in 1990, is a small and sober memorial to those who died in December 1989. This was followed in 2005 by the larger and more prominent *Memorial of Rebirth.* In addition, other elite actors (including the army and the Orthodox Church) also erected a range of monuments in various locations in Bucharest. In other cities which played an important role in the revolution (particularly Timişoara, Braşov and Sibiu), the local authorities have erected monuments to local events. In addition, a range of non-state actors (including non-governmental organizations and private individuals) has been active in memorialising the events of December 1989, particularly

---

[45] Although the remembrance of the anti-communist resistance is sometimes contested. See Monica Ciobanu, "Rewriting and Remembering Romanian Communism: Some Controversial Issues," *Nationalities Papers*, 39:2 (2011): 214-216.

[46] Craig Young and Duncan Light, "Multiple and Contested Geographies of Memory: Remembering the 1989 Romanian 'Revolution'," in *Memories of War, Place and Identity*, eds. Danielle Drozdzewski, Sarah de Nardi and Emma Waterton (London: Routledge, 2016).

in Bucharest. As such, the commemorative landscape is eclectic and multi-layered, reflecting the contested interpretations and meanings of the 1989 Revolution.

What is particularly significant is that the state's efforts to memorialise the 1989 Revolution have largely failed to become the focus of popular allegiance or support. While the *Memorial of Rebirth* in Revolution Square is the focus of official commemorations of the revolution, the *Memorial* itself has attracted widespread public derision. It has been roundly criticised on aesthetic and architectural grounds, and holds little resonance for many Romanians who interpret the events of December 1989 as a coup d'état more than a genuine popular revolution. Instead, popular remembrance of the Revolution in Bucharest is focused in a different space: University Square. This location is notorious for the events of June 1990, when young people who gathered to protest at the persistence of the communist elite in Romania's post-communist government were savagely attacked by Jiu Valley miners, resulting in many deaths. Here a wide range of unofficial monuments have been erected by individuals and civil society groups to produce a commemorative landscape which refutes and contests the official narrative of the 1989 Revolution. University Square has therefore become an important site of countermemory,[47] in opposition to official commemorative agendas. More broadly, it is now firmly established as a space of protest against officialdom and authority.

This overview of the use of monuments, plaques, statues, and memorials is not intended to be exhaustive, but instead seeks to demonstrate the range of types of memorialisation practices which attempt to place transitional justice into the public arena. There is not space here to discuss in detail the design and symbolism of each of these sites (although this is an important subject for further research). Moreover, we know relatively little about the public reaction to, and reception of, such commemorative landscapes. However, the examples above give hints of how even what might appear to be a straightforward process – condemning communism and commemorating its victims in public space – can be contested and subject to debate. Bucharest's *Memorial of Rebirth* illustrates that while political elites may seek to shape transitional justice projects and the remembrance of the victims of communism, they may not always succeed. Instead, projects to shape commemoration and public memory can sometimes be contested and challenged by the populace. The public reception of sites and practices of memorialisation remains a neglected aspect of transitional justice.

---

[47] Young and Light, "Multiple and Contested Geographies of Memory."

Museums and Tourism

To fully appreciate the role of museums in transitional justice projects it is important to recognise that museums are not simply collections of objects put on public display for the education and entertainment of visitors. Instead, museums have always had a broader ideological purpose. They are a form of public culture through which political elites tell a society about itself and where it has come from. In particular, museums that are sponsored by the state have an important role in "telling the national story." They are institutions that are intended to be visited by the citizenry, and which have a clearly articulated educational mission. They aim to communicate a particular understanding of the past and thus play a significant role in the making (and remaking) of public memory. More broadly, as a means of 'staging' the nation[48] museums contribute to the formation of collective identities, and their importance within nation-building projects is widely acknowledged.[49] As the earlier discussion noted, communist regimes were fully aware of the educative and propagandist role of museums in communicating their political agenda (and the associated narrative of national history) to a broad public.

In the post-communist context, museums are important "vehicles of memory"[50] within projects to memorialize the communist past. In particular, museums can tell the story of the oppression, human rights abuses, and suffering inflicted by communist regimes. This, obviously, is a story that has not been formally told before (since it was not something that communist regimes were likely to draw attention to). Moreover, museums can interpret the communist period from the perspective of the people who lived through it. This is a bottom-up narrative of history that focuses on everyday lives of ordinary people, rather than the macro-political agenda of the communist state and its leading party. Memorial museums also interpret communist rule for future generations who did not experience it themselves in order to help them understand the experiences that shaped their parents' and grandparents' generation. Museums can also be locations for ceremonies and rituals intended to commemorate the victims of communist rule. Overall, memorial museums that are

---

[48] Tim Edensor, *National Identity, Popular Culture and Everyday Life* (Oxford: Berg, 2002), 85.

[49] Donald Horne, *The Great Museum: The Re-presentation of History* (London: Pluto, 1984), 165-179, as well as Fiona McLean, "Museums and the Construction of National Identity: A Review," *International Journal of Heritage Studies* 3:1(1998): 244-252.

[50] Jelin, "Public Memorialization in Perspective," 141.

established as part of transitional justice projects are institutions intended to encourage remembrance, reflection and civic engagement.[51] But they are not just about the communist past: museums can also be used to make an unambiguous statement about a state's post-communist political identity and aspirations. In this context, they are sites for "performances of democracy, not static representations of national identity."[52] The use of museums in this way is as ideological as anything seen during the communist period, but for entirely different ends.

What is important, but frequently overlooked, is the role of tourism in this process. Memorial museums are intended to be visited (and as such they function as visitor 'attractions' even if their subject matter is far from attractive). Some of the visitors to memorial museums will be children and young people, studying the communist period as part of their educational curriculum. However, most people will be visiting during their leisure time. Furthermore, many of these people will be tourists (conventionally defined as people staying away from their home area for at least 24 hours) who can be both domestic (citizens of a country travelling within that country) and international (visitors from other countries). Although political scientists may be inclined to dismiss tourism as trivial and with little to offer in understanding politics, there is growing interest within the discipline of tourism studies in the ways that tourism can contribute to broader political projects and objectives.[53] For example, visiting historic buildings and monuments is a means of 'connecting' with the broader community of the nation.[54] As such, tourism can be identified as one form of banal nationalism.[55] Tourism can also be used to project political identities to an external audience. For example, a number of studies have explored the ways in which the Central and Eastern European countries have used their state-sponsored tourism promotional materials to project a distinctly *post*-communist political identity to the wider world.[56]

---

[51] Barsalou and Baxter, *The Urge to Remember,* 14.

[52] Liz Sevcenko, cited in Barsalou and Baxter, *The Urge to Remember*, 14.

[53] Michael C. Hall, *Tourism and Politics: Policy, Power and Place* (Chichester: Wiley, 1994); Nigel Morgan and Annette Pritchard, *Tourism, Promotion and Power: Creating Images, Creating Identities* (Chichester: Wiley, 1998); and Michael C. Hall, *Tourism: Rethinking the Social Science of Mobility* (London: Routledge, 2005).

[54] Catherine Palmer, "An Ethnography of Englishness: Experiencing Identity through Tourism," *Annals of Tourism Research*, 32:1 (2005): 11.

[55] Michael Billig, *Banal Nationalism* (London: Sage, 1995).

[56] Morgan and Pritchard, *Tourism Promotion*; Derek Hall, "Destination Branding, Niche Marketing and National Image Projection in Central and Eastern Europe," *Journal of Vacation Marketing*, 5:3 (1999): 227-237; Derek Hall, "Brand

In the context of transitional justice projects, tourism at memorials and museums can be used to communicate a message about the communist past and the post-communist future. Moreover, many of the visitors to such places will be heritage tourists who are interested in, and receptive to, learning during their leisure time.[57] For domestic tourists, the visit to a memorial museum performs the same role as other monuments and memorials: it is a reminder of the traumas of the recent past, a recognition of the victims of that past, a warning to future generations, an affirmation of the rejection of communism, and a commitment to broader 'European' values. However, international tourists are an equally important (and sometimes numerically dominant) audience (and for this reason most memorial museums make extensive use of displays and interpretation in the English language, and often in a range of other European languages). Most international visitors will have no direct experience of living under communist rule (and often little background knowledge or understanding of communism). Therefore, museums are a way of telling such visitors the story of "what we lived through" and "the events that shaped us." This is also a way of affirming and legitimating a commitment to the same political and economic agendas that have underpinned European integration since World War II.

Some formerly communist countries have been active in using museums as a way to remember the abuses and victims of Communist Party rule. Perhaps the best examples are Estonia's Museum of Occupations (which opened in 2003 in a purpose-built structure), the Museum of the Occupation of Latvia (opened in 1993), and Lithuania's Museum of Genocide Victims (established in 1992 in the former headquarters of the Soviet security service). Each is located in the respective capital city, and all are run by private foundations benefiting from state support. The displays of these museums focus on the nature of totalitarian rule; its impact on politics, economy and domestic life; the nature of domestic repression and human rights abuses; the activities of resistance groups; and the struggle for, and achievement of, independence in the early 1990s. All

---

Development, Tourism and National Identity: The Re-imaging of Former Yugoslavia," *Brand Management* 9:4-5 (2001): 323-334; Duncan Light, "Romania: National Identity, Tourism Promotion and European Integration," in *Tourism in the New Europe: The Challenges and Opportunities of EU Enlargement*, eds. Derek Hall, Melanie Smith and Barbara Marciszewska (Wallingford: CABI, 2006), 256-269.

[57] Duncan Light, "Heritage as Informal Education," in *Heritage, Tourism and Society*, ed. David T. Herbert (London: Mansell, 1995), 117-145.

these museums receive large numbers of foreign tourists, and are often included in the itineraries of visiting politicians and dignitaries.

However, Romania has not followed the model of the Baltic states. As yet there is no state-sponsored museum in the capital city, which addresses the communist period (although the Presidential Commission for the Analysis of the Communist Dictatorship called in 2006 for the establishment of such a museum[58]). Most of Bucharest's National History Museum is closed for a lengthy refurbishment (although it has hosted temporary exhibitions, largely intended for Romanians, about everyday life under communism). The only museum in the capital which addresses the communist era is the Museum of the Romanian Peasant, which contains a small basement room themed around the abuses associated with forced collectivisation in the 1950s. In the capital city, the role of museums within transitional justice projects has yet to be recognised. This, in itself, demonstrates Romania's ambivalent approach to transitional justice. Moreover, as Jones notes, the notion of a central/national museum dedicated to the communist period is something that divides both political elites and the wider public.[59]

The situation is little different outside Bucharest, where many regional and local museums continue to be silent about the communist era. There are a few exceptions: the Teleorman County Museum in Alexandria includes a small display on collectivisation in the local region,[60] while a small museum opened in Timişoara is dedicated to the 1989 Revolution. Elsewhere, memorial museums have opened in buildings that were formerly prisons or were associated in other ways with the repressive apparatus of the communist regime. The conversion of such buildings into memorial museums is a form of symbolic 're-inscription' that is intended to give them a new use for memorialising the practices that they formerly hosted. For example, a small museum was opened in Gherla prison by the Association for Former Political Prisoners in 1997 (although only organised groups can visit).

However, the best-known example is the Memorial to the Victims of Communism and to the Resistance in Sighetu Marmaţiei in the far north of

[58] Vladimir Tismaneanu, Dorin Dobrincu and Cristian Vasile, eds., *Raport final al Comisiei Prezidentiale pentru Analiza Dictaturii Comuniste din România* (Bucureşti: Humanitas, 2007).

[59] Sara Jones, "Uneasy Heritage: Remembering Everyday Life in Post-Socialist Memorials and Museums," in *Encounters with Popular Pasts: Cultural Heritage and Popular Culture*, eds. Mike Robinson and Helaine Silverman (Cham: Springer, 2015), 221.

[60] Stan, *Transitional Justice in Post-Communist Romania*, 218.

Romania. This opened in 1998 in a building that had formerly been used as a prison and in which the majority of the pre-World War II Romanian political, military, social and academic elite had been imprisoned after the communist regime took control of the country. It features displays (in the former cells) about those who were imprisoned there but also deals with the nature of (and abuses committed by) Romania's communist regime. It also includes a chapel and monument in the former prison's courtyard. The museum was developed by the Civic Academy Foundation, a non-governmental organization, with the financial support of the Council of Europe. It hosts summer schools for young Romanians and publishes regular volumes of academic study about the communist era.[61] Its significance as a site of public remembrance of the human rights abuses of the communist regime was recognised by the Romanian government, which declared it a site of national interest in 1997. However, its peripheral and inaccessible location means that the number of visitors (whether Romanian or international) is relatively small.

Memorial museums are not without their critics. Although tourism is one of the principal means through which memorial sites are encountered, there has long been a tendency to dismiss the practices of visitors to such places as trivial or insignificant. At best, tourists who visit places associated with trauma or tragedy are regarded as passive and unquestioning consumers incapable of fully appreciating the significance of the story presented to them and, at worst, as shallow thrill-seekers motivated by "a morbid and senseless curiosity."[62] However, recent research in the disciplines of tourism studies and anthropology has demonstrated that the behaviour of visitors to memorial places is far more purposeful and significant than is often appreciated, and that visitors can undertake highly meaningful acts of remembrance and engagement with the subject matter they encounter.[63] Other authors accept that visits to memorial museums may be associated with short term learning,

---

[61] Bădica, "The Black Hole Paradigm," 96-101, as well as "Memorialul Victimelor comunismului şi al Rezistenţei," available at: http://www.memorialsighet.ro/, accessed on 18 October 2013.

[62] Joy Sather-Wagstaff, *Heritage that Hurts: Tourists in the Memoryscapes of September 11* (Walnut Creek: Left Coast Press, 2011), 77.

[63] Sather-Wagstaff, *Heritage that Hurts*, 115-170; Laurajane Smith, "The Cultural 'Work' of Tourism," in *The Cultural Moment in Tourism*, eds. Laurajane Smith, Emma Waterton and Steve Watson (London: Routledge, 2012), 219-229; Andrea Witcombe, "Using Immersive and Interactive Approaches to Interpreting Traumatic Experiences for Tourists," in *Heritage and Tourism: Place, Encounter, Engagement*, eds. Russell Staiff, Robyn Bushell and Steve Watson (London: Routledge, 2013), 152-170.

understanding and changed attitudes, but they question the longer-term impacts of such visits in bringing about deeper learning and a broader engagement with the issues of transitional justice.[64] Overall, the 'consumption' of memorial museums by their visitors is clearly a subject that merits much fuller research.

Conclusion

Issues of memorialisation and the reformulation of public memory are often considered to be 'soft' aspects of transitional justice, and consequently they have not received as much academic attention as the 'hard' politics of truth commissions, lustration, or restitution. However, we argue that the cultural politics of transitional justice also deserves much fuller attention, particularly the issue of shaping public memory through commemorative practices and landscapes. Transitional justice is not only played out in the spaces of courtrooms, legislatures, and administrations but is also worked out in public squares, memorial landscapes, and museums. Moreover, while processes such as lustration and even restitution symbolically show that post-communist states are acting to address past injustices, in societal terms their impact may be relatively limited. Not everyone in society was able to reclaim property or necessarily had a personal connection to key figures who were placed on trial. Hence, such practices arguably may have a limited impact on the everyday lives and practices of the majority of the population. However, monuments and commemorative landscapes can reach far more people in the course of their daily lives, and can address their wish for justice in a much more immediate and visible way. Furthermore, memorial landscapes potentially have a much longer-term role than other practices of transitional justice in that they are able to shape public memory across multiple generations.

In Romania, the role of monuments, memorials, and museums as forms of public remembrance of the communist past is complex and contested. In turn, this reflects the broader ambivalence among the country's political elite towards the communist regime and its legacies. It is clear that the state has not taken the lead in the remembrance of the communist period (with the exception of commemorative monuments dedicated to the events of December 1989). Consequently, the use of memorials and museums as a way of coming to terms with communism is less well developed in

---

[64] Hamber, Ševčenko and Naidu, "Utopian Dreams or Practical Possibilities?," 145-148.

Romania than in many other formerly communist states of Central and Eastern Europe. Instead, it is non-state actors (particularly civil society groups and non-governmental organizations) that have led the process: indeed, Stan describes the extent of the non-state sector's contribution as "astonishing,"[65] particularly given the lack of enthusiasm of the central authorities for any form of reckoning with the communist past. It is civil society groups that have led the way in commemorating the abuses and victims of the communist regime and popular resistance to Communist Party rule. Furthermore, individual citizens have also been active in remembering the events of the 1989 Revolution (particularly in Bucharest), and the events that followed in June 1990 as a result of the former communist elite retaining its hold on power.

One issue that arises from this survey of commemorative practices and landscapes in post-communist Romania is the need to explore the public's reception of, and responses to, practices of memorialisation. This is something that has been little researched: indeed, as Barsalou and Baxter argue, "the impact of *all* transitional justice processes – memorialisation among them – remains under-researched."[66] Thus, we need to address questions such as the ways in which citizens relate to memorials and landscapes linked to transitional justice projects within their everyday lives. Do memorials work effectively as vehicles of transitional justice or do they simply become a backdrop to the everyday use of space in the city? We also need to address the ways in which elite-sponsored memorialisation can be contested by ordinary citizens, since memorial landscapes can be regarded with apathy or even simply ignored (Bucharest's *Memorial of Rebirth* is a striking example). Some authors are sceptical about the long-term impact of museums on the public consciousness.[67] Furthermore, as Clark suggests, there is a danger that too much memorialisation may inhibit societies' ability to move on.[68] Moreover, different generations may have very different responses to the ways in which commemorative landscapes function as part of transitional justice, responses shaped by interactions between the generations mediated through the family, mediatisation and representations of history.

In short, while commemoration and memorialisation are fundamental processes of transitional justice, there is much that we do not know about whether and in what ways such practices achieve their intended aims.

[65] Stan, *Transitional Justice in Post-Communist Romania*, 231.

[66] Barsalou and Baxter, *The Urge to Remember,* 3.

[67] Hamber, Ševčenko, and Naidu, "Utopian Dreams or Practical Possibilities?," 415-418.

[68] Clark, "Reconciliation through Remembrance?," 133-134.

Therefore a focus on the popular reception, negotiation and contestation of memorialisation intended to right the wrongs of the communist era is an important research agenda for scholars of transitional justice.

CHAPTER EIGHT

THE ROLE OF ART IN DEALING WITH THE COMMUNIST PAST

CATERINA PREDA

Growing numbers of studies have been recently published on the topic, but the role of art in dealing with the recent past has remained understudied in political science in general, and in the field of transitional justice more specifically.[1] This observation is particularly true in the case

[1] Among others, Peter D. Rush and Olivera Simić, eds., *The Arts of Transitional Justice* (New York: Springer, 2014); Clara Ramirez-Barat, *Transitional Justice, Culture and Society: Beyond Outreach* (New York: Columbia University Press, 2014); Rebecca Atencio and Nancy Gates-Madsen, "Art and Transitional Justice," in *Encyclopedia of Transitional Justice*, eds. Lavinia Stan and Nadya Nedelsky (New York: Cambridge University Press, 2013), 1:117-123; Lizelle Bisschoff and Stephanie Van der Peer, eds., *Art and Trauma in Africa: Representations of Reconciliation in Music, Visual Arts, Literature and Film* (London: I.B. Tauris, 2013); Sanja Bahun, "Transitional Justice and the Arts: Reflections on the Field," in *Theorizing Transitional Justice*, eds. Claudio Corradetti, Nir Eisikovits and Jack Volpe Rotondi (London: Routledge, 2015); Ewald Mengel and Michela Borzaga, eds., *Trauma, Memory and Narrative in the Contemporary South African Novel* (Amsterdam: Rodopi, 2012); Vikki Bell, "Contemporary Art and Transitional Justice in Northern Ireland: The Consolation of Form," *Journal of Visual Culture*, 10:3 (2011): 324-353; Viki Bell and Mario Di Paolantonio, "The Haunted Nomos: Activists-Artists and the (Im)Possible Politics of Memory in Transitional Argentina," *Cultural Politics*, 5:2 (2009): 149-178; Rosemarie Buikema, "Performing Dialogical Truth and Transitional Justice: The Role of Art in the Becoming Post-Apartheid of South Africa," *Memory Studies*, 5:3 (2012): 282-292; Louis Bickford, "Memoryscapes," in *The Art of Truth-Telling about Authoritarian Rule*, eds. Ksenija Bilbija, Jo Ellen Fair, Cynthia Milton, and Leigh Payne (Madison: University of Wisconsin Press, 2005), 96-102; Michael Lazzara, *Chile in Transition: The Poetics and Politics of Memory* (Gainesville: University Press of Florida, 2006); Ana Longoni, "Crossroads for Activist Art in Argentina," *Third Text*, 22:5 (2008): 575-587; Diana Taylor, *The Archive and the Repertoire:*

of the former communist countries and especially Romania, where only two studies have pondered over the link between art and the process of coming to terms with the legacy of the communist regime of 1945-1989.[2] To address this lacuna, this chapter investigates the extent to which artistic interpretations such as films, theater plays, and paintings reproduce the public discourse on the need to reckon with the recent past and provide a missing or alternative perspective on it. It also explores whether art can represent a form of "poetic justice" by providing a documentary source of understanding the past that can supplement court depositions, truth commission reports, secret archival documents, and the like.

Art can help us to understand the recent past beyond the traditional sources of information considered reliable and valuable by political science or transitional justice studies. "Whether artistic interventions into memory politics are produced within official channels (as in the case of state-sponsored monuments and memorials) or outside of them (in galleries or on the streets),"[3] art gives flesh to memory through its symbolic power of reconstructing past reality, or the alternative to reality it proposes. One approach to study the role of art in dealing with the communist past considers the "art of memory" or "art of memorialization" as a specific form of cultural memory. This chapter discusses a specific type of "art of memory" that portrays the former agents of the Securitate, the Romanian communist secret political police, and points out the missing or incomplete justice that has been meted out since 1989 for the human rights abuses perpetrated by the communist regime (for this point, see Chapter 5 in this book).

The art's role as a tool of understanding the recent past is also noticeable in Romania, where since 1989 numerous artistic productions have engaged with the communist regime and its legacy of human rights abuses. These artistic productions range from movies to theater productions and paintings to art installations.[4] Compared to their counterparts

---

Performing Cultural Memory in the Americas (Durham: Duke University Press, 2003); James Young, *At Memory's Edge: After-Images of the Holocaust in Contemporary Art and Architecture* (New Haven: Yale University Press, 2000).

[2] Anca M. Pusca, *Post-Communist Aesthetics* (London: Routledge, 2016), and Caterina Preda, "Looking at the past through an artistic lens: art of memorialization" in *History of Communism in Europe. Politics of memory in Post-communist Europe*, 1 (Bucharest: Zeta Books, 2010), 129-148.

[3] Atencio and Gates-Madsen, "Art and Transitional Justice," 1:117.

[4] *A fost sau nu a fost* (12:08 East of Bucharest), 2006, artistic movie directed by Corneliu Porumboiu; *Nunta muta* (Silent Wedding), 2008, artistic movie directed by Horatiu Malaele; *Comedie Roșie* (Red Comedy), 2006, directed by Alexandru

elsewhere in Central and Eastern Europe, Romanian artists have probably been just as interested in assuming the communist period as a reference point for their creations. However, as noted above, transitional justice scholars have devoted less attention to Romanian artistic contributions.

The chapter first reviews Romania's modest record of dealing with the legacy of its communist regime through judicial methods. The second section explains the link between art and memory, and the role art can play in reckoning projects centered on communist human rights abuses. The third section discusses in depth twelve Romanian artistic productions with explicit memory dimensions that seek to portray the communist perpetrators (seven artistic movies, documentaries, and plays) and to reenact justice for past crimes (five movies and paintings). These examples were chosen because they discuss topics that are overlooked by research on the art of memory (which generally focuses on the portrait of Nicolae Ceauşescu). Because they offer a positive, nostalgic remembering of life under communism, these examples can help us to better grasp the role of the perpetrators, the reasons why justice is absent, and the ways in which art can supplement this absence. The conclusion explains the lessons that transitional justice scholars can draw from the Romanian case.

"Forget your past": dealing with communism in Romania

"Forget Your Past" was a graffiti stencil sprayed on the Buzludzha memorial in Bulgaria, a monument the communist regime built in 1981 to mark the site where the socialists secretly founded in 1891 the forerunner of the Bulgarian Communist Party. This stencil captures what I believe to

---

Tocilescu; *1989 – Anul care a dispărut* (1989 – The Year That Disappeared), 2016, directed by Ana Mărgineanu; and *Cum mi-am petrecut sfârşitul lumii* (How I Spent the End of World), 2006, artistic movie directed by Cătălin Mitulescu; *Amintiri din epoca de aur* (Tales from the Golden Age), 2009, artistic movie directed by Hanno Höfer, Răzvan Mărculescu, Cristian Mungiu, Constantin Popescu, and Ioana Uricaru. Theater productions include *Comedie Roşie* (Red Comedy), 2006, directed by Alexandru Tocilescu at National Theater of Bucharest, and *1989 – Anul care a dispărut*, 2015, directed by Ana Mărgineanu at Teatrul Mic of Bucharest. Artworks include paintings or other media depicting Nicolae Ceauşescu such as *89*, exhibition by Mircea Suciu opened in 2007 at h'art Gallery, Bucharest; *Posthumous Dialogue with Nicolae Ceauşescu*, video by Ion Grigorescu, exhibited at The Museum of Modern Art, New York in 2016; *Understanding History*, 2009, a series of paintings by Dragoş Burlacu; *Three colours*, 2007-2008, video by Istvan Laszlo; or *Ceauşescu*, *Nicolae* and *Study for the boogyman*, three paintings by Adrian Ghenie produced in 2007, 2009 and 2010, respectively.

represent the dominant approach to dealing with the communist past promoted by the Romanian state actors after 1989. Indeed, Romania still lacks state-funded museums dedicated to the communist regime, and relies instead on a handful of museums and exhibitions organized by non-state foundations and dedicated mostly to the memory of the victims of the communist regime (for example, the Sighet memorial organized in a former political prison, and the so-called "Plague" hall set up in the Museum of the Peasant in Bucharest). The absence of such state-funded memorialization projects is complemented by the late condemnation of the communist regime by the Romanian state actors, and the absence of reconciliation among former victims, victimizers and bystanders.

The official efforts of the Romanian post-communist governments to come to terms with the recent past have included only a handful of court trials. The legally flawed show-trial of Nicolae and Elena Ceaușescu was hastily organized in December 1989, being followed by the trials of former high-ranking Communist Party members conducted in the early 1990s. Gheorghe Crăciun, the commandant of the Aiud prison, was also brought to trial, but died before the court could formulate a verdict. In 1993, former Minister of Interior Alexandru Drăghici and three Securitate officers were accused of human rights violations, but the trial did not lead to their conviction. Four years later, eight militia and Securitate officers were convicted for two killings that occurred in 1981. In 2002, the courts considered the case against those responsible for the death of engineer Gheorghe Ursu, who was killed in the Bucharest militia dungeon in 1985. Thus, from 1990 to 2010 only four indictments of crimes committed by former members of the Securitate were drawn, of which only two were finalized. More recently, in 2016 Alexandru Visinescu, a former guard at the Ramnicu Sarat, Mislea and Jilava prisons during the 1950s, was found guilty for the murder of twelve political prisoners.

Raluca Grosescu and Raluca Ursachi argue that the longevity of the communist regime and the fact that most of the crimes took place during the 1950s, that is, three decades before the collapse of the communist regime allowed the courts to hear such cases, have limited the number of trials.[5] Even more important explanatory factors were represented by the amnesty granted during the late 1980s by the Ceaușescu regime, the statute of limitation for certain crimes, and the post-communist courts' refusal to

[5] Raluca Ursachi and Raluca Grosescu, "Transitional Criminal Justice in Post-Communist Romania," paper presented at the Crimes of the Communist Regimes conference, 24-26 February 2010, Prague; as well as Raluca Grosescu and Raluca Ursachi, *Justitia penala de tranzitie: de la Nurnberg la postcomunismul romanesc* (Iasi: Polirom, 2009).

frame communist-era human rights crimes and abuses as impresciptible. Lavinia Stan explains Romania's unimpressive transitional justice record by the large number of Communist Party members (3.8 million in a total population of 23 million), and Securitate secret informers (between 400,000 and 1 million) who retained political clout after the collapse of the communist regime, and used their positions of power and influence to block efforts to reckon with a political regime they had loyally served.[6] Furthermore, Stan argued, transitional justice has pitted the society against the state.[7] Whereas state actors have proved reluctant, even hostile, toward de-communization, civil society organizations, especially victims groups, have vocally promoted lustration, access to the Securitate archives, the creation of the Presidential Commission for the Study of the Communist Dictatorship in Romania, and the condemnation of the communist regime as "illegitimate and criminal" by President Traian Basescu in late 2006, among other transitional justice methods.[8]

Vladimir Tismăneanu acknowledges that a democracy cannot work on the basis of lies, denial and amnesia.[9] Tismaneanu and the other members of the Presidential Commission who drafted its Final Report "passed moral judgment on the defunct dictatorship and invite[d] reckoning with the past throughout a painful, albeit inevitable, acknowledgment of its crimes against humanity and other forms of repression" perpetrated by the communist regime.[10] Nevertheless, the Report was unable to gain the support of important political forces, some civil society groups, the former victimizers, and even some victims who opposed it for personal reasons. That was because the Report failed to acknowledge alternative ways to interpret the communist regime in a more positive light, and insisted on its criminal character and on passing a moral condemnation that did not fit well with the Report's self-avowed academic perspective. More broadly, Alexandru Gussi considers that the discourse on the recent past of the Romanian civil society ranges from open opposition to the condemnation of communist crimes to declared nostalgia for the communist regime, whereas state actors have generally promoted transitional justice policies

---

[6] Lavinia Stan, "Romania," in *Transitional Justice in Eastern Europe and the Former Soviet Union*, ed. Lavinia Stan (London: Routledge, 2009), 128-151.

[7] Ibidem, 147.

[8] Lavinia Stan, *Transitional Justice in Post-Communist Romania: The Politics of Memory* (New York: Cambridge University Press, 2013).

[9] Vladimir Tismăneanu, "Democracy and Memory: Romania Confronts Its Communist Past," *The Annals of the American Academy of Political and Social Science*, 617:1 (2008): 166.

[10] Ibidem, 169.

that encourage forgiving and forgetting and have used memory for their electoral and political advantage[11] (see also Chapter 4 in this book).

In fact, besides the memory programs championed by the victims of the communist regime, which underscored the negative aspects of dictatorial repression, various state and non-state actors have promoted a positive depiction of communism during 2005-2015. Studied as a form of nostalgia or *ostalgia,* this phenomenon encompasses several personal and collective manifestations. Among these, note the personal and nostalgic memory put forward by the private initiatives to open a Museum of the Communist Consumer in Timişoara and a Museum of Daily Life under Communism in Botoşani, which would present the "normality" of life under a dictatorial regime where most citizens suffered from economic deprivations more than political persecution. This nostalgia also infuses a number of advertising and marketing projects used by various pubs, restaurants, and commercials to attract consumers longing for long-discontinued goods, as well as the internet-based blog analyzed by Cristina Petrescu (see Chapter 9 in this book). Finally, nostalgia is also noticeable in the arts, where a number of films and artworks are taking issue with it.[12]

The significant repressive role played by the Securitate, especially during late communism (the 1980s), has been extensively discussed by the literature on communism and post-communism.[13] This attention has echoed the increased preoccupation of post-communist governments with the need to deal with the institutional legacy of the communist regime. This need stems from the suspicion, widely shared by the Romanian public, that the secret agents of the former Securitate and of the various post-communist intelligence services have maintained a constant presence in politics, the economy and the judiciary. In his 2010 documentary movie *Kapitalism, Our Secret Recipe* (Kapitalism, reteta noastra secreta), Alexandru Solomon presented politically influential Romanian businessmen, who used their close ties to the Securitate to build vast financial empires. Money, power and the communist past helped these "magnates" to build Kapitalism, which departs from its Western counterpart because of its

---

[11] Alexandru Gussi, "Political Uses of Memory and the State in Post-Communism," *Studia Politica. Romanian Political Science Review,* XIII:4 (2013): 724 and 722.

[12] Caterina Preda, "Le rôle de la nostalgie dans la mémoire artistique du passé communiste dans la Roumanie contemporaine," *Canadian Slavonic Papers*, 57:3-4 (2015): 268-283.

[13] Dennis Deletant, *Romania under Communist Rule* (Bucharest: Center for Romanian Studies, 1999), Stan, "Romania," and Tismaneanu, "Democracy and Memory."

roots in the communist regime.[14] The documentary is an artistic rendering of the belief commonly held in Romania that former secret agents have joined the post-communist political and economic elites. This belief enforces the public perception that state actors have embraced a policy of forgetting the recent past, instead of coming to terms with it by prosecuting former victimizers and removing them from government and public administration. In this documentary, art has produced a response that reflects popular views about the role of the Securitate in post-communist society. Other cases discussed below prove that art can depict alternatives to the general public perspectives on the recent past.

The role of art in dealing with the communist past

Besides more consecrated memorialization practices (such as the opening of museums, the building of memorials and monuments, the celebration of anniversary dates, and the renaming of localities, streets, and parks, some of which are discussed in Chapter 7 of this book), cultural forms and artistic renderings of the past are created in the aftermath of dictatorial regimes, civil wars, and other traumatic events. Paul Ricoeur distinguishes seven types of remembering and forgetting. His typology includes blocked memory, manipulated memory, forced memory, ordered memory, happy memory, appeased memory, and reconciled memory.[15] The activity to remember is incomplete when societies and individuals forget the past actively or passively, erase the memory of it, and have partial or selective memory of it. All these, for Ricoeur, amount to "a strategy of avoidance, of eluding, of running away, an ambiguous, active but also passive form of forgetting."[16] Ricoeur's theories are relevant for the Romanian case because they suggest that democratic governments refusing to construct a comprehensive memory policy can support partial remembering (manipulated memory), or can completely annul any memory of the past (blocked memory).

Societies never have a unique shared memory of the past; instead, they see the emergence of several collective memories. Of these memories, of interest for our investigation is cultural memory. Cultural forms of

---

[14] *Kapitalism, reteta noastra secreta*, 2010, documentary movie directed by Alexandru Solomon. Also "Kapitalism – our secret recipe," Medias Central European Film Festival, 2015, available at: http://www.meceff.ro/kapitalism-our-secret-recipe.aspx, accessed on 1 May 2016.

[15] Paul Ricoeur, *Memory, History, Forgetting* (Chicago : Chicago University Press, 2004).

[16] Ibidem, 429.

remembrance are increasingly produced in this present that is oversaturated with residues of the past, not only in post-communist Central and Eastern Europe, but also in other regions of the world marked by conflict and non-democratic experiences. Scholars of cultural memory have insisted on the specificity of these practices. Cultural memory, as Jan Assman and John Czaplicka argued, refers to those "texts, images and rituals specific to each society in each epoch, whose 'cultivation' serves to stabilize and convey that society's self-image."[17] For Alexander Etkind, "cultural memory is close to the concept of collective memory, but is significantly broader," because "the turn from 'collective memory' to 'cultural memory' de-emphasizes the remembering collective and focuses on the materials of which memory is made."[18]

The specificity of each media that shapes cultural memory is therefore important, but the impact of these diverse media depends on their reach to the public: if the media are widely seen or read then they have a significant influence on cultural memory; otherwise they have little, even zero, impact on it.[19] In studying the media of memory, Etkind talked about "multimedia collages" of cultural memory: historical studies, the Internet, novels, songs, archives, the family photo album, all participate in shaping memory.[20] Etkind also discussed the diverse character of the arts of memory and distinguished between "soft" and "hard" memory. While "soft" memory includes texts, history and other written narratives, "hard" memory is emphasized through monuments. She suggests that in Eastern Europe "novels, films and debates about the past vastly outpace and overshadow monuments, memorials and museums."[21] This is also the case in Romania, where "hard" memory is not so rich, but "soft" memory is increasingly abundant.

Going a step further, note that post-memory or secondary memory constructed by the next generation, as Marianne Hirsch theorized, has photographs as main artistic practice. Post-memorial work, as Hirsch argued, "strives to reactivate and re-embody more distant social/national

---

[17] Jan Assman and John Czaplicka, "Collective Memory and Cultural Identity," *New German Critique*, 65:1-2 (1995): 132.

[18] Alexander Etkind, *Warped Mourning. Stories of the Undead in the Land of the Unburied Cultural Memory in the Present* (Stanford: Stanford University Press, 2013), 40.

[19] Astrid Erll, "Literature, Film and the Mediality of Cultural Memory," in *Cultural memory studies. An international and interdisciplinary handbook*, eds. Astrid Erll and Ansgar Nunning (Berlin: Walter de Gruyter, 2008), 389-398.

[20] Etkind, *Warped Mourning*, 40.

[21] Ibidem, 176.

and archival/cultural memorial structures by reinvesting them with resonant individual and familial forms of mediation and aesthetic expression."[22] To this secondary memory, Alison Landsberg added a new form of memory, "prosthetic memory," which is specific to modernity and enacted at public sites such as museums or in the cinema. This type of memory combines the personal experience of the viewer with events the viewer did not live directly to create a new form of memory, which affects that individual's stance on the past.[23] This mechanism can work for media other than cinema or museums, as shown by the theater plays inspired by the trial of the Ceaușescus discussed below.

In this line of thought, Andreas Huyssen's "art of memory" refers mainly to photography as the most common practice seen in the visual arts that deal with the past. This chapter makes use of diverse artistic practices that belong to the larger corpus of art of memory. Artistic expressions help bring about the different perspectives on the past because, as Huyssen recalls, there cannot be "a memory consensus about a national trauma that pitted the majority of a society against a relatively small minority drawn from all ethnic and social backgrounds."[24] In South America, for example, the topic of art of memory as an important practice for dealing with a traumatic past is more commonly employed and researched because it is assumed by those who were persecuted by the dictatorship, that is, those who fell victim to the repression of the military regimes.[25]

Thus, the art of memory is an important part of cultural memory practices. Art is a way of not forgetting, of remembering the past in countries that are keen to forget it, of moving forward and away from it. As Cynthia Milton noted, "art reminds audiences of the ongoing tensions of the unresolved past in the present."[26] At the same time, counter-history and counter-memory also use cultural forms to reconstruct the recent past and to challenge official stances on it by giving a voice to subjects

---

[22] Marianne Hirsch, "The Generation of Post-Memory," *Poetics Today*, 29:1 (2008): 111.

[23] Alison Landsberg, *Prosthetic Memory. The Transformation of American Remembrance in the Age of Mass Culture* (New York: Columbia University Press, 2004), 2.

[24] Andreas Huyssen, *Present Pasts, Urban Palimpsests and the Politics of Memory* (Stanford: Stanford University Press, 2003), 102.

[25] Idem, Macarena Gomez-Barris, *Where Memory Dwells. Culture and State Violence in Chile* (Berkley, CA: University of California Press, 2009), and Elisabeth Jelin, *Los trabajos de la memoria* (Lima: Instituto de Estudios Peruanos, 2012).

[26] Cynthia Milton, ed., *Art from a Fractured Past: Memory and Truth-Telling in Post-Shining Path Peru* (Durham: Duke University Press, 2014), 2-3.

marginalized by grand state-controlled narratives of the past (minorities, victims, or losers of the conflict). When discussing the documentary fiction of Chris Marker's films, Jacques Rancière reminded us that memory is made not of all the memories of a conscience, but of a more limited group of signs, traces, and monuments: "memory is a work of fiction."[27] Although noticing the fiction of documentary renderings, Rancière also observed that Marker's films recall the need to remember and not to forget. These needs also form the background of the Romanian examples discussed below.

These examples, which are discussed as instances of the art of memory, can be understood as one of the types of artistic expressions that Anca Pusca analyzed under the general heading of "post-communist aesthetics," which she understood as a set of "circumstances, events, and interventions, which disrupt normal/expected forms of perception and visibility and create/open a space where new and often unexpected meanings, interpretations and opportunities emerge."[28] These different gazes conform to the multimedia collages theorized by Etkind and illustrate the diversity of artistic renderings of the past. Such diversity contrasts with the monolithic discourses recognized and analyzed by social sciences in general.

The power that images have to forge our understanding of the world, and of the past, should not be overlooked. According to Murray Edelman, we live in a world created by images of paintings, literature, and films.[29] This is why, paradoxically, the artistic rendering of the past as depicted in a movie like *Schindler's List*[30] is known to a wider public than the direct testimonials of Holocaust survivors who describe their traumatic experiences. Similarly, Astrid Erll acknowledged that "fictions, both novelistic and filmic, possess the potential to generate and mold images of the past which will be retained by whole generations. Historical accuracy is not one of the concerns of such 'memory-making' novels and movies; instead, they cater to the public with what is variously termed 'authenticity' or 'truthfulness'."[31] It is then important to note in which form the art of memory approaches the past, the angle from which it

[27] Jacques Rancière, *La fable cinématographique* (Paris: Ed. Du Seuil, 2011), 201-202.
[28] Pusca, *Post-Communist Aesthetics*, 1.
[29] Murray Edelman, *From Art to Politics. How Artistic Creations Shape Political Conceptions* (Chicago: University of Chicago Press, 1995).
[30] *Schindler's List*, 1995, artistic movie directed by Steven Spielberg.
[31] Erll, "Literature, Film and the Mediality of Cultural Memory," 389.

chooses to discuss that past, and the degree to which it relates to broader public debates.

This chapter argues that art is a form of poetic justice, and could even be considered as a supplementary documentary source that might facilitate a better understanding of the past. This capacity is best illustrated by the documentary film *Fernando ha vuelto*, which discusses the case of an individual disappeared by the Chilean dictatorship, whose family found his remains after a long search. In the movie, a forensic anthropologist states that even if the identification of Fernando's remains will not serve the justice process, it "will remain at least for history, if not for justice."[32] The documentary film is a form of justice, because it insists on the lack of justice for the disappeared and truth about their fate, and thus shows the limits of the state-led national reconciliation program. In their work, Peter Rush and Olivera Simić discussed art as justice in terms of "affective justice" or "melancholy justice," which is apparently "forever deferred to an indefinite future."[33] Milton further thinks that art can bear witness to past human rights violations, but this role is problematic: "can we 'trust' art and images to recount the past? Yes and no.... Art does not necessarily result in a singular narrative or even a coherent one. Rather, art may inscribe and promote multiple memories and meanings and implicitly counters the homogenizing tendencies of institutional memories."[34]

The art of memory in Romania

As noted earlier, the fact that in Romania few communist crimes have been prosecuted, and only a handful of former perpetrators have assumed responsibility for their crimes is attributable to the reluctance of successive post-communist governments, and other state actors, to embrace transitional justice as the best way for the country to move forward. Non-state actors have called for resolute transitional justice, not reconciliation. As a result, different discourses of reconciliation with the communist past and retribution for communist crimes have been present in the public space of post-communist Romania. This section asks whether the art of memory merely reproduces these public perspectives or provides an alternative reading of the past. As stated earlier, the media used by these artistic renderings of the past differ in terms of their interaction with the public. Film, theater and painting have different reach and elicit different

---

[32] *Fernando ha vuelto*, 1997, documentary film directed by Silvio Caiozzi.

[33] Rush and Simić, eds., *The Arts of Transitional Justice*, vi-vii.

[34] Milton, ed., *Art from a Fractured Past*, 17-18.

emotions. There is a further difference in the timing of the artistic renderings of the past discussed below, between the early films of Lucian Pintilie, and the more recent plays of Gianina Cărbunariu.

Portraits of perpetrators

The fact that few Securitate agents and former prison guards have been indicted and sentenced for their past human rights violations is the topic of several artistic representations of the communist past. Let's comparatively analyze several films and theater plays produced after 2000 that present both the torturers who inflicted abuse and the communist repression system that created and supported their actions. These artistic renderings insist on the importance of publicly discussing and understanding the role that perpetrators played in the communist repressive apparatus. The representation of perpetrators is a form of "poetic justice" because it allows a confrontation, albeit aesthetically mediated more than legally grounded, with the past wrongdoings.

One of Romania's most respected film directors, Lucian Pintilie, has produced two artistic films that present the Securitate and its agents: *The Oak* (whose Romanian title is Balanța, more accurately translated as The Scale) and *The Afternoon of a Torturer* (Dupa-amiaza unui tortionar).[35] In another movie, *Niki and Flo* (Niki Ardelean, colonel in rezerva), a former Army colonel is confronted with his past abuses, and the loss of privileges, social status, and respect after 1989.[36] However, this third movie is not discussed in this section, which focuses mainly on the portrayal of the former Securitate and its agents. While *The Oak* was released in 1992, shortly after the regime change, the other two movies were produced in 2001 and 2003, respectively, more than a decade after the collapse of the communist regime. This time difference makes an imprint on the way in which the communist regime is depicted in each one of them.

The Oak, an adaptation of the novel with the same name,[37] tells the story of Nela, the daughter of a recently deceased Securitate colonel. The plot happens during the late 1980s, under Ceausescu's rule, when the regime refrained from imprisoning dissenters and trouble-makers and instead encouraged them to emigrate or placed them under Securitate surveillance. Therefore, an important, but (almost) unseen, character in the

---

[35] *Balanța*, 1992, artistic movie directed by Lucian Pintilie, and *Dupa-amiaza unui tortionar*, 2001, artistic movie directed by Lucian Pintilie.

[36] *Niki Ardelean, colonel in rezerva*, 2003, artistic movie directed by Lucian Pintilie.

[37] Ion Băieșu, *Balanța* (Bucharest: Minerva, 1985).

film is the ubiquitous Securitate. Leaving Bucharest by train, Nela takes a job as a teacher in the tiny Transylvanian mining town of Copşa Mică, where she is gang-raped upon arrival, before she meets physician Mitică, who helps her. Even in that remote town, far from the capital, Nela cannot escape the reach of the Securitate, which remains a constant background presence. The film portrays the Securitate as an omnipotent surveillance institution, exemplified by the numerous threats Nela receives by phone, and as the maker of an absurd world where there is no right or wrong. The complex relationship between Nela and the secret agents assigned to monitor her is best described when Nela and Mitică travel to a nearby village to burry one of Mitică's deceased patients, and their truck gets stuck in the mud. The secret agents who followed them closely by car help them to get unstuck. All these shenanigans end with a dinner offered by the village mayor at his house, during which Mitică acknowledges that the Securitate agents came to the village as a sort of James Bond, but returned like a vegetable store (by bringing back what food they can). "This is the current situation of the city dweller in Romania, and especially of the most privileged type, the Securitate agent," the film comments.[38]

Here Mitică was referring to the chronic food shortage of the 1980s, which emptied stores of most items needed for bare survival (see Chapter 10 in this book). Villages, where peasants could engage in limited subsistence economy by growing vegetables and raising animals, were privileged sites where urban dwellers could find food. This is, however, not the only way in which the movie comments on life during communist times and the impact of the Securitate on the lives of ordinary people. Toward the end of the movie, the secret agents are seen shooting a bus full of children and their kidnappers, a reference to a real-life situation that occurred in August 1981 in Timisoara in which the Securitate confronted three young individuals who took commuters on a bus as hostages. After their arrest, the three "terrorists" were murdered by the Securitate at the order of Ceausescu and in the absence of a fair trial. This early post-communist movie presents an absurd, mixed, and complicated portrait of the mysterious, dark, and omnipresent Securitate.

The Afternoon of a Torturer, also based on a book,[39] presents the interview conducted by a young journalist and an elderly unnamed former political prisoner with former prison guard Franţ Ţandără, the only one among the former communist torturers who wanted to publicly acknowledge his wrongful deeds, rather than keeping silent about them, as

---

[38] *Balanţa*, 1992, artistic movie directed by Lucian Pintilie.

[39] Doina Jela, *Drumul Damascului* (Bucharest: Humanitas, 1999).

all other guards preferred to do. The interview takes place near Giurgiu, a small town in southern Romania where Țandără welcomes them, and then takes them to his shack in the fields where he lives with his almost blind wife. They are interrupted by angry phone calls that threaten Țandără for giving the interview and by the arrival of his son accompanied by youngsters who scream slogans against the former torturer. As the torturer declares, "We were big beasts, lady. Yes but [us, the guards] were forced to torture. Obligated? Nobody was forced, mam. This is what I accepted. I wasn't threatened with 'if you don't do it, you will get hurt or something'. This I can say before God. I would lie to say somebody pressured me."[40] He then describes his torture methods and the way they changed him as an individual, thus showing us that communism turned persons into monsters. The portrait of the perpetrator depicted in this movie is comparable to those outlined in other ideological contexts, such as those of South America, that help us to identify commonalities between the transformation of torturers. Țandără calls his son his punishment, and reveals that his wife and son are against him telling what he did in communist times. Thus, the movie comments on both the communist crimes and the way in which the former torturer relates to his past crimes, family, and former victims in post-communist times. Note that the movie portrays a real, not fictional, character. Țandără died on 2 May 2004 in Giurgiu without ever being indicted for his communist-era crimes.

According to the director, the film expresses the impossibility of finding peace by only confessing publicly, the punishment of never being punished, and the torture of living daily with the guilt of the past, because "hell is on earth."[41] Pintilie's touching portrayal of the torturer somehow excuses Țandără's behavior by presenting some mitigating factors for his cruelty: the family traumas he endured, including the killing of his father and its impact on Țandără's life, and the hatred shown towards him by his own son. We are presented with a perpetrator who has few regrets for his past wrongs, and who transmogrifies from the privileged but reprehensible tool of the dictatorial communist regime into one of the many individuals who lost financially and socially during post-communist times, but who is still free to live by himself in the fields close to Giurgiu. We are shown a man who suffers, had a difficult life, and who confesses, but Pintilie

[40] *Dupa-amiaza unui tortionar*, 2001, artistic movie directed by Lucian Pintilie.
[41] Lucian Pintilie, "După-amiaza unui torționar. Câteva idei fixe după terminarea filmărilor," *22*, 17 September 2013, available at: http://revista22.ro/31225/bucurestiul-cultural-nr-127----dupa--amiaza-unui-tortionar-câteva-idei-fixe-dupa-terminarea-filmarilor.html, accessed on 29 May 2016.

creates no monster that audiences can easily hate. The film shows us, through Țandără's portrayal, that the Romanian society chose not to remember and is therefore still marked by the legacy of past wrongdoings.

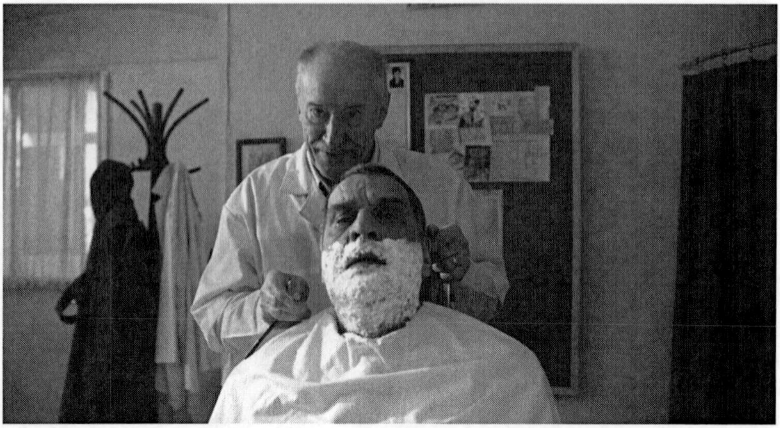

Figure 1. *Tuns, ras și frezat [Half shaved]* (2013) by Bogdan Mureșanu

The short film *Half Shaved* (Tuns, ras și frezat), directed by Bogdan Mureșanu, depicts the confrontation with the communist past that occurs in a barbershop in March 1991, as the radio announces in the opening scenes.[42] While waiting for clients, barber Vasile Bodoran is suddenly visited by a client he believes to be his former torturer, General Nicolae Pleșiță, who enters his shop. The barber tells Pleșiță that his desire of meeting him, the former torturer, is finally accomplished after twenty years of waiting. Bodoran takes advantage of this unexpected encounter to challenge his former torturer, to threaten to punish him for his previous crimes, to recall his former suffering, including the many interrogations and beatings he endured, and to describe them all to the client whom he suspects of being his former torturer. In the end, the client turns out not to be Pleșiță, and thus issues of memory, remembering, accusing, and administering self-justice, when justice is not delivered through the courts, come together in this film only from the viewpoint of the former victim.

As Pintilie in *The Afternoon of a Torturer*, Mureșanu uses the real name of a real Securitate agent to frame his take on the communist past and give authenticity to his cinematographic narrative. Pleșiță (1929-2009) was an important Securitate officer and police investigator who, as head of

[42] *Tuns, ras și frezat*, 2013, short movie directed by Bogdan Mureșanu.

the Foreign Intelligence Service from 1980 to 1984, monitored, intimidated and even killed members of the Romanian diaspora critical of Ceausescu's policies. The fact that he was a "die-hard communist and a ruthless chief of the Securitate secret police"[43] did not prevent Pleşiţă from becoming a frequent and apparently respected contributor of popular television talk shows during post-communist times. Whereas Ţandără was never brought before the courts to account for his crimes, Pleşiţă was tried in the 1990s but was eventually found not guilty by the courts, despite publicly describing the cruel beatings he administered to dissident writer Paul Goma. Whereas in *The Afternoon of a Torturer* the torturer does all of the talking, in *Half Shaved* the torturer is silent, since he is not even present.

Pleşiţă also features in Alexandru Solomon's documentary *Cold Waves* (Război pe calea undelor), which describes the monitoring of the Radio Free Europe (RFE) by the Securitate before 1989.[44] The radio station was an important source of alternative information for news-starved Romanians at a time when the Ceauşescu regime was tightly controlling any means of communications, including foreign radio and television programs. The movie, which uses both raw communist-era footage and interviews with former Securitate officials and RFE correspondents, shows the Securitate's efforts to stop the RFE transmissions that challenged the official communist propaganda. After 1989, the former Securitate members who had been responsible for monitoring the RFE retained their political influence, the film suggests, and impeded Romania's efforts to confront its past. The director believes that it is paramount to understand the reasons why these individuals do not regret their past decisions. The documentary shows Pleşiţă, who was never convicted for the human rights violations he perpetrated as a Securitate officer, as a guest of the very popular Mirror TV station defending his past actions. The film also presents post-communist deputy Ilie Merce, another Securitate officer involved in monitoring radio stations, in his parliamentary office, defending his past efforts against the RFE.

This documentary film anticipates Solomon's contention, also presented in his *Kapitalism, Our Secret Recipe*, of the continuity of power holding by the former Securitate officers after 1990, their impunity, and their popular support. Solomon's documentary films, which express his viewpoint on the communist historical context (in accordance with Rancière's

[43] Alison Mutler, "Feared Romanian Securitate Chief Plesita Dies," *Pittsburgh Post-Gazette*, 3 October 2009, available at: http://www.post-gazette.com/news/obituaries/2009/10/03/Obituary-Nicolae-Plesita-Feared-Romanian-secret-police-chief/stories/200910030131 accessed on 29 May 2016.
[44] *Razboi pe calea undelor*, 2007, directed by Alexandru Solomon.

perspective recalled earlier), are the artistic expression of the belief commonly held in post-communist Romania that the democratic transformation started in 1989 failed to be brought to completion and the new democracy was hijacked by representatives of the former communist regime. Solomon's films directly comment on the absence of reckoning with the communist past as the deliberate choice of the Romanian post-communist power holders.

In addition to film, theater plays make another important contribution to the art of memory in Romania. Two plays directed by Gianina Cărbunariu, *Xmm from Ykm* (produced in 2011) and *Typographic Majuscule* (2013), comment on the Securitate and memory by using the Securitate secret files that the director accessed.[45] Documentary theater is a common practice in Central and Eastern Europe as well as other post-traumatic societies in other regions of the world.[46] *Xmm from Ykm* is inspired by the case of writer Dorin Tudoran, who in 2010 published documents from his Securitate file as a victim.[47] Cărbunariu's play is based on the Securitate transcription of a discussion that took place at the Bucharest Municipal Committee of the Romanian Communist Party on 25 March 1985 between Tudoran, the president of the Writers' Union Dumitru Radu Popescu, and the Party Propaganda Secretary Nicolae Croitoru. To these three characters, which are played interchangeably by several actors, is added another character, the TO, whose acronym is referring to the Operative Technician who most probably registered the discussion. The play uses the file creatively not so much to recreate the communist past, but rather to present it from as many perspectives as possible. The actors play with the file in an effort to show different angles of the communist reality, prove that every historical truth is constructed, supplement the file with additional information, and highlight deleted or revised text. The play comments on the secret files and their capacity to tell the truth and depict past reality, as much as it reflects on their effects on the Romanian post-communist society.

Typographic Majuscule was part of the regional theater project "Parallel Lives – The 20th Century through the Eyes of the Secret Police," which reunited theaters and directors from the Czech Republic, Hungary,

---

[45] *Xmm from Ykm*, 2011, theater play directed by Gianina Cărbunariu, and *Typographic Majuscule*, 2013, theater play directed by Gianina Cărbunariu.

[46] Among others, Olivera Simic, "Stories We Tell: Documentary Theater, Performance and Justice in Transition," in *Post-Communist Transitional Justice: Lesson from Twenty-Five Years of Experience*, eds. Lavinia Stan and Nadya Nedelsky (New York: Cambridge University Press, 2015), 252-275.

[47] Dorin Tudoran, *Eu, fiul lor. Dosar de Securitate* (Iasi: Polirom, 2010).

Slovakia, Germany, Poland, and Romania. The play tells the story of Mugur Călinescu (1965-1985), whom the Securitate investigated in 1981 in Botoşani for writing in chalk anticommunist messages on the city walls and fences. The young man died of leukemia four years after being interrogated by the secret agents. Besides the Securitate files, the director used interviews with Mugur's mother and the secret agents who questioned him. As in *Xmm from Ykm*, Cărbunariu makes the actors interpret different roles throughout the play. The theatrical representation uses lights and new media (video) to tell Mugur's story, and one of the characters always records what is going on the scene, thus reproducing the original Securitate monitoring. We see Mugur and his mother being interrogated, the agents parading, and the young man writing messages of freedom and solidarity. We are confronted with the concreteness of surveillance, and the absurd nature of the repressive regime, whose agents noted all details about the life of Mugur and his mother, irrelevant information about trivial daily activities, intimate discussions, and personal thoughts. The omnipresence of surveillance forms the background for Mugur's life, and the lives of all those around him. This way, the play recreates the illusion of the perfect surveillance conducted by a secret eye, which helped the Ceausescu regime to maintain control over the country during the 1980s.

Figure 2. Gianina Cărbunariu, *Typographic Majuscule* (2013)

For Cristina Vatulescu, the relationship between the secret police and the artists placed under surveillance amounted to "police aesthetics," a term she used to analyze the way in which the Soviet secret police influenced the artists, and surveillance practices created new aesthetic strategies.[48] In the same vein, Cărbunariu produces theater plays that use the tools offered by the secret police (the secret files) to discuss the Securitate's control over the ordinary citizen. Cărbunariu's works, which constitute good examples of "police aesthetics," seek to challenge the power exercised by the Securitate on the society and to make use of the instruments provided by those who carried out surveillance. For Anca Pușca, Cărbunariu's works exemplify the reactions of those who did not experience communism directly but instead invent ways of provoking discussions about it, in accordance with Hirsch's "post-memory." In her two plays, Cărbunariu approaches the past to demystify the existence of "an only true and valid reading of the past" as the inherently good interpretation of a multifaceted reality.[49]

Reenacting justice

The 1989 show-trial of Nicolae and Elena Ceaușescu marked in a dramatic way the establishment of the new democratic regime and its relation to the communist past. Its impact remains important, although commemorations of the 1989 Revolution celebrate the victims of the Ceausescu regime, not the Ceausescu family members, who themselves were victims of the revolutionary upheaval. The filmed version of the trial is available on the Internet, together with its transcript.[50] The Ceaușescus were accused of genocide (for allegedly killing over 60,000 Romanians), undermining state power by organizing the armed repression of the protests, and damaging public property by destroying buildings, subverting national economy, and attempting to flee the country with over one billion dollars deposited in foreign banks. The Ceausescus received the death penalty, and their wealth was confiscated. In defiance of basic

---

[48] Cristina Vatulescu, *Police Aesthetics: Literature, Film, and the Secret Police in Soviet Times* (Stanford: Stanford University Press, 2010).

[49] Pusca, *Post-Communist Aesthetics*, 51-52.

[50] "Procesul si executia sotilor Ceausescu," Youtube, 21 June 2014, available at: https://www.youtube.com/watch?v=584UW7dTTT4, and *Transcriptul 'procesului' Nicolae si Elena Ceausescu*, Ceausescu.org, 25 December 1989, available at: http://www.ceausescu.org/ceausescu_texts/revolution/trial-ro.htm, both accessed on 29 May 2016.

legal principles, their sentence was considered final and definitive in the absence of an appeal, and they were executed on 25 December 1989 hours after the death penalty was pronounced. In 2013 the army garrison of Târgoviște, where the trial took place, became a museum included in the so-called "red tours" together with other communist markers.[51] The rooms where the two were kept can be visited, as well as the site of their execution where their silhouettes are drawn in chalk on the sidewalk.

Several artistic productions show how the Romanian artists have dealt with this traumatic event, and how their reinterpretations can help us to understand the past. These cases suggest that art can function as a form of poetic justice by reenacting past events, and provide a supplementary documentary source. The theater play *The Last Hours of Ceaușescu* (Ultimele ore ale lui Ceausescu), directed by Milo Rau and Simone Eisenring, and the docu-fiction film *Three Days until Christmas* (Trei zile pana la Craciun), directed by Radu Gabrea, use the transcript to reenact the trial.[52] The paintings of Adrian Ghenie, *The Trial* and *Study for a Trial*, document the erasure of the iconic image of the Ceaușescu couple seated at the table of the "so-called tribunal" during the trial, an image that many Romanians recognize as emblematic for the trial hearings.

Twenty years after the 1989 Revolution, the International Institute for Political Crimes in Berlin produced the documentary theater *The Last Hours of Ceaușescu* and staged it at Odeon Theater. The play started with a prologue consisting of six monologues delivered by direct participants in the Revolution: writer Ana Blandiana, actor Ion Caramitru, a youngster from Timișoara, the city where the Revolution began, and three other direct participants in the trial, including Army General Victor Stănculescu. At the time the play was produced, Stănculescu, one of the masterminds of the Ceausescu trial, was serving a prison term for his involvement in the Revolution, and the loss of life that accompanied it. He was allowed to leave the prison to participate in the play and the ensuing discussion. The monologues, which alternated with images from the Revolution, were followed by the detailed reenactment of the trial, including Ceaușescu's refusal to respond to accusations unless he was brought in front of the

[51] Duncan Light, "Gazing on Communism: Heritage Tourism and Post-Communist Identities in Germany, Hungary and Romania," *Tourism Geographies: An International Journal of Tourism Space, Place and Environment*, 2:2 (2000): 157-176.

[52] *Ultimele ore ale lui Ceaușescu*, 2009, documentary theater produced by Milo Rau and Simone Eisenring, and *Trei zile pana la Craciun*, 2012, documentary theater produced by Radu Gabrea.

Great National Assembly.[53] The trial and the actors were placed in a décor similar to the army barracks where the trial took place, with its bright light and uncomfortable chairs. By reenacting the trial and its traumatic memory the actors highlighted the trial's shortcomings, the unfair and inaccurate indictment that was supported by no concrete evidence, and the rushed and legally untenable execution, which transformed the accused into victims. In 2010 the couple's only surviving son, Valentin Ceaușescu, sued the theater in an attempt to stop the play on grounds that he alone had rights over the use of the brand Ceaușescu, but in 2011 he lost the trial.

Three Days until Christmas blends fiction with a documentary approach by using interviews with direct participants to the trial and archival material from December 1989. It shows the Ceaușescu couple running away from Bucharest to their home in Snagov, a small village close to the capital, and finally to Târgoviște, where they were also arrested. We see the trial and what happened to the two Ceausescus before and after it. The two are shown in a dormitory in the desolate army barracks, interacting with the young soldiers and with each other. The dictator and his wife are humanized in Gabrea's story, and the trial is rapidly depicted, highlighting especially the well-known image of Elena taking care of Nicolae and their refusal to acknowledge the court's authority. Their execution is not shown in Gabrea's film, as it was not included at the moment of the transmission of the filmed version of the trial in December 1989. The audience is presented with the dictatorial couple as human beings, not the extremely negative images that sometimes depict them.

These two examples illustrate "prosthetic memory" because, by reenacting the memory of the trial, they provide another access point to an event that was widely presented by the Romanian media. As all the other plays and movies discussed here, they too impact the new generations born after 1990, which have no direct experience with the trial as broadcast on television in 1989.

Last, Ghenie's paintings use the image of the staged trial with the two Ceauseșcus sitting at an improvised defendants' bench in the garrison, but erase the contours, the details, and the faces of the two accused. Ghenie thus focused on the Ceaușescus' rich winter coats that contradicted the image of modesty and frugality that the dictator sought to publicly project

---

[53] Cristina Modreanu, "Cronica de teatru/Dupa 20 de ani de la revolutie - Procesul sotilor Ceausescu vazut ca performance I," *Ziarul de Duminică,* 16 December 2009, available at: http://www.zf.ro/ziarul-de-duminica/cronica-de-teatru-dupa-20-de-ani-de-la-revolutie-procesul-sotilor-ceausescu-vazut-ca-performance-i-5183980/, accessed on 1 May 2016.

at the time of the trial. Ghenie painted the dictator just before his execution, and declared that he was impressed by how Ceaușescu conducted himself during the trial, and almost felt sorry for him.[54] The bursting of Ceaușescu's head after the shooting is also alluded to by Ghenie's use of splattered color. Thus, Ceaușescu's trial is also the moment of truth for the artist, who spotted the real person behind the dictator's much-vilified public image. Anca Pușca notes that the televised image of the killed Ceaușescu has accompanied Ghenie's generation, which witnessed the show-trial and understood it as a masquerade.[55]

Figure 3. Adrian Ghenie, *The trial* (2010)

Through such reenactments and the inherent humanization of the Ceaușescus, these Romanian artists have disavowed the largely accepted responsibility and blame placed on Nicolae and Elena in a trial orchestrated by new revolutionary leaders who pointed towards the Ceaușescus as the only ones responsible for the wrongdoings of the communist regime. This political strategy implicitly pardoned the other Communist Party figures who participated in the communist human rights abuses.

---

[54] Adrian Ghenie, "Painting a dictator in the moment before his execution," San Francisco Museum of Modern Art video interview, 15 October 2012, available at: https://www.youtube.com/watch?v=2f8IlnRnL8U, accessed on 1 May 2016.
[55] Pusca, *Post-Communist Aesthetics*, 30.

Conclusion

The artistic evocation of the communist past is a recurrent art form that involves theater, cinema, the visual arts, music, or performative strategies deployed in the public sphere in an effort to dwell on the past and question its relationship with the present. Documentary artistic forms such as photography, film, and theater are widely used in post-communist Europe and other settings that come to terms with past wrongdoings. The Romanian examples also bring forward fiction as a supplementary source of documenting the past through artistic means.

As this chapter suggests, post-communist Romania has faced an official policy of forgetting the communist human rights abuses and a late condemnation of the criminal character of the communist regime, and has disregarded other aspects of the past that remain important to a significant segment of the population. The chapter has argued that different types of artistic renderings of the past serve as a form of "poetic justice" by compensating for much-needed court trials, and as additional documentary source of "truth" for understanding the past. The chapter highlighted the role of artistic mediations of the past in understanding the communist regime, and presented art projects as key facets of reckoning with a past that is not forgotten or forgiven. By employing concepts drawn from the study of cultural memory, I identified a "multimedia collage" of memory formed of post-communist films, documentaries, theater plays, and paintings that constitute diverse facets of memorializing the communist past. Some of the works analyzed here are good examples of post-memory, whereas others are examples of the artists' own memory experiences. The plays of Gianina Cărbunariu, for example, use theater to question the legacy of the communist past and restage it in an effort to show the existence of multiple viewpoints on the past.

As in other post-dictatorial countries, documentary theater is a privileged form of dealing with the past. In South America, truth commissions issued reports on the basis of which compensation for the abuses against human rights was granted, and in Argentina, Chile, Uruguay, and Paraguay national reconciliation was promised by the new democratic elites. The plays of theater directors who have worked with this past and its legacy employ performativity to talk about the past, and use in their performance practices material traces that help to articulate the memory of the dictatorship. In Romania, by contrast, documentary theater practices are scarcer, but still able to construct a new memory of the communist regime through the interaction with the public, including audiences born after 1989. The theatre plays discussed above showed that the Securitate molded the lives of citizens under the communist regime though its surveillance mechanisms, an example of "police aesthetics." The restaging of the trial of the Ceausescus is artistically used to question the court proceedings and the death sentence. Film, I argued, could serve as a form of poetic justice by confronting the past, as shown by the works of Pintilie, Mureşan, and Solomon, which ridicule the perpetrators, instead of presenting them as omnipresent and feared. We see them as human beings, and as artisans of surveillance and suffering; they are everywhere and everybody is suspected of working for the Securitate. Film provides access to various personal viewpoints about living under communism that are easier to comprehend than official reports or academic writing. Poetic justice involves the identification of those who were guilty through documentary or fictional means. Equally, painting Nicolae and Elena Ceausescu, Ghenie erases their features, and this way he makes us see the demystified portraits of those who were ultimately held responsible for all of the communist wrongdoings.

PART 3.

VICTIMS AND COLLABORATORS

CHAPTER NINE

NOSTALGIA, IDENTITY AND SELF-IRONY IN REMEMBERING COMMUNISM

CRISTINA PETRESCU

Romania is an atypical case of remembering an atypical communist past.[1] Before 1989, the country was in many respects different from the other Soviet satellites, yet remaining in essence a Soviet-inspired left-wing dictatorship.[2] Three different features of its recent past generated the atypical process of remembering: (1) the profound economic crisis of late communism during the 1980s; (2) the violent nature of the 1989 regime change; and (3) the difficult transition to democracy resulted from the prolonged political domination of the former party bureaucrats.[3] Given this

[1] Cristina Petrescu and Dragoş Petrescu, "The Piteşti Syndrome: A Romanian Vergangenheitsbewältigung?," in *Postdiktatorische Geschichtskulturen im Süden und Osten Europas: Bestandsaufnahme und Forschungsperspektiven*, ed. Stefan Troebst (Göttingen: Wallstein Verlag, 2010), 502–618.

[2] Kenneth Jowitt, *Revolutionary Breakthroughs and National Development: The Case of Romania, 1944-1965* (Berkeley: University of California Press, 1971); Michael Shafir, *Romania - Politics, Economics and Society: Political Stagnation and Simulated Change* (London: Frances Pinter, 1985); Trond Gilberg, *Nationalism and Communism in Romania: The Rise and Fall Ceauşescu's Personal Dictatorship* (Boulder, CO: Westview Press, 1990); Dennis Deletant, *Ceauşescu and the Securitate: Coercion and Dissent in Romania, 1965-1989* (London: M.E. Sharpe, 1995); Vladimir Tismăneanu, *Stalinism for All Seasons: A Political History of Romanian Communism* (Berkeley, CA: University of California Press, 2003); and Dragoş Petrescu, *Explaining the Romanian Revolution of 1989: Structure, Culture, and Contingency* (Bucharest: Editura Enciclopedică, 2010).

[3] Cristina Petrescu and Dragoş Petrescu, "The Canon of Remembering Romanian Communism: From Autobiographical Recollections to Collective Representations," in *Remembering Communism: Private and Public Recollections of Lived Experiences in Southeast Europe*, eds. Maria Todorova, Augusta Dimou and Stefan Troebst (Budapest: Central European University Press, 2014), 43-70.

"exceptionalism," public representations have focused on the criminal and illegitimate nature of the Romanian communist regime in order to mark a break with this past.[4] At the same time, nostalgic memories of everyday life without repression are considered a syndrome of a long lasting societal disease, which communism once caused and post-communist transition cannot cure.[5] Not only in Romania, but also everywhere else in the former Soviet bloc, the individuals who never got entangled with the secret police remember to have lived "perfectly normal lives."[6] These nostalgic memories reflect sentiments toward the post-communist transition more than the communist regime. While the rapid European integration of Southern Europe produced prosperity and attachment to democracy,[7] the protracted transition in Central and Eastern Europe generated various emotions, including nostalgia for the communist past.[8] However, what came to be called "post-communist nostalgia" in Central and Eastern Europe is neither a desire to restore the past, like in the Soviet Union,[9] nor an unhealthy denial of communist crimes. It is a lament for the loss perceived by the individuals who have faced the transition.[10] Moreover, since the remembrance of the things "lost in transition" originates in a

---

[4] Vladimir Tismăneanu, Dorin Dobrincu and Cristian Vasile, eds., *Comisia Prezidenţială pentru Analiza Dictaturii Comuniste din România. Raport Final* (Bucharest: Humanitas, 2007), as well as James Mark, *The Unfinished Revolution: Making Sense of the Communist Past in Central-Eastern Europe* (New Haven: Yale University Press, 2010).

[5] INSCOP-Adevărul, "Barometrul despre România: Atunci vs. Acum," December 2014, available at: http://www.inscop.ro/wp-content/uploads/2014/12/INSCOP-Dec.2014.-Acum-vs.-Atunci1.pdf, and Diana Toea, "Românii, încă nostalgici după Ceauşescu: Explicaţiile unui istoric," Ziare.com, 18 December 2014, available at: http://www.ziare.com/nicolae-ceausescu/comunism/romanii-inca-nostalgici-dupa-ceausescu-explicatiile-unui-istoric-1339109, both accessed on 10 April 2016.

[6] Mary Fulbrook, *The People's State: East German Society from Hitler to Honecker* (New Haven: Yale University Press, 2005), 2-5.

[7] Juan J. Linz and Alfred Stepan, *Problems of Democratic Transition and Consolidation: Southern Europe, South America, and Post-Communist Europe* (Baltimore: The Johns Hopkins University Press, 1996).

[8] Maruška Svašek, ed., *Postsocialism: Politics and Emotions in Central And Eastern Europe* (New York: Berghahn Books, 2006), 11-13.

[9] Svetlana Boym, *The Future of Nostalgia* (New York: Basic Books, 2001).

[10] Frances Pine, "Retreat to the Household? Gendered Domains in Postsocialist Poland," in *Postsocialism: Ideals, Ideologies and Practices in Eurasia*, ed. Chris M. Hann (London: Routledge, 2002), 95-113; as well as Maria Todorova and Zsuzsa Gille, eds., *Post-communist Nostalgia* (New York: Berghahn Books, 2010).

desire for a fairer world,[11] it does not undermine the democratic consolidation.

This chapter argues against Romanian commonplace interpretations of nostalgia for the pre-1989 past, which explain this phenomenon either in terms of amnesia and denial of the communist crimes, or in terms of admiration for the alleged communist achievements in social or foreign policies. These views have proliferated – so arguments often develop – due to the very limited effects of transitional justice and the quasi non-existence of a consistent public policy towards the communist past.[12] Thus, the fundamental difference between a communist regime and a democratic one remains obscure, while nostalgia for the pre-1989 past flourishes and endangers the never-ending transition. In contrast, this chapter argues that the nostalgia generated by the Romanian transition to democracy does not represent a dangerous mourning for the communist past, but a sentiment perfectly compatible with the belief in democratic values. The first consistent corpus of nostalgic memories, whose authors spontaneously collected testimonials on the internet with the manifest desire to remember the past before it is forever lost, illustrates this argument. More precisely, this chapter is a micro-level analysis of a popular website that attracts urban and educated individuals, who contribute significantly to the richness of the personal memories preserved on this blog.

This website was created by art and web designer Cristian Vasile on 3 March 2006, at 18:53 hours precisely, when he suddenly realized that the soda fountain shop around the corner had disappeared. Thus, a picture of a soda syphon was among the first items posted on this blog. "I have started Latrecut.ro because I have forgotten my childhood, so I needed a collective effort to remember it," confesses Cristian Vasile, known to most of his blog fans by the alias Igu.[13] Initially, this website had neither its own

---

[11] Mitja Velikonja, "Lost in Transition: Nostalgia for Socialism in Post-Socialist Countries," *East European Politics and Societies*, 23:4 (2009): 533-551.

[12] Elena Dragomir, "In Romania, Opinion Polls Show Nostalgia for Communism," Balkananalysis.com (27 December 2011), available at: http://www.balkanalysis.com/romania/2011/12/27/in-romania-opinion-polls-show-nostalgia-for-communism/, and Raluca Beşliu, "Communist Nostalgia in Romania," Opendemocracy.net (13 April 2014), available at: https://www.opendemocracy.net/can-europe-make-it/raluca-besliu/communist-nostalgia-in-romania, both accessed on 10 July 2016.

[13] Ionela Ilie, "Nostalgia lui Igu," *Esquire*, December 2007, available at: http://www.esquire.ro/articole/reportaje/nostalgia-lui-igu.htm, accessed on 10 July 2016.

internet domain nor a logo, for it spontaneously emerged from its creator's impulse to trigger "the remembrance of things past." Anyone could post practically anything related to the times that seemed to have passed away, images or texts, without disclosing his or her real name. However, the blog attracted especially authors who represent (like the author of this chapter) the youngest generation who experienced communism as pre-adulthood individuals. The heydays of the blog were the years 2006 and 2007, when around 30,000 visitors entered the blog every month. Ever since, around 1,000 postings and tens of thousands of related comments transformed the website into arguably the most beloved venue of exchanging memories from the recent-but-not-exclusively-communist past, while Latrecut.ro established itself as the website where individuals could post "naïve memories" about the communist period. A few other websites are dedicated to images of everyday life under communism, but none attracted the witty comments posted on Latrecut.ro. What makes the contributors to this blog different is their capacity to make fun of rather grim memories, recuperate the humor that helped Romanians survive those difficult times, and thus distance themselves from a past nostalgically remembered.

Unlike the recollections of older generations, which primarily refer to the extraordinary times of repression (1945-1964), the memories of this younger generation speak of "ordinary" times (1964-1989). In particular, they focus on the adversities experienced during the profound economic crisis in the 1980s, which distorted daily routines and family life. Thus, these memories are free from the secret police, but still illustrative for the arbitrariness of party decisions. Unlike peers from neighboring countries, who remember childhood as an age free of problems, Romanians recall schooldays as intrinsically mixed with hardships and deprivations. Although nostalgic, these memories evoke the in-depth, continuous penetration of the party-state into the daily existence of the common and complying citizens.[14] Therefore, they are complementing, not contradicting the morally correct narrative that focuses on the victims of terror and the heroes of resistance. Moreover, their nostalgia for the past is comparable with the nostalgia expressed by peers in older democracies, and thus compatible with the desire to build a democratic future. In short, this chapter argues that these on-line memories represent a longing not for the pre-1989 world, but for the world that predated the internet.

---

[14] Jürgen Kocka, "Eine durchherrschte Gesselschaft," in *Die Sozialgeschichte der DDR*, eds. Hartmut Kaelble, Jürgen Kocka and Hartmut Zwahr (Stuttgart: Klett-Cotta, 1994), 547-543.

In the year 2000, when we will no longer be children

This verse opened one of the songs included in the compulsory musical repertoire for schools and universities in Ceauşescu's Romania. The lyrics were considered non-ideological for not talking about the Communist Party, its supreme leader, or the motherland – "Partidul, Ceauşescu, România," the three key words of the official ideology in the late 1970s and the 1980s. The song referred to the hypothetical bright future Romanian children would supposedly live one day. Drawing from the lyrics, teachers used to ask children to imagine, in words or drawings, how the future would look like. A blog entry best epitomizes personal experiences in communism and post-communism: "[This was] a song that we used to sing before the revolution, which inspired us to draw the most amazing pictures of year 2000. What a huge disappointment 2000 was, compared to the spaceships and the cities on the moon which we imagined!"[15] Another comment voices even more clearly disappointment with the present: "How full of expectations we were when we used to sing this song. Yet, in 2000 I have lost my job and had to interview with employers who were at odds with the law and the common sense."[16] Frustration with not coping well with the challenges of post-communist transition, not the perceived benefits of communism, made these authors return to the past. As Laura Nostalgica wrote, it is the passing of their innocent youth that these individuals regret: "although those times were inferior to today in terms of rights, services, etc., we experienced more intensely the joys of life, we were happier, less sinful, more naïve."[17] These nostalgic memories are symptomatic for the time of remembering, that is, for the transition from communism to capitalism and democracy, not for the time they remember.

The authors of these blog entries belong to the third generation that experienced communism, if one considers those who were already adults at the end of World War II as the first generation, and those born

---

[15] Sirg, "Noi in anul 2000," Latrecut.ro, 25 April 2008, available at: http://www.latrecut.ro/2008/04/noi-in-anul-2000/#comments, accessed on 27 May 2016. Note that most of the blog authors quoted in this chapter are using nicknames, not their real names.

[16] Alice, Comments # 11, Latrecut.ro, 15 June 2008, available at: http://www.latrecut.ro/2008/04/noi-in-anul-2000/#comments, accessed on 27 May 2016.

[17] Laura Nostalgica, "fascinantii ani '80", Latrecut.ro, 7 February 2008, available at: http://www.latrecut.ro/2008/02/fascinantii-ani-80/#comments, accessed on 9 July 2016.

immediately after the communist takeover of 1945 as the second. Until these first nostalgic memories were posted electronically, the older generations had primarily conveyed memories about the terror, the armed resistance, or the hardships of daily life characteristic of the 1945-1964 period.).[18] The dissemination of recollections about victims and heroes was a top post-communist priority in a country where the regime change of 1989 was so painful and the post-communist transition so tortuous. Accordingly, those involved in the organization of memory, from civil society groups, such as the Associations of the Former Political Prisoners in Romania or the Civic Academy, to various professionals and institutions, such as the National Council for the Study of the Securitate Archives or the Institute for the Investigation of the Communist Crimes, believed that the remembrance of the recent past must emphasize the criminal nature of the communist regime.[19] Their narrative of communism represented a tragedy centered on victims and heroes, which conveyed what they believed to be the morally correct interpretation of the past.[20] During democratization such instrumental narrative made nostalgic recollections seem indecent, even disrespectful, to the numerous innocent victims. Thus, until the third generation spontaneously engaged in remembering its own past, the positive memories from communism were conveyed mostly privately[21]

The oldest in this generation include the numerous "children of the decree" (*decreţei*), born after abortion was officially banned by Decree 770/1966.[22] They represented the largest age group among those who lost

---

[18] Gabriela Cristea and Simina Radu-Bucurenci, "Raising the Cross: Exorcizing Romania's Communist Past in Museums, Memorials and Monuments," in *Past for the Eyes: East European Representations of Communism in Cinema and Museums after 1989*, eds. Oksana Sarkisova and Péter Apor (Budapest: Central European University Press, 2008), 275-306; Monica Ciobanu, "Reconstructing the History of Early Communism and Armed Resistance in Romania," *Europe-Asia Studies*, 66:9 (2014): 1452-1481; and Monica Ciobanu, "Piteşti: A Project in Reeducation and its Post-1989 Interpretation in Romania," *Nationalities Papers: The Journal of Nationalism and Ethnicity*, 43:4 (2015): 615-633.

[19] Alexandru Gusi, *La Roumanie face a son passe communiste: Mémoires et cultures politiques* (Paris: l'Harmattan, 2011).

[20] Tzvetan Todorov. *Hope and Memory: Reflections on the Twentieth Century* (London: Atlantic Books, 2003), 187-197.

[21] David Kideckel, "The Unmaking of an East-Central European Working Class," in *Postsocialism: Ideals, Ideologies and Practices in Eurasia*, ed. Chris M. Hann, (London: Routledge, 2002), 114-132.

[22] Gail Kligman, *The Politics of Duplicity: Controlling Reproduction in Ceauşescu's Romania* (Berkeley, CA: University of California Press, 1998).

their lives in the 1989 Revolution.[23] The youngest segment includes those old enough in 1989 to have personal memories about the shootings or the unintelligible talk about "liberty and victory," as a blog comment mentions.[24] As mentioned, these internet recollections refer to everyday life during the 1980s, when the terror was long gone, but the hardships of daily life were more challenging than in other communist countries.[25] An unmatched economic crisis was accompanied by an unusually tight ideological control, which imposed much less allegiance to Marxist-Leninism than to nationalist views.[26] However, these memories are not conveying a purely negative image of the recent past, though their authors agree that "communism was bad." In content and message, these on-line stories are complementing the recollections of the older generations about the injustice and the abuses committed by the communist regime in the name of a bright future. Because this generation exited communism before it became embittered by it, its narrative on the communist past is ironic more than tragic.[27]

One could link the timing of this novel trend in remembering communism to Romania's acceptance into the European Union in January 2007, the symbolic moment when the goals of the 1989 Revolution were finally achieved, and the dictatorial past seemed irremediably left behind. It is probably not just a simple coincidence that the blog was created and became quickly popular around that time. By then, the daily landscape had totally changed with the disappearance of small communist items and consumer goods from private houses and the appearance of post-communist advertisements and graffiti in public spaces. The release of the popular movie *Amintiri din Epoca de Aur* [Memories from the Golden Age] reinforced this new trend of remembering the past, and highlighted the passing of time. Its directors revealed the difficult problems posed by

---

[23] Marius Mioc, *Revoluţia din Timişoara şi falsificatorii istoriei* (Timişoara: Sedona, 1999), 226-241.

[24] Analuchian, Comment # 16, 24 December 2006, available at: http://www.latrecut.ro/2006/12/generatia-x/#comments, accessed on 27 May 2016.

[25] Dragoş Petrescu, *Entangled Revolutions: The Breakdown of the Communist Regimes in East-Central Europe* (Bucharest: Editura Enciclopedică, 2014).

[26] Jowitt, *Revolutionary Breakthroughs and National Development*, 273-292; Shafir, *Romania - Politics, Economics and Society*, 47-63; Gilberg, *Nationalism and Communism in Romania*, 47-57; as well as Katherine Verdery, *National Ideology under Socialism: Identity and Cultural Politics in Ceauşescu's Romania* (Berkeley, CA: University of California Press, 1991).

[27] Hayden White, *Metahistory: The Historical Imagination in the Nineteenth Century Europe* (Baltimore: The Johns Hopkins University Press, 1973).

the hitherto transformation of the everyday landscape.[28] The communist-era clothing and house interiors were reconstructed by public collection of artifacts, while the streets of Bucharest were digitally restored. As the past became "another country," the blog contributors engaged in a collective yet chaotic endeavor of preserving in electronic format communist-era objects that could be found in dusty attics or forgotten drawers. There is a concerted effort to remember the types of bread or pastry, the best brands of chocolate or ice cream, the games children used to play, or the most popular books. In short, this internet remembering of the communist past has begun by immortalizing small items of everyday life before they disappear. Memory, as Pierre Nora noted, is attached to sites and artifacts, whereas history is anchored in events.[29] Thus, nostalgia for the communist times is associated in Central and Eastern Europe with the commercial trend of reviving popular communist products and their corresponding consumerist esthetics, and efforts to catalogue objects, artifacts, and recipes of the past. The commercialization of communism has occurred in Romania too, but there was no systematic effort of cataloguing the items from that period before this internet type of remembering emerged.[30]

The frantic revisiting of the past has also been accelerated by the coming of age of the generation that never experienced communism. In reaction, the blog authors realized that their greatest asset is their double identity: "we can consider ourselves the happiest people because .... we know how it was before and how it is now from experience, not from the stories of others.... We are the end of one life-style and the beginning of another."[31] The authors know they witnessed an irreversible change, which they conceptualize not as a regime change, but as a change in everyday routines. The end of communism meant the end of membership in the Pioneers' Organization, the local non-alcoholic beverages, the smuggled video-cassettes that offered an alternative to the two-hour official television program, and the games played outdoors. In contrast, the beginning of democracy was marked in children's life by the arrival of Coca Cola, the 24-hour multi-channel television, and internet games. As

[28] Florentina Ciuvercă, "Epoca de Aur a renăscut în chinuri," *Evenimentul Zilei*, 26 September 2009, available at:http://www.evz.ro/articole/detalii-articol/869213/Epoca-de-Aur-a-renascut-in-chinuri-VIDEO, accessed on 10 April 2016.

[29] Pierre Nora, "Between Memory and History: Les Lieux de Mémoire," *Representations*, 26 (Spring 1989): 7-24.

[30] Dragoş Petrescu, "Peitsche und Zuckerbrot: Erinnerung an die Ceauşescu-Ära in Rumänien," *Osteuropa Zeitschrift*, 63:5-6 (2013): 355-366.

[31] Dr. Me, Comment # 4, Latrecut.ro, 13 December 2006, available at: http://www.latrecut.ro/2006/12/generatia-x/#comments, accessed on 27 May 2016.

one post noted, "we were a generation of (...) 'first-timers'!"[32] The simultaneous identity of "the last" and "the first" has driven the blog authors to make a virtue out of necessity, and reevaluate their double personal experience with communism and democracy: "While I was thinking that we were a generation of losers, you gave me all the reasons to understand that after all we are the winners, because we moved this country to the next century, where the old ones will never arrive, while the young ones will never know how it was before."[33]

The blog postings refer primarily to school and other related activities. There is a collective endeavor to remember communist school objects, and to catalogue textbooks, stationery, uniforms, and transcripts.[34] Relevant for this chapter are the formal and informal aspects of education. The authors agree that education was better under communism, though its content and methods were often derided. Perhaps most telling are the funny recollections triggered by a text included in the school curricula of the late 1980s.[35] The Romanian communist ideology implied learning about the nation more than class struggle, as the compulsory readings praised the motherland as much as the Communist Party and its leader. The piece most intensely remembered on the blog was authored by reputed poet Ana Blandiana, who later turned into a critic of Ceaușescu's personality cult.[36] The text spoke of Romania's geography, which the poetess thought to resemble a bouquet of flowers fastened by the ribbon of the Danube River, and immersed in the vase of the Black Sea. The green fields stood for leafs, while the yellow hills, the brownish mountains with white cliffs, and the other geographical symbols resembled the flowers. The text suggested that no other country in the world supports such a wonderful comparison. The textbook included also homework assignments related to this text, which was explicitly intended to make children proud of the motherland. One of these tasks required pupils to imagine with what else could they compare

---

[32] Meda, Comment # 4, Latrecut.ro, 31 December 2007, available at: http://www.latrecut.ro/2007/07/urme-in-zapada-amintiri-de-mic-copil/#comments, accessed on 9 July 2016.

[33] Hedes Mihai, Comment # 12, Latrecut.ro, 12 December 2006, available at: http://www.latrecut.ro/2006/12/generatia-x/#comments, accessed on 27 May 2016.

[34] See *Archive for the 'Scoala' Category*, Latrecut.ro, 2006-2015, available at: http://www.latrecut.ro/category/scoala, accessed on 27 May 2016.

[35] Scrintin, "manuale de citire/romana din clasele primare," Latrecut.ro, 26 April 2006, available at: http://www.latrecut.ro/2006/04/manuale-de-citireromana-din-clasele-primare/#comments, accessed on 9 July 2016.

[36] Cristina Petrescu, *From Robin Hood to Don Quixote: Resistance and Dissent in Communist Romania* (Bucharest: Editura Enciclopedică, 2013), 339-340.

"Romania and its beauties."[37] Many blog contributors remembered that most children reiterated variations of the text, for they knew that was expected of them, but also admitted that they thought Romania resembled a fish, an obvious comparison if one looked at the map horizontally, not vertically as the poetess did. For one commentator, this exercise showed that "not everyone perceives the same thing in the same way."[38] Yet, the most revealing memory refers to the children who were naïve enough to openly compare the country with a fish and even stretch their imagination to embellish it by arguing that the fish was a tasty and fatty carp, while its scales represented the counties.[39] The teachers' reaction to this "ideological deviation" was virulent up to the point of granting a failing grade and asking parents to come to school, for education was meant to transmit the official dogma, not to stir the imagination and develop critical thinking. The laughter of the children who complied with the text illustrates that pupils learned early on to hold back what they really thought and got used to the inherent duplicity of communism.

Thus, inasmuch as the communist education system appears to have been better, the memories of this age group suggest that this perception has less to do with what teachers transmitted and more with what children learned by default: how to get along with others. An intensive socialization inside and outside the school through sports, games, or other leisure activities created strong bonds among individuals. Children's games feature frequently in the recollections of these individuals who were the last to play in-between the apartment blocks games that required nothing more than a ball.[40] Accordingly, the school-related memories go beyond educational activities and evoke a lifestyle that had long disappeared due to the emergence, availability and affordability of new technologies (laptops, mobile phones) and informational sources (internet).[41] Worth

[37] *Citire: Manual pentru clasa a IV-a* (Bucharest: Editura Didactică şi Pedagogică, 1987), 10-11.
[38] GayRo, Comment # 16, Latrecut.ro, 22 September 2006, available at: http://www.latrecut.ro/2006/04/manuale-de-citireromana-din-clasele-primare/#comments, accessed on 27 May 2016.
[39] Costi, Comment # 15, Latrecut.ro, 31 August 2006, available at: http://www.latrecut.ro/2006/04/manuale-de-citireromana-din-clasele-primare/#comments, accessed on 27 May 2016.
[40] Flintobert, "Jocuri pierdute," Latrecut.ro, 4 January 2009, available at: http://www.latrecut.ro/2009/01/jocuri-pierdute/#comments, accessed on 9 July 2016.
[41] Sirg, "Cărți de joc educative," Latrecut.ro, 6 October 2006, available at: http://www.latrecut.ro/2007/10/carti-de-joc-educative-muzica/#comments, accessed on 9 July 2016.

mentioning are the recollections about the difficulty of coping with daily life in the absence of adequate child support. Most schools finished classes around noon, when parents were still at work. Children had to return home by themselves, and parents used to hang the house key around children's neck to minimize the risk of losing it. This habit stirred many self-mocking memories. Some remember they chewed the thread to which the key was attached, because it had a good salty taste from their own sweat, others that children differed according to the key type, which said something about the house in which they lived and implicitly their family status. These adversities of daily life offered them the possibility to spend quality time with friends and peers after school.[42] Thus, the authors' nostalgia expresses a longing for the more consistent social interactions of communist times.

Finally, one could not overlook the nostalgic remembering of books that were frantically read for lack of alternative modes of acquiring knowledge about the world. Remembered are not the ideological books included among compulsory readings, but books that constituted an alternative, ad-hoc literary canon and stirred genuine interest. The most popular book of all times, a veritable site of memory in itself judging by the numerous comments it attracted, was *Cireşarii* [The People of the Cherry Tree], a five-volume book written between 1956 and 1968.[43] The book, which was published in almost 1 million copies during communist times,[44] narrates the fabulous adventures of a group of teenagers with whom all children in Romania identified. These adventures were primarily set in an imaginary little town that was hard to locate on the map, and reminded of the interwar more than the communist times. The main characters acted as if the communist system did not exist. In short, the book's main quality, remembered as such by its readers, was the capacity to stimulate the imagination, which the communist education system tried to stifle. One contributor noted that: "all those who wrote on this site would like to leave for the 'great adventure' on the footpaths of our beloved people of the cherry tree (...), but for the greatest majority this was

[42] Mande, "Cheia de gat," Latrecut.ro, 4 March 2006, available at: http://www.latrecut.ro/2006/03/cheia-de-gat/#comments, accessed on 27 May 2016.

[43] Constantin Chiriţă, *Cireşarii*, 5 vols. (Bucharest: Editura Tineretului, 1956-1968).

[44] Alex Ştefănescu, "La o nouă lectură: Cireşarii," *România literară*, 9 (March 2003), available at: http://www.romlit.ro/constantin_chiri, accessed on 10 April 2016.

a beautiful dream that vanished with childhood."[45] Reading allowed people to transcend the grim communist reality and travel to places where they were not allowed to go. Paradoxically, the abusive communist policies favored an intense reading activity. While in Romania of the late 1980s the television program was highly ideological and drastically reduced to cut household consumption of electricity, individuals could escape the daily misery through books. An author remembered this restriction: "Just imagine that you no longer have internet or television after 22:00 ... nothing, maybe not even electricity. How do you think it was?"[46] A reply suggested that this nostalgia was for a time of passionate book reading and intense friendship, which coincided with deprivations: "it was better in a way, we used to read more. We used to communicate directly more, not only through the internet or phone."[47]

All of these recollections show that their authors, like many others in the world, are longing for childhood, an age free of the problems specific to adulthood. It was good then because they were young, not because the communist regime offered a sheltered existence, social equality, and everyday stability. This is longing for a lifestyle that gradually disappeared when new technologies and means of communication spread and brought the world closer than ever, while socially separating and alienating individuals from each other. Two comments convey this nostalgia: "Reading and writing these memories – would you believe – I began longing for those times. A simple life, in which any new thing more colorful or just different was a source of joy, and in which there was more solidarity and trust between individuals."[48] And "If we are no longer so close, it is because we now have a television set with hundreds of programs and a computer. Thus, we see each other only on the internet, we discuss with each other on the internet, forgetting what means to see your friends daily."[49] In short, this generation remembers melancholically the

---

[45] Micutza, Comment # 24, Latrecut.ro, 25 April 2010, available at: http://www.latrecut.ro/2006/04/ciresari-adevarati/#comments, accessed on 27 May 2016.

[46] Sirg, "Inchiderea programului," Latrecut.ro, 2 April 2008, available at: http://www.latrecut.ro/2008/04/inchiderea-programului/#comments, accessed on 9 July 2016.

[47] Bb, Comment # 12, Latrecut.ro, 2 December 2008, available at: http://www.latrecut.ro/2008/04/inchiderea-programului/#comments, accessed on 27 May 2016.

[48] Iani, Comment # 10, Latrecut.ro, 22 April 2008, available at: http://www.latrecut.ro/2006/12/amintiri/comment-page-1/#comments, accessed on 27 May 2016.

[49] Dan Adrian, Comment # 41, Latrecut.ro, 22 April 2008, available at:

world before the internet. However, while older generations conveyed their memories in print, these authors use the internet. The next section illustrates even more convincingly why this generation's longing for the past has little to do with communism, which is remembered with irony.

In Romania, colder than the cold water is the hot water

This haiku-like joke in the above title epitomizes the humor of communist times, which was present throughout Central and Eastern Europe and helped individuals to laugh the communist system out of existence.[50] The joke, heard in Romania during the 1980s, was posted by the blog initiator in 2010.[51] The above-mentioned recollections of the formal and informal education are mixed with aspects of everyday life in Romania in the 1980s, when the economic crisis modified consumption patterns and daily routines. For critics of Alltagsgeschichte (the history of everyday life), these recollections romanticize the past by emphasizing the small joys instead of remembering the suffering.[52] But in the memories analyzed here, used as sources for the history of everyday life in Ceauşescu's Romania, small suffering overshadows the small joys of the past. However, these on-line memories refer to a period when suffering had a different meaning than in the 1950s, and thus they allow for a return to the past without the desire to make justice. These stories do not refer to communist officials, except Ceauşescu and his wife, whose personality cult was enforced through education. Also absent is the infamous secret police, the Securitate, which turned Romanian communism into a tragedy.[53] An entry asked: "What has childhood to do with the Securitate? We never heard of it when we were children, we only heard of it in

---

http://www.latrecut.ro/2006/12/amintiri/comment-page-1/#comments, accessed on 27 May 2016.

[50] Ben Lewis, *Hammer & Tickle: The History of Communism Told Through Communist Jokes* (London: Weidenfeld & Nicholson, 2008), 1-3.

[51] "Bancuri din perioada de dinainte de 'astia' – Top 10," Latrecut.ro, 19 January 2010, available at: http://www.latrecut.ro/category/social/bancuri/, accessed on 27 May 2016.

[52] Alf Lüdtke, ed., *The History of Everyday Life: Reconstructing Historical Experiences and Ways of Life* (Princeton: Princeton University Press, 1995), 12-15.

[53] Ruxandra Cesereanu, *Gulagul în conştiinţa românească: Memorialistica şi literatura închisorilor şi lagărelor comuniste* (Iaşi: Polirom, 2005); as well as Ruxandra Cesereanu, ed., *Comunism şi represiune: Istoria tematică a unui fratricid naţional* (Iaşi: Polirom, 2006).

1990."[54] In comparison with older generations, the blog contributors were too young to develop a traumatic relation with the dictatorial past. Although deeply marked by the experience of the 1980s, they were the first to look back without resentment and to recover the humor of those years of deprivation. Self-mockery helped then individuals to cope with daily misery. In contrast, after the collapse of 1989, older generations remembered communism only in a tragic mode. Two decades after 1989, the last generation who outlived communism returns to its past to regard it with self-irony, as shown below.

The gloomy 1980s singled Romania out not for ideological control but for endemic shortages and a profound crisis in its unreformed centrally planned economy. The most colorful on-line memories refer to the scarcity of goods, or the cold and the darkness in private dwellings. These childhood experiences differentiate the Romanians from others in the communist bloc. Even queues – the quintessence of the faulty planned economy as manifested in everyday life – are remembered differently in post-communist Romania.[55] Throughout Central and Eastern Europe people lined up to buy scarce goods, but in Romania of the 1980s shortages were chronic. The regime's decision to repay the foreign debt triggered the reintroduction of rations of basic foodstuff and other essential products, such as gasoline.[56] Queues became a "way of life," the sole mode of survival.[57] This exceptional situation required the involvement of children, whose parents asked them to participate in the continuous effort to muddle through. Before or after school, while parents worked, children had to hunt for basic food, sharing shifts with their retired grandparents. Queuing for exotic fruits was mostly the children's job in communist Europe, since oranges or bananas were considered luxury goods, not essential for daily meals. However, the Romanian children had to stay in line for basic foodstuff – bread, milk or meat. It is not incidental that the comments related to queues were among the first to be posted on the blog.

The most common memory relates to the strategies employed by those lagging behind in the queue, which in time shaped distribution patterns.

---

[54] Leu, Comment # 6, Latrecut.ro, 7 January 2008, available at: http://www.latrecut.ro/2007/12/amintirile-mele-la-30-ani/#comments, accessed on 27 May 2016.

[55] "Aliments," "Gasoline," "Meat," "Queue," "Ration," "Supplies," *Martor. The Museum of the Romanian Peasant Anthropology Review*, No. 7 (2002), 20-22, 75-78, 101-104, 132-138, 140-141, 164-165.

[56] Petrescu, *Entangled Revolutions*, 290-293.

[57] Pavel Câmpeanu, *România – Coada pentru hrană: Un mod de viață* (Bucharest: Litera, 1994).

Usually people shouted to the sellers to "give only 1 kilo per person, so everyone would have a share," a comment recalled.[58] Those who had less to lose, like the elderly, could swear at Ceauşescu, another commentator noted about his grandfather.[59] Such unusual strategy provoked the withdrawal from the queue of those who feared possible arrest, since conventional knowledge maintained that all lines were infiltrated with Securitate agents. Sometimes, queuing produced out-of-the-ordinary events, as the accidental killing of a person who desperately tried to reach a truck of bread.[60] In contrast, those who never witnessed such tragic events ridiculed the uncivil behavior in the line: "When someone cried 'chicken at the grocery store' [*a băgat pui la Alimentara*], one could effectively see people, children and mature persons, running from all directions toward the shop. Then, the 'fun' started, for those who had been there already for 4-5 hours tried to hamper others from cutting in front of the line."[61] These memories show that the faulty supply of basic goods modified social norms and codes of conduct up to the point of eliminating good manners and civil behavior.

Beyond memories that reconstruct the everyday struggle of overcoming imposed adversities, the capacity of many contributors to distance themselves from their own absurd past behavior reflects their way of remembering. A comment adds a telling story about the value of the food rations. When her mother slipped on ice and injured her head, on their return from buying the monthly quantity of cooking oil for the family, she reassured her mother that no bottle was crushed in the fall.[62] At the same time, the recollection of the early awakenings and the long hours in line made many recognize that queues were a formative experience that marked them for life: "If there was something annoying, it was to be sent to stay in line and waste time. Even now, after 1990, I hate to stay in line. For instance, I preferred to have no bread for the Easter of 2007 than wait

---

[58] Adina, Comment # 6, Latrecut.ro, 31 March 2006, available at: http://www.latrecut.ro/2006/03/cozi, accessed on 27 May 2016.

[59] Razvanx, Comment # 17, Latrecut.ro, 10 January 2007, available at: http://www.latrecut.ro/2006/03/cozi./, accessed on 27 May 2016.

[60] Eh, Comment # 1, Latrecut.ro, 7 March 2006, available at: http://www.latrecut.ro/2006/03/cozi./, accessed on 27 May 2016.

[61] Pe vremea mea, Comment # 14, Latrecut.ro, 11 September 2006, available at: http://www.latrecut.ro/2006/03/cozi./#comments, accessed on 27 May 2016.

[62] Anca, Comment # 29, Latrecut.ro, 7 January 2010, available at: http://www.latrecut.ro/2007/12/1980-1989-amintiri-de-atunci/#comments, accessed on 27 May 2016.

in line, so I ate without bread for two days" until shops reopened.[63] These recollections on queuing also convey a sense of loss: the abundance characteristic of the market economy turned meaningless the act of acquiring groceries that once produced so much joy because it was accomplished only by overcoming considerable difficulties: "We used to find joy in everything (...) When I received a chocolate, I first played with it a while and quite some time must have passed until I could find the courage to open it (...) Maybe we are a generation that appreciates better what we have."[64] These childhood memories suggest that everyday deprivations conferred a different meaning to happiness, which could be reached easier.

More than the lack of food, the strategies of coping with other arbitrary measures, such as the shortages of electricity, gas, heating and hot water, characterized the Romanian "exceptionalism" of the 1980s.[65] To some extent, the supply of services specific to modern urban life was inadequate in all communist countries. In Romania, a country of peasants before 1945, industrialization and urbanization gained momentum in the 1960s and followed the already-obsolete Stalinist model. Its result was the creation by 1970s of an "advanced late nineteenth-century economy," based on industries such as steel, organic chemistry or electric machinery, and outdated western technologies that required high energy consumption.[66] In reaction, the party decided in the 1980s to cut the household energy consumption, which nonetheless represented only a small fraction of total consumption. This decision led to "de-modernization." Basic household electric appliances – television sets, refrigerators, vacuum cleaners, irons, washing machines – became available in the 1960s, but their usage was officially discouraged in the 1980s to spare energy.[67] The height of this absurd method of saving energy at the expense of the population was reached with the drastic cut in public utilities. This measure led to a fundamental change in everyday life, as the temperature in apartments in winter time dropped to 15°C, the gas pressure was so low that even an egg was hard to boil, electricity cuts occurred every evening, running water

---

[63] Pirpirel, Comment # 19, Latrecut.ro, 21 February 2010, available at: http://www.latrecut.ro/2006/03/cozi./, accessed on 9 July 2016.

[64] Sorin, Comment # 30, Latrecut.ro, 11 January 2010, available at: http://www.latrecut.ro/2007/12/1980-1989-amintiri-de-atunci/#comments, accessed on 27 May 2016.

[65] Petrescu, *Explaining the Romanian Revolution*, 155-173.

[66] Daniel Chirot, ed., *The Crisis of Leninism and the Decline of the Left: The Revolutions of 1989* (Seattle: University of Washington Press, 1991), 4-9.

[67] Vlad Georgescu, *The Romanians: A History* (London: I. B. Tauris, 1991), 272.

was provided only a couple of hours a day, and hot water became a luxury. Thus, each family was compelled to find inventive solutions to cope with the totally inadequate public utilities provided by the communist state.[68]

The generation that in the 1980s had a pre-adult age remembers this de-modernization in a self-mocking vein and makes fun of the abnormalities of everyday life under communism. Nostalgia remains present in these memories, but the blog entries represent veritable caricatures of those times. Under the title "Ză darc said" (the Romanian transliteration of "the dark side"), an entry commented: "One of the saddest memories of my childhood is the gas lamp, near which we were forcing our eyes to do the homework when electricity was forcefully spared. In the same category are the bricks heated in the gas oven [to warm the bed during the night] or the habit to sleep all in the same room because we could not heat the whole apartment. Middle Age landscape, in a block of flats…"[69] This comment is associated with the picture of a gas lamp, which was a hallmark of Romanian communism in the 1980s. Besides this method of coping with electricity cuts, which required the use of a scarce product like kerosene, the blog contributors reiterated other more modern and ingenious solutions that ranged from using battery lanterns to using a car battery to light a bulb. As for the reaction of those who had to endure these arbitrary measure, a comment reminds of the cry of disappointment emerging from all apartments, whenever the communist authorities enforced electricity cuts unexpectedly, for instance, in the middle of a soccer game.[70] Children's reaction was not entirely bitter, for they could turn it into a blessing in disguise, if used as an excuse for not doing their homework: "power cuts made me happy because I could skip homework, and there wasn't much [to watch] on television anyway. By candle light, I used to secretly read or to dream with eyes open. I liked the dance of light on the wall and the [shadows of] animals I invented with my fingers."[71] Like any other measure introduced by a communist regime, electricity cuts

[68] Shafir, *Romania – Politics, Economics and Society*, 117-118.
[69] Grim Riper, "Za darc said," Latrecut.ro, 31 March 2006, available at: http://www.latrecut.ro/?s=darc+said, accessed on 27 May 2016.
[70] Dienutza, Comment # 29, Latrecut.ro, 27 July 2009, available at: http://www.latrecut.ro/2006/03/za-darc-said/#comments, accessed on 27 May 2016.
[71] Ionut, "Amintiri din copilarie," Latrecut.ro, 3 August 2007, available at: http://www.latrecut.ro/2007/08/amintiri-din-copilarie/#comments, accessed on 27 May 2016.

respected the party hierarchy, as the neighborhoods where nomenklatura families lived were spared the ordeals that ordinary individuals endured.[72]

Even more spectacular are the memories related to daily cooking, which was seriously disturbed by the reduction of gas pressure as most cooking machines in communist Romania worked with gas. As all public utilities, the natural gas supply was strictly controlled by the state. During the cold season, people used to turn the cooking machines into alternative gas heaters for the freezing apartments, so the authorities deliberately reduced the pressure in the centralized pipeline system to prevent the consumption of a precious fuel like natural gas. Thus, the home pressure regulators became useless. The measure practically affected every family, but only indirectly the children who did not cook. Some memories depict burlesque situations, like the return to the primitive rural-type of cooking, directly on a fire settled between the apartment blocks when time permitted. Such a situation, so strange that it remained engraved among the author's kindergarten memory, is described on the blog: "I woke up around six and, while my mother was pushing me to drink the tea made on a gas cylinder, I saw our neighbor making eggs and potato chips on an improvised fire behind the block. This impressed me profoundly because such method is used in the countryside. In cities, we had gas cookers. After all, it is good that this is over."[73] When people warmed their cold apartments with the cooking machine, the low gas pressure during the day pushed Romanians to cook during nights. This situation turned tragic during preparations for Christmas, a religious feast that was not officially banned, but intentionally discouraged in communist Romania. There was no free working day, but children already were on their winter holiday. There were no Santa Claus, Christmas tree or carols. Instead, alternative carols were officially sung (including for the Ceauşescu family) on the New Year, when a winter tree was decorated with the presents from Grandfather Frost [Moş Gerilă in Romanian, the equivalent of the Soviet Ded Moroz].[74] Christmas was nonetheless observed in the family. Preparations for the related party and the warm atmosphere within the

[72] Calin, Comment # 22, Latrecut.ro, 13 April 2007, available at: http://www.latrecut.ro/2006/03/za-darc-said/#comments, accessed on 27 May 2016.

[73] Ceasuri, Comment # 23, Latrecut.ro, 31 July 2008, available at: http://www.latrecut.ro/2007/12/1980-1989-amintiri-de-atunci/#comments, accessed on 27 May 2016.

[74] Peter Molloy, *The Lost World of Communism: An Oral History of Daily Life Behind the Iron Curtain* (London: BBC Books, 2009), 126; and "Carol," "Christmas," "Jack Frost," "'Pluguşor'," *Martor*, 37-38, 40-41, 93, 122-123.

family, which contrasted with the almost insurmountable hardships imposed by the communist regime on the people, triggered nostalgic memories among the blog authors. Scarcity did not spoil the joy, rather enhanced it, as Romanians used to store on food for this occasion for months, so that Christmas was turned into an extraordinary event in more ways than one. The low gas pressure made the baking of special cakes a real adventure and provoked drama when it failed, as everyone is reminded by a touching and highly popular entry among blog readers, which illustrates the limits of the party-state penetration in society.[75] Before 1989, most Romanians continued to celebrate Christmas, despite the atheistic propaganda, for this feast represented a relief valve for the frustration of facing the daily petty adversities of life.

Finally, the low indoor temperatures in winter, the endless cold that made older generations "look back in anger,"[76] provoked burlesque memories among the blog contributors. They reiterated their parents' methods of coping with the situation. A common method was to use supplementary electric appliances, which nevertheless seriously raised the electricity bill. More ingenious solutions required connections abroad and access to non-marketed goods, as this blog entry narrates: "My parents managed to get (from abroad, with great difficulty ...) some kerosene filter lamps. They made a thick smoke (...) but in the end it was warmer." The use of such devices required a tank and a reserve of kerosene, neither of which could be bought on the market. As the same blog contributor remembers, his parents had to install a custom-made tank of 500 liters in their tiny apartment balcony.[77] These artisan-like methods of coping with cold could hardly solve the problem, another entry noted: "Only two rooms were really heated: the kitchen by the cooking machine and the bedroom by an auxiliary electric radiator. In the sitting room we used to enter wearing a thick winter coat."[78] The most problematic time was the night, when the outside temperatures often dropped well below zero. As

---

[75] Horia Gârbea, "Poveste românească de Crăciun sau Moartea şi învierea lui Moş Crăciun," Latrecut.ro, 17 May 2006, available at: http://www.latrecut.ro/2006/05/poveste-de-craciun/#comments, accessed on 28 May 2016.

[76] "Cold," "Heating," "Tent (in the House)," *Martor*, 44-45, 81-82, 171-172.

[77] Andreika, "1980-1989, amintiri de-atunci," Latrecut.ro, 27 December 2007, available at: http://www.latrecut.ro/2007/12/1980-1989-amintiri-de-atunci/#comments, accessed on 28 May 2016.

[78] Alex33, Comment # 18, Latrecut.ro, 21 August 2006, available at: http://www.latrecut.ro/2006/03/za-darc-said/#comments, accessed on 28 May 2016.

another blog contributor remembered, the preparation for sleep required thus supplementary arrangements: "We used to have some sheets made of mouton fur and military tent fabric ... [these were] very good against cold. This is how we used to sleep!"[79]

The same person posted also a comical memory about lack of hot water. While cold water was running according to the daily schedule, there were residential quarters where hot water was not supplied on a daily basis. Thus, bathing could at best occur weekly and children had to sacrifice for this event any other more pleasurable activity, like playing with friends outdoors or going to a movie. The bathing required a lengthy ritual of preparation, which involved the entire family for several hours. "My father made a tank in the bathroom about 20 liters, we boiled the water [in the kitchen], we opened all doors to the bathroom to have freeway and then we rapidly fetched the heavy pots with heated water to the bathroom." There, the hot water was mixed with cold water, an activity which had its own routine: "Even today I remember the ratio: 20 parts of boiled water to 9 parts from the tap, cold as ice, obviously! In the bathroom, winter freeze, certainly!"[80] Others solved the problem by illegally emptying the radiators, in which specially treated and thus really expensive water run, for its temperature was anyway not high enough to heat the apartment. "In our apartment block, all [residents] used to take hot water from the radiator, for there was slim chance to see it running from the tap," an entry stated.[81]

On the whole, these memories depict the return to a way of life specific to pre-modern times more than the end of the twentieth century. They illustrate the utter failure of the communist social policies. The communist regimes in East Germany and Czechoslovakia, while no less coercive, promoted the general social and economic well-being of their populations, and thus turned into "welfare dictatorships."[82] Communist regimes that were unable to maintain this dimension of care, like those in Poland and Hungary, tried to accommodate the population's demands to a certain

---

[79] Iuliduli, Comment # 10, Latrecut.ro, 14 January 2008, available at: available at: http://www.latrecut.ro/2007/12/1980-1989-amintiri-de-atunci/#comments, accessed on 28 May 2016.

[80] Ibidem.

[81] Balqan, Comment # 12, Latrecut.ro, 12 April 2006, available at: http://www.latrecut.ro/2006/03/za-darc-said/#comments, accessed on 28 May 2016.

[82] Konrad Jarausch, ed., *Dictatorship as Experience: Towards a Socio-Cultural History of the GDR* (New York: Berghahn Books, 1999), 6.

extent, and downplayed coercion.[83] By contrast, Romanian communism relied on tight social control and disregarded consumption. It was sufficiently atypical in the region to stir atypical childhood memories that could hardly emerge in other former communist countries. Wherever individuals remember their youth under a communist regime, their memories seem comparable to those emerging from democratic countries, as it is the case in East and West Germany.[84] Even the recollections from the 1980s analyzed above echo those of peers from the "free world" to the extent that both age groups recall reading the same books or watching the same movies. Charles Dickens or Walt Disney might be equally remembered on both sides of the former Iron Curtain, but the Romanians' atypical memories betray the fundamental difference between democratic and non-democratic societies. These atypical memories of everyday life highlight what others from Central and Eastern Europe during the 1980s tend to obscure: the fact that the communist regimes relied on the unlimited power by one political party that freely interfered into the lives of individuals down to the level of family life and personal relations.

Conclusion

The on-line memories of the last generation that experienced Romanian communism illustrate a longing for the time before the internet, the time of intense reading of books and close friendships that have disappeared from both sides of the Iron Curtain almost simultaneously. Most contributors to the blog agree on the relationship between past and present: "Under communism it was worse than now. This means neither that now might be fine nor that then one could not have been happy.... We lived through those times, but understood them only later, when we could compare [them] with what followed."[85] Because they are challenged by the hardships of living in the highly competitive environment of the never-ending transition – for which neither parents, nor teachers ever prepared them – these blog contributors are longing for their lost childhood. This

---

[83] Herbert Kitschelt, Zdenka Mansfeldova, Radoslaw Markowski and Gábor Tóka, *Post-Communist Party Systems: Competition, Representation, and Inter-Party Cooperation* (Cambridge: Cambridge University Press, 1999), 24-25.

[84] Jana Männig, *Bei Oma schmeckt's besser* (Gudensberg; Wartberg Verlag, 2009), 4.

[85] Ovidiu, Comment # 18, Latrecut.ro, 8 June 2006, available at: http://www.latrecut.ro/2006/05/poveste-de-craciun/#comments, accessed on 9 July 2016.

exercise in collective remembering is related to the problem of identity.[86] Its purpose is to transmit to the next generations that never lived under communism what the blog authors consider to be their most valuable asset: their dual and unique life experience with both dictatorship and democracy. Although longing for the past, this generation agrees that "one cannot really compare,"[87] for "whatever one might say, nothing can be compared with liberty!"[88] The exercise of remembering the common past has played a curative function[89] for them. By bringing this generation together on the internet, it has given its members the certitude that there are others that feel and think alike. In short, the return to the pre-1989 past has helped the last generation that experienced Romanian communism to build and assume a collective identity. For the internet represent the main source of information for the young generation of today, these on-line stories about youngsters' everyday life under late Romanian communism are more popular than those expressed in printed form. Consequently, such stories turned into a valuable teaching support material, for these narratives about the hardships of the youth under communism do not conflict but complement those conveyed by textbooks. Their stories illustrate that, whatever the problems faced in the process of democratic consolidation might be, their solution is not backward-looking. These recollections vividly remind everyone that the communist regimes were dictatorships ready at all times to infringe basic rights, disregard the rule of law and deprive human beings of their dignity. In short, such recollections support (not undermine) the process of democratic consolidation.

[86] Chris Hann, "Transition, Tradition, and Nostalgia: Postsocialist Transformations in a Comparative Framework," *Collegium Atropologicum*, 36:4 (2012): 1119-1128.

[87] Zaqk, Comment # 9, Latrecut.ro, 17 February 2011, available at: http://www.latrecut.ro/2009/01/amintiri-din-acei-ani/#comments, accessed on 28 May 2016.

[88] Babilonul imobiliar, Comment # 11, Latrecut.ro, 20 January 2008, available at: http://www.latrecut.ro/2007/12/1980-1989-amintiri-de-atunci/#comments, accessed on 9 July 2016.

[89] Todorova and Gille, *Post-communist Nostalgia*, 8.

CHAPTER TEN

REMEMBERING THE GULAG: RELIGIOUS REPRESENTATIONS AND PRACTICES

MONICA CIOBANU

A commonly recurring theme that unites the lived experiences of Stalinism in Romania with mnemonic practices is the representation of early communism from a religious, spiritual or mystical perspective. Post-communist debates on Gulag-style repression (imprisonment, deportations and torture) have become and remain integrated in a Christian Orthodox and nationalist framework. In Romania, themes that dominated official nationalist-communist propaganda during the 1980s (ethnic nationalism, national victimization, or the myth of an exceptional historical destiny) have resurfaced and are embraced by victims and their descendants, as well as by politicians, intellectuals, civic associations, the media, and the general public.

This chapter analyzes religious symbols and liturgical practices that characterize both individualized and collective representations of the Gulag by looking at the role of religion in furthering reconciliation and strengthening post-communist liberal democracy. The focus here is on two distinctive but interconnected types of processes of remembering and their historical reconstruction. The first refers to memoirs and autobiographical accounts written by individual victims. These include former political prisoners of different socio-occupational and political backgrounds, members and supporters of the armed anti-communist resistance, students affiliated with the interwar nationalist and fascist Iron Guard who were subjected to political reeducation through torture experiments in the Piteşti prison, and also victims of the 1951 forced deportations into the arid Bărăgan region. The second takes into account collective representations, including the activities of memorialization that involve civic associations, the media, museums and exhibitions, artistic movies and documentaries, and official commemorations.

In order to establish a framework for this analysis first some information on the significance of the Gulag in the post-communist politics of memory with an emphasis on the Orthodox Church is given. This is followed by an examination of autobiographical accounts of the victims of repression and how these individual experiences have been publicly presented in exhibitions, documentaries, and various forms of official representations. The next section analyzes the way in which these memorialization activities have led to an extreme sacred, religious and mythological narrative of the Gulag as particularly embodied by the prison saints movement. Lastly, some conclusions are drawn regarding the impact of these religious practices and representations on promoting or inhibiting the advancement of liberal democracy based on values of inclusiveness and tolerance.

The Gulag and the Orthodox Church in the post-1989 politics of memory

Scholars of Romanian communism are unanimous in considering two successive stages of communist history that correspond to different styles of repression and two distinctive versions of communist ideology. The first stage saw a Stalinist Gulag-style repression (1944-1964), which was followed in a second stage by a nationalist-communist regime that persisted until December 1989.[1] The August 1944 coup against General Ion Antonescu (Hitler's wartime ally), organized by King Michael in alliance with the historical parties and a few members of the Communist Party, was followed by a rapid dismantling of democratic institutions. This process culminated in the proclamation of the Popular Republic of Romania in December 1947 set up to replace constitutional monarchy. From 1947 until 1964, the year when the last political prisoners were released, the regime can accurately be described as Soviet-style Stalinist communism. Repression and terror, which were widely used, indiscriminately targeted all "class enemies" regardless of their social class, ethnic and religious affiliations, occupation, level of education, as well as political affiliations or sympathies. The machinery of the Gulag, which consisted of

---

[1] Vladimir Tismăneanu, *Stalinism for all Seasons: A Political History of Romanian Communism* (Berkeley: University of California Press, 2003), and Dennis Deletant, *Romania under Communist Rule* (Iaşi: Center for Romanian Studies and Civic Academy Foundation, 1999).

a network of prisons, forced relocations, deportations and labor camps, achieved the complete Sovietization and communization of the country, as well as the consolidation of the new communist regime through violence and terror.[2] A special department within the Ministry of Internal Affairs led by Gheorghe Pintilie (an agent of the Soviet secret service) was set up in August 1948 as the General Directorate of People's Security (Direcţia Generală a Securităţii Poporului, more commonly referred to as the Securitate). The Securitate engaged in interrogations, torture and physical intimidations against political prisoners and their families, friends, co-workers, and even whole communities where the armed resistance or opposition to collectivization was seen as posing a threat to the regime.[3] By far the most dehumanizing treatment was utilized in the Piteşti prison against members of the Iron Guard.[4] As one of the main goals of the regime was to establish a fully atheist society, policies were soon enacted to strip the Romanian Orthodox Church of its social and spiritual role. Official placed under strict surveillance major public religious celebrations, such as Easter and Christmas. Teaching religion was banned in public schools. The presence of the Soviet military until 1958 significantly contributed to this forced Stalinization.[5]

It is estimated that the total number of victims of repression included 600,000 political prisoners and 200,000 administrative detainees.[6] Among the victims were many priests, nuns and monks who refused to collaborate with the regime, or, as was the case with those belonging to the Greek Catholic Church, refused to convert to Orthodoxy. In fact, the Greek Catholic Church was dismantled in late 1948 and its assets were turned over to the majority Orthodox Church. Although several other denominations had been granted official recognition, the Orthodox Church alone enjoyed legal status. Through ambiguous and subtle strategies combining both repression and cooptation, the regime succeeded in subordinating the Church's senior hierarchy to its own ends. The repression of the Orthodox Church intensified during the 1950s, when a

---

[2] Ion Bălan, Regimul Concentraţionar din România: 1945-1964 (Bucharest: Civic Academy Foundation, 2000).

[3] Marius Oprea, *Banalitatea răului. O istorie a Securităţii în documente* (Iaşi: Polirom, 2003).

[4] Mircea Stănescu, *Reeducarea în România Comunistă. Aiud, Suceava, Piteşti, Braşov* (Iaşi: Polirom, 2010).

[5] Cristian Vasile, *Biserica Ortodoxă Română în primul deceniu comunist* (Bucharest: Curtea Veche, 2005).

[6] Romulus Rusan, *Chronology and Geography of Communist Repression in Romania* (Bucharest: Civic Academy Foundation, 2007).

large number of priests were arrested for refusing to submit to government authority.[7] The most targeted were former Iron Guard members and supporters, some categories of theology students, theologians, intellectuals, and clergy involved in parallel but unofficial spiritual and religious practices. The spiritualist movement known as the Burning Bush (Rugul Aprins) was perceived as dangerous to the socialist-atheist order and condemned as a fascist-legionary group. This community of meditation, prayer and intellectual debate brought together lay intellectuals together with theologians and clergy who sought the revival of spiritual Orthodoxy as means to oppose Sovietization and communization. Its leader, Sandu Tudor, was arrested in 1958 and sentenced to twenty-five years imprisonment. Other principal members including Benedict Ghiuş, Valeriu Anania, Dumitru Stăniloae, and Arsenie Papacioc were also interrogated, arrested and imprisoned.[8]

The passing of Decree 410 in 1959 by the communist authorities escalated further this wave of repression by severely diminishing the number of nuns and monks permitted to live in monasteries. The top echelon of the Orthodox Church failed miserably in any attempt to defend their fellow clergy. Patriarch Justinian (1948-1977) responded by reforming monastic life in accordance with official ideology. Labeled by some as the "Red Patriarch," Justinian Marina (known during the war as Ioan Marina, and sympathetic and supportive to the communist cause), was an extraordinarily complex and rather ambivalent character. As Lavinia Stan and Lucian Turcescu argue, "Justinian can be described as both opponent and collaborator" who in following a strategy of accommodation with the government prevented the wholesale dismantling of the Church.[9]

Following the release of the last political prisoners in 1964, the regime relaxed to a degree and began to establish itself as partly rooted in national historical traditions and independent from Soviet hegemony. In the same year, the leader of the Communist Party, Gheorghe Gheorghiu-Dej, issued a declaration of independence from Moscow. This nationalist trend was continued under Dej's successor, Nicolae Ceauşescu, the general secretary of the Communist Party from 1965 until 1989. By the 1980s this trend had

---

[7] Lavinia Stan and Lucian Turcescu, *Religion and Politics in Post-Communist Romania* (New York: Oxford University Press, 2007).

[8] Cristian Vasile, "Autorităţile comuniste şi problema mănăstirilor ortodoxe în anii '50," in *Anii 1954-1960: Fluxurile şi Refluxurile Stalinismului*, ed. Romulus Rusan (Bucharest: Civic Academy Foundation, 2000), 179-189.

[9] Lucian Turcescu and Lavinia Stan, "Church Collaboration and Resistance under Communism Revisited: The Case of Patriarch Justinian Marina (1948-1977)," *Eurostudia*, 10:1 (2015): 100.

reached a peak and had resulted in an official rhetoric expressing an extreme nationalist-communist ideology which was highly xenophobic and incorporated some of the themes and beliefs of the pre-World War II Iron Guard legionary doctrine.[10] Moreover, after a brief period of liberalization that lasted only until the mid-1970s, Ceauşescu gradually imposed a deeply repressive and personalized rule, subordinating the Securitate apparatus to himself and relying increasingly on family members and loyal followers in the top echelon of the party for support.

Unlike the previous era, however, political opponents were pursued in subtler and more refined ways. Physical terror was partially replaced by psychological repression carried out through insidious threats of blackmail. The Securitate began to use better educated employees, and gradually became heavily dependent on informers and collaborators who were recruited in exchange for personal favors and material benefits.[11] In fact, in December 1989 it was revealed that while the number of Securitate's full-time employees was not especially impressive, the number of informers had reached such a level that there was one for every 57 members of the population.[12] This is significant as it indicates that late communism was heavily dependent on cooptation (involving both the increasingly mass character of the Communist Party and the growing civilian involvement with the Securitate), as well as widespread repression. However, when faced with a number of courageous, but rather isolated, acts of opposition and dissidence, the Securitate never hesitated to use physical coercion and imprisoned or sent such individuals to psychiatric hospitals. By December 1989 when a popular uprising resulted in a violent and abrupt overthrow of Ceauşescu's personal rule there was no organized opposition at all, or any credible political alternative, and power descended almost inevitably into the hands of former second rank communist officials rallying around the National Salvation Front (FSN).

From 1964 until 1989, the history of the Romanian Orthodox Church paralleled and mirrored the highly nationalist and personalized features of the communist regime. In 1974, when the Church became part of the advisory body to the Communist Party (the Socialist Unity and Democracy Front) it was nothing less than entirely absorbed into the official structures of the party-state. Many archimandrites, hierarchs and lower-level clergy became collaborators and informers. Some betrayed the

---

[10] Katherine Verdery, *Identity and Cultural Politics in Ceauşescu's Romania* (Berkeley: University of California Press, 1991).

[11] Mihai Albu, *Informatorul: studiu asupra colaborării cu Securitatea* (Iaşi: Polirom, 2008).

[12] Oprea, *Banalitatea răului*, 48.

secrets of confession.[13] The Synod for its part made no attempt to protect fellow priests whose anti-communist activities had led to their imprisonment. Nor did it oppose the demolition of twenty-two churches and monasteries. The regime rewarded this submissive compliance by consolidating the position of the Orthodox Church as the national autocephalous church. Between 1955 and 1989, nineteen saints were canonized and Saint Andrew the Apostle was proclaimed the evangelizer of Romania.[14] At the same time, the principal religious celebrations continued to be performed by the church with the tacit consent of the authorities. In some instances, party officials themselves participated in certain religious ceremonies including burials and baptisms. In the 1980s it was quite common to see the Patriarch, Teoctist Arăpaşu (the leader of the Orthodox Church from 1986 until 2007), side by side with top communist officials during public ceremonies. In December 1989, when the anti-communist revolution began in the city of Timişoara, Teoctist was quick to send Ceauşescu a telegram in support of any use of repressive measures. After 1989, the Church repudiated this episode.

When the communist regime collapsed in December 1989, many former political prisoners were quick to join the Association of Former Political Prisoners (AFDPR) under the leadership of former political prisoner Constantin "Ticu" Dumitrescu. Together with the three re-established historical parties – the Liberal Party (PNL), the Peasant Christian Democratic Party (PNŢCD), and the Social-Democratic Party (PSD) – the AFDPR became part of the anti-communist opposition and at the same time the most vocal actor in revealing the atrocities of the Stalinist Gulag, which had remained unspoken for more than two decades. They found strong allies among some civic associations, public intellectuals and former dissidents who sought to challenge the ongoing dominance of the Communist Party successors in public life during the 1990s and early 2000s.

At the same time, they tried with some success to manufacture the historical narrative of a national anti-communist resistance. This was to elevate their anti-communist dissident credentials (also known as "resistance through culture" in the case of humanist intellectuals) to the point of establishing the existence of a larger scale opposition to the

[13] Lavinia Stan and Lucian Turcescu, "The Devil's Confessors: Priests, Communists, Spies, and Informers," *East European Politics and Societies*, 19:4 (2005): 655-688.

[14] Iuliana Conovici, "Re-weaving Memory: Representations of the Interwar and Communist Periods in the Romanian Orthodox Church after 1989," *Journal for the Study of Religion and Ideologies*, 12:35 (2013): 118-119.

communist regime before 1989. For many, the focus on Stalinist repression in an open public debate represented a convenient way of avoiding the uncomfortable discussion of collaboration and passive acquiescence that had characterized late communism.[15] Some were to describe Stalinism as a genocide against the nation or as the Christian Holocaust.[16] As scholars of religion and remembering point out, although the use of religious language in the face of mass atrocities is quite common, there is still an ambiguity about it. Broudhalm and Cushman argue that "the use of traditional religious language and concepts (…) can become a barrier against an open encounter with the atrocity of mass murder."[17] Further in the chapter we will see how the remembrance of Gulag repression and suffering as an experience of the sacred became instrumental in manufacturing a narrative of victimization.

As for the Romanian Orthodox Church, the main immediate challenge it faced in the aftermath of the December 1989 revolution was to reassert itself as the national church by pledging allegiance to the revolution and the new regime. Given Patriarch Teoctist's overt support for the Communist Party during the popular uprising of December 1989, this was a rather uneasy undertaking. But the post-communist politicians and their governments realized that by cultivating close relationships with the Church, and by participating in religious ceremonies alongside sundry resurrected officers of the Church, they could improve their public image and boost their popularity among a population that had reasserted its religious faith after more than four decades of forced atheism. In this context, the Church tried to address the embarrassing allegations of the collaboration of priests with the secret police, and Teoctist's resignation and controversial return in 1990, by attempting to shield the identities of the Orthodox clergy who had acted as Securitate agents and informers during communism. Through propaganda and cautious, if limited, truth-telling the Orthodox Church also began to promote the idea that in fact it did nothing more than engage in small and innocuous compromises before

---

[15] Cristina Petrescu and Petrescu Dragoş, "The Canon of Remembering Romanian Communism," in *Remembering Communism: Private and Public Recollections of Lived Experience in Southeast Europe*, eds. Maria Todorova, Augusta Dimou and Stefan Troebst (Budapest: Central European University Press, 2014), 29-42.

[16] Gheorghe Boldur-Lăţescu and Filip-Lucian Iorga, *Genocidul Comunist în România: Reeducarea prin Tortură* (Bucharest: Albatros, 2003).

[17] Thomas Broudholm and Thomas Cushman, "Introduction: the Religious in Responses to Mass Atrocity," in *The Religious in Responses to Mass Atrocity: Interdisciplinary Perspectives*, eds. Thomas Broudholm and Thomas Cushman (Cambridge: Cambridge University Press, 2009), 4.

1989 in order to salvage itself and its future and to keep faith alive among its congregations.[18] As Conovici shows, by indulging in "selective memory" and emphasizing only the persecutions it suffered under communism, while not addressing the issue of collaboration, "the Orthodox Church thus defined itself as a martyr of the communist regime."[19] By identifying itself as an innocent martyr, the Orthodox Church could easily reclaim its status as a "collective agent" and publicly articulate the experience of communism as a monstrous collective trauma that had threatened and disrupted the life of the nation. In 2004, when a monument dedicated to communist heroes was removed from the Freedom Park (Parcul Libertății) in Bucharest, the Patriarchate attempted to replace it with a Cathedral of Redemption. As in other instances, the Orthodox Church leaders attempted to advertise among the public the idea that communism could only be exorcised through religion.[20]

Personal accounts of lived religion in prisons

Scholars of memory emphasize that when major changes take place in society individuals readjust and reconstruct their biographies in order to fit them into the new social order through which new ideologies, belief systems, collective affiliations, and identities emerge.[21] Narratives reestablish meaning and identity for those whose lives suffered major disruptions and dislocations. When certain experiences cannot easily be explained or incorporated into the natural order, "religion responds to a human need to make sense out of something that is experienced as meaningless or even as destroying our sense of meaning."[22]

The abrupt and forced communization and collectivization of the country after 1944, legitimized through the imposition of an essentially

---

[18] Stan and Turcescu, *Religion and Politics in Post-Communist Romania.*

[19] Conovici, "Re-weaving Memory," 116-117.

[20] Lavinia Stan and Lucian Turcescu, "Politics, National Symbols and the Romanian National Cathedral," *Europe-Asia Studies*, 58:7 (2006): 1119-1139.

[21] Aleida Assman and Linda Short, eds., *Memory and Political Change* (New York: Palgrave Macmillan, 2012); Allan Megil, "History, Memory and Identity," *History of the Human Sciences*, 11:3 (1998): 37-62; and Eviatar Zeruvabel, *Collective Memory and the Social Shape of the Past* (Chicago: Chicago University Press, 2003).

[22] Arne Gron, "The Limits of Ethics - The Ethics of the Limit," in *The Religious in Responses to Mass Atrocity: Interdisciplinary Perspectives*, eds. Thomas Broudholm and Thomas Cushman (Cambridge: Cambridge University Press, 2009), 22.

atheist ideology enforced by indiscriminate repression, was perceived by many at the time as a fundamental break with the established traditional order. A new Criminal Code based on the Soviet model was introduced in February 1948. It featured a new criminal category of "counterrevolutionary," which permitted the authorities to pursue mass arrests among undesirable social and political elements labeled as enemies of the new regime. Their physical elimination was further facilitated by Law 16 of 1949, which established capital punishment for treasonous activity. As a result of this legislation, the penitentiary system and later associated work colonies were fully subordinated to the regime by their transfer from the jurisdiction of the Ministry of Justice to the Ministry of Internal Affairs. A further legal decision issued by the Council of Ministers in July 1951 invested the General Directorate of Penitentiaries and Work Colonies (DGPCUM) with the principal mission of isolating socially dangerous elements, and with their reeducation in accordance with the principles of Marxist ideology and socialism. The old penitentiary staff was replaced with personnel primarily recruited from the poor peasantry and the industrial working class, a move obviously undertaken for their now desirable class origins and also their willingness to join the Communist Party. Moreover, the increasing influence of the Communist Party and the Securitate in the internal affairs of the DGPCUM created far harsher detention conditions for political prisoners than before. The prison system was typically characterized by overcrowding, inadequate nutrition, lack of basic hygiene and medical care, sleep deprivation, physical and mental abuse, isolation from the outside world, and constant surveillance. Each prison was governed by a dual leadership structure of commandant and political officer that overlapped and confused the lines of administrative authority. In this way, the Securitate rapidly managed to gain control over the administration of the prison system.[23] The ultimate goal of the prison system was the political reconversion of socially dangerous elements, referred to by prisons officials as "bandits" "traitors" or "animals," in order to domesticate or pacify them and render them harmless.

In these extreme circumstances religion, naively or complexly felt, became both an escape from prison life and a mechanism of resisting the authorities. Most autobiographical accounts acknowledge the role of religious faith in building personal resilience and in keeping alive a sense of humanity. Collective prayers, Sunday masses, and the celebration of Christmas and Easter built solidarity and community ties among fellow prisoners of different religious denominations (Orthodox, Roman Catholic,

---

[23] Bălan, *Regimul concentraționar*, 175-209.

Greek Catholic, Protestant, and Jewish). Especially on Easter and Christmas, religious hymns and prayers developed some sense of freedom and defiance among prisoners in all types of detention facilities and forced labor camps. Such episodes of "collective effervescence" or enthusiasm, as the classical French sociologist Emil Durkheim put it, are narrated in many of the memoirs written by former political prisoners. Some, including those published by Virgil Maxim, Nicole Valery-Grossu, Aspazia Oțel Petrescu, and Ioan Ioanid, provide vivid and graphic descriptions of these moments.[24] In his *Elementary Forms of Religious Life*, Durkheim analyses the importance of commemorative rituals for strengthening social solidarity and to "awaken certain ideas and sentiments, to attach the present to the past or the individual to the group."[25] Indeed, these religious ceremonies provided political prisoners a spiritual and solidary means to reconnect to their previous lives in a brief respite from coercion and to resist ideological reconversion. Even former atheists embraced prayer or converted to Christianity in open ceremonies. The best-known cases include Richard Wurmbrandt and Nicolae Steinhardt.[26] Both converted from Judaism and became fervent Christian believers. These acts of rebellion did not go unnoticed by prison authorities, who in response attempted to ban prayers and other religious symbolism from the cells. But political detainees continued to pray, to manufacture crosses and icons, and to conduct Bible readings.

Among the more devoted inmates, prison experience represented a voyage towards a sense of spiritual and religious exaltation. When faced with extreme situations such as long-term solitary confinement, terminal illness, or imminent threat of death prayers brought comfort and salvation.[27] By invoking the presence of saints, angels, the Virgin Mary, or Christ traumatic episodes were often explained and understood by inmates as part of a providential plan or a necessary test of faith.[28] Similarly, when

---

[24] Nicole Valery-Gross, *Binecuvânatată fii închisoare* (Bucharest: Universul, 1997); Virgil Maxim, *Imn pentru crucea purtată: abecedar duhovnicesc pentru un frate de cruce* (Bacău: Babel, 2012); Aspazia Oțel Petrescu, *Strigat-am catre tine, Doamne…* (Botoşani: Axa, 2012); and Ioan Ioanid, *Închisoarea noastră cea de toate zilele*, vol. 1, 1949, 1952-1954 (Bucharest: Humanitas, 1999).

[25] Emil Durkheim, *The Elementary Forms of Religious Life* (London: George Allen and Unwin, 1915), 420.

[26] Nicolae Steinhardt, *Jurnalul Fericirii* (Cluj: Dacia, 1991), and Richard Wurmbrandt, *Torture for Christ* (Bartlesville: Living Sacrifice Book Company, 1998).

[27] Conovici, "Re-weaving Memory," 118-119.

[28] Dumitru Radu Bordeianu, *Mărturisiri din Mlaştina disperării* (Bucharest: Scara, 2001); Ioan Ioanolide, *Deținutul profet* (Bucharest: Bonifaciu, 2009); Eugen

entire collectivities underwent an unexpected and violent disruption of their lives the explanatory framework they resorted to a shared logic of deity. In an oral history study of the deportations in Bărăgan from 1951, Smaranda Vultur pointed out how former deportees described this episode in biblical terms of the original myth of the end of the world as symbolized by Noah's ark.[29]

Religious language was used in a redemptive fashion by former prisoners when describing the tortures and interrogations inflicted on them or on fellow prisoners. Some interpreted it in extreme terms as justifying the benign strength of God, despite the presence and ugliness of evil. According to Jennifer Geddes, this is a form of redemptive language and theodicy, which justifies suffering in the name of a higher cause.[30] Those who particularly embraced a monastic life or were to become archimandrites or priests after their release presented the inhumanity of the prison as essentially part of a larger providential plan that ultimately would aid the purpose of serving God against the forces of evil. For example, Justin Pârvu - a former Iron Guard militant who spent twelve years in prison and later became a conservative Orthodox activist and the superior of Petru Vodă Monastery - saw the death of many young believers as an integral part of a revivalist national and Christian movement.[31] Victims were described as saints and martyrs. As Arsenie Papacioc put it in mystical terms: "communism filled the heaven with saints."[32] He was a former member of the Burning Bush movement, a political prisoner from 1958 until 1964, and then confessor at the hermitage Sfânta Maria Tomis from 1976 until his death in 2011.

Embracing a monastic life or joining the clergy became a means of redemption and seeking forgiveness for those who compromised in some way or betrayed a cause during imprisonment either as Securitate informers or direct participants in the reeducation process. A well-known

---

Mărgirescu, *Moara dracilor. Amintiri din Închisoarea de la Pitești* (Alba Iulia: Fronda, 1994); Nicolae Purcărea, *Urlă haita…* (Bucharest: Fundația Sfinții Închisorilor, 2012).

[29] Smaranda Vultur, *Istoria trăită – Istoria povestită: Deportare în* Bărăgan (Timișoara: Amarcord, 1997), 38.

[30] Jennifer Geddes, "Religious Rhetoric in Response to Atrocity," in *The Religious in Responses to Mass Atrocity: Interdisciplinary Perspectives*, eds. Thomas Broudholm and Thomas Cushman (Cambridge: Cambridge University Press, 2009), 27-29.

[31] Justin Pârvu, "Aiudul, jertfă și sfințenie," in *Din Temnițe spre Sinaxare*, ed. Justinian Chira (Galați: Egumenița, 2008), 4-7.

[32] Arsenie Papacioc, *Ne vorbește părintele Arsenie*, vol. 1 (Făgăraș: Agaton, 2004).

case involved Gheorghe Calciu-Dumitreasa, a former medical student and Iron Guard member, who became an informer while in Gherla prison. But after release in 1963 Calciu graduated from a theological seminary and was openly critical of Ceauşescu's campaign of demolishing the churches. This led to his arrest and imprisonment in 1979. However, international pressure resulted in his release five years later and eventual emigration to the United States in 1985. Until 2006 he served as pastor of the Romanian Orthodox parish in Alexandria, Virginia. Others who followed a similar path were Justin Paven, Tudor Stănescu, and Nagy Geza.[33]

Following the same pattern of explanation based on a simple dichotomy of good versus evil, prison guards, interrogators, Securitate officers, and informers were demonized and described in quite monstrous terms. Representing an atheist ideology and acting as instruments of Soviet repression individuals such as these could not in any circumstance be considered as part of the national community. The prison memoirs describe them as belonging to an underclass or underworld, illiterate and ruthless upstarts lacking all fear of God. The most brutal among them were seen to lack human characteristics and usually presented as sadists or Judas figures. Eugen Ţurcanu, a student who initiated the infamous torture in Piteşti; Vasile Ciolpan, a former director of Sighet prison; Petrache Goiciu, commandant of Gherla penitentiary from 1952 until 1959; Alexandru Vişinescu, commandant of Râmnicu-Sărat prison from 1956 to 1963 and sentenced to twenty years in prison for crimes against humanity in 2016. All are explicitly named and witnessed to in several of these writings.[34] Overall, the prevailing image of communism is the figure of an "anti-Christ." This demonizing schema uses the language of religion as a way of making sense of a senseless and extreme brutality that otherwise cannot be understood in any coherent narrative. Ultimately the forces of good are thought to prevail and evildoers are punished in a transcendent justice that metes out ill fortune, ill health, or lethal accidents as retribution.[35]

These aspects of religion as lived experience were incorporated in the broader narratives of the Gulag manufactured by both state and non-state actors after 1989. They became the focus of public representations of Stalinist repression centered on the principal themes of individual and

[33] Monica Ciobanu, "Piteşti: A Project in Reeducation and its Post-1989 Interpretation in Romania," *Nationalities Papers,* 43:4 (2015): 626-627.

[34] Dumitru-Cătălin Rogojanu, *Imaginea torţionarului comunist reflectată în memorialistica universului concentraţionar românesc (1947-1989)* (Târgovişte: Cetatea de Scaun, 2014).

[35] Vultur, *Istoria trăită*, 36-37.

collective suffering, sacrifice and faith, spiritual strength and the moral superiority of those persecuted by the regime. I turn now to these aspects of memorialization.

Public representations of the Gulag

More than twenty-five years after the fall of communism public representations of the Stalinist repression of the 1950s have shifted from first-hand biographical accounts of lived experience to a broader narrative of collective anguish. The latter has been broadly disseminated by both civic groups and public officials. Religious imagery initially employed to express both political persecution and affiliation with the anti-communist and national Christian community has been expanded from a small-scale level involving only former political prisoners and their families and local communities to a larger historical narrative of a struggle for national survival. The cross as the symbol of Christian faith is always visible in some form in exhibitions, museums or other public venues, monuments and private or official commemorations, at anniversaries of the victims of communism, or in mass media accounts and artistic representations. As Gabriela Cristea and Simina Radu-Bucurenci argue, "only Christian symbols are powerful enough" to shape the sense of national identity.[36] Anti-communist rhetoric is now part of mainstream official discourse and the Orthodox Church has become a major supporter of this ongoing narrative. The presidential inauguration of Klaus Iohannis in December 2014 (an ethnic German Lutheran and the former mayor of Sibiu) was, for example, blessed by Patriarch Daniel in an Orthodox ceremony. Iohannis's first public act was to award the Romanian Star (Ordinul Steaua României) to Octavian Bjoza, the leader of the Association of Former Political Prisoners, for keeping alive the memory of the victims of communism and their sacrifice.[37] The honor was bestowed on the 25th anniversary of the 1989 uprising. This official anti-communist rhetoric had begun in 2007 when President Traian Băsescu endorsed the report of the Presidential Commission for the Analysis of Romanian Dictatorship.

---

[36] Gabriel Cristea and Simina Bucurenci, "Raising the Cross: Exorcising Romania's Communist Past in Museums, Memorials and Monuments," in *Past for the Eyes*, eds. Oksana Sarkisova and Peter Apor (Budapest: Central European Press, 2008), 275-315.

[37] "Octav Bjoza, decorat cu cea mai înaltă distincție a statului," Digi24.ro, 22 December 2014, available at: http://www.digi24.ro/Stiri/Digi24/Special/1989+Anul+care+a+schimbat+lumea/Octav+Bjoza+decorat+Klaus+Iohannis, accessed on 21 March 2016.

Given that at the time the report was not unanimously endorsed by Parliament, its recommendations were only partially implemented and subsequent transitional justice mechanisms have had only limited results.[38] Similarly, it was only twenty-five years after the end of communism that former political prisoners were formally included in the government. In October 2014, the head of the AFDPR, Bjoza, was appointed under-secretary of state at the Secretariat for Recognizing the Special Merits of Fighters against the Communist Regime.[39] The establishment in May 2016 of a national monument to the anti-communist resistance under the auspices of the AFDPR, now endorsed by the state, seems to suggest that anti-communism has finally been legitimized and integrated into the official historical narrative.[40]

In the aftermath of December 1989, and in the absence of a state-led interest in addressing the communist past, the principal actors engaged in publicly articulating the experience of Stalinist repression were gathered under the umbrella of a vocal anti-communist civil society movement that sought to oppose the continuing dominance of old regime elites in public life. They included political prisoners represented by the AFDPR, which was led by Ticu Dumitrescu until his death in 2008. He was a previous member of the National Peasant Party and a former political prisoner. The civil society movement also included the Civic Academy Foundation set up in 1994 and ran by the well-known poet and dissident, Ana Blandiana. Both urged revealing the truth about the past, which had been suppressed and distorted by communist authorities and ignored by the new regime in the 1990s. Over eighty monuments, constructed since 1991 under the auspices of the AFDPR with private funding, were included in an

---

[38] Vladimir Tismăneanu, Dorin Dobrincu and Cristian Vasile, eds., *Raport Final: Comisia Prezidențială pentru Analiza Dictaturii Comuniste din România* (Bucharest: Humanitas, 2007). For the impact of the report on the politics of memory, see Lavinia Stan, *Transitional Justice in Post-Communist Romania* (New York: Cambridge University Press, 2013) and Chapter 4 in this volume.

[39] "Hotărîrea Guvernului no. 563/2014 privind organizarea si functionarea Secretariatului de stat pentru recunoașterea meritelor luptătorilor împotriva regimului comunist instaurat în România în perioada 1945-1989," *Monitorul Oficial*, 72, 19 October 2014, available at: http://lege5.ro/en/Gratuit/gqydgobqge/hotararea-nr-563-2014-privind-organizarea-si-functionarea-secretariatului-de-stat-pentru-recunoasterea-meritelor-luptatorilor-impotriva-regimului-comunist-instaurat-in-romania-in-perioada-1945-1989, accessed on 26 April 2016.

[40] "Prezentele presedintelui," 19 April 2016, available at: http://afdpr.ro/categorie/prezentele-presedintelui, accessed on 26 April 2016.

anniversary album published in 2004.[41] The introduction noted that memorials built near detention centers in mountainous regions where there had been armed resistance, as well as in villages where peasants revolted against collectivization, represented sites of remembering those described as "hero-martyrs." The majority of these monuments incorporate the cross or a skull and crossbones motif on official maps of Romania. Some combine several crosses that together represent the two world wars, the communist period and the December 1989 revolution. Such symbolic images are meant to show an historical continuity of national sacrifice.

The same themes and images dominate the Memorial of the Victims of Communism and of the Resistance in Sighet. This is a small town located in northwestern Romania, where pre-World War II political elites were imprisoned. The memorial was set up in 1997 by the Civic Academy Foundation and designated a year later by the Council of Europe as a principal site of memory in Europe.[42] The prison was transformed into a memorial museum, whose most important symbol is represented by a Cortege of the Sacrificed Victims. This was a statuary group consisting of eighteen human silhouettes led by a headless character towards a wall that blocks the horizon. The chapel dedicated to prayer and silence was built in the backyard of the museum, the design selected through an architectural competition. Revealingly, the competition was conducted on the theme: "I could not have survived in prison had I not believed in God."[43] A cross was also placed in the auditorium and called "resurrection." It is marked by the well-known biblical verse: "You will find the truth and the truth will set you free." Religion is thus seen as redeeming suffering.

The cross is also an important instrument for removing and obliterating all physical and spiritual traces of the old regime. Cristea and Radu-Bucurenci carefully show how the Peasant Museum in Bucharest, which was designed in 1990 to replace the Museum of the History of the Communist Party, embraced the cross as "the organizing principle of the museum." They describe an extraordinary moment when priests performed a religious ceremony to exorcise all the old ghosts of communism.[44]

The symbol of divine perfection and completeness as represented by the number seven in the Christian tradition complements the cross and

---

[41] Ionel Nicu Save, ed., *Album Memorial – Monumente închinate jertfei, suferinței și luptei împotriva comunismului* (Bucharest: Ziua and AFDPR, 2004).

[42] "Memorialul Victimelor Comunismului si ale Rezistentei," 5 July 2011, available at: http://sighet.ro/?page_id=557, accessed on 26 April 2016.

[43] Romulus Rusan, ed., *Memorialul Victimelor Comunismului și al Rezistenței: ghid și activitate* (Bucharest: Academia Civică, 2014), 11-12.

[44] Cristea and Bucurenci, "Raising the Cross," 18-19.

reinforces the message of national rebirth through sacrifice. For example, the monument built at Aiud prison incorporates seven double crosses that sustain a larger cross embodying the sacrifice of political prisoners. The significance of the number seven is featured in the book dedicated to the Bărăgan deportations written by young student Tatiana Maria Cernicova, titled *Anno Domini 1951*. The book was based on a prize-winning essay on the question "What would it feel like to be a refugee?," organized in Bucharest in 2000 by the United Nations High Commissioner for Refugees. In order to document this experience, she chose to interview seven individuals whose childhoods had been disrupted by forced relocation. Cernicova acknowledges the significance of the number seven as "the symbol of eternal life, perfection, harmony and luck."[45] The same interpretation of deportation as an abnormal and disruptive event is represented in the photograph album *Deportații Via Dolorosa Bărăgan*, which consists of 51 paintings by Radu Bercea with captions written by Nicolae Ianași (both former political prisoners). One painting presents an anguished deportee asking: "Lord, why did you punish us and let communism come over us?"[46] These paintings are currently housed in the Drobeta Turnu-Severin Museum (Muzeul Regiunii Porților de Fier) in southwestern Romania, where many were subject to deportation because of the region's proximity to Yugoslavia and the potential threat of "Titoism."

In both instances the use of religious language is evident in an "aphopatic" manner that "signals that something outside of the ordinary in human life had occurred requiring language that is out of the ordinary to respond to it."[47] In this way, the experience of lived religion in prison has been transmitted by means of public representations (in museums, public exhibitions, photo albums, documentaries) to a younger generation that had never lived under communism. Through forms of education like this, the "generation of postmemory" – as Marianne Hirsch (2012) refers to the children of Holocaust victims – can understand the history of early communism through the particular interpretations of religious experience.[48] Yet the children of political prisoners in the Gulag (considered at the time potentially dangerous elements by the regime) continued to be kept under surveillance by Securitate and were denied equal rights to education and

[45] Tatiana Maria Cernicova, *Anno Domini, 1951* (Timişoara: Mirton, 2003), 84.

[46] Radu Bercea and Nicolae Ianaş, *Deportați via Dolorosa Bărăgan, 18 iunie 1951* (Drobeta Turnu Severin: Profin, 2010).

[47] Geddes, "Religious Rhetoric," 26.

[48] Marianne Hirsch, *The Generation of Post-Memory* (New York: Columbia University Press, 2012).

employment. This constitutes for many of them a strong incentive towards preserving and disseminating the memory of repression.

The artistic work of the well-known film director Nicolae Mărgineanu (the son of reputable psychologist, who was imprisoned from 1948 until 1967) illustrates how the lived experience of prison life is presented to a larger audience. Two of his films – *Blessed Are You, Prison!* (Binecuvîntată fii, Închisoare!) released in 2002 and *White Gate* (Poarta Albă) in 2014 - powerfully convey the message of redemption though religion.[49] The first tells the story of a young intellectual, Nicoleta Bruteanu, who later wrote her autobiography under the name of Valery-Nicole Grossu. It narrates how she found the strength to resist interrogation, torture, and solitary confinement by rediscovering her faith. She wrote that she was "never closer to God than I was in prison."[50] *Poarta Albă* portrays the experience of forced labor at one of the main sites named by communist dictator Gheorghe Gheorghiu-Dej as the "cemetery of the bourgeois": the Danube-Black Sea Canal (Canalul Dunărea-Marea Neagră). The film begins and ends with the image of an icon representing the Virgin Mary holding the infant Jesus dressed in prison clothes. The central character is Father Arsenie Boca, born in 1910 in what was at the time the Austro-Hungarian Empire. He was a monk, theologian and artist. During communism he was arrested several times and imprisoned for allegedly helping the anti-communist resistance in the mountains. Boca died in 1989 just before the December revolution, which he had allegedly predicted. Some consider him a legendary figure or a "prison saint" because of the exemplary life he is said to have led in prison and because of his alleged miracles and prophecies. Others dismiss or criticize Boca for his alleged fascist sympathies. It is to this type of spiritual or mystical memorialization promoted by religious groups and parts of the church that we turn now.

The prison saints movement

The various mnemonic practices discussed above convey the religious and spiritual dimensions of prison experiences to a lay audience in secular settings. The prison saints movement, however, brings this undertaking directly into the religious sphere. I use the "prison saints movement" here as a catch-all term that includes religious civic associations that promote the canonization of clergy or other Christian believers persecuted by

---

[49] Nicolae Mărgineanu, *Binecuvîntată fii Închisoare*, DVD, 2002 and *Poarta Albă*, DVD, 2014.

[50] Nicole Valery-Gross, *Binecuvîntată fii închisoare*, 1997. (see footnote 24).

communist authorities. These were individuals who led exemplary lives, engaged in sacrifices for fellow prisoners or believed to perform miracles either during imprisonment or after their release. The clearest evidence of a "prison saint," however, is the alleged finding of relics (bodily remains that show some characteristics of the living) that are said to explain the performance of such miracles after death. In conjunction with this campaign of beatification, these various associations also advocate religious education and national rebirth. The most active among them are the Arsenie Boca Foundation (Fundația Arsenie Boca), the Prison Saints Foundation (Fundația Sfinții Închisorilor), the Professor George Manu Foundation (Fundația Profesor George Manu), and the Rost Association (Asociația Rost).[51] More recently these initiatives have been consistently pursued and coordinated by the Areopag Group, consisting of several Christian intellectuals led by theologian and writer Danion Vasile. Vasile is a follower of Justin Pârvu. Pârvu - the de facto spiritual founder of the group – was a former political prisoner, Iron Guard activist both before and after 1989, and archimandrite at the Petre Vodă monastery until his death in 2013. Since its inception in 2008, Areopag has been involved in documenting and disseminating information about the "prison saints" through mass media and various other publications and pilgrimages.[52]

The many pilgrimages, which are often organized by the Basilica travel agency (an agency under the patronage of the Orthodox Patriarchate), expose large audiences to the phenomenon of prison saints. Mass-media propaganda attracts pilgrims seeking spiritual comfort in even higher numbers. According to Apostol, Cristea and Dosescu, one of the newest pilgrimage destinations – the tomb of Father Arsenie Boca at the Prislop monastery – exceeded 50,000 people in 2014.[53] Other popular destinations are the Petru Vodă monastery, where Father Pârvu spent his last years as

---

[51] For information regarding these foundations see "Părintele Arsenie Boca (1910-1989)," 2016, available at: http://www.arsenieboca.ro; "Fundația Sfinții Închisorilor," 2015, available at: http://www.fundatiasfintiiinchisorilor.ro, "Fundația Profesor George Manu," no date, available at: http://www.fgmanu.ro; "Asociația Rost," 2016, available at http://www.rostonline.ro/asociatia-rost/, all accessed on 28 April 2016.

[52] Danion Vasile, "Avva Justin Parvu si Sfintii Inchisorilor," Iasi, 19 March 2014, video available at: https://www.youtube.com/watch?v=IXrAEwKHXFM, accessed on 21 March 2016. For the history and ideology of the Iron Guard see Roland Clark, *Holy Legionary Youth: Fascist Activism in Interwar Romania* (Ithaca: Cornell University Press, 2015).

[53] Mihaela-Simona Apostol, Adriana Anca Cristea and Tatiana Corina Dosescu, "The Tomb of Father Arsenie Boca at Prislop Monastery," *Knowledge Horizons - Dimitrie Cantemir Christian University*, 7:3 (2015): 153.

an abbot and confessor, and the Elevation of the Holy Cross skete (Schitul Înalțarea Sfintei Cruci). This is located at a cemetery on the poor outskirts of Aiud where the remains of political prisoners are said to be anonymously buried. Their remains, now named "relics," are exhibited in the basement of the skete. While conducting an ethnographic study there Monica Grigore met a number of women visiting the ossuary who expressed what she described as a "strange devotion." What appealed to them was less the fact that the remains were victims of communism than their perceived ability to perform miracles. As Grigore points out "history, memory, and religion intermix in Aiud while an active group of actors (guides, priests, journalists, and writers) attempt to popularize the devotion to the 'saints' in order to obtain their canonization."[54]

In fact, such attempts at conjoining religion and the memory of communist repression, tying them into a coherent narrative of national Christian victimhood, is not unique to Romanian Orthodoxy. At Lozhok in Russia, a Gulag camp that operated from 1929 to 1956 became a site of regional pilgrimage where many locals and visitors came to consider the natural spring of Iskitim as holy.[55] This is not to say that religious believers are indifferent to the main goals of transitional justice (reconciliation and truth-telling). In a cross-regional comparative study, Daniel Philpott shows that religious actors are likely to make a highly positive impact on the politics of memory, especially when they are independent of the state and willing to espouse a theology of reconciliation.[56] However, as discussed earlier in the chapter, under communism the Romanian Orthodox Church has always been closely connected to the government. Moreover, after 1989 the Church distributed propaganda that emphasized only its *own* repression and victimization, while remaining silent over collaborationism and the involvement of clergy with the Iron Guard before World War II.

The prison saints movement illustrates this pattern well. Christian intellectuals belonging to the Areopag group justify the questionable past of their candidates for sainthood by arguing that those who embraced a religious and spiritual message cannot be considered extremists or

---

[54] Monica Grigore, "The Aiud Prison Saints. History, Memory and Lived Religion," *Eurostudia*, 10:1 (2015), 41.

[55] Jeanmarie Rouhier-Willoughby, "The Gulag Reclaimed as Sacred Space: The Negotiation of Memory at the Holy Spring of Iskitim," *Laboratorium*, 7:1 (2015): 51-70.

[56] Daniel Philpott, "What Religion Brings to the Politics of Transitional Justice," *Journal of International Affairs*, 61:1 (2007): 93-109.

criminals.[57] This apologetic, if that is what it is, parallels the increased popularity of the prison saints' cause since the mid-late 2000s. In contrast, during the 1990s and the early 2000s, the topic was not openly addressed. In fact, according to Vasile in 1999 when representatives of political prisoners, together with the Christian organizations Anastasia and the Orthodox Brotherhood (Frăția Ortodoxă), joined forces to lobby for canonization, the Holy Synod warned them that an apology for the legionary movement is dangerous and could jeopardize any canonization.[58]

However, Patriarch Teoctist was open towards the idea of canonization and suggested Vasile read a 1950 article by theologian Liviu Stan discussing the criteria for canonization.[59] These criteria were as follows: ongoing Orthodox faith until death; strength to endure danger or repression in the name of faith; the ability to perform miracles both during and after life; the preservation of the body after death; and a spontaneous and popular cult for the saint as manifested by believers. This last was crucial, as it would confer popular legitimacy to any act of canonization endorsed by the Church. The increased interest in Stalinist repression, shown in the growing number of public commemorations and wider participation in pilgrimages to sacred sites, seems to illustrate the emergence of a popular cult. Since 1989 non-state actors and the Romanian Orthodox Church appear to have worked together in subtle ways to shape a type of lived religion embedded in a national-Christian historical narrative of victimization.

Conclusion

This analysis of the role of religious representations and practices in the process of remembering the Gulag leads us to several conclusions regarding the interplay between memory, religion and politics in shaping a post-communist historical and national narrative. The three distinctive mnemonic practices presented here – autobiographical accounts, public representations, and the prison saints – seemingly indicate that when both state-and non-state actors embrace a common interpretive framework regarding the history of repression, previous ideologies manifested in non-democratic settings tend to reproduce themselves in the post-communist context. The religious and mystical tone used in the autobiographies and

[57] Grigore, "The Aiud Prison Saints," 45.

[58] Danion Vasile, "Criteriile canonizării sfinților închisorilor," in *Din Temnițe spre Sinaxare*, ed. Justinian Chira (Galați: Egumenița, 2008), 19-25.

[59] Liviu Stan, "Despre canonizarea sfinților în Biserica ortodoxă - noțuni introductive," *Ortodoxia*, 2 (1950).

memoirs of political prisoners published in the early 1990s and the early 2000s has become one of the main focuses of public representations of communist repression. The prevailing dichotomies presented in the individualized accounts of prison experience - good versus evil, Soviet communism versus national suffering, Christian versus non-Christian - have been refined in the work of painters, photographers and curators and subsequently displayed at various sites of memory. At the same time, the self-styled propaganda of resistance and victimization disseminated by the Orthodox Church has further consolidated this version of the past. Finally, the increasing appeal of the prison saints movement and the most recent official recognition of the anti-communist resistance suggest that the myth of suffering under Soviet communism has become the standard or official memory of communism during post-communist times. The almost perfect symbiosis between Christian devotion, patriotism and the rejection of foreign or alien repression resembles the old Romanian myth of historical exceptionalism manufactured well before 1989 and constructed on the basis of ideas characteristic of interwar fascism. Ironically now the post-communist establishment attempts to revitalize these ideas within the unlikely terms of an anti-communist liberal ideology.

Such a political condition inhibits the growth of a more subtle, nuanced and inclusive discussion regarding victims, perpetrators and resistance to oppression. The effort to confine or limit religious persecution to the Orthodox clergy and the experience of repression itself to Christian believers alone, who are then said to represent the majority of Romanians, entirely excludes the memories of other religious, and ethnic, groups from this newly emerging master narrative.

CHAPTER ELEVEN

COMING TO TERMS WITH THE CONTROVERSIAL PAST OF THE ORTHODOX CHURCH

CRISTIAN VASILE

During the twenty-five years that followed the collapse of the communist regime, Romanian historians have written numerous studies in an effort to shed light on the sufferings endured by various religious denominations present in the country, especially the Romanian Orthodox Church, which commands the allegiance of over 80 percent of the population.[1] Most of this growing body of research examined the persecution of religious groups by the communist state, and as such it is safe to say that the Romanian historiography has failed to describe accurately the other facet of the church-state relationship: the Church leaders' cooperation with, submission to, and conformism toward the communist state authorities. After the 1989 Romanian Revolution the leadership of various religious denominations, mainly that of the Orthodox Church, contributed to what I call the "politics of fear" by calling for archival documents and other sources that are either public (stored with the National Archives and the State Secretariat for Religious Denominations) or ecclesiastical (the Holy Synod, that is, the collective leadership of the Orthodox Church) to remain under lock instead of being made available to researchers or members of the general public.

This chapter examines the efforts of post-communist Romanian historiographers to reveal the collaboration of prominent church leaders with the communist political police, the Securitate, and the Communist Party and, in this way, to redress communist-era human rights injustices

[1] This work was supported by a grant of the Romanian National Authority for Scientific Research and Innovation, CNCS – UEFISCDI, project number PN-II-RU-TE-2014-4-2922.

perpetrated especially against Orthodox and Greek Catholic clergy members. The chapter further focuses on the way in which since 1989 historians unaffiliated with religious denominations have contributed to transitional justice efforts to reckon with the controversial past of the Orthodox Church through the rewriting of history books and efforts to enable public access to secret archives relevant to post-World War II church history. The efforts of these historians also revealed the post-communist reticence of church leaders to come to terms with the communist past (1945-1989). This reticence also manifested in their attitude toward the *Final Report* of the Presidential Commission for the Analysis of the Communist Dictatorship in Romania, which was released in late 2006 (for the Commission and its *Final Report*, see below).[2] The Commission's mandate was to identify the institutions and methods that made possible the human rights crimes and abuses of the communist regime, and to document the role communist officials played in supporting and perpetuating that regime.

The *Final Report* included a much-discussed chapter on the relationship between religious denominations and communist authorities. That chapter generated fierce criticism from the Orthodox Church leadership, which alleged that it breached the *sine ira et studio* principle in historical writing. This principle, which translates as "without hate and zealousness," reminds historians to refrain from being carried away by emotion when they write about crimes and war. In response to the *Final Report*, the Holy Synod of the Orthodox Church established a history commission entrusted with the task of defending the church and its clergy, accused by the Presidential Commission of collaborating with the communist authorities. In 2009, church historians published their report, which accused the members of the Presidential Commission of putting together a "dubious historiographical scenario" of church-state collaboration and suggested that those experts were comparable to the heretics of the Middle Ages in their critical views on the Church.[3]

That chapter in the *Final Report* did not avoid controversial topics such as the collaboration of the Orthodox leaders with the Securitate and the Communist Party, which the Orthodox Church has consistently tried to

---

[2] Vladimir Tismaneanu, Dorin Dobrincu, and Cristian Vasile, eds., *Raport final* (Bucharest: Humanitas, 2007).

[3] George-Eugen Enache, Adrian-Nicolae Petcu, Ionuţ-Alexandru Tudorie, and Paul Brusanowski, "Biserica Ortodoxă Română în anii regimului comunist. Observaţii pe marginea capitolului dedicat cultelor din *Raportul final* al Comisiei Prezidenţiale pentru Analiza Dictaturii Comuniste din România," *Studii Teologice*, 2 (2009): 7-104.

downplay after 1989. From this viewpoint, the *Final Report* expressed symbolically a separation of church and state that the Orthodox Church is yet to embrace and challenged the church's official history during communist times, promoted especially under Patriarch Teoctist Arăpaşu (1986-2007) by the church's press, journals, and radio and television programs. This chapter analyzes these aspects in an effort to find out the extent to which the *Final Report* influenced the writing of church history and to assess Orthodox attempts to reform the official church historiography.

Church and state during communism

Let me describe briefly the nature of collaboration between the Orthodox Church and the communist state in order to show that the communist period was characterized by both church repression and church collaboration, and to identify the legacies that have burdened church-state relations during post-communist times.[4]

The Romanian communist laws did not explicitly uphold the separation of the communist state from the majority Orthodox Church. In this respect, Romania differed from Bulgaria, another predominantly Orthodox country in Central and Eastern Europe, where the Constitution and the Law on Religious Denominations of 1949 proclaimed such separation. The Romanian Orthodox Church was only prohibited from having a presence in the schools, but even this prohibition was enacted only in 1952, that is, four years after the Bulgarian communist authorities instituted it. How can one explain the difference between these two countries that were so similar in terms of the nature of their political regime and religious majority? Some scholars have noted that the independence of state from church (and church from state) is a Western idea that historically was not seen as a necessity or even desirable, by the Orthodox Churches of Russia and Eastern Europe, for a number of reasons.[5] As such, by the time predominantly Orthodox countries in the region became communist at the end of World War II, neither the dominant churches nor even the communist state was used to, or appreciated the advantages of, such independence and separation.

---

[4] Cristian Vasile, "The Orthodox Church and the State in Romania: Experiences with Interference and Separation," paper presented at the Churches and State Authority / Violence in Central and Eastern Europe conference, Berlin, 7 December 2012.

[5] Thomas Bremer, ed., *Religion and the Conceptual Boundary in Central and Eastern Europe: Encounters of Faiths* (Basingstoke: Palgrave Macmillan, 2008), 4.

A number of reasons could explain this state of affairs in Romania during early communism, but the most important consideration might have been the fact that the communist authorities refrained from imposing church-state separation because they wanted to avoid weakening the position of Patriarch Justinian Marina, a known pro-communist church figure whom the communists had elevated as leader of the Romanian Orthodox Church in mid-1948, after the death of Patriarch Nicodim.[6] Faced with resistance and opposition from among the clergy, many of whom had declared anti-communist leanings, the communist authorities organized a hostile takeover of the Romanian Orthodox Church that ultimately benefited Justinian to the detriment of other candidates to the patriarchal see. The communist regime seemingly wanted to avoid turning the Orthodox believers left dissatisfied by Marina's win against itself at a time when the regime launched what it saw as key political initiatives such as the nationalization of industry, the collectivization of land, and the suppression of the minority Greek Catholic Church.[7] For these policies to be brought to completion, the regime realized it needed the help, or at least the neutrality, of the dominant Orthodox Church. As in the case of Bulgaria, however, the Romanian communist officials maintained an ambivalent position toward the majority Church. On the one hand, the Orthodox Church was recognized as an important institution that historically contributed to the state-building process. On the other hand, Orthodoxy and other religions were treated with suspicion, especially during the early years of communist rule.[8] Nevertheless, the provisions on church-state relations of both the Constitution of 1952 and the special law of 1948 remained unchanged until the collapse of the communist regime in 1989.

Many of the abuses, harassment, and other acts of aggression perpetrated by the Romanian communist regime against the Orthodox priests had a legal basis. In addition, to a certain extent they were condoned by the

---

[6] For a new perspective on Justinian, see Lucian Turcescu and Lavinia Stan, "Church Collaboration and Resistance under Communism Revisited: The Case of Justinian Marina (1948–1977)," *Eurostudia. Revue Transatlantique de Recherche sur l'Europe*, 10:1 (2015): 75–103.

[7] On collectivization, see Gail Kligman and Katherine Verdery, *Peasants under Siege: The Collectivization of Romanian Agriculture, 1949-1962* (Princeton: Princeton University Press, 2011). On the dismantling of the Greek Catholic Church, see Ioan-Marius Bucur, *Din istoria Bisericii Greco-Catolice Române, 1918-1953* (Cluj: Accent, 2003), 133-262.

[8] Carsten Riis, *Religion, Politics, and Historiography in Bulgaria* (Boulder: Columbia University Press, 2002), 103.

Orthodox leadership, which punished the offending priests with forced dismissal, retirement or suppression even before those priests were persecuted by the communist authorities. The repression was sometimes facilitated by changes in the organizational structures of some important ecclesiastical bodies, including church assemblies, and amendments to the pre-communist legislation that pertained to the life of religious denominations.[9] After 1947, for example, the membership of the Holy Synod was changed to benefit the clergy who supported the communist regime. The following year a number of institutional innovations were introduced. Among them was the appointment of the so-called *împuterniciti*, who were government representatives authorized to maintain contact with the Church at the local level. Their responsibilities made these special delegates for religious affairs akin to the *cadres* or the *commissioners* in the Soviet Union.

Stalin's death in 1953 and the appointment of Nikita Khrushchev led to changes in the way in which the communist regime in the Soviet Union, and also in the Central and Eastern European satellites, related to society more broadly and the faithful more specifically. Probably under Khrushchev's influence by the end of the 1950s the Romanian communist authorities became increasingly preoccupied to curb monasticism in the Orthodox Church, the more so many young people had started to visit various monasteries, thus irritating the communist regime. After some consideration, the total ban was considered unrealistic, being abandoned in favor of a policy of infiltration, subversion, and containment through the use of internal rules imposed by the church leadership. This policy had the final goal of consistently decreasing both the intensity of religious life and the number of monasteries in Romania, and indirectly the number of monks and nuns living in them.

At the same time, another trend was becoming noticeable. Given the fact that it was forbidden to offer religious schooling and religion was no longer a subject in public schools, the Romanian Orthodox Church started to adopt some of the practices embraced by other religious denominations. For instance, after the country turned communist the Romanian Catholics had replaced ecclesiastical schools with Sunday catechism. Nevertheless, these frail attempts at emulating the Catholic example were rapidly discouraged by the state authorities. For the Ministry (later State Secretariat) of Religious Denominations, the government structure that

[9] Central Historical National Archives (ANIC), Fond Preşedinţia Consiliului de Miniştri – Stenograme (1949–1959), File 2/1947, p. 57; ANIC, Fond Direcţia Generală a Poliţiei, File 36/1943, p. 3.

supervised and controlled religious life in Romania, such attempts represented a great danger.

At the end of the 1980s, the Orthodox Church was under strict state control in terms of personnel policy, as well as the appointment, transfer and promotion of clergy members and church leaders. Almost all of these were entirely decided by the religious affairs inspectors (*împuterniciţi*) mentioned above, and the Bucharest-based functionaries of the Religious Denominations Department who supervised the Church at the local level. Nevertheless, since the early days of the communist rule the Romanian Orthodox leaders managed to establish mechanisms for negotiating with the state authorities policies relevant to the church. These mechanisms were quite different in the 1950s and the 1980s because communist persecution of the Church diminished in late communism, thus allowing clergy more leverage in relation to state authorities than during early communism. Such negotiation sometimes also involved open cooperation alliances established by the Orthodox Church leaders with various factions of the Communist Party leadership. The Church further engaged in negotiations with the local delegates of the Religious Denominations Department, and took advantage of the corruption that marred the Department to retain its presence in the life of the believers. At the same time, the Orthodox Church was weakened by its own corruption, by the many clergy who had been tainted by a pro-fascist past, and thus had become prisoners of their own biographies and subjects of possible blackmail. Note that at least some of these tainted clergy were rehabilitated after their release from prisons, where they ended up during the early communist rule as punishment for their fascist past, and were even allowed to join the ecclesiastical diplomacy after the 1960s.

In 1961, the Romanian Orthodox Church became a member of the World Council of Churches, an ecumenical organization that gathered a number of Orthodox churches in communist Europe. This membership allowed the Romanian Orthodox Church to pursue an ecclesiastical diplomacy that often complemented Ceauşescu's maverick foreign policy.[10] This church diplomacy integrated well-known theologians and priests who had been political prisoners during the 1950s. Among them were Fr Dumitru Stăniloae, a respected theologian, and Fr Antonie Plămădeală, who became Metropolitan of Transylvania in 1982.[11] During

[10] Kaisamari Hintikka, *The Romanian Orthodox Church and the World Council of Churches, 1961-1977* (Helsinki: Luther Agricola Society, 2000).

[11] For the biography of Antonie Plămădeală, see Cristina Plămădeală, "The Use and Misuse of the Securitate's Files: The Case of Plamadeala," *Eurostudia*, 10:1 (2015): 125-139.

the late 1970s and the early 1980s, however, some events endangered and threatened the bilateral cooperation between the communist state authorities and the dominant religious group (which also included support for the Soviet-type "struggle for peace" that was less about promoting peace and more about devaluing Western efforts in that regard). A number of priests and monks refused to praise the achievements of the Romanian communist regime, and criticized the urban systematization policy, which was a euphemism for the destruction of many historical monuments, including church buildings, in Bucharest and other major cities across the country. Fr Gheorghe Calciu-Dumitreasa protested against church demolitions in Bucharest, and was imprisoned from 1979 to 1984 as a result.[12] As a consequence, the few theology institutes and Orthodox seminaries still allowed to function in communist Romania were kept under closer scrutiny by the Securitate.[13]

Some important communist leaders played a significant role in the appointment of the leaders of the Ministry of Religious Denominations (which in 1957 changed its name to the Religious Denominations Department and then changed it again in 1990 to the State Secretariat for Religious Denominations), and also of the church leaders and administrators (including those few who had enthusiastically supported the dismantling of the Greek Catholic Church in 1948). Such appointments, however, could not decisively contribute to the complete subordination of the Orthodox Church to the whims of the communist regime. As suggested earlier, more important from this point of view was the changing of the legislative framework governing the relationship between church and state, and the appointment of the *împuterniciţi*, the field cadres of the Ministry.

Prime Minister Petru Groza after World War II and the president of the Romanian communist republic after 1952 linked the church as an institution to the state structures. Groza insisted that he was not a communist, but rather the leader of the tiny pro-Soviet formation, the Front of the Ploughmen (Frontul Plugarilor), and a member of some of the Orthodox Church's top ecclesiastical bodies (the Metropolitan Synod of

[12] Ana Maria Cătănuş, *Vocaţia libertăţii. Forme de disidenţă în România anilor 1970–1980* (Bucharest: Institutul National pentru Studiul Totalitarismului, 2014), 130–143.

[13] "Reţeaua informativă a Securităţii din învăţământul teologic la sfârşitul anilor '70 şi începutul anilor '80," *Arhivele totalitarismului*, XI, 40–41:3–4 (2003): 47–53.

Transylvania and the Church National Congress).[14] Groza was one of the politicians who constantly urged the church to try to identify a *modus vivendi* with the communist regime, rather than openly defy its policies. As the Orthodox Church leadership endeavored to make itself useful to the new communist leaders, it was spared from the brutal repression faced by the Greek Catholic Church, for example.

The Romanian Orthodox Church probably depended on state support to a larger extent than the Russian Orthodox Church, which represented the dominant religious denomination in the former Soviet Union. That was because the Romanian Orthodox Church benefited from the suppression of the sister and rival Greek Catholic Church in December 1948, when as a result it received over 2,000 church buildings, parishes, and monasteries, and welcomed within its ranks over one million believers. This move amounted to a successful but paradoxical proselytism carried out by a self-avowed atheistic regime for the benefit of the majority religion. This is not the only reason for the church's dependence on the state, but perhaps is one of the most significant.

A similar move took place in the Soviet Union two years earlier with the dismantling of the Ukrainian Greek Catholic Church under the pretext of unifying them with the Russian Orthodox Church. I believe, however, that the Romanian Orthodox Church suffered less atheistic aggression for a shorter period of time. In a way, the Romanian Orthodox hierarchs became even more closely tied up with the communist regime after the Greek Catholics were deprived of official recognition and as a result went underground. The communist authorities, therefore, succeeded in binding the Orthodox hierarchy tight to a state whose policies had benefited the majority religion. In addition, historians like Anca Şincan saw the official recognition of the neo-Protestant denominations in 1950 as another way in which the communist authorities were blackmailing the Orthodox Church leaders. However, for the communist political police a more successful way of blackmailing Orthodox clergy was to unveil their pro-fascist political allegiances during pre-communist times. It was only rarely that the Securitate failed to coopt them as its tools.

Before Romania turned communist a significant number of Orthodox clergy supported extreme-right, ultra-nationalist, anti-Semitic, anti-capitalism, and pro-Orthodox political parties such as the Legionary Movement (also known as the Iron Guard) or the National Christian Party (the former National-Christian Defense League). According to the *Final*

[14] Dorin Liviu Bîtfoi, *Petru Groza, ultimul burghez. O biografie* (Bucharest: Compania, 2004).

Report of the International Commission on the Holocaust in Romania, which investigated the country's involvement in the Holocaust: "The Romanian Orthodox Church itself had strong anti-Semitic leanings, both in its senior hierarchy and among local clergy. Miron Cristea, did not speak out against anti-Semitism. On the contrary, he demonized the Jews and called for their departure from Romania."[15] Cristea served as Orthodox Metropolitan of Romania in 1919-1925 and as Patriarch in 1925-1939. [16] Even Teoctist Arăpaşu admitted before his death that he was a sympathizer of the Iron Guard in his youth.[17]

Therefore, it is no surprise that an ideologue of the Legionary Movement such as Nae Ionescu, the charismatic philosophy professor who was recognized as a mentor of the "Young Generation" during the 1930s, was mentioned even after 1989 in official church publications as a positive hero of inter-war Romania. His evocation was uncritical, focusing exclusively on his pedagogical and cultural merits with no mention of his involvement in the Iron Guard. Ionescu fully understood the significance of being an Eastern European and an Orthodox, as *Ziarul Lumina*, the daily published by the Romanian Patriarchal See, claimed in 2011.[18] None of the top leaders of the Romanian Orthodox Church hurried to publicly praise the controversial Ionescu as a model, but the publication of such statements in the official church newspaper suggested that they endorsed this uncritical praise.

The *Final Report* on church collaboration

The Presidential Commission for the Analysis of the Communist Dictatorship in Romania was created in 2006, that is, two years after the International Commission for the Study of the Holocaust in Romania completed its *Final Report*, which denounced Romanian fascism and revealed the country's involvement in the Holocaust. The Presidential Commission has been widely known as the Tismaneanu Commission after its chair, Vladimir Tismaneanu, professor at the University of Maryland,

[15] Tuvia Frilling, Radu Ioanid and Mihail E. Ionescu, eds., *Final Report* (Iasi: Polirom and International Commission on the Holocaust in Romania, 2005), 19.
[16] Lucian N. Leustean, *Orthodoxy and the Cold War Religion and Political Power in Romania, 1947-65* (Basingstoke: Palgrave Macmillan, 2009), 40-44.
[17] Boris Buzilă, *Un patriarh în oglinda vremii sale* (Iasi: Timpul, 2009), 23–24.
[18] Dan Chiţoiu, "Ce trebuie să cauţi la un gânditor ca Nae Ionescu," *Ziarul Lumina*, 3 October 2011, available at: http://ziarullumina.ro/opinii/ce-trebuie-sa-cauti-la-un-ganditor-ca-nae-ionescu. Accessed on 4 March 2013.

College Park.[19] The Presidential Commission was established in April 2006 by President Traian Băsescu to draw up a report documenting the crimes of the 1945-1989 period that would allow the official condemnation of the Romanian communist regime. The Final Report had to focus on the institutions and the methods that allowed the communist regime to retain control over the country and perpetuate itself over more than four decades. It included also a chapter that discussed religious denominations under communist rule.

As mentioned earlier, this particular chapter stirred fierce criticism from the Orthodox Church leadership, which alleged that the *Final Report* breached the *sine ira et studio* principle of historical writing. In response to the chapter, the Holy Synod established a commission of historians with the mission to defend the Orthodox Church and its leaders accused by the Presidential Commission of collaborating with the communist regime. In 2009, the church historians published their counter-report. That document accused the members of the Presidential Commission of displaying Novatian's heresy.[20] The *Final Report* came under heavy attack for two reasons. First, it questioned the traditional definition of national identity, which centered on Orthodox religious identity and Romanian ethnic identity. This definition promoted a national history, including post-World War II church history, in which the victims of the communist regime were essentially Orthodox and ethnic Romanians. Second, it disturbed the Orthodox post-communist relentless campaign to forge a new narrative about church-state relations under the communist regime. This narrative has sought both to exonerate Patriarch Teoctist and the Orthodox Church as an institution of collaboration, and to rewrite the history of the Church as a victim of communist repression.

Key to this historical rewriting has been an insistence on the fate of Romanian monasticism, and especially of the Vladimireşti monastery, which the communist authorities disbanded in 1955-1956. After 1990 at numerous ecclesiastical services and other religious anniversaries a group of former nuns from the Vladimireşti monastery disturbed the meetings by shouting against Patriarch Teoctist, whom they denounced as an "Anti-Christ and communist."[21] These nuns were repeatedly silenced and then

---

[19] Vladimir Tismaneanu, "Democracy and Memory: Romania Confronts Its Communist Past," *The Annals of the American Academy of Political and Social Science*, 616:1 (2008): 166-180.

[20] Enache, Petcu, Tudorie, and Brusanowski, "Biserica Ortodoxă Română în anii regimului comunist," 12.

[21] "Manastirea Recea: Parintele Ioan Iovan," *Lumea credintei*, no. 10, October 2005, available at: http://www.lumeacredintei.com/reviste/lumea-credintei/lumea-

even sued, but they continued to voice their criticism until 2006, the year when the Presidential Commission conducted its research activities.

The *Final Report* tried to understand the origin of these disputes. In the mid-1950s the communist authorities considered the Vladimireşti monastery a center that spread mysticism and gathered so-called "enemies of the people." Such accusations were directed especially against two individuals: Veronica Gurău Barbu, the abbess of the monastery, and monk Fr Ioan Iovan, the monastery's priest confessor. The Securitate accused the two Vladimireşti representatives of offering moral and material support to the anticommunist resistance groups, which had formed at the end of World War II in the hope of toppling the communist regime and reinstalling democracy.[22] As a consequence, in March 1955 Abbess Veronica and Fr Ioan Iovan were arrested. Early the following year the Securitate troops took the monastery by storm and then disbanded it, obliging all nuns to leave. Even before the repression the Holy Synod discouraged any Orthodox support for the monastery by pretending that the Vladimireşti nuns and Fr Iovan had breached Orthodox dogma by engaging in insubordination, erroneous devotion to the Holy Eucharist (*împărtăşanie deasă*), and public confession (*mărturisirea în public*).[23] On 25 January 1955 Fr Iovan dismissed such allegations and sent to Patriarch Justinian a memo in which he confronted the Orthodox leaders and accused them of being coward and obedient to the communist authorities. Fr Iovan also mentioned that vicar Teoctist Arapasu had hindered his devotion to the Holy Eucharist in 1952, when Arapasu was the president of the Orthodox Theological Institute in Bucharest.[24] Iovan's memo was mentioned and also commented on in the *Final Report*.

Immediately after President Basescu officially condemned the communist regime on 18 December 2006, the Holy Synod openly protested against the *Final Report*. It also convinced Fr Iovan, who had reconciled with the Orthodox leaders after his release from the prison during communist times, to write to Tismaneanu in January 2007 in order to provide corrections of some of the Final Report's conclusions regarding the 1950s. Soon afterwards, the Holy Synod's commission of historians

---

credintei-anul-iii-nr-10-27-octombrie-2005/manastirea-recea-parintele-ioan-iovan/. Accessed on 26 March 2016.

[22] Romanian Information Service Archives (ASRI), fond Documentar, file no. 2487, p. 82. See also *Final report*, cit., p. 275.

[23] George Enache, *Ortodoxie şi putere politică în România contemporană* (Bucharest: Nemira, 2005), 586-587.

[24] Archives of the State Secretariat for Religious Denominations (ASSC), fond Justinian Marina, file no. 2; See also *Final report*, cit., p. 276.

used Iovan abjuration to target the work of the Presidential Commission and argue that both the Orthodox clergy who opposed and those who condoned the crimes of the communist regime had served the church as an institution by allowing to survive and remain active under a self-avowed atheistic dictatorship. The Presidential Commission admitted that sources of oral history such as Fr Ioan Iovan's post-communist declarations must be complemented by an analysis of his 1955 memo which accused Orthodox leaders of collaboration with the communist regime. In 2009, the Presidential Commission published Iovan's memo in its entirety.

The moral verification of Orthodox clergy

The historians appointed by the Holy Synod never explained why the Romanian Orthodox Church kept its archives closed even after 1989. In a recent book, historian Şerban Pavelescu suggests that during the past twenty-five years the archives of the Orthodox Church that pertained to the pre-communist and communist periods have remained stuck in a continuous, never-ending reorganization process as a result of which important documents remain inaccessible to researchers, especially to the historians who are independent from the Orthodox Church leadership and unwilling to cover up past church collaboration with the repressive regime.[25] In fact, the reorganization turned out to be just a pretense, as in reality the Holy Synod had made the decision to block access to the archives, but was unwilling to admit it publicly. In 2008, two years after the release of the *Final Report*, the Orthodox Church leadership also succeeded to impede the verification of Orthodox clergy by the National Council for the Study of Securitate Archives. According to Law 187/1999, as the new custodian of the Securitate archives, the Council was to use secret documents and information collected from other sources to ascertain whether specific categories of public officials, including the priests of religious denominations that accept government subsidies for salaries and pensions, had served as secret informers during communist times. The verification process was moral more than practical, as it led to no job loss.

Anca Şincan and other historians stressed the fact that until 1989 the Orthodox Church was under the strict control of the communist authorities in terms of its personnel policy, since the appointment, transfer and promotion of priests were almost entirely decided by the inspectors for

---

[25] Şerban Pavelescu, *Stat şi Biserică în reconstrucţia politică a societăţilor postcomuniste din Balcani. Elemente pentru o sociologie politică a ortodoxiei* (Bucharest: Editura Militară, 2013), 43.

religious affairs (*împuterniciți*), who were special delegates supervising the church at the local level.[26] At the same time, we should not forget that throughout the communist period the Orthodox clergy conducted negotiations with state officials for the benefit of the church. An example of such negotiations is represented by the fact that in 2008, two years after the *Final Report* was released, the Orthodox Church and its supporters decisively influenced the Juridical and Legal Affairs Committee of the Romanian Senate and Chamber of Deputies to exclude priests from the social categories screened by the National Council for the Study of Securitate Archives. To paraphrase Bremer's suggestion that "the role of religion was to change radically" in Central and Eastern Europe after 1989, one could say that in Romania "the role of the Orthodox Church hierarchy changed radically" after the collapse of the communist regime.[27] Its influence over Parliament demonstrates the enormous political clout the Orthodox Church has enjoyed during post-communist times.

Let me briefly present how the Orthodox Church influenced debates in the Romanian Parliament, especially in the Senate. In 2008, the parliamentary committee discussed a number of amendments to Law 187/1999, which governed the activity of the National Council and access to the Securitate secret files for ordinary citizens, historians and journalists. These discussions were in fact conducted in defiance of the *Final Report* and its recommendation to expand access to the archives produced by the communist state agencies, not restrict it further. For example, the law stipulated that every Romanian citizen (as well as every non-governmental organization, mass-media outlet, political party, and public institution) had the right to be informed by the National Council about the past of some individuals. Among those who could be thus screened for their past involvement with the Securitate as officers, collaborators, agents, or informers were the Orthodox Patriarch, metropolitans, bishops, and priests. As mentioned earlier, in 2008 the Senate adopted an amended bill which limited the public's right to access

---

[26] Anca Şincan, "Of Middlemen and Intermediaries: Negotiating the State Church Relationship in Communist Romania. The Formative Years," PhD Thesis (Budapest: Central European University, 2011), 116, and Anca Sincan, "Silencing the Archive – A Methodological Insight into the Research for the Study 'A Day in the Life of an Inspector for Religious Denominatinos'," *Anuarul Institutului de Cercetari Socio-Umane 'Gheorghe Sincai'*, 15 (2012): 144-155.

[27] Thomas Bremer, "Religion and the Conceptual Boundary in Central and Eastern Europe: Introductory Remarks," in Thomas Bremer, ed., *Religion and the Conceptual Boundary in Central and Eastern Europe: Encounters of Faiths* (Basingstoke: Palgrave Macmillan, 2008), p. 2.

files by reducing the scope of the screening of the clergy.[28] It specified that the clergy could be screened exclusively at the request of the leadership of the religious denomination to which they belonged.[29] Somehow predictable, to date the Orthodox Church leadership did not formulate any demand for screening the Holy Synod members or their subordinates. This analysis should not single out the Romanian Orthodox Church, since with a handful of exceptions the leadership bodies of other religious denominations have behaved similarly. In this respect, one could detect some connections with the official narrative regarding church history under communism. I focus on the screening of clergy members because the transitional justice methods carried out by the National Council, and other state agencies, might have put pressure on the Holy Synod and the church historians to review the Orthodox narrative on recent history.

The Greek Catholic issue and the politics of fear

Since the collapse of the communist regime, the Holy Synod and its Orthodox intellectual supporters have showed a constant aversion toward the Greek Catholic Church, which was officially reinstated in December 1989. The Greek Catholic Church, as well as the Orthodox Church, counted within its ranks hundreds of martyrs, both clergy and laymen, who had been persecuted, imprisoned and even killed by the communist regime. However, those Greek Catholic clergymen killed and persecuted by the communist authorities were ignored, for no serious reasons, and not included in *Martyrologium*, a dictionary of martyrs published in 2007 and jointly edited by the Orthodox and the Roman Catholic Churches.[30] This reference volume also represented a response to the *Final Report* in that it countered the report's story of church collaboration with a long list of church victims. The Greek catholic martyrs were probably ommited from the dictionary because their biographies of suffering were contested by the

---

[28] Lucian Turcescu and Lavinia Stan, "The Romanian Orthodox Church and Democratisation: Twenty Years Later," *International Journal for the Study of the Christian Church*, 10:2 (2010): 8.

[29] "Legea nr. 293/2008 pentru aprobarea Ordonantei de urgenta a Guvernului nr. 24/2008 privind accesul la propriul dosar si deconspirarea Securitatii," *Monitorul Oficial*, Part I, 800 (18 November 2008).

[30] Ciprian Câmpineanul, Adrian N. Petcu, Sebastian Ilfoveanul, Corneliu Bârlădeanul, Visarion Răşinăreanul, Toma Rădulescu, Ionel Popescu, Florin Şerbănescu, Ştefan Lupu, Cristinel Fodor, Hermann Pitters, eds., *Martiri pentru Hristos, din România, în perioada regimului comunist* (Bucharest: Editura Institutului Biblic şi Misiune al Bisericii Ortodoxe Române, 2007).

Orthodox leaders, and especially by Patriarch Teoctist. The Greek Catholics accused Teoctist of attempting to convert their bishops to Orthodoxy in the late 1940s.

Greek Catholic historians have even suggested that these tensions with the Orthodox, which regard the interpretation and evaluation of the communist past, are partly responsible for the decision to keep the Holy Synod archives under lock and block any historiographical reform within the Orthodox Church. The archives contain documents regarding the 1948 forced transfer of property from the then disbanded Greek Catholic Church to the Orthodox Church. This transfer has been the object of numerous legal disputes since 1989, as many Greek Catholic parishes have asked the courts to order the return of their ecclesiastical properties. As such, we are perhaps not talking only about the rewriting of church history, but also about matters of political and ecclesiastical importance.

In general, the main political parties of post-communist Romania have supported, mostly for electoral reasons, the proposals coming from the Orthodox Church leadership. It is important to point out that Ion Iliescu, who served as President of post-communist Romania during 1990-1996 and 2000-2004, and Patriarch Teoctist had known each other for many years before 1989. They met during the 1970s in Iasi, where they were dignitaries. Iliescu was the Secretary of the Iasi branch of the Communist Party, whereas Teoctist was the Metropolitan of Moldova.[31] In 1990, Teoctist was able to retain his position as leader of the Romanian Orthodox Church, after various church leaders and members contested his leadership and criticized his collaboration with the communist regime. He returned to office in part with the support of Iliescu, elected as Romania's first post-communist president. Moreover, the interests of the Orthodox hierarchy have coincided with those of the post-communist political elites, both those promoting an anticommunist discourse (Emil Constantinescu and his Democratic Convention of Romania) and those extolling the virtues of the communist regime (Ion Iliescu and his Social Democrats, the successors of the former Communist Party). One such matter where the interests of the church converged with the interests of the political elites was history writing more broadly, and in particular the examination of the archival records pertaining to the recent past. This amounted to the "politics of fear"[32] and a politics of oblivion, the fear generated by an unusable past. Iliescu and his Social Democrats showed no empathy for

---

[31] Florica Dobre, ed., *Membrii CC al PCR 1945–1989. Dicţionar* (Bucharest: Editura Enciclopedică, 2004), 322-323.

[32] Alexandru Gussi, *La Roumanie face à son passé communiste. Mémoires et cultures politiques* (Paris: Editions L'Harmattan, 2011), 60.

the Greek Catholic property restitution cause, and blocked every attempt to return to the Greek Catholics the church buildings that had been confiscated by the communist regime in 1948.

Valeriu Anania's memoirs

The younger generations of Orthodox historians failed to define themselves as an alternative to the official historiographical viewpoint promoted by the Romanian Orthodox Church. Paradoxically, the most visible and significant attempt to challenge the main paradigm of the official church history writing belonged to former Metropolitan of Cluj, Bartolomeu Valeriu Anania, who also took a firm anti-Greek Catholic stand in the property restitution controversy that divided the Orthodox and the Greek Catholic Churches. The paradox arose from his controversial past. During the 1930s Anania joined the Iron Guard, but three decades later he was allowed to leave communist Romania for the United States to pursue an official spiritual and political mission. Anania insisted that he never adhered to the Iron Guard, but rather to the less benign Blood Brotherhoods (*Frăţiile de Cruce*), the youth organization of the Movement. However, his involvement with the Iron Guard is well documented and therefore beyond dispute. His official appointment to a post outside of Romania was curious, given the fact that the communist regime denied visas to former Guard members and former political prisoners, and also allowed very few citizens in general to travel to capitalist countries. Perhaps his mission to the United States had an important political dimension: to undermine the Bishop of the Romanian Orthodox Episcopate in America, Valerian Trifa, another former member of the Iron Guard.[33] In his memoirs, a sort of personal subjective history of the post-World War II Romanian Orthodox Church, Anania broke some historiographical taboos, and breached the rule of silence on sensitive issues pertaining to church life and his own life as well. In his book almost all of the important Orthodox leaders (Patriarch Teoctist included) were portrayed in a rather unfavorable light.[34] The only exception was Patriarch Justinian, Anania's spiritual benefactor. The book stirred fierce debates and controversies. Anania died in 2011, three years after the publication of his memoirs.

---

[33] Gerald J. Bobango, *Religion and Politics: Bishop Valerian Trifa and His Times* (Boulder: Columbia University Press, 1981).
[34] Bartolomeu Valeriu Anania, *Memorii* (Iasi: Polirom, 2008), 665.

The opening of some documents regarding Orthodox leaders, especially Patriarch Teoctist, after 2006 and the publication of Anania's memoires fuelled this "politics of fear." On 5 July 2012 the Holy Synod reacted to these leaks of information by adopting Decision 5944 on access to the Orthodox Church archives. According to the Decision, in order to preserve and honor the memory of the Holy Synod members the demands received by the Romanian Patriarchal See from various institutions and researchers interested in studying the documents regarding the personal life and activity of the Orthodox leaders, documents stored both by the Holy Synod and the archives of the Orthodox bishoprics, had to be reviewed and approved only by the Holy Synod. This meant that the Orthodox bishops lost the right to approve such demands, which they had exercised before the Decision was enforced.[35] It also meant that historians known for maintaining a critical or neutral stance toward the Orthodox Church no longer qualify for access to documents, allowing therefore the church historians a virtual monopoly over the information contained in the archives.

The *Final report*, the Romanian Presidential Commission, the screenings carried out by the National Council, together with other transitional justice initiatives that have negatively affected the reputation of some important Orthodox leaders and clergy members, have determined the radicalization of the church hierarchy, which has adopted increasingly inflexible and polarized views on the need to come to terms with the legacy of communist human rights abuses. To counteract these reckoning efforts, the Orthodox Church created its own history commission, closed its archives even to bona fide Orthodox historians, and applied increased pressure on Parliament for amending some key pieces of legislation.

Public access to (ecclesiastical) archives

Given this context, let me analyze several shortcomings that have plagued Romanian historiography during the past twenty-five years. Since 1989, the archives of the State Secretariat for Religious Denominations have not been opened, so that what are essentially public records and documents could be studied by all researchers without discrimination. Instead, these archives have turned into exclusive spaces reserved for a

[35] Sidonia Bogdan, "De ce se intră atât de greu în arhivele «sfinte» ale Bisericii," *România Liberă*, 4 February 2015, available at:
http://www.romanialibera.ro/special/dezvaluiri/de-ce-se-intra-atat-de-greu-in-arhivele-sfinte-ale-bisericii-366292; accessed on 28 March 2016.

few privileged historians. In addition, under the influence of compromised clergy and theologians the writing of the history of religious denominations in Romania has generally favored one church over the other and has been marred by the lack of critical and unbiased assessment.

From a legal viewpoint, the Romanian Orthodox Church should allow the transfer of its archives, mainly of the Holy Synod Archives, to the National Archives.[36] The 1996 Law on public archives also stipulates that, in certain circumstances, the Orthodox Church is allowed to keep its archives with the approval of the National Archives. Apparently, the Orthodox Church leadership never explicitly asked from the National Archives permission to retain possession of its documents that pertain to the communist and post-communist periods. Given the exceedingly large size of the Holy Synod Archives, and the National Archives' shortage of available space, shelves, and resources, the National Archives leaders have apparently avoided to confront the Holy Synod on this issue. Instead, the National Archives representatives have advised individual researchers to address the Orthodox Church because, legally, the Church had the obligation to ensure free access for historians and other social science experts.

For many historians, access to the Holy Synod Archives is essential when trying to document sensitive topics such as the case of Fr Gheorghe Calciu-Dumitreasa and the forced defrocking of other vocally critical Orthodox priests during communist rimes. Often such defrocking initiated by the church leaders preceded the priest's imprisonment by the state authorities. Since 1989, the Orthodox Church has refused to allow independent historians access the Holy Synod Archives. Furthermore, according to some reports some documents in those Archives were purged or even destroyed immediately after December 1989.[37] Another category of documents apparently met with the same destiny – documents compiled by the Securitate on former monk Daniel Ilie Ciobotea, who became Patriarch Daniel in 2007. Shortly after Ciobotea succeeded Teoctist, the Romanian mass media alleged that the former Securitate had destroyed

---

[36] The Law no. 16/1996 (Law of the National Archives) stipulated that "The documents created in time by the state authorities, public or private economic, social, cultural, military and religious organizations, as well as documents created by individuals are considered to be historical sources and form the National Archive Fund of Romania. These documents are granted special protection from the state, under the conditions of this law."

[37] "Seminarul Teologie si politica, Cheia, 16–18 octombrie 2003," *Revista istorică*, 5–6 (2004): 231–233, and Cristian Vasile, *Biserica Ortodoxă Română în primul deceniu comunist* (Bucharest: Curtea Veche, 2005), 272.

Ciobotea's file on 23 December 1989, during the Romanian Revolution. The press took the lead from a statement made by Mircea Dinescu, then leader of the National Council for the Study of Securitate Archives, who allegedly had access to relevant secret documents.[38] Since the file was lost, it is unclear whether it portrayed Ciobotea as a victim or a collaborator of the communist secret political police.

The State Secretariat for Religious Denominations preserved another important archive, which gathered documents issued by the communist state agency that supervised religious affairs between 1945 and 1989. For more than two decades the State Secretariat Archive was opened to only a handful of privileged researchers with political connections, whose access was approved by the leaders of the State Secretariat. Somewhat paradoxically, there were several positive aspects of such an arbitrary and un-transparent access, since even it created a breakthrough in historiography as the newly published documents contributed to the general advancement of knowledge. In 2006, the members of the Presidential Commission invoked this precedent when they themselves sought access to the State Secretariat Archive in order to write the *Final Report*. They were not met with a refusal. By the time this chapter went to the press part of the State Secretariat Archive had already been transferred to the National Archives, where it was deposited in the archival fond Ministry for Religious Denominations, Division for Documentary Studies. Since 2011, historians can access all of these documents. However, the integrity of the State Secretariat Archive remains under question, as important documents are still missing. For example, in 2006 the experts of the Presidential Commission did not find the personal file of Patriarch Teoctist, although he had served as bishop starting with 1950. Accidentally, the researchers of the Presidential Commission identified another relevant document, *Notes on the Orthodox Bishops*, probably an excerpt of the aforementioned personal file.[39] That document was recently published in Hungarian.[40]

---

[38] "Dinescu vrea audierea patriarhului Daniel la CNSAS," *România Liberă*, 16 October 2007, available at:
http://www.romanialibera.ro/actualitate/eveniment/dinescu-vrea-audierea-patriarhului-daniel-la-cnsas-108799 (accessed on 23 March 2016).

[39] ASSC, fond Departamentul Cultelor, Note privind episcopii, pp. 61–64.

[40] "A Roman Ortodox Egyház és a kommunista rezsim. Új történelmi források nyomában," in *Állam és egyház kapcsolata kelet-közép-Európában 1945 és 1989 Között. Intézmények és módszerek* [The Relationship Between State and Church in Central and Eastern Europe, 1945–1989: Institutions and methods of control] (Budapest: METEM, 2014), 79–93.

The document, an informative note dated 19 April 1962, revealed Teoctist's early pro-communist attitudes (during the 1946-1948 period) and even his alleged support for the Romanian branch of the Soviet International Red Aid. The future patriarch was credited by the communist officials as trustworhy because he supported the suppression of some monasteries situated near villages targeted by communist propaganda. He was further appreciated by the government officials for his stand on the "morbid Orthodox mysticism." Also the document revealed that, with the approval of the communist authorities, Teoctist was invited by the Romanian Radio to speak during the "Peasants' Hour" program both in favor of the Soviet-oriented Peace Movement and the collectivization campaign unleashed in Romania. Somehow the document announces Teoctist's ascent to the leadership of the Orthodox Church. As a result of the church elections organized in 1962, he was promoted from the position of deputy bishop to the post of bishop of Arad (a county located in Western Romania) with the support of the communist authorities. The following year, in 1963, government support helped Teoctist's nomination as bishop of the Romanian Orthodox Church in America (with the see located in Detroit). However, the American authorities refused to grant him the necessary visa. Two decades later, Teoctist became the Romanian Orthodox patriarch.

Conclusion

After 1989 the (symbolic) competition for the position of "national church," the desire to retain the Greek Catholic assets obtained in 1948, and the preservation of a biographical comfort were some of the factors which allowed for a certain continuity in the historiographical narrative regarding the history of the church during communist times. In Stan's opinion, among Central and Eastern European countries Romania followed the middle road of adopting a moderate transitional justice program – more substantive than the programs adopted in most former Soviet republics, but also more modest and less vigorous than the ones in Central Europe.[41] The same observation seems to be valid with respect to the efforts to come to terms with the controversial recent history of the Romanian Orthodox Church. Whereas Bulgaria was confronted by a split of its dominant Orthodox Church (between a canonical Patriarchate

[41] Lavinia Stan, *Transitional Justice in Post-Communist Romania: The Politics of Memory* (New York: Cambridge University Press, 2013), 3.

recognized by other Orthodox sister churches and an alternative Synod[42]), the Romanian Orthodox Church has remained united both as an institution and in regard to the history writing that it officially recognizes. Although the Romanian Orthodox Church leadership severely restricted public access to church archives, today the recent history of the Church can be researched by accessing significant archives other than those controlled by the Church.

As explained earlier, since 2011 an important part of the Archives of the State Secretariat for Religious Denominations has become available for public access at the National Archives. (However, the aforementioned document concerning Patriarch Teoctist apparently remains locked in the State Secretariat Archives.) As a result of this transfer, historians and other researchers can study a wealth of documents that reveal the collaboration of the Orthodox Church with the communist authorities. Public access to the secret files of the former Securitate that document religious life during communism was further granted by the National Council for the Study of Securitate Archives. In 2006, in the context of establishing the Presidential Commission, President Traian Băsescu also ordered the transfer to the National Council of more than one million secret files in view of being opened to the Romanian citizens.[43] Among these files there were many documents regarding clergymen, nuns, and monks who suffered persecution under communist rule. In some cases, the real identity of the informers from within religious denominations can be determined.

Despite being officially contested by the Orthodox Church, the "spirit" of the *Final Report* penetrated both the *History of the Romanians* (Istoria romanilor), a treatise edited by the Romanian Academy,[44] and the important *History of Communism in Romania* (O istorie a comunismului din Romania), an innovative handbook for high schools published in 2008 by the Institute for the Investigation of Communist Crimes in Romania.[45] Nevertheless, the recent history of the Orthodox Church and the

---

[42] Lavinia Stan and Lucian Turcescu, *Church, State, and Democracy in Expanding Europe* (New York: Oxford University Press, 2011), 25.

[43] Stan, *Transitional Justice in Post-Communist Romania*, p. 58. According to other authors this process of files transfer began in 2005. In fact, until now the number of files exceeds 2,000,000.

[44] Cristian Vasile, "Biserica şi regimul comunist (1944-1948)," in Dinu C. Giurescu, and Florin Şperlea, eds., *Istoria românilor*, vol. 9, *România în anii 1940-1947* (Bucharest: Academia Română and Editura Enciclopedică, 2008), 873-907.

[45] Mihai Stamatescu, Raluca Grosescu, Dorin Dobrincu, Andrei Muraru, Liviu Plesa, and Sorin Andreescu, *O istorie a comunismului din România. Manual pentru liceu* (Iasi: Polirom, 2008), 86-87, 108.

collaboration of religious denomination with communist authorities have remained taboo topics for many Romanian historians.

The efforts of the independent researchers to challenge the Church's official history writing have revealed the reluctance of church leaders to come to terms with the recent past. However, one must notice a number of significant historiographical concessions made by the representatives of the Orthodox Church. For instance, the counter-report drafted by the Orthodox Church historians in 2009 admitted for the first time ever that year 1948 marked the *suppression* of the Greek Catholic Church instead of a voluntary *unification* of the Orthodox and Greek Catholic Churches, as official Orthodox documents have asserted all along.[46]

[46] Enache, Petcu, Tudorie, and Brusanowski, "Biserica Ortodoxă Română în anii regimului comunist," 14.

CHAPTER TWELVE

PAIN AND POLITICS IN VICTIM TESTIMONIALS

DELIA POPESCU

The rise of memory studies has prompted an exploration of the political and public process of memory as history. To say that public memory is constructed, forged in the socio-political interaction of competing meanings and structures, has become conventional in the increasingly cross-disciplinary academic literature.[1] As Wertsch notes, "instead of being some sort of steady-made attribute of individuals or groups, collective remembering turns out to involve an array of complex relationships between active agents and the narrative tools they employ."[2] This approach has been useful in identifying memory not as a hermeneutic monolith, but as a contested set of dialectical processes that continue to be unpacked.[3] The idea that we can more accurately speak of memor*ies* rather than Memory has opened the door to considering what the public, state, and private individuals each concomitantly privilege when it comes to ascribing meaning and importance to the past. Moving between these private - public, civic society - state memory tiers results in a rich interaction of aims and opportunities that, at any given time, can allow one version of memory to subdue another.[4] As Pakier and Strath argue, there is a memory war waged over the (claim of) universal validity of one memory

---

[1] James Wertsch, *Voices of Collective Remembering* (Cambridge: Cambridge University Press, 2002), and Cristian Tileaga, "What Is a 'Revolution'? National Commemoration, Collective Memory, and Managing Authenticity in the Representation of a Political Event," *Discourse and Society*, 19:3 (2008): 359-382.

[2] Wertsch, *Voices of Collective Remembering*, 148.

[3] Charles S. Maier, *The Unmasterable Past: History, Holocaust, and German National Identify* (Cambridge, MA: Harvard University Press, 1998), as well as Kevin O'Neall and Alexander L. Hinton, eds., *Genocide: Truth, Memory, and Representation* (Durham, NC: Duke University Press, 2009).

[4] James Johnson, "The Arithmetic of Compassion: Rethinking the Politics of Photography," *British Journal of Political Science*, 31:3 (2000): 621-643.

narrative.[5] The "agents" of memory fight for mnemopolitical hegemony. This now dominant account relies on a political interpretation of what it means to "construct" memory for collective consumption.[6] To understand an attempt to shape public memory is to place it between the push and pull of socio-political forces.

In this context, documentary filmmaking acts as an intervention in a contemporary political world dominated by visual culture.[7] Documentaries seek to speak truth to power and elicit political results.[8] Following this logic of reconciling messages and interpreting aims as political acts, this chapter analyzes *The Memorial of Pain*, a Romanian documentary series that includes dozens of victim testimonies over thousands of hours of footage, to critically assess the practice of documentary-making as an insight into transitional justice efforts. The stated goal of the filmmaker, Lucia Hossu Longin, was to mount investigations and unearth hitherto unseen documents, shed light on injustices by bringing witnesses to the public eye, and "ask for the right to truth" in an effort to ultimately "recover history."[9] The telling subtitle of the series is "A history that is not learnt in school."[10] *The Memorial* is an explicit effort to take on the existing historical account and propose a different dominant mnemopolitical narrative that poses questions of justice and power meant to yield legal results and end impunity. *The Memorial* is construed to live in this

[5] Malgorzata Pakier and Bo Strath, *A European Memory: Contested Histories and Politics of Remembrance* (New York: Bergham Books, 2010).
[6] Tileaga, "What Is a 'Revolution'?"
[7] James Johnson, "The Arithmetic of Compassion: Rethinking the Politics of Photography," *British Journal of Political Science*, 31:3 (2000): 621-643.
[8] Bill Nichols, *Representing Reality: Issues and Concepts in Documentary* (Bloomington, IN: Indiana University Press, 1991); Alison Landsberg, *Prosthetic Memory: The Transformation of American Remembrance in the Age of Mass Culture* (New York: Columbia University Press, 2004); as well as Sara Jones, "Memory on Film: Testimony and Constructions of Authenticity in Documentaries about the German Democratic Republic," *European Journal of Cultural Studies*, 16:2 (2012): 194-210.
[9] Lucia Hossu Longin, *Memorialul Durerii: O istorie care nu se invata la scoala* [*The Memorial of Pain: A History Not Taught in School*]. Book and 10-DVD set. Bucharest: Humanitas, 2007, 421 and 424. With one exception, all references in this text are for the 2007 edition of Hossu Longin's transcript book.
[10] The Romanian verb "*a invata*" means both *to learn* and *to teach*, hence the phrase can be interpreted to mean "A history not learnt in school" or "A history not taught in school," and only context can clarify the meaning. The ambiguous phrasing of the subtitle enhances this double meaning, something that Hossu Longin would have been aware of. All translations from Romanian are my own.

interstitial space between memory and justice, and address them simultaneously: it is both an effort to reconstruct a national narrative of memory, and explicitly aimed at extracting legal redress.

The transitional justice literature has gradually accommodated a broader, less legalistic understanding of the tools involved in reckoning processes.[11] Starting with the reconciliation focus of some truth commissions, transitional justice assessments have incorporated civic society initiatives and other, more informal ways of enlarging the sphere of truth-telling. Documentary film also represents an effort to record, investigate, comment on, and critique the movement of justice. Tyson argues that "cinematic intervention" is part of the discussion about the "politics of memory and forgetting" and often aims at "narrowing the gap of impunity," but can be "antagonistic" and risk victim re-traumatization.[12] Consequently, we should constantly assess the tools and objectives of documentary film in order to judge its political role in justice efforts. This chapter contributes to the critical evaluation of transitional justice as it is reflected by civil society aims and demands through visual representation and witness testimony. Adopting an interpretive approach grounded in critical discourse analysis, I focus on the interaction between the choices, voices, and tools of conveying the message of the documentary, while also considering the background social and political circumstances.[13] The point is to problematize civic interventions and provide a richer picture of civil society within transitional justice debates.

Context and document: *The Memorial of Pain*

The first documentary episode of *The Memorial of Pain* was broadcast on 4 August 1991, only twenty months after the bloody 1989 Romanian

---

[11] Payam Akhavan, "Justice in the Hague, Peace in the Former Yugoslavia? A Commentary on the United Nations Crimes Tribunal," *Human Rights Quarterly*, 20:4 (1998): 737-816; Kieran McEvoy, "Transitional Justice from Below: Towards a Thicker Understanding of Transitional Justice," *Journal of Law and Society*, 22:4 (2007): 489-513; Christine Bell, "Transitional Justice, Interdisciplinarity and the State of the 'Field' or 'Non-field'," *International Journal of Transitional Justice*, 33:1 (2009): 5-27; Catherine Turner, "Delivering Lasting Peace, Democracy, and Human Rights in Transition: The Role of International Law," *International Journal of Transitional Justice*, 2:2 (2008): 126-151.

[12] Adam Tyson, "Genocide Documentary as Intervention," *Journal of Genocide Research*, 17:2 (2015): 194.

[13] I generally draw on the critical discourse analysis framework proposed by Norman Fairclough, *Media Discourse* (London: Edward Arnold, 1995).

Revolution. The series' first iteration reached 120 episodes,[14] but in 2008 the series was rebroadcast and new episodes were added, including the so-called "Black Series" in 2013 (interviews with perpetrators and torturers), and "The Bucharest Memorial" (about the communist demolition project initiated by Nicolae Ceausescu) pushing the episode count to 150.[15] Each episode generally revolves around the participation of particular individuals in anti-communism throughout their lives. The stories narrated in the documentary animate the progression and message of each chapter of anti-communism. The series starts with the "Resistance in the Mountains" (during the 1940s and the 1950s), moves to the early communist efforts to purge the pre-communist regime (show trials, deportations, suppressing cultural and religious practice), and continues to the communist prison system, the brutal Pitesti re-education experiment and the dissident efforts of the 1980s. The array of stories does not include accounts of pre-1940s opposition (either anti-communist or anti-fascist),[16] and relatively little attention is paid the events of the 1989 Revolution, which were the focus of public attention and made the subject of most communism-related trials organized after 1989.

The website of TVR2, the Romanian public television channel that rebroadcast the series in 2008, maintains an episode listing and an introduction which notes: "*The Memorial of Pain* lingered in the collective memory of the Romanian people, and twenty years after the first episodes were broadcast, it is more than a TVR brand; it is a symbol for the fight to keep Romanian memory alive."[17]

When the series reached one hundred episodes, in recognition of its relevance, it was solicited by the Hoover Archives and the Library of Congress in Washington, DC. Parts of the series have received international acclaim, and some episodes have been broadcast on France's TV5 and the French-German channel ARTE.[18] The popularity of the series also led to a distribution effort in Romania in 2007, when several episodes

---

[14] Hossu Longin, *Memorialul Durerii*, 2007.

[15] *Memorialul Durerii*, TVR2, 2013, available at: http://tvr2.tvr.ro/emisiuni/memorialul-durerii_4182.html, accessed on 28 April 2016.

[16] Bucur notes that the omission of early anti-communism fragments the story of anti-communism in counterintuitive ways. Maria Bucur, *Heroes and Victims: Remembering War in Twentieth-Century Romania* (Bloomington, IN: Indiana University Press, 2009).

[17] *Memorialul Durerii*, 2013.

[18] Awards are listed on the inside of the title page, Hossu Longin, *Memorialul Durerii*, 2007, 2.

appeared in a boxed DVD set. That set, which is the focus of this chapter, contains 36 episodes selected out of the first 120 broadcasted and presented on 10 DVDs that are accompanied by a transcript book of the episodes.[19] The selection was done by Hossu Longin and her team, with an eye to creating a "history textbook" by recording in writing "with minimal interventions" the words on the screen.[20] The DVD collection omits the 1989 events altogether.

To punctuate the importance of the collection, each DVD cover (five covers for every two DVDs) displays a note of critical acclaim from prominent political, journalistic, and intellectual figures. The mix of voices reflects a consideration for both the visual craft and the political message. Film critic Eugenia Voda comments that "*The Memorial of Pain* no longer represents a TV series; it first and foremost represents a (moral and political) phenomenon and only then a documentary film," echoing the comments of historian Adrian Cioroianu who calls it an "unprecedented publicistic effort" and writer-dissident Monica Lovinescu's point that it reveals a "rare repertoire of courage." Journalist Dan Goanta urges that the documentary should be mandatory viewing in schools, as Khmer Rouge video documents are in Cambodia, and dissident Flavia Coposu Balcescu calls it "the most illuminating thing in the national conscience" in a decade. Adding to the point, in the published version of the DVD transcripts, the preface is replaced by an open letter from acclaimed Romanian film director Lucian Pintilie, who comments that the "colossal merit" of *The Memorial* was to "uncover the monstrous historical lie" according to which Romania had no anti-communist resistance, and "completely revise this unjust and humiliating image" of Romanian silence and submission. It is "absolutely ravaging," Pintilie adds, "to find out that Romania had one of the most consistent resistance movements in the East."[21]

The assessment and accolades are representative of a substantial part of civil society reactions,[22] especially from dissident circles, but the trajectory

---

[19] Hossu Longin, *Memorialul Durerii*, 2007.

[20] Ibidem, 425. The "interventions" are mostly explanatory notes about gestures or sounds (for example, a note about the person on the screen crying). Since the filmmaker herself did the selection, I take the 36 episodes to be representative of the broader message and intent of the entire series.

[21] Longin, *Memorialul Durerii*, 5.

[22] In dissident as well as literary and cultural circles the series was met with acclaim. Even some critics of Hossu Longin's career trajectory or post-communist political choices acknowledge the merit of the series; see the interview with Gabriel Liiceanu, "Nesansa mea sau a Luciei Hossu Longin a fost ca am cunoscut-

and impact of the series was affected by a significant degree of pushback, primarily from the successor of the Communist Party, the National Salvation Front, later re-baptized the Social Democrat Party. The "fight to keep memory alive" is documented by Hossu Longin's afterword to the book paired with the DVDs.[23] The short piece reads like a journal entry reflecting on the process of making the series and its importance. Hossu Longin's evaluation of political obstacles is relevant because it comments on the early post-revolutionary Romania and because it sets the tone of the documentary and explains its pointed demand for justice. She mentions that governmental institutions like the Ministry of Internal Affairs, the Ministry of Justice, and the State Security Archives offered no support in her investigative endeavors, but that she "relentlessly asked for the right to truth," and three long years later her calls "literally opened the previously locked gates of prisons about which nothing was known before 1991."[24] She entered "unknown territory," and was "fighting against the clock" of old age, demolitions, and governmental interference:

> as it happened at the Galati penitentiary, where the cells of death row inmates were becoming stylish rooms, painted in pastels, outfitted with heaters and "Relaxa" mattresses, and, if in'91 and '92 the torturers still considered explaining their actions, in time, they realized that nobody, no official body, no justice institution would ask them for a "mea culpa," or put them under surveillance, or inconvenience their old years. They had nothing to be afraid of. They could slam the door in our faces.[25]

As this passage suggest, the political context of Romanian post-communist politics presented a particular challenge to transitional justice in that country. Much of that context makes the subject of chapters in this volume. Importantly for the present discussion, the issue of criminalizing the past has been addressed remarkably slowly in Romania. Politically, transitional processes were plagued by the prominent role of old regime loyalists (turned social democrats) in the post-revolutionary government.[26]

---

o ca persoana!" [My Bad Luck or That of Lucia Hossu Longin Was that I knew Her As a Person], *Adevarul*, 6 October 1998. Reception was not as warm in some political corners, and downright hostile in others.

[23] Longin, *Memorialul Durerii*.

[24] Ibidem, 421.

[25] Longin, *Memorialul Durerii*, 421.

[26] Vladimir Tismaneanu, *Stalinism for All Seasons: A Political History of Romanian Communism* (Berkley, CA: University of California Press, 2003); Lavinia Stan, *Transitional Justice in Post-communist Romania: The Politics of Memory* (New York: Cambridge University Press, 2013); as well as Monica

Additionally, the economic downturn and uncertainty that came on the heels of the revolutionary change resulted in a great deal of anxiety about economic survival, and a degree of apathy toward "old" political problems. The 1989 revolution amplified the cleavages within a civil society that continued to suffer from the legacy of "ever depleted reserves of interpersonal trust and social capital."[27] As both Dennis Deletant and Lavinia Stan observe, Romanian social and political life was caught between the experience of the most restrictive Stalinist regime in Eastern Europe, and the reality that Romania had "the highest percentage of Communist Party members among all European communist countries."[28] Beyond the perceived ambiguity of separating Romanian society into victims and perpetrators, the events of 1989 emerged as the main act in need of rhetorical definition (much has been made of the question whether or not it was a revolution or a coup). Over 1,000 people died in 1989,[29] and their public and bloody passing appeared to require justice with an immediacy that the previous forty-five years did not seem to demand.

Adding to the public hesitation to demand official justice was the notion that the government was not to be trusted. The distrust resulted not only from the abuses of the previous regime, but it from the composition of the post-communist political elite, dominated by many who had occupied notable positions in the old regime (including the first post-communist president, Ion Iliescu). The topic of narratively reconstructing the truth (instead of finding those responsible for communist atrocities) took center stage, and resulted in a mnemopolitical competition complicated by the Romanian historical evolution from fascism to communism to revolutionary change. As Lavinia Stan notes, the past was compartmentalized according to political interests and this resulted in the conviction of "some politicians and civil society groups that these pasts were in fact competing for the rather meager resources that the post-communist reform program made available to the working-through-the-past project."[30] The clash of memories was a contest for social, political, and economic capital.

Ciobanu, "Criminalizing the Past and Reconstructing Collective Memory: The Romanian Truth Commission," *Europe-Asia Studies*, 61:2 (2009): 314.

[27] Stan, *Transitional Justice in Post-communist Romania*, 6.

[28] Ibidem, 14. Also Dennis Deletant, "Romania, 1945-1989: Resistance, Protest, and Dissent," in *Revolution and Resistance: Challenges to Communist Rule*, eds. Kevin McDermott and Matthew Stibbe (Oxford: Berg, 2006), 81-100.

[29] Peter Siani-Davies, *The Romanian Revolution of 1989* (Ithaca, NY: Cornell University Press, 2006).

[30] Stan, *Transitional Justice in Post-communist Romania*, 17.

In this context, segments of the ruling elite depicted communism as either the idiosyncratic progeny of its own time and hence to be put behind uncritically, or as a political stance with some essentially respectable ideas tarnished by ill-intentioned practice. As a result, only in 2006 did the president institute a Commission for the Study of the Communist Dictatorship. Overall, in Romania the contribution of civil society in revealing the stories of those who suffered was far greater than the contribution of the state. As Lavinia Stan documents, the civil society initiatives were many, happened earlier, and affected society more deeply. Most Romanians were unaware of significant acts of dissidence, and accounts of these events (such as the expulsion of writer Paul Goma or the miners' strike in the 1970s) were met with great interest.[31]

The Memorial belongs to the early efforts that, very soon after the Revolution, attempted to rescue a vision of the past that included the early years of anti-communist opposition, and demanded justice for communist crimes. The series is focused on the beginning of anti-communism, insists on its very early roots, and privileges a continuity of resistance that does not tip the balance of memory and justice in favor of the 1989 events. The present was hijacked by the recent past, as Hossu Longin argued, and this led to political obstacles. We know now that thousands of classified documents were destroyed in the government building and the Securitate archives. Files disappeared and, later on, records were legally rationed to provide very limited access. Given these challenges, Hossu Longin conceived of the documentary as an effort to recover, before they were lost, proofs of the Romanian gulag, and connect them with the participation of the survivors, many of whom were part of the post-communist elite. The afterword of the book highlights the obstacles she faced, and ties them to the structural corruption affecting the political process. In one account, Hossu Longin is called to the Prosecutor's Office, presumably to offer video evidence, but when she shows ten tapes of testimonies she is "cautioned" (her word) that her interviews are liable to cause heart attacks to Alexandru Nicolschi and Vasile Ciolpan, two prominent Securitate officials and known torturers.[32] After receiving inadequate information, she concludes that the justice system is functionally dependent on the communist lawyers and prosecutors, those ready to obfuscate facts and benefit from the newly gained freedom by building "grandiose legal practices" to defend the tormentors. She also reports public threats by legislators, and requests for the Romanian public

[31] Bucur, *Heroes and Victims*, 224.
[32] Hossu Longin, *Memorialul Durerii*, 422.

TV channel to stop the broadcast. The situation in the Soviet Union in 1991 put additional pressure on Romania's democratization, and Hossu Longin notes the taunting comments she received about her eventual fate if anti-democratic forces succeeded in Russia.[33]

Despite the obstacles, the series was broadcast and well received. Because of its impact and prominence, the series is mentioned by all serious studies on transitional justice in Romania, which recognized it as a major contribution to the creation of a public narrative, although none analyzed it in depth.[34] The documentary offers a unique blend of testimonial and narrative commentary. The narrative provided by the interviewer, Lucia Hossu Longin, edited with the aid of the director and her husband, Valentin Hossu Longin, serves as a type of explanatory frame that often breaks into overt calls for justice directed at the post-communist regime. The interplay between the narrative tone, frame and symbols in this documentary is the focus of this chapter.

Narrative and documentary image

The documentary is staged as a discussion between the interviewer and her main interlocutors, victims of communist prisons and persecution.[35] Testimonies are parceled as distinct episodes focusing on particular people and events. The episode format allows Hossu Longin to create, each time, a finite story-telling universe, with a beginning, middle and an end punctuated by archival material, images, voices, and commentary. The title of the series is first introduced with what sounds like three loud, echoing thuds on a heavy metal door, suggestive of a prison gate or a cell door. The theme music is a classical piece with musical surges and crescendos evocative of emotional turmoil. We know, from the start, that we are in the "concentrationary universe" and the leitmotif is suffering. The subtitle, also displayed on the screen, reads like a motto – "A history we do not learn in school" – and projects the feeling that the audience is about to gain privileged access to concealed knowledge.

The actual interviews are allowed to flow relatively freely, as Hossu Longin asks few questions and mostly allows the interviewee to tell her story. Hossu Longin sometimes asks for clarifications, other times she

---

[33] Ibidem, 423. Jilava is an infamous communist prison.

[34] See Vladimir Tismaneanu, Dorin Dobrincu, and Cristian Vasile, eds. *Comisia Prezidentiala pentru Analiza Dictaturii Comuniste din Romania. Raport Final* (Bucharest: Humanitas, 2007); Bucur, *Heroes and Victims*; as well as Stan, *Transitional Justice in Post-communist Romania.*

[35] I use "victim" to reflect the word-choice and message of the documentary.

asks the interlocutor to comment on feelings, but most of the interpretive work is done "outside" the interview. While the interviewee is allowed to recount events and impressions with little interruption, the rest of the episode engages an impressive array of tools to explain, amplify, and streamline the message. The beginning of most episodes provides a collage of photos, on screen text, and voice-over commentary meant to set the stage for each story the audience is about to see and hear. Documents corroborating the testimonies are interspersed throughout the episode, by way of clarification, sometimes interrupting the flow of the interview. Many testimonies are set against music that changes with the "mood" of the story: romantic music for childhood or generally positive biographical accounts, and sharp, anticipative, or emotionally pitched music for stories of suffering and persecution.

Sound plays an important role in story construction, and the sound mix of the series is remarkably diverse, from church bells, to the sound of wind and running water, to electronic mixes meant to startle or stress specific moments. To amplify the emotional pull, many episodes include theatrical readings of victim journals or poetry, performed by prominent Romanian actors.[36] The theatrical elements create a sense that every effort has been made to summon the images, feeling, and sounds of the past and render a thick description of how "it really was."

Most interviews are shot in the private homes of those who testify, increasing the feeling of descending into a private, inner world, evocative of profound sharing and inner truth. Landsberg argues that this extension of private feeling through the apparent transparency of the film creates a "prosthetic memory" – the feeling that the viewer "takes on a more personal, deeply felt memory of a past event through which he or she did not live." [37] The quiet and mournful atmosphere of testimonials is punctuated by the sharp interference of video documents: photos, images of prisons, dark corridors, piles of files, and archival footage. The intrusion of document and proof reminds the viewer that this is not about an exercise in imagination, but about the very real need to redress these wrongs now by piecing together the chain of evidence. The effort to reconstitute the truth, across both the personal and judicial is carried to its

[36] For example, in the first episode, *The First Partisans* ("Primii Partizani"), actress Leopoldina Balanuta reads the journal of Maria Cenusa, a participant in the mountain resistance; Balanuta also recites a religious passage in the episode "The Trial of Political Elites" (Procesul Elitelor Politice); in "The Demon in the Inkwell" (Demonul din Calimara) and "Collectivization in Vrancea" (Colectivizare in Vrancea), actors Victor Rebengiuc and Claudiu Stanescu both recite poetry.

[37] Landsberg, *Prosthetic Memory*, 2.

logical conclusion by staged reconstitutions: Hossu Longin takes victims to prisons, mines, mental institutions, graveyards, to the forests, fields, and villages where they had been hunted, tortured, and confined, and asks them to retrace their steps.[38] The sense of reliving the experience lends the documentary a type of experiential authenticity, although it was not filmed when the original events happened.[39] To strengthen the evidentiary account, Hossu Longin introduces reports and analysis provided by historians,[40] some of which read directly from the files of those interviewed. To put it all together, she provides bookend commentary, and a couple of interventions throughout each episode, when the "voice of God" of the Narrator is clarifying the movement and meaning of events. Consequently, each episode carefully moves back and forth between the private account of suffering, the historical and documentary context in which that account is embedded, and the message – a call directed at the audience to take note and act.

An analysis: history and memory

Documentary film is an effort to reconstruct reality; it is a "claim to the real"[41] that transforms events into "individual signifiers."[42] The visual reconstruction is subject to constraints that compress and modify reality into the *intention* of reality – the meaning of the lived experience. Documentaries intend to convey meaning as much as (if not more than) the circumstances that made that meaning possible. Bill Nichols argues that "the world, as we see it through a documentary window is heightened, telescoped, dramatized, reconstructed, fetishized, miniaturized, otherwise modified"[43] to serve a particular story or argument. The stories of the best documentaries capture our imagination, while "their own structure remains virtually invisible, their own rhetorical strategies and strategic choices

---

[38] In only one case, the reconstruction of the Pitesti experiment, the staging is done by an actor and with the aid of drawings, to suggest the impossibility of (re)presenting the enormity of what had happened.

[39] Jones, "Memory on Film," 205.

[40] Liviu Taranu, Floria Banu, Claudiu Secasiu, Victor Neumann, Iuliu Cracana, and Dennis Deletant.

[41] Allison J. Levine, *Framing the Nation: Documentary Film in Interwar France* (New York: Continuum, 2010), 8; Alan Renov, *Theorizing Documentary* (New York: Routledge, 1993); as well as Nichols, *Representing Reality*.

[42] Christian Metz, *Film Language: A Semiotics of the Cinema* (New York: Oxford University Press, 1974), 36.

[43] Nichols, *Representing Reality*, 112.

largely unnoticed."[44] The hidden structures that strategically weave together meaning through images, scenarios, reconstructions, accounts, documents, and commentary amount to narrative frames. The overarching arguments are comprised in master frames built through a deliberately crafted interaction between the methods of bringing in information (testimonies, documents, witnesses, experts, and archival footage) and the interpretation provided to contextualize and critique this information. This interplay sets the stage between the "two protagonists: the subject (or actor) and the object (or acted-upon)."[45]

I identify two master frames in *The Memorial*: a narrative of recovering national identity ("national history as Christian martyrdom") and a call for justice ("collective memory requires justice"). The coexistence of these two master frames is not always unproblematic, and to smooth out the hermeneutic path Hossu Longin creates an edifice of proxies: she associates nationalism with national identity with anticommunism and justice, and ultimately with legal action in the present. The past is meant to leap into the present so that the viewer can conceive of a just present as an expiated past. The main narrative frames are further complicated by the presence of multiple voices: of the narrator, experts (historians), the victims, sometimes perpetrators, and witnesses. These voices must be corralled by the "interpreter," corroborated with documents, archival footage, and expert testimony, and finally disciplined into a core diagnostic message. To unpack the process of frame construction, I follow Rothberg's advice and critically consider the documentary as a virtual performance with all its markers (elements like the interlocutors, sites, and language).[46]

Voices and frames

The prominent voices of the series can be subsumed under what I call the Narrator's Voice (primarily Hossu Longin and her avatars: expert narrative, documents, archival footage), and the Teller's Voice (victims, perpetrators, witnesses, and family members). The principal framing voice, that of the Narrator, adds meaning and purpose to the Teller's message. The two voices do not always coexist comfortably. At times, the message of Teller testimony is enhanced by the Narrator's voice, but at

[44] Ibidem, x.

[45] Tzvetan Todorov, *Hope and Memory* (Princeton, NJ: Princeton University Press, 2003).

[46] Michael Rothberg, *Traumatic Realism: The Demand of Holocaust Representation* (Minneapolis: University of Minnesota Press, 2000).

other times the Narrator's frame subdues the Teller's message. For Jones, documentary aims at historical authenticity, but the question is who has the authority to authenticate.[47] The construction of authenticity is a question of power, and victim-witness accounts can be "harnessed" toward a particular frame.

To outline the interplay between voices and the "harnessing" of messages through frames, I identify key themes that can be consistently traced through the series. These themes can be grouped under the two frames mentioned above. The "national history as Christian martyrdom" frame subsumes religion, nationalism, and martyrdom. The second frame, "collective memory requires justice," includes forgiveness, justice, and an indictment of post-communist politics. Each frame integrates the three themes in logical packages that construct one another in a hermeneutic feedback loop.

National history as Christian martyrdom

Religion has a prominent place in the series, through the voices of both Narrator and Teller. Episodes are explicitly dedicated to the communist suppression of religion ("The Tragedy of the Greek-Catholic Church") or the importance of religious ritual as a frame for resistance ("Easter Night in the Lead Mines"). Several testimonies are laced with religious language. The former detainees describe their life in prison and reliance on faith for survival. Those victimized often comment on the saintly character of other detainees, the importance of reading the Bible, and God's protection in those harsh circumstances. In a few striking instances, former detainees thank God for casting them as victim rather than torturer, and giving them the chance to go to prison and understand their faith ("With God in the Catacombs"). Conspicuously, the Narrator voice takes on the mantle of religious language and values in order to reflect the expression of those victimized and create solidarity of authenticity. The religious interpretation permeates biographical detail. Talking about Vasile Motrescu (a peasant leader of the mountain resistance) Hossu Longin comments that his journal discussion of sin and virtue "is reminiscent of the ladder of virtues or the ladder of heaven at Sucevita monastery, with that contrast between the kind order of heaven and the frightening wrath of Hell," and she adds that

[47] Jones, "Memory on Film," 195, and Edward M. Brunner, "Abraham Lincoln as Authentic Reproduction: A Critique of Postmodernism," *American Anthropologist*, 96:2 (1994): 400.

"Motrescu did not escape that diabolical weighing of the soul."[48] Personal descriptions of dissidents also take on religious tones: pastor Wurmbrand is "a living martyr, a true apostle Paul behind the Iron Curtain," writer Mircea Vulcanescu is "a saint leaping from an icon" with "something of Noah in him," and airforce pilot Tudor Greceanu steps into "the aura of glory only in heaven."[49]

In other commentary interventions, religious language is used to aid in the creation of a moral mood. Prison suffering is "hell," and the prison system is a "diabolical" scheme against humanity.[50] In a fragment on collectivization, Hossu Longin comments that "village life is centered on the protecting, loving and strong holy church" and asks whether or not God will stop the evil that oppressed these villagers for decades.[51]

In at least one episode, religious ritual becomes the narrative frame. In the episode "Easter Night in the Lead Mines" the name of the mine where the "politicals" (that is, political prisoners) were convicted to hard work, the "Devil's Mill," is used as the overarching metaphor when presenting the reconstruction of a clandestine Easter night service inside the mine. The mine is a hell ("although," Hossu Longin comments, "Hell itself also exists"[52]) and the service is an anti-hell: a story of resistance and redemption. In moments of "extreme despair" some of the detainees showed that "they can reach exceptional Christian moral values."[53] Their personal faith becomes the reference point of the Narrator's interpretative message. The loaded language elevates the moral profile of victims to martyrs: not just individual victims but willing, tragic sacrifices for the nation.[54]

The audience is invited to connect faith and strength, morality and survival, and godly virtue against hellish criminality. The use of religious

---

[48] Hossu Longin, *Memorialul Durerii*, 24.
[49] Ibidem, 290, 105, and 328, respectively.
[50] Ibidem, 128, 308, 383, as well as 96, 344.
[51] Ibidem, 203.
[52] Ibidem, 221.
[53] Ibidem, 227.
[54] It was suggested that the heavy iconography of the series can be recognized as an extension of Hossu Longin's pre-89 career in TV, when she was responsible for building heroic images of a different sort, for productions such as "Homage from the country to the beloved leader" (about Nicolae Ceausescu), "Heroes of freedom and hope" (about communist heroes), and "Song to Romania" (Cantarea Romaniei; an ode to communist nationalism). See Liiceanu, "Nesansa mea sau a Luciei Hossu Longin a fost ca am cunoscut-o ca persoana!" In other words, the methods she applies to *The Memorial* problematically fall in line with what she learned building communist nationalism.

referents creates a bridge of empathy with victims and viewers. The Narrator is an extension of the victims: the transition between journal readings and narrator commentary is often seamless, and the viewers are unsure whose words they are hearing. The integration presents a cohesive story meant to be told with one "voice," that of the victim – the voice of authentic experience. The unity of language is meant to reflect a unity of authenticity. The victim's experience and the subjective authenticity of the account are extended and objectivized through the Narrator's voice striving to embody, through language, the moral choices of the subject-victim.

The effort to extend the testifier's persona is further reflected in the use of archaisms and regionalisms in the comments related to the mountain (and generally peasant) resistance. Consistently, Hossu Longin makes conspicuous use of the same verbiage employed by the peasants.[55] The regional and archaic language lends the commentary not only the feeling of intimate connection with its subjects, but also a poetic tone that enhances the emotional weight of the remarks. Language choices build into an expressive crescendo that, at times, ends in the reading of poetry passages.[56] The bond between emotion and tradition builds the archetype of the Romanian peasant: a kind and romantic soul guided by faith, emotionally connected to nature, and profoundly patriotic.[57] Poetic language captures the imagination and builds a mental map leading the audience to the nexus between depth of feeling, personal character, and the character of the nation:

> A generation went happy to die because of love of country, love for those persecuted, love for God; in this climate thirsty for freedom and national consciousness were born the heroes of later times. As it was to be proven, the nation, the country needed the pathetic sacrifice of their living beings.[58]

The emerging frame of martyrdom in the service of the nation is punctuated by commentary connecting love of country, faith in God, and

[55] Words like: fiare, grai, milostiv, culcus, pribegie, osanda, urgie, datini.

[56] For examples, see Hossu Longin, *Memorialul Durerii*, transcript pages 90-91, 128, 249, 258-259, 265, 270, and 278.

[57] Throughout the commentary, Hossu Longin connects the character of the Romania peasant with both religion and patriotic feeling; see, for instance, Hossu Longin, *Memorialul Durerii*, 12, 21, 46, 50, and 107.

[58] Ibidem, 44.

sacrifice.[59] The resistance movement is "formed in the luminous atmosphere of Christian moral, in respect for traditions (datini), and the melodious sound of bells."[60] Describing Ion Gavrila Ogoranu, a member of the fascist Iron Guard and a leading resistance figure, Hossu Longin mentions that he received "an exacting education: duty to the country, moral life, and faith in God."[61] The connection between religion and country lends a Christian profile to the story of resistance. Hossu Longin comments on Christian resistance members whose "martyrdom is worthy of the first century," overlapping the history of Christianity with the fight against communism, while simply ignoring many of these people's links with the Iron Guard. The Christian profile ignores other religions present in Romania in an attempt to homogenize the nation, to strengthen one dominant interpretation of history, and to create an opposing (national) narrative to atheist communism. Several testimonies reinforce the predominantly Christian character of the Romanian people, and emphasize the connection between atheism and communism as proof of outside intervention. In a typical comment that defines this frame, one former detainee suggests that the founders of the communist regime were "only foreigners and no Romanians," and as proof, they were willing to sacrifice territory to other countries against the "sacred duty" of the "nationalist sentiment" natural to a "small country surrounded by enemies."[62] Some of the worst atrocities of the regime are put in a foreign context: the "brain of this operation" is not in Romania, says one political detainee about the Pitesti experiment, pointing out its application in Russia[63]; those conducting abusive searches "did not speak Romanian well"[64]; and the background of prison system directors, Securitate agents, and prison torturers is exposed as Russian, Jewish, or Roma.[65]

The communist government in Romania is described as an imposition from Moscow, its agents brought from outside and buttressed by the threat of Russian intervention, despite the fact that by 1953 many pro-Muscovite

---

[59] See, for example, transcript page 47 about the connection between the archetypical Romania peasant and Christianity.
[60] Hossu Longin, *Memorialul Durerii*, 46.
[61] Ibidem, 329.
[62] Ibidem, 86.
[63] Idem.
[64] Ibidem, 94. The torturer Alexandru Nicholski, a Securitate officer, is identified as Russian and recognized by an inmate cited by Hossu Longin because of his "Mongolian cheekbones and the stunted Romanian language he was speaking" (p. 94).
[65] Hossu Longin, *Memorialul Durerii*, 139, 311, 176, 181, as well as 267.

agents were marginalized by the Romanian elements gathered around Gheorghe Gheorghiu-Dej. Communist policy outcomes are portrayed as "events of non-national history"[66] that obscure the "authentic" national past evidenced through the continuous opposition mapped by the series. The effort to connect the dots of resistance moments and chart continuity is meant to underscore the relentless presence of a Romanian imaginary in contrast with foreign communist imposition. The frame of the authentic nation, whose truthful existence is embodied by resistance, is integrated via similes into a larger narrative of history and myth that serves as insight into the profile of the Romanian spirit. For instance, the deaths connected to the mountain resistance are described as a "true Catyn of the Fagarasi mountains," a Securitate action in 1950 is assessed as a "true Tiananmen," the building of the Danube-Black Sea Channel is compared to building the Egyptian pyramids, a Romanian Union movement is dubbed a "true Romania Gdansk," dissident Paul Goma is described as "a Romanian Solzhenitsyn," Vasile Paraschiv as a "Romanian Walesa," and fascist writer Radu Gyr as a "Homer of prison."[67] Albeit unknown, the formative moments of Romanian-ness, forged in opposition, are meant to stand out as historically significant.

Collective memory requires present justice

The series (re)frames Romanian nationhood as an identity of resistance that requires both acknowledging the existence of an authentic Romanian self and the necessity to reclaim its political reality. In other words, if the authentic profile of the nation was suppressed, present politics and society have a "sacred duty" to recover it. In this context, the Narrator's voice is the voice of justice here and now, requiring us to act on behalf of both the nation and the victim. The two are conceived as inseparable because one's profile was built through the other's sacrifices. This interdependence collapses two justice categories: private and public. Hossu Longin

---

[66] Peter Apor, "Master Narratives of Contemporary History in Eastern European National Museums," in Dominique Poulot and Felicity Bodenstein, eds., *Great Narratives of the Past. Traditions and Revisions in National Museums: Conference Proceedings from EuNaMus, European National Museums: Identity Politics, the Uses of the Past and the European Citizen, Paris 29 June – 1 July and 25-26 November 2011*, EuNaMus Report No. 4, Linkoping University Electronic Press, Linkoping, Sweden, 2012), 569-586. Available at:
http://www.ep.liu.se/ecp/078/ecp11078.pdf, accessed on 22 May 2016.

[67] Hossu Longin, *Memorialul Durerii*, 37, 45, 260, 384, 339, 380, as well as 90, respectively.

constructs an account of justice that requires public intervention to render justice to the victims, and ultimately to the nation that they represent. The personal is political here, because personal sacrifice stood in the service of national identity.

The hermeneutic leap to the public duty to recover justice leaves little room for an account of private forgiveness, and builds tension in the narrative fabric. A significant number of testimonials express personal forgiveness: from writer Mircea Vulcanescu's call "Do not avenge us!," to religious calls for forgiveness, to those who express the impossibility of finding relevant punishment.[68] An important anchor for the discourse of transcending (if not forgiving) past deeds is represented by Petre Tutea, a prominent intellectual imprisoned for years in the gulag, and an influential voice after 1989. Interviewed on his hospital bed, Tutea is adamant that accounts of suffering should not be made public because they taint national memory. He connects the idea of moving past communist abuses with the notion of duty toward the mother country:

> LHL: "Do you think that the truth of the prisons should be brought out to light?"
>
> Tutea: "No, for the pride of the Romanian people."
>
> LHL: "But do you think that the torturers represent the Romanian people?"
>
> Tutea: "These events occurred inside the Romanian nation and they reflect on its shine. I don't want to humiliate, by wailing, the Romanian people."
>
> LHL: "And yet, we should, professor, write a history of these four decades of communism (should we not)?"
>
> Tutea: "This can be written in abstract, I don't want to participate to its making, because of my national pride."
>
> LHL: "But your life was there during all those years, a part of your life was there."
>
> Tutea: "Can I say, madam, that I was slapped, can I possibly, I would have to commit suicide if I declare that."
>
> LHL: "There are so many young people, after the revolution, very confused. What would you advise them, professor?"
>
> Tutea: "To stop tormenting their peers, because it's a shameful and a dishonoring act."
>
> LHL: "Do you believe in the future of this country?"
>
> Tutea: "I do. That's why I suffered; Even now if you take me out and shove me to the wall for the Romanian people I will shout 'Excelsior!'"

[68] Ibidem, 105, 184, 295, 299, 317, 373, as well as 88 and 163.

Like Tutea, other interwar intellectual figures express the need for a protective silence meant to preserve the honor of the Romanian people (also suggesting that this *is* about Romanians, not outsiders). For them, rescuing the national image requires putting the ugly past behind. The son of diplomat and political detainee Nicolae Margineanu points out that "he never wanted to share the ugly things, because he said he didn't want to bring, even for a second, an insult to the Romanian people."[69]

But the documentary frame exposes the past, and as such, it is incompatible with the message of silence. Hossu Longin also chooses to strongly echo the voices demanding public denunciation and legal justice.[70] The project of collective testimony requires an arbiter of outcome, and the master frame reflects that choice. The Narrator's voice distills the intention of the documentary into a call for action and puts aside dissonant voices. Hossu Longin points outs, repeatedly, that post-communist Romania is unwilling to deal with the injustices of the past. The stories of communism's victims show the failures of the present as much as those of the past. The vast majority of Hossu Longin's political commentary reflects on the fact that the 1989 Revolution did not bring the "remedy they hoped for," and that "historical injustices have yet to be redressed."[71] While former detainees die in poverty and desperation, their torturers prosper in a country that threatens no punishment for their crimes, propped by a corrupt political power.[72] The tragedy of injustice is "not at all accidental," Hossu Longin argues, because "although we seem to live in freedom and democracy" former Communist Party leaders still hold power, perpetuate crimes and lie about the past, while the true revolutionaries have no chance to lead the new democratic state.[73] The commentary goes as far as mentioning the political party and the new leaders who are to blame for this state of affairs, including President Ion Iliescu and a number of state prosecutors.[74] It also implicates the Orthodox

[69] Ibidem, 102. Corneliu Coposu, former political detainee and post-89 political figure, expresses a similar sentiment. Hossu Longin, *Memorialul Durerii*, 286.

[70] Several voices explicitly demand punishment, and one former detainee specifically says that "however, Christian Tutea is…I will not forgive…not for myself…but for the suffering of innocent others" (327-328).

[71] Hossu Longin, *Memorialul Durerii*, 32, 33, 92, 305.

[72] Ibidem, 128, 333, and 337.

[73] Ibidem, 160, 207, 337, 289, and 218.

[74] Ibidem, 339, 400-403.

Church leadership for being complicit in forced demolitions and pressures on other religious denominations like the Greek Catholic Church.[75]

In Hossu Longin's view, the unwillingness to render justice leads to a stultified historical memory. One Narrator avatar, writer Octavian Paler, remarks that Romanians know nothing of their own resistance, and take no pride in the sacrifice of their countrymen, as if they are "cursed," allowing outsiders to believe that Romanians are "a people of cowards."[76] Although a number of victim statements express personal forgiveness, the message of the series turns that on its head: it is precisely because of these victims, rendered larger than life by their very ability to sacrifice and forgive, that we must pursue vigorous justice. The commentary is framed as an appeal embedded in the argument that a larger issue is at stake: the recovery of national memory. The Narrator's voice is militant, relentless, and focused on connecting past and future in a cycle of injustice that needs to be explicitly and publically stopped.

The memory of history

In a discussion of traumatic realism, Rothberg comments on the importance of representation in history.[77] Traumatic realism, he argues, sheds light on the past and puts through the hermeneutic filter of the present. We recall, reconstruct, and represent the past in terms intelligible to today, and at the same time we shed light on what today means by creating connections with moments in the past. History is constructed and reconstructed – it is represented to an audience, and present understandings of the past are grounded in a "constellation" of elements that make up the time we are in. The construction of history, its memory so to speak, is the object of present interpretations, but also a projection of the past employed to illuminate the present. Documentaries might tell us much about the past, but they also reveal much about the present.

The enormity of some past events presents a problem of representation. Much has been written about attempts to represent the Holocaust and the limitations of communicating such experiences.[78] An important upshot of

[75] Ibidem, 365, and 180. These comments contributed to the aggressive reaction of some prominent religious and political figures of the day.
[76] Ibidem, 42.
[77] Rothberg, *Traumatic Realism*.
[78] Claude Lanzman, *Shoah: An Oral History of the Holocaust* (New York: Pantheon Books, 1985); Lawrence Langer, *Versions of Survival: The Holocaust and the Human Spirit* (Albany: State University of New York Press, 1982); Lawrence Langer, *Holocaust Testimonies: The Ruins of Memory* (New Haven:

this discussion is the observation that documentaries, even those based primarily on testimony, are "a representational medium that is mediated and governed by conventions just as is written work."[79] The superimposed narrator commentary offers an ordering principle for the testimonies, a way to discipline them into a message. The narrator's words are interpretations that assert the interpreter's "authority over the witness."[80] A version of history is actively made "when we speak of the survivor instead of the victim and of martyrdom instead of murder" and "we draw on an arsenal of words" to project "verbal fences."[81] Documentaries participate in the work of understanding the past, but they are problematic as historical record. They are interpretive pieces that reflect on the past, rather than merely reproducing it. The mediation of narrative determines how and what we remember, and elicits a certain type of political response from the viewer who is cast as a vicarious witness.

Much of Hossu Longin's work seeks to bring the present to bear on the past by applying standards of legal justice. She identifies present political problems: the defiant attitude of the ruling elite in dealing with the past, and the ignorance of the Romanian people regarding the history of anti-communist resistance. She tackles these political problems by crafting an indicting and urgent message of action. Those who suffered are dying, as are those who tortured, and much evidence is disappearing. Justice cannot be staged in the absence of victims and perpetrators. Those responsible for the workings of justice, the political leaders, must be taken to task. The documentary unifies past voices into a present political call that delegitimizes those in power and demands redress. Hossu Longin proposes the series as a way to understand the past and a means of building a historical record employed for the purpose of justice.[82] She urges the viewer to put together the documents, reconstitutions, testimonies, expert commentary and draw her same conclusions: that the system is broken and the past swept under the rug. Yet her effort is not historical record inasmuch as it "narrates history" by "imposing structural principles on the

---

Yale University Press, 1991); Tzvetan Todorov, *Facing the Extreme: Moral Life in the Concentrations Camps* (New York: Henry Holt, 1996); as well as Rothberg, *Traumatic Realism.*

[79] Rothberg, *Traumatic Realism*, 118.

[80] Ibidem, 121.

[81] Langer, *Holocaust Testimonies*, 6.

[82] She specifically says that in the end. For a critique of transforming a moral point into a law, see Mark Osiel, *Mass Atrocity, Collective Memory and the Law* (New Brunswick, NJ: Transaction Publishers, 1997).

chaos of historical experience."[83] By proposing an interpretation of present justice as an expression of corruption and willful neglect, *The Memorial* represents a "competitor socializer,"[84] a source of meaning and knowledge meant to subdue other possible narratives: that justice is not needed, that it should take a form different than trials, that there were too many involved to speak of meaningful justice, that forgiveness is more important for moving forward, or that it is better to focus on the future than dwell on the past. While many of these positions are supported by the testimonies she covers, Hossu Longin's choices streamline historical meaning into a frame of legal justice as the sine-qua-non of nationhood and democracy. Demand for a modern understanding of justice leads to an institutional understanding of the requirements of justice that privileges institutional justice over societal reconciliation.[85] The documentary thus participates in the cultural production of one understanding of justice, focused on institutional solutions. While that is not surprising, as it is consistent with transitional justice patterns in the region,[86] it is also not a predetermined choice, especially when judged by the standard of the very testimonials it contains. The commentator virtually never asks the interviewees about what they want, or what they would like to see legally done. The documentary message is inferential: it assumes that logic alone points in the direction of legal justice and treats the testimonies as an integral part of that message.

The question is not whether Hossu Longin is right in proposing legal justice as the measure of redress, but to what extent her attempt at framing that message reduces the voices of her subject testimonies, diminishes their weight, and interpretively affects their message. In other words, the question is to what extent history is subordinated to a particular goal of memory. As Cioroianu aptly points out, history is uncertain, but memory is always certain.[87] The leap between memory and history requires an imposition of collective certainty that sits in an uneasy balance with the plurality of individual memory. The Narrator becomes the moral authority, while dissenting or nuanced messages are left to linger behind a unified

[83] Hayden White, *The Content of the Form: Narrative Discourse and Historical Representation* (Baltimore, MA: Johns Hopkins University Press, 1990), 5.

[84] Michael Shafir, "Memory and History in Postcommunism: Preliminary Theoretical Remarks," *Sfera Politicii*, 120-121-122 (2006), available at: http://www.sferapoliticii.ro/sfera/120-121-122/art21-shafir.html, accessed on 28 April 2016.

[85] Rothberg, *Traumatic Realism.*

[86] Stan, *Transitional Justice in Post-communist Romania.*

[87] Adrian Cioroianu, *Focul ascuns in piatra* (Iasi: Polirom, 2000), 29.

lesson of memory. Furthermore, laying bare the testimony of pain does not necessarily lead to societal outrage and a renewed sense of mobilization for justice. As Hossu Longin confirms, civil society responses were mixed, and even those sympathetic to the project "reproached us the tears."[88] Re-traumatization risks psychological retreat rather than mobilization. Documentary films also open the possibility of prolonging victimhood by exposing it publicly. The "moral witness" may inspire "political mimesis,"[89] but it may also tip the balance of shame and guilt to produce the opposite effect.

This ties into the issue of forgiveness, the subject of an energetic debate in transitional justice. Starting from Arendt's remarks on the political place of forgiveness, current discussions cover the interaction between public and private dimensions of forgiveness.[90] These insights are relevant here because they problematize the extent to which the Narrator can not only speak in the name of victims, but can extend political action and public forgiveness in their stead. The issue is not meant to be settled here, but note that framing voices do more than select messages: they project courses of action that may be privately and individually incompatible in a way that undermines the very goal of justice. Answering the question "Justice for who?" results in strategic choices that privilege some notions of justice over others, some voices over others, and some understandings of the nation over others.

Documentaries also reflect the difficulty of creating a historical record with limited access and partial knowledge. Hossu Longin consistently comments on the difficulties she encountered while putting together the series. As she acknowledges in the afterword of the first edition of the transcript book, she is given access to prisons three years after the documentary started airing. In a telling afterword to the newest edition of

---

[88] Hossu Longin, *Memorialul Durerii*, 2007, 423.

[89] Jane M. Gaines, "Political Mimesis," in *Collecting Visible Evidence*, eds. Jane M. Gaines and Michael Renov (Minneapolis: University of Minnesota Press, 1999), 90.

[90] Hannah Arendt, *The Human Condition* (Chicago: University of Chicago Press, 1958); Martha Minow, *Between Vengeance and Forgiveness: Facing History after Genocide ad Mass Violence* (Boston: Beacon Press, 1998); Amy Gutmann and Dennis Thomson, "The Moral Foundations of Truth Commissions," in *Truth vs. Justice*, eds. Robert Rothberg and Dennis Thompson (Princeton, NJ: Princeton University Press, 2000), 22-44; Todorov, *Hope and Memory*; Charles Griswold, *Forgiveness: A Philosophical Exploration* (New York: Cambridge University Press, 2007); Bas Van Stokkom, Neekle Dorn, and Paul van Togeren, *Public Forgiveness in Post-Conflict Contexts* (Cambridge: Intersentia, 2012).

episode transcripts, she makes reference to a particular situation when she interviewed a deceased detainee's brother, who talked to her with tears in his eyes, later to find out from his file that he was the one who turned his brother in to the secret police.[91] The construction of emotive capital on imperfect information undermines the legitimacy of a claim to justice. That claim has to be constantly assessed and put in the context of what documentaries can assert and achieve.

Perhaps the most important intervention of Hossu Longin's documentary activism is the construction of a version of national myth. As Bucur argues, after the fall of communism in Romania, "the most important debates in politics and culture were about authenticity, rebirth, traditions, and truth that needed to be uttered in order to restore moral order in a Romanian society deeply corrupted by the communist regime."[92] The lack of trust in the political system allowed for a public reorientation toward the "subterranean truths and authentic forms of resistance" expressed by personal accounts. *The Memorial* was an important participant in the creation of counter-myths, "greatly impacted a whole generation of young people," and "fundamentally influenced how victimization and resistance under communism were to be viewed."[93] The documentary achieved this, Bucur continues, "by placing the recollections of the documentary's simple heroes at center stage in this narrative."[94] While the assessment praises the impact of the series, it takes the testimony of "simple heroes" at face value, and underplays the degree to which the production of heroes is a labor of creative construction through which *The Memorial* privileged a certain ethnic and religious version of national myth. The movement between testimony and narrator commentary allows the series to piece together a homogeneous image of the Romanian nation. As shown above, statements were selected and elevated into the narrative metaphors of

[91] Lucian Hossu Longin, *The Memorial of Pain: A History Not Taught in School* (Memorialul Durerii: O istorie care nu se invata la scoala), 2nd ed. (Bucharest: Humanitas, 2013), 7.

[92] Bucur, *Heroes and Victims*, 223. See also Claus Offe, "The Politics of Social Policy in East European Transitions," *Social Research*, 60:4 (1993): 649-684; Andrei Pippidi, *Despre Statui si Morminte: Pentru o Teorie a Istoriei Simbolice* [On Statues and Tombs: Toward a Theory of Symbolic History] (Iasi: Polirom, 2000); Constantin Iordachi and Balázs Trencsényi, "In Search of a Usable Past: The Question of National Identity in Romanian Studies, 1990-2000," *East European Politics and Societies*, 17:3 (2003): 415-453; and Shafir, "Memory and History in Postcommunism."

[93] Bucur, *Heroes and Victims*, 243.

[94] Idem.

stories and episodes. This reveals the uneven power relationship between Narrator and testimony especially in the context of its great impact on the young generation. Nationalism and the effort to "recover" a heroic national image can feed into political disputes and prop marginalization.

Documentaries with great impact do not just reflect on the present by framing the past, they also inform the future by framing the present. The construction of public-collective memory must negotiate the creation of dominant myths and guard against legitimizing a discourse of exclusion. It is in this regard that documentary tools are at their most vulnerable: the emphasis on message, the requirement of an understandable, streamlined aesthetic and narrative frame compels a translation effort that propels one version of memory over another. As Shafir argues, "the search for a "usable past" in transitional societies and the need for myth replacement might well lead into *mis*-replacements."[95] The digital age has brought the sharing of visual accounts to our fingertips, and arguably has democratized the sources of myth creation at the expense of both professional historians and the state. At the same time, the privatization of memory creation has opened the door to interpretive acts and broader competition between authentic memory sources in ways that still need to be explored.

---

[95] Shafir, "Memory and History in Postcommunism."

CONCLUSION

LAVINIA STAN AND LUCIAN TURCESCU

Taking stock of post-communist Romania's trajectory seems appropriate, since the country continues to be largely overlooked by transitional justice experts and practitioners. Whereas numerous studies have focused on the coming to terms with the communist past in Germany, Poland, the former Yugoslavia, and the Baltic states, there are still only a handful of titles that pay explicit and exclusive attention to Romania.[1] In addition, to date there are no other volumes that bring together scholars and decision-makers from inside and outside of Romania; look at both judicial and symbolic reckoning, state and non-state actors, or early and late initiatives; or highlight theoretical and empirical insights that could help us to open new avenues for research or put to rest some long-standing debates. The present volume seeks to address this gap with the help of contributions that draw on the first twenty-five years of post-communist transitional justice experience.

This concluding chapter seeks neither to summarize all the major points made by our expert contributors, nor to offer an evolution, history, chronology or periodization of reckoning efforts in post-communist Romania. Rather the focus here is on the insights that the twelve chapters are able to offer to scholars of transitional justice in Romania and other post-communist and post-dictatorial settings. These insights open new avenues for future research and practice, and show the value of studying not only the countries that position themselves as the leaders of de-communization, but also the countries that have pursued a more cautious, even ambiguous, path. Romania's position relative to transitional justice is comparatively assessed by Horne in Chapter 3, which argues that the country largely mimicked its immediate neighbors, Bulgaria and Albania,

---

[1] Only one of these is published in English. See Lavinia Stan, *Transitional Justice in Romania: The Politics of Memory* (New York: Cambridge University Press, 2013). A number of chapters are scattered in different books dedicated to various transitional justice methods, and a slightly larger number of academic articles have been published to date.

which in turn situate themselves somewhere between the Central European transitional justice leaders and the former Soviet laggards. Horne's empirical data suggests that larger political and geographical phenomena might determine the pace and scope of post-communist reckoning, a point that needs further investigation.

Let us briefly present below four major insights gathered in this volume. They cut across different chapters, being often revealed with the help of different readings of post-communist developments that are informed by different theoretical and methodological frameworks. Note that these are not the only themes that readers can grasp from our volume, since chapters also talk about the discrepancy between official and vernacular reckoning initiatives, the degree to which the religious majority has (not) reckoned with its own past, the competition between the Greek Catholic and the Orthodox Churches for official recognition as victims of communist repression, as well as the timing of transitional justice and its impact on the efficacy of coming to terms with the communist past. A full review of all these themes, and the insights gained from closely looking at them, is beyond the scope of this concluding chapter. The four insights presented below are what we consider to be the most promising from a theoretical and empirical viewpoint.

The power of definitions

Several contributors suggest that the narrow definitions on which some transitional justice analyses rely seriously limit the practical and theoretical impact of these assessments and might even make them unpalatable to members of the public whose memory of communism diverges from the canon. Rather than abandoning the underlying terms and concepts that have been employed to date, our contributors call for greater awareness of definitional limitations and more concerted efforts to consider alternative conceptions. Tileaga, Turcescu and Stan, as well as Cristina Petrescu directly and indirectly address this larger theme in Chapters 1, 2 and 9. This is the first new insight offered by our volume.

The 2006 official condemnation of the communist regime in Romania had a relatively limited impact partly because, as Tileaga tells us in Chapter 1, it was based on a narrow "archival" understanding which ignored alternative forms of memory of the troubled communist past. Similarly, the Final Report released by the Presidential Commission for the Study of the Communist Dictatorship in Romania (the so-called Tismaneanu Commission) proposed a "synthetic and rational account of the history of communism" that aimed at facilitating "the creation of a unified collective memory of communism capable of overriding lay, individual experiences or perspectives," but at the same time relied exclusively on an "archival" framework that understood memory as "storage of information, encoding and retrieval." Tileaga first distinguishes among "archival," "relational" and "psychosocial" conceptions of memory, and then argues that transitional justice experts should consider these three understandings of memory as "complementary, mutually informing, positions" that should be used concomitantly with greater theoretical and practical benefit. An understanding of the ways in which these different conceptions of memory relate to "acts of remembering and forgetting, preservation and loss, expression and repression might help us to appreciate both official (formal) and vernacular (ordinary) mnemonic stances and activities." Employing a combination of understandings allows for a more comprehensive and nuanced reevaluation of the past, in all its complexity.

In Chapter 9, Cristina Petrescu takes Tileaga's theoretical considerations one step further by providing a wealth of examples of vernacular "relational" and "psychosocial" mnemonic stances which have usually been ignored by transitional justice scholars (mostly the historians) who privileged "archival" memory. These stances, which reconstruct everyday life under communism sometimes in great and nuanced detail, do not connect it to the dictatorship, repression, human rights abuses, property requisitions, police surveillance, and the other past wrongs that were invoked by the Tismaneanu Commission when calling for the official condemnation of communism as illegitimate and criminal. Such nostalgic memories may have been brushed aside by official reckoning initiatives because they emphasized continuity with, not resolute break from, the communist regime, the values it promoted, and the society's acquiescence of it. As Petrescu reminds us, in Romania and other former communist countries, "the individuals who never got entangled with the secret police remember to have lived 'perfectly normal lives'." Such nostalgic normalcy of life sits rather awkwardly with official and unofficial efforts to reckon with past human rights abuses, since it recognizes few, if any of them. However, to ignore its existence means to brush aside a significant number of voices and memories and thus to run the risk of presenting a historical narrative with which large segments of the society do not necessarily identify. Central and Eastern European "post-communist nostalgia," Cristina Petrescu posits, is "neither a desire to restore the past, nor an unhealthy denial of communist crimes," but rather "a desire for a fairer world" and "a lament for the loss perceived by the individuals who have faced the [post-1989] transition."

Terms like collaboration and resistance, dissent and consent have been frequently invoked by transitional justice scholars who work on post-communist Europe, but to date surprisingly very little effort has been made to unpack these concepts, define them with some rigor and dispassion, and catalogue empirical cases. Chapter 2 surveys the available literature in search for these elusive definitions. Turcescu and Stan argue that, while a plethora of studies have dealt with the above concepts under Nazism, these very studies found terms like "collaboration" and "resistance" to be increasingly dissatisfactory and proposed their refinement or replacement with other, more nuanced concepts. However, the scholarship on communism, first of all, has tended to ignore the scholarship on resistance and collaboration under Nazism, its passionate disagreements over definitions, and the refinements it proposed. Second, the same scholarship dealing with communism has tended to focus instead on concepts like dissent and consent and the formation of a Central and Eastern European civil society as a result of dissent. However, such forms of opposition and collaboration were representative more of the second half of the communist period, especially after 1970, but ignored the armed resistance often raised against the communist regime during its first decades. Third, Turcescu and Stan also make the point that definitions have been formulated for legal purposes in various legislative pieces generally in the absence of a rigorous scholarship conducted by historians, political scientists, and others. As a result, during post-communist times definitions of resistance and collaboration, dissent and consent have been formulated primarily by history commissions (like the Tismaneanu Commission), transitional justice legislation created by parliaments, and verdicts handed down by the courts. In this sense, these definitions have been imbued with political motivations focused on the post-communist present more than the communist past.

Assessing communism through post-communist lenses

Whether the absence, presence, speed and scope of post-communist transitional justice are rooted in the nature of the communist past, the type of regime change (exit, as Huntington put it), or the "politics of the present" has been a perennial debate during the last three decades.[2] It is

[2] See, among others, Samuel Huntington, *The Third Wave: Democratization in the Late Twentieth Century* (London: University of Oklahoma Press, 1991); Eva Jaskovska and John P. Moran, "Justice or Politics? Criminal, Civil and Political Adjudication in the Newly Independent Baltic States," *Journal of Communist*

generally accepted that the balance of communist and anticommunist forces in state structures after 1989 represents a powerful determinant of the appetence for reckoning, and that post-dictatorial political reality (sometimes disproportionally) impacts transitional justice programs. Nevertheless, both Gussi and Cristina Petrescu show that additional traits of the post-communist present color individual assessments and interpretations of the communist past in more ways than one. They make reference to severe economic hardship, dramatic loss of social status, persistent democratic deficit, long-term institutional inconsistency and major institutional failures, endemic high-level political corruption, dysfunctional rule of law, moral relativism, and a perceived generalized political chaos as constituting post-communist lenses that indirectly improve individual estimates of the communist past and obscure its most severe shortcomings. They therefore suggest new ways in which the present – in the form of satisfaction with the social, political and economic effects of various post-communist institutional reform programs, the quality of the post-dictatorial democracy, and the post-communist economic progress or regress – affects the reconstruction of the past and the selective reading of communist reality. This is the second new insight offered by our volume.

In Chapter 4, Gussi focuses on the effects of some Romanian delayed and incomplete transitional justice programs on (lack of) post-communist democratic legitimacy and (lack of) credibility of the new democratic state born out of revolutionary ashes. In doing so, he also talks about post-communist interpretations of the communist period (1945-1989) and of the Romanian Revolution of December 1989. For him, "without reflecting nostalgia for communism, perceptions of the 1989 Revolution still reflect the public's general attitudes towards the political regime that emerged from it." In particular, negative assessments of the dictatorial past have resulted from "dissatisfaction with the post-communist present and the economic hardships it brought along" more than nostalgia for the communist regime. In Chapter 9, Cristina Petrescu makes a similar argument when she asserts that positive assessments of daily life under the

---

Studies and Transition Politics 22:4 (2006):485-506; John P. Moran, "The Communist Torturers of Eastern Europe: Prosecute and Punish or Forgive and Forget?," *Communist and Post-Communist Studies* 27:1 (1994):95-109; Nadya Nedelsky, "Divergent Responses to a Common Past: Transitional Justice in the Czech Republic and Slovakia," *Theory and Society* 33:1 (2004):65-115; Lavinia Stan, ed., *Transitional Justice in Eastern Europe and the Former Soviet Union: Reckoning with the Communist Past* (London: Routledge, 2009); Helga Welsh, "Dealing with the Communist Past: Central and East European Experiences after 1990," *Europe-Asia Studies* 48:3 (1996):419-428.

communist regime reflect dissatisfaction with post-communist reality and disappointment with a new democratic regime that failed to fulfil its promise of bettering the lives of ordinary citizens. This position underscores, to a certain extent, the reverse of Ana Blandiana's well-made point that "memory helps us understand what is happening to us today," cited in Chapter 4, since it reveals that current reality colors and reconstructs memory of the past in sometimes unexpected ways. A legal, institutional and rhetorical construct, Gussi points out, post-communism has falsely "proclaimed the end of the one-party regime and the beginning of the democratization process." The break between the present and the past was less resolute than this overused term implied. In reality, the Revolution permitted the reproduction of the communist elite, "which many Romanians believed had hijacked the revolutionary discourse and the state itself," and the continuation of some key state institutions, policies, practices, and actors that have undermined the post-communist democracy. Therefore, the Revolution led to a "transition without transition" that re-legitimized the personnel and institutional structures of the *ancien regime* and made the narrow, insufficient transitional justice initiatives they initiated and implemented palatable to the larger population.

Commission of some truth, but no reconciliation

For a number of reasons, truth commissions have been generally overlooked in the post-communist space. The handful of bodies created in Germany, the Baltic republics, the Republic of Moldova, and Romania were mostly academic in focus, heavily reliant on "archival memory," and rather ignored by the general public.[3] Tileaga and Gussi, two independent researchers not connected with the Presidential Commission for the Study of the Communist Dictatorship in Romania, as well as Vasile, the Commission's secretary and co-author of its final report, offer additional insight in Chapters 1, 4, and 11. They explain the reasons why the Presidential Commission was set up by state officials with considerable delay and reluctance, why victims groups insistently called for such a transitional justice institution since the early 1990s, why its mandate and methods of data collection and analysis were rather narrowly conceived, and why this body was ultimately unable to change the way in which key

---

[3] For a fuller discussion, see Lavinia Stan, "Truth Commissions in Post-Communism: The Overlooked Solution?," *Open Political Science Journal*, 2 (2009): 1-13.

state institutions and large segments of the civil society (including prominent victims groups and all of the former victimizers) relate to the recent communist past. This is our volume's third major insight.

Of all contributors, Gussi offers the more extensive and nuanced analysis of the Presidential Commission, its final report, and the resulting official condemnation of the communist regime by President Traian Basescu in December 2006. As an independent scholar not connected with the Commission, Gussi is able to critically evaluate the process, the actors, and the effects in order to contextualize this transitional justice institution and connect it with Romania's broader reckoning trajectory. For him, the Commission, the report and the ensuing condemnation reflected the "defensive anticommunism" of key state officials, "concealed the past, and prevented the state from assuming guilt." It legitimized state institutions only for the briefest moment because "the promises included in the condemnation speech were never fulfilled," and "the emphasis on condemnation obscured the state's need to take responsibility for past crimes and its post-1989 continuity." That was largely because the final report and the condemnation were "designed by anticommunists for the benefit of anticommunists" in view of proclaiming "a radical break with the past that implicitly downplayed the need to assume responsibility" for it, and they echoed the policy of oblivion "by neglecting victims, forgetting state continuity, and ignoring the need for redress." Whereas for the anticommunist civil society groups the condemnation (and the Presidential Commission) constituted the first step toward re-launching reckoning efforts, a point of view insistently put forward by some Commission members after 2006, for the state officials engaged in defensive anticommunism they seemingly represented the end of de-communization. Few of the Commission's recommendations were acknowledged by President Basescu in his official statements, and even fewer were translated into reality after 2006.

The three contributors assess the value of the final report somewhat differently. Tileaga criticizes its reliance on "archival memory," and failure to reflect other narratives about the past proposed by former victimizers and bystanders (which include the on-line commentators analyzed by Cristina Petrescu). Vasile, who was personally involved in drafting the final report, documents its rejection by the majority Romanian Orthodox Church, whose memory of communism draws on cases of resistance and defiance of repression, downplaying instances of collaboration and consent and casting them as a necessary compromise required by the very survival of the Church. As he writes when looking at the report's public reception, "despite being officially contested by the

Orthodox Church, the 'spirit' of the *Final Report* penetrated both the *History of the Romanians* (Istoria românilor), a treatise edited by the Romanian Academy, and the important *History of Communism in Romania* (O istorie a comunismului din România)," a high school textbook published in 2008 by the Institute for the Investigation of Communist Crimes. He nevertheless concedes that "the recent history of the Orthodox Church and the collaboration of religious denomination with communist authorities have remained taboo topics for many Romanian historians," thus admitting that the report's conclusions were not embraced by large segments of the Romanian academia, and were largely ignored by the public.

Gussi, in turn, notes that the textbook reached few Romanian pupils, and the report had only a minimal impact over the state officials and the members of the general public unaffiliated to the intellectual groups from which the Commission members and experts were primarily drawn. For Gussi, it is erroneous to see the final report of the Presidential Commission as the country's "official narrative" on communism because it failed to change the way in which state institutions relate to communism. The report was never fully accepted by the state institutions called to fulfill the promises of the presidential condemnation: the Ministry of Education never introduced as obligatory the textbook on the history of communism, choosing instead to remove the *History of Communism in Romania* (O istorie a comunismului din România) textbook from the curriculum in 2012; the Ministry of Culture never created an official museum of communism; the Ministry of Interior never re-wrote its own history, refused to remove the portrait of a former communist minister notorious for his human rights violations, and repeatedly tried to block independent historians from accessing sensitive collections housed with the National Archives; and the Romanian Presidential Office no longer makes the final report freely available on its website. The final report, hence, had very limited echo within a post-communist state apparatus that exhibited strong continuity with its communist predecessor.

The importance of leadership

The importance of leadership remains largely ignored by transitional justice scholars. In another book, Grodsky notes that political leaders engage in reckoning, or avoid it, depending on the perceived costs and benefits attached to various transitional justice programs.[4] Some legal

[4] Brian Grodsky, *The Costs of Justice: How New Leaders Respond to Previous Rights Abuses* (Notre Dame: University of Notre Dame Press, 2010).

scholars suggested that transitional justice could not be implemented without a sympathetic judiciary, thus pointing to other relevant dimensions of leadership.[5] The present volume suggests additional insights into this neglected, but important topic. In Chapters 1, 4, 5, 6 and 11, Tileaga, Gussi, Grosescu and Fijalkovski, Dragos Petrescu, as well as Vasile talk about the crucial input of state officials in pushing official transitional justice programs forward. In Chapters 7, 8, 10, and 12, Light and Young, Preda, Ciobanu, as well as Popescu identify non-state actors, including individuals and groups working within the post-communist civil society, who facilitate processes of coming to terms with the communist past. Thus, these two sets of chapters provide complementary views on the relevance of leadership. This is the fourth insight offered by the present volume.

In addition to the state officials who were instrumental in setting up the Presidential Commission and the Institute for the Investigation of Communist Crimes (mentioned in the chapters signed by Tileaga, Gussi, and Vasile), Chapters 5 and 6 discuss the role of the judiciary and of the leaders of the National Council for the Study of Securitate Archives in implementing transitional justice programs. There are three main ideas that provide new evidence for the way in which leadership (or lack thereof) matters.

First, Gussi identifies the 2000s as a period of "policy competition" with respect to transitional justice, when an increasingly active and persuasive civil society forced the political elite and some key state institutions to consider an ever increasing number of relevant reckoning policies. Such competition facilitated the opening of the archives of the Securitate and of the Communist Party's Central Committee, the creation of the Institute and of the Presidential Commission, the official condemnation of the communist regime, and several transitional justice bills. President Băsescu made the most radical reckoning gestures because his Democrat allies were, together with the Social Democrats, the most vulnerable to anticommunist challenges as successors to the former Communist Party. He thus became in many ways the country's transitional justice champion. However, the condemnation he delivered in front of the Romanian Parliament "concealed the ambiguities of the Romanian post-communist state structures, political parties, political elites, and even Băsescu himself." As in other post-communist cases documented by

[5] Wojciech Sadurski, *Rights before Courts: A Study of Constitutional Courts in Postcommunist States of Central and Eastern Europe* (Dordrecht: Springer, 2014), 2nd edition.

Grodsky, Nalepa and Welsh, Basescu was a politician concerned more with boosting his own legitimacy, credibility and popularity than with rectifying past wrongs.[6]

Second, in Chapter 5 Grosescu and Fijalkowski emphasize the importance of the judiciary in delivering justice to former victims, punishing former victimizers, and "mediating the conflict between the duty to prosecute severe violations of human rights and the duty to respect the basic principle of non-retroactivity of law." According to them, whether a country's judiciary acts as a facilitator or an impeder of transitional justice programs (prosecutions of former communist decision-makers, cases of property restitution and just compensation) depends mainly on the legal culture shared by the judiciary, more precisely, on the "legal experts' education and approaches to constitutionalism, international human rights law, and international criminal law." In post-communist Romania, a judiciary that included magistrates educated, recruited, and promoted under the communist regime of Nicolae Ceausescu slowed down, and sometimes even completely blocked, transitional justice initiatives. As the two authors note, "the debates concerning crimes against humanity showed that both the judiciary and the legal experts of the Ministry of Justice lacked commitment towards, and awareness of, international law." The domestic legislation was harmonized with the international law with considerable delay and mainly at the prompting of the political elite and the civil society. Prosecutions of communist victimizers have been extremely few, and completed with considerable delay. While today Romania has a new generation of legal scholars who have transnational experience and are sympathetic to court trials for redress, they might already work outside the temporal "window of opportunity" for transitional justice, since most communist-era victims and victimizers are already deceased.

Last, Dragos Petrescu documents the way in which the National Council for the Study of the Securitate Archives (CNSAS) unexpectedly became a leader in the implementation of what he calls "informal lustration" in the form of public exposures of the former secret collaborators of the once feared Securitate. His argument, which merits particular attention for the fact that Petrescu is the head of the National Council and therefore offers a unique perspective on the internal workings of this important Romanian transitional justice institution, shows that the National Council has been

---

6 Grodsky, *The Costs of Justice*; Monika Nalepa, *Skeletons in the Closet. Transitional Justice in Post-Communist Europe* (New York: Cambridge University Press, 2010); Welsh, "Dealing with the Communist Past."

able to navigate a generally adverse political climate and to interpret a restrictive legal framework in innovative ways that partly supplement the lack of a radical lustration program akin to those implemented in Central Europe. Since 2015, the National Council has filed over one hundred legal cases against individuals who acted as former Securitate collaborators, but denied their past. Nevertheless, one should remember that prosecution is sought for these individuals' decision to lie in official statements meant to illuminate their past, not for their communist-era activity and their infringement of fundamental human rights. In addition, the Romanian citizens have the right to find out the real names of those who informed on them before 1989, and this is why the National Council unveils the identity of the informers directly to the victims, who in turn can make these names public. Credit is due to the historians affiliated with the Council, who individually and collectively act as leaders of this "informal lustration" process.

The role of the civil society leaders is documented in Chapters 7, 8, 10, and 12 in addition to the internet comments analyzed in Chapter 9. Light and Young, Preda, Ciobanu, Popescu, and Cristina Petrescu speak about the importance of symbolic reckoning through memorialization (memoryscapes), commemorations, art projects, museums and exhibitions, as well as oral history documentaries. Documentary maker Lucia Hossu-Longin, painters Adrian Ghenie and Radu Bercea, theater director Gianina Carbunariu, movie directors Lucian Pintilie and Nicolae Margineanu, the Orthodox nuns of the Prislop Monastery, writers and former victims Virgil Maxim, Nicole Valery-Grossu, Aspazia Oțel Petrescu and Ioan Ioanid, the community leaders of the urban neighborhoods who called for the removal of communist landscape symbols (statues, monuments, and street names), poet Ana Blandiana, and the Civil Society Foundation have all helped to redefine the communist past in ways that reflect the memory of various social, ethnic, and religious groups. These initiatives have sometimes complemented the efforts of state officials, and other times completely replaced them. More importantly, the five chapters that touch on these themes suggest the great diversity of collected – individual and collective – mnemonic experiences proposed and promoted by the civil society. Different, often completely opposed, interpretations of the past that draw on very selective readings of communist reality have impeded the civil society to speak with one voice when confronting the post-communist political elites.[7]

[7] These findings complement those of David Backer, "Civil Society and Transitional Justice: Possibilities, Patterns, and Prospects," *Journal of Human*

Taken together, these insights suggest that Romania, not long ago considered by many as nothing more than a non-case of transitional justice, represents an important example that merits further consideration. Its layered dictatorial recent pasts, unique exit from communism, and mixed record of transitional justice initiatives have the potential to provide unique insights into some of the most important questions with which transitional justice scholars and practitioners have struggled.

Rights 2:3 (2003): 297-313; and Olivera Simic and Zala Volcic, eds., *Transitional Justice and Civil Society in the Balkans* (New York: Springer, 2013).

BIBLIOGRAPHY

"A Roman Ortodox Egyház és a kommunista rezsim. Új történelmi források nyomában." In *Állam és egyház kapcsolata kelet-közép-Európában 1945 és 1989 Között. Intézmények és módszerek* [The Relationship Between State and Church in Central and Eastern Europe, 1945–1989: Institutions and methods of control], 79–93. Budapest: METEM, 2014.

Act No 451/1991 in Czechoslovakia, cited in Pavel Zacek, "Lustration Laws in the Czech Republic. The application of Act No 451/1991 Coll. and Act No 279/1992 Coll.," no date, available at: http://etickakomisecr.cz/data/pdf/clanky/zacek-lustrace.pdf accessed on October 30, 2016.

"Act Regarding the Records of the State Security Service of the former German Democratic Republic of December 20, 1991 (Stasi Records Act)," Berlin, 2013, available at: http://www.bstu.bund.de/DE/BundesbeauftragterUndBehoerde/Rechtsgrundlagen/StUG/StUG_englisch/StUG_englisch_pdf.pdf?__blob=publicationFile accessed on October 30, 2016.

Adorno, Theodor. "What Does Coming to Terms with the Past Mean?" In *Bitburg in moral and political perspective*, edited by Geoffrey Hartman, trans. T. Bahti and G. Hartman. 114-129. Bloomington, IN: Indiana University Press, 1986.

Akhavan, Payam. "Justice in the Hague, Peace in the Former Yugoslavia? A Commentary on the United Nations Crimes Tribunal." *Human Rights Quarterly* 20:4 (1998): 737-816.

"Albanian High Court Annuls Lustration Law." *BalkanInsight*, February 2, 2010.

Albu, Mihai. *Informatorul: studiu asupra colaborării cu Securitatea*. Iaşi: Polirom, 2008.

Alderman, Derek H. "Memory and Place: Geographies of a Critical Relationship." *Social and Cultural Geographies* 5:3 (2004): 347-355.

"Aliments." *Martor. The Museum of the Romanian Peasant Anthropology Review* 7 (2002): 20-22.

Anania, Bartolomeu Valeriu. *Memorii*. Iasi: Polirom, 2008.

Ancel, Jean. *The History of Holocaust in Romania*. Jerusalem: Lincoln University of Nebraska Press and Yad Vashem, 2011.

Anderson, Benedict. *Imagined Communities: Reflections on the Origin and Spread of Nationalism*, 2nd edition. London: Verso, 2006.

Andreescu, Gabriel. *Carturari, opozanti si documente: Manipularea Arhivelor Securitatii*. Iasi: Polirom, 2013.

Andrews, Molly. *Shaping History: Narratives of Political Change*. Cambridge: Cambridge University Press, 2007.

Apor, Peter. "Master Narratives of Contemporary History in Eastern European National Museums." In *Great Narratives of the Past. Traditions and Revisions in National Museums: Conference Proceedings from EuNaMus, European National Museums: Identity Politics, the Uses of the Past and the European Citizen, Paris 29 June – 1 July and 25-26 November 2011*, edited by Dominique Poulot and Felicity Bodenstein. Linkoping: Linkoping University Electronic Press, 2012, 569-586. Accessed May 22, 2016. http://www.ep.liu.se/ecp/078/ecp11078.pdf.

Apostol, Mihaela-Simona, Adriana Anca Cristea and Tatiana Corina Dosescu. "The Tomb of Father Arsenie Boca at Prislop Monastery." *Knowledge Horizons - Dimitrie Cantemir Christian University* 7:3 (2015): 151-153.

Arendt, Hannah. *The Human Condition*. Chicago: University of Chicago Press, 1958.

Argenbright, Robert. "Remaking Moscow: New Places, New Selves." *The Geographical Review* 89:1 (1999): 1-22.

"Armistice Agreement between the German High Command of the Armed Forces and the French Plenipotentiaries, Compiagne, June 22, 1940," Lillian Goldman Law Library, Yale Law School, 2008, available at: http://avalon.law.yale.edu/wwii/frgearm.asp, accessed October 29, 2016.

"Asociația Rost." 2016. Accessed April 28, 2016. http://www.rostonline.ro/asociatia-rost/.

Assman, Aleida and Linda Short, eds. *Memory and Political Change*. New York: Palgrave Macmillan, 2012.

Assman, Jan and John Czaplicka. "Collective Memory and Cultural Identity." *New German Critique* 65:1-2 (1995): 125-133.

Atencio, Rebecca and Nancy Gates-Madsen. "Art and Transitional Justice." In *Encyclopedia of Transitional Justice*, edited by Lavinia Stan and Nadya Nedelsky. 1:117-123. New York: Cambridge University Press, 2013.

Austin, Robert. "Albania." In *Encyclopedia of Transitional Justice*, edited by Lavinia Stan and Nadya Nedelsky. 2:7-14. New York: Cambridge University Press, 2013.

Austin, Robert and Jonathan Ellison. "Post-Communist Transitional Justice in Albania." *East European Politics and Societies* 22:2 (2008): 373-401.

Azaryahu, Maoz. "The Power of Commemorative Street Names." *Environment and Planning D: Society and Space* 14:3 (1996): 311-330.

Bădica, Simina. "The Black Hole Paradigm: Exhibiting Communism in Post-Communist Romania." In *History of Communism in Europe: Volume 1 Politics of Memory in Post-Communist Europe*. 83-101. Bucharest: Zeta Books, 2010.

Bahun, Sanja. "Transitional Justice and the Arts: Reflections on the Field." In *Theorizing Transitional Justice*, edited by Claudio Corradetti, Nir Eisikovits and Jack Volpe Rotondi. 153-166. London: Routledge, 2015.

Băieșu, Ion. *Balanța*. Bucharest: Minerva, 1985.

Backer, David. "Civil Society and Transitional Justice: Possibilities, Patterns, and Prospects," *Journal of Human Rights* 2:3 (2003): 297-313.

Bălan, Ion. *Regimul Concentraționar din România: 1945-1964*. Bucharest: Civic Academy Foundation, 2000.

Barsalou, Judy and Victoria Baxter. *The Urge to Remember: The Role of Memorials in Social Reconstruction and Transitional Justice*. Washington DC: United States Institute of Peace, 2007). Accessed October 3, 2013. http://www.usip.org/publications/the-urge-remember-the-role-of-memorials-in-social-reconstruction-and-transitional.

Bartlett, Frederic. *Remembering: A Study in Experimental and Social Psychology*. Cambridge: Cambridge University Press, 1932/1995.

Bell, Christine. "Transitional Justice, Interdisciplinarity and the State of the 'Field' or 'Non-field'." *International Journal of Transitional Justice* 33:1 (2009): 5-27.

Bell, James. "Redefining National Identity in Uzbekistan: Symbolic Tensions in Tashkent's Official Public Landscape." *Ecumene* 6:2 (1999): 183-213.

Bell, John. *French Legal Cultures*. London: Butterworths, 2001.

Bell, Vikki. "Contemporary Art and Transitional Justice in Northern Ireland: The Consolation of Form." *Journal of Visual Culture* 10:3 (2011): 324-353.

Bell, Viki and Mario Di Paolantonio. "The Haunted Nomos: Activists-Artists and the (Im)Possible Politics of Memory in Transitional Argentina." *Cultural Politics* 5:2 (2009): 149-178.

Bercea, Radu and Nicolae Ianaş. *Deportaţi via Dolorosa Bărăgan, 18 iunie 1951*. Drobeta Turnu Severin: Profin, 2010.

Berindei, Mihnea, Adriana Colombes and Anne Planche. *Roumanie: le livre blanc. La réalité d'un mouvement néocommuniste*. Paris: La Découverte, 1990.

Beşliu, Raluca. "Communist Nostalgia in Romania." Opendemocracy.net. April 13, 2014. Accessed July 10, 2016. https://www.opendemocracy.net/can-europe-make-it/raluca-besliu/communist-nostalgia-in-romania.

Bickford, Louis. "Memoryscapes." In *The Art of Truth-Telling about Authoritarian Rule*, edited by Ksenija Bilbija, Jo Ellen Fair, Cynthia Milton, and Leigh Payne. 96-102. Madison: University of Wisconsin Press, 2005.

Billig, Michael. *Freudian Repression*. Cambridge: Cambridge University Press, 1999.

—. "Discursive, Rhetorical and Ideological Messages." In *The Message of Social Psychology*, edited by Craig McGarty and S. Alexander Haslam. 210-221. Oxford: Blackwell, 1997.

—. *Arguing and Thinking: A Rhetorical Approach to Social Psychology*, 2nd ed. Cambridge: Cambridge University Press, 1996.

—. *Banal Nationalism*. London: Sage, 1995.

Billig, Michael, Susan Condor, Derek Edwards, Mike Gane, David Middleton and Alan Radley. *Ideological Dilemmas: A Social Psychology of Everyday Thinking*. London: Sage, 1988.

Bisschoff, Lizelle and Stephanie Van der Peer. eds. *Art and Trauma in Africa: Representations of Reconciliation in Music, Visual Arts, Literature and Film*. London: I.B. Tauris, 2013.

Bîtfoi, Dorin Liviu. *Petru Groza, ultimul burghez. O biografie*. Bucharest: Compania, 2004.

Bjoja, Octav. Intervention at Scoala Memoriei, Sighet, July 2013. Document with Alexandru Gussi.

Bobango, Gerald J. *Religion and Politics: Bishop Valerian Trifa and His Times*. Boulder: Columbia University Press, 1981.

Bobek, Michal. "Judicial Transformations in Post-Communist Societies: A Study in Institutions, Administration and Interpretation." *CAS Working Paper Series* 4. 2011. Accessed May 10, 2016. http://www.cas.bg/uploads/files/Shaken%20Order/M.%20Bobek.pdf.

Bodnar, John. "Public Memory in an American City: Commemoration in Cleveland." In *Commemorations: The Politics of National Identity*, edited by John R. Gillis. 74-89. Princeton: Princeton University Press, 1994.

—. *Remaking America: Public Memory, Commemoration, and Patriotism in the Twentieth Century*. Princeton: Princeton University Press, 1992.

Bogdan, Sidonia. "De ce se intră atât de greu în arhivele «sfinte» ale Bisericii." *România Liberă*, February 4, 2015. Accessed March 28, 2016. http://www.romanialibera.ro/special/dezvaluiri/de-ce-se-intra-atat-de-greu-in-arhivele-sfinte-ale-bisericii-366292.

Boldur-Lățescu, Gheorghe and Filip-Lucian Iorga. *Genocidul Comunist în România: Reeducarea prin Tortură*. Bucharest: Albatros, 2003.

Bordeianu, Dumitru Radu. *Mărturisiri din Mlaştina disperării*. Bucharest: Scara, 2001.

Borneman, John. *Settling Accounts. Violence, Justice and Accountability in Postsocialist Europe*. Princeton: Princeton University Press, 1997.

Boym, Svetlana. *The Future of Nostalgia*. New York: Basic Books, 2001.

Bremer, Thomas. ed. *Religion and the Conceptual Boundary in Central and Eastern Europe: Encounters of Faiths*. Basingstoke: Palgrave Macmillan, 2008.

Brems, Eva. "Transitional Justice in the Case Law of the European Court of Human Rights." *The International Journal of Transitional Justice* 5:2 (2011): 282-303.

Brockmeier, Jens. "After the Archive: Remapping Memory." *Culture & Psychology* 16:1 (2010): 5-35.

Broudholm, Thomas and Thomas Cushman. "Introduction: the Religious in Responses to Mass Atrocity." In *The Religious in Responses to Mass Atrocity: Interdisciplinary Perspectives*, edited by Thomas Broudholm and Thomas Cushman. 1-20. Cambridge: Cambridge University Press, 2009.

Brown, Steven D. "Two Minutes of Silence: Social Technologies of Public Commemoration." *Theory & Psychology* 22:2 (2012): 234-252.

Brown, Steven D. "The Quotation Marks Have a Certain Importance: Prospects for a 'Memory Studies'." *Memory Studies* 1:3 (2008): 261-271.

Brown, Steven D. and Paula Reavey. *Vital Memory and Affect: Living with a Difficult Past*. London: Routledge, 2015.

Brown, Steven D. and Paula Reavey. "Experience and Memory." In *Research Methods for Memory Studies*, edited by Emily Keightley and Michael Pickering. 45-59. Edinburgh: Edinburgh University Press, 2013.

Bruner, Jerome S. *Actual Minds, Possible Worlds*. Cambridge, MA: Harvard University Press, 1986.

Brunner, Edward M. "Abraham Lincoln as Authentic Reproduction: A Critique of Postmodernism." *American Anthropologist* 96:2 (1994): 397-415.

Buchet, Constantin and Cristian Troncotă, "Colaborator," in *Romania 1945-1989. Enciclopedia Regimului Comunist: Represiunea*, ed. Octavian Roske (Bucharest: Institutul National pentru Studiul Totalitarismului, 2011), vol. 1: 335-336.

Bucur, Ioan-Marius. *Din istoria Bisericii Greco-Catolice Române, 1918-1953*. Cluj: Accent, 2003.

Bucur, Maria. *Heroes and Victims: Remembering War in Twentieth-Century Romania*. Bloomington, IN: Indiana University Press, 2009.

—. "Gendering Dissent: Of Bodies and Minds, Survival and Opposition under Communism," *Oxford Slavonic Papers* 7 (2008): 9-26.

Buikema, Rosemarie. "Performing Dialogical Truth and Transitional Justice: The Role of Art in the Becoming Post-Apartheid of South Africa," *Memory Studies* 5:3 (2012): 282-292.

"Bulgaria: Constitutional Court Decision on the Panev Law, Constitutional Court Case No. 32, Decision No. 1 (February 11, 1993)." In *Transitional Justice*: *How Emerging Democracies Reckon with Former Regimes*, edited by Neil Kritz. 300-302. Washington, DC: United States Institute of Peace Studies, 1995.

"Bulgaria: Law for Temporary Introduction of Some Additional Requirements for the Members of the Executive Bodies of Scientific Organizations and the Higher Certifying Commission ("Panev Law") December 9, 1992." In *Transitional Justice*: *How Emerging Democracies Reckon with Former Regimes*, edited by Neil Kritz. 296-299. Washington, DC: United States Institute of Peace Studies, 1995.

"Bulgaria: Law on Banks and Credit Activity, No. 25 of March 18, 1992." In *Transitional Justice*: *How Emerging Democracies Reckon with Former Regimes*, edited by Neil Kritz. 3: 293. Washington, DC: United States Institute of Peace Studies, 1995.

Bulgarian Dossier Commission. "The Curtain Is Raised." 2010. Accessed August 26, 2016. http://www.comdos.bg/p/language/en/.

Bulgarian Dossier Commission website. Accessed May 2, 2014. http://www.comdos.bg/.

Bulgarian Parliamentary Debates. Accessed March 26, 2013. http://www.parliament.bg/pub/StenD/2012121210500530031990_4.pdf.

Bulgarian Registrar. No date. Accessed September 13, 2016. http://agentibg.com/index.php/bg/.

Bunce, Valerie and Sharon L. Wolchik. "International Diffusion and Post-Communist Electoral Revolutions." *Communist and Post-Communist Studies* 39:3 (2006): 283-304.

Bundesbehörde für die Stasi-Unterlagen (BStU). *The European Network of Official Authorities in Charge of the Secret Police Files: A Reader on their Legal Foundations, Structures and Activities*. 2nd revised edition. Berlin: BStU, 2013.

Burrin, Philippe. *France under the Germans: Collaboration and Compromise*. New York: The New Press, 1998.

Butler, William. *Soviet Law*. London: Butterworths, 1988.

Buzilă, Boris. *Un patriarh în oglinda vremii sale*. Iasi: Timpul, 2009.

Byford, Jovan and Cristian Tileagă. "Accounts of a Troubled Past: Psychology, History, and Texts of Experience." *Qualitative Psychology*, in press.

Campbell, Sue. "The Second Voice." *Memory Studies* 1:1 (2008): 41-48.

Câmpeanu, Pavel. *România – Coada pentru hrană: Un mod de viaţă*. Bucharest: Litera, 1994.

Câmpineanul, Ciprian, Adrian N. Petcu, Sebastian Ilfoveanul, Corneliu Bârlădeanul, Visarion Răşinăreanul, Toma Rădulescu, Ionel Popescu, Florin Şerbănescu, Ştefan Lupu, Cristinel Fodor, Hermann Pitters. eds. *Martiri pentru Hristos, din România, în perioada regimului comunist*. Bucharest: Editura Institutului Biblic şi Misiune al Bisericii Ortodoxe Române, 2007.

Carey, Henry F. "From Big Lie to Small Lies: State Mass Media Dominance in Post-Communist Romania." *East European Politics and Societies* 10:1 (1996): 16-45.

"Carol." *Martor. The Museum of the Romanian Peasant Anthropology Review* 7 (2002): 37-38.

Cătănuş, Ana Maria. "Disidenţă," in *Romania 1945-1989. Enciclopedia Regimului Comunist: Represiunea*, ed. Octavian Roske (Bucharest: Institutul National pentru Studiul Totalitarismului, 2011), vol. 1: 567-580.

—. *Vocaţia libertăţii. Forme de disidenţă în România anilor 1970–1980*. Bucharest: Institutul National pentru Studiul Totalitarismului, 2014.

Cernicova, Tatiana Maria. *Anno Domini, 1951*. Timişoara: Mirton, 2003.

Cesereanu, Ruxandra. *Decembrie 89. Deconstructia unei revolutii*. Iasi: Polirom, 2009.

—. "The Final Report on the Holocaust and the Final Report on the Communist Dictatorship in Romania." *East European Politics and Societies* 22:2 (2008): 270-281.

—. ed. *Comunism şi represiune: Istoria tematică a unui fratricid național*. Iaşi: Polirom, 2006.

—. *Gulagul în conştiința românească: Memorialistica şi literatura închisorilor şi lagărelor comuniste*. Iaşi: Polirom, 2005.

Cezar, Iulius and Răzvan Popa. "Directorul Arhivelor Naţionale a desecretizat fără drept informaţii." *Adevărul,* April 21, 2009. Accessed September 16, 2016. http://www.evz.ro/directorul-arhivelor-nationale-a-desecretizat-fara-drept-informatii-848048.html.

Chiriță, Constantin. *Cireşarii*, 5 vols. Bucharest: Editura Tineretului, 1956-1968.

Chirot, Daniel. ed. *The Crisis of Leninism and the Decline of the Left: The Revolutions of 1989*. Seattle: University of Washington Press, 1991.

Chiţoiu, Dan. "Ce trebuie să cauţi la un gânditor ca Nae Ionescu." *Ziarul Lumina*, October 3, 2011. Accessed March 4, 2013. http://ziarullumina.ro/opinii/ce-trebuie-sa-cauti-la-un-ganditor-ca-nae-ionescu.

"Christmas." *Martor. The Museum of the Romanian Peasant Anthropology Review* 7 (2002): 40-41.

Church, Gordon. "Bucharest: Revolution in the Townscape Art." In *The Socialist City: Spatial Structure and Urban Policy*, edited by R.A. French and F.E.I. Hamilton. 493-506. Chichester: Wiley, 1979.

Ciobanu, Monica. "Piteşti: A Project in Reeducation and its Post-1989 Interpretation in Romania." *Nationalities Papers: The Journal of Nationalism and Ethnicity* 43:4 (2015): 615-633.

—. "Reconstructing the History of Early Communism and Armed Resistance in Romania." *Europe-Asia Studies* 66:9 (2014): 1452-1481.

—. "Rewriting and Remembering Romanian Communism: Some Controversial Issues." *Nationalities Papers: The Journal of Nationalism and Ethnicity* 39:2 (2011): 205-221.

—. "Communist Regimes, Legitimacy and the Transition to Democracy in Eastern Europe." *Nationalities Papers: The Journal of Nationalism and Ethnicity* 38:1 (2010): 3-21.

—. "Criminalising the Past and Reconstructing Collective Memory: The Romanian Truth Commission." *Europe-Asia Studies* 61:2 (2009): 313-336.

Cioflâncă, Adrian. "Politics of Oblivion in Post-Communist Romania." *Romanian Journal of Political Science* 2:2 (2002): 85-93.

Ciorioianu, Adrian. *Focul ascuns in piatra*. Iasi: Polirom, 2000.

Citire: Manual pentru clasa a IV-a. Bucharest: Editura Didactică şi Pedagogică, 1987.

Ciuvercă, Florentina. "Epoca de Aur a renăscut în chinuri." *Evenimentul Zilei*, September 26, 2009. Accessed April 10, 2016. http://www.evz.ro/articole/detalii-articol/869213/Epoca-de-Aur-a-renascut-in-chinuri-VIDEO.

Clark, Janine N. "Reconciliation through Remembrance? War Memorials and the Victims of Vukovar." *International Journal of Transitional Justice* 7:1 (2013): 116-135.

Clark, Roland. *Holy Legionary Youth: Fascist Activism in Interwar Romania*. Ithaca: Cornell University Press, 2015.

Cleary, Matthew and Susan Stokes. *Democracy and the Culture of Skepticism: Political Trust in Argentina and Mexico*. New York: Russell Sage, 2006.

"Codul Penal din 1968," 1968. Accessed May 9, 2016. http://lege5.ro/Gratuit/he2demzw/codul-penal-din-1968.

Colceru, Daniel. "L'entrée du totalitarisme dans les manuels roumains." *Histoire et Liberté. Les cahiers d'histoire sociale* 42 (2010): 45-53.

"Cold." *Martor. The Museum of the Romanian Peasant Anthropology Review* 7 (2002): 44-45.

Coman, Ramona. *Réformer la justice dans un pays post-communiste. Le cas de la Roumanie*. Brussels: Université de Libre Bruxelles, 2009.

Conovici, Iuliana. "Re-weaving Memory: Representations of the Interwar and Communist Periods in the Romanian Orthodox Church after 1989." *Journal for the Study of Religion and Ideologies* 12:35 (2013): 109-131.

Consiliul National pentru Studierea Arhivelor Securitatii. *Raport de Activitate privind anul 2015*. Bucharest: CNSAS, 2016. Accessed July 8, 2016. http://www.cnsas.ro/documente/rapoarte/Raport%20CNSAS%202015.pdf.

Consiliul National pentru Studierea Arhivelor Securitatii. *Raport de Activitate privind anul 2014*. Bucharest: CNSAS, 2015. Accessed May 26, 2016. http://www.cnsas.ro/documente/rapoarte/Raport%20CNSAS%202014.pdf.

Consiliul National pentru Studierea Arhivelor Securitatii. *Raport de Activitate privind anul 2012*. Bucharest: CNSAS, 2013. Accessed January 30, 2016. http://www.cnsas.ro/documente/rapoarte/Raport%20CNSAS%202012.pdf.

Consiliul Național pentru Studierea Arhivelor Securității. *Raport de Activitate privind anul 2007*. Bucharest: CNSAS, 2008. Accessed July 9, 2016. http://www.cnsas.ro/documente/rapoarte/Raport%202007.pdf.

Consiliul Național pentru Studierea Arhivelor Securității. *Raport de Activitate privind anul 2006*. Bucharest: CNSAS, 2007. Accessed July 9, 2016. http://www.cnsas.ro/documente/rapoarte/Raport%202006.pdf.

Consiliul Național pentru Studierea Arhivelor Securității. *Raport de Activitate privind anul 2005*. Bucharest: CNSAS, 2006. Accessed June 20, 2016.
http://www.cnsas.ro/documente/rapoarte/Raport%202005.pdf.

Consiliul National pentru Studierea Arhivelor Securitatii website. No date. Accessed August 26, 2016. http://www.cnsas.ro/.

Constantinescu, Emil. *Timpul dărâmării, timpul* zidirii. 3 vols. Bucarest: Universalia, 2002.

Control Corps of the Ministry of Interior. *Report 2015.796*, 20 July 2009, unpublished document with Alexandru Gussi.

Converse, Philip E. "The Nature of Belief Systems in Mass Publics." In *Ideology and discontent*, edited by David Apter. 206-261. New York: Free Press, 1964.

Cotterrell, Roger. "The Concept of Legal Culture." In *Comparing Legal Cultures*, edited by David Nelken. 13-31. Aldershot: Darmouth, 1997.

Couso, Javier A. "The Transformation of Constitutional Discourse and the Judicialization of Politics in Latin America." In *Cultures of Legality. Judicialization and Political Activism in Latin America*, edited by Javier A. Couso, Alexandra Huneeus and Rachel Sieder. 141-160. Cambridge: Cambridge University Press, 2010.

Cristea, Gabriela and Simina Radu-Bucurenci. "Raising the Cross: Exorcizing Romania's Communist Past in Museums, Memorials and Monuments." In *Past for the Eyes: East European Representations of Communism in Cinema and Museums after 1989*, edited by Oksana Sarkisova and Péter Apor. 275-315. Budapest: Central European University Press, 2008.

Crowley, David and Susan E. Reid. "Socialist Spaces: Sites of Everyday Life in the Eastern Bloc." In *Socialist Spaces: Sites of Everyday Life in the Eastern Bloc*, edited by David Crowley and Susan E. Reid. 1-22. Oxford: Berg, 2002.

Irina Culic, "The Strategies of Intellectuals: Romania under Communist Rule in Comparative Perspective," in *Intellectuals and Politics in Central Europe,* ed. Andras Bozóki (Budapest: Central European University Press, 1999), 50-53.

Curtea Constitutionala a Romaniei. "Decizia nr. 820 din 7 iunie 2010 referitoare la obiecția de neconstituționalitate a dispozițiilor Legii lustrației, privind limitarea temporară a accesului la unele funcții şi demnități publice pentru persoanele care au făcut parte din structurile de putere şi din aparatul represiv al regimului comunist în perioada 6 martie 1945–22 decembrie 1989." *Monitorul Oficial al Romaniei* 420 (June 23, 2010). Accessed July 14, 2016. http://www.legex.ro/Decizia-820-2010-105400.aspx.

Curtea Constitutionala a Romaniei. "Decizia nr. 51 din 31 ianuarie 2008 referitoare la excepția de neconstituționalitate a dispozițiilor Legii nr. 187/1999 privind accesul la propriul dosar şi deconspirarea poliției politice comuniste." *Monitorul Oficial al Romaniei* 95 (February 6, 2008): 2–8. Accessed July 9, 2016. http://www.cnsas.ro/documente/cadru_legal/DECIZIE%2051_2008.pdf.

Curtea de Apel Bucureşti, Secția a VIII-a Contencios Administrativ şi Fiscal, "Sentința civilă nr. 671, Ședința publică din data de 5 februarie 2010," Dosar nr. 22502/3/2008. Accessed July 8, 2016. http://www.cnsas.ro/documente/monitoare/2013/Voiculescu%20Dan.pdf.

"Czech Republic: Constitutional Court Decision on the Screening Law (November 26, 1992)." In *Transitional Justice: How Emerging Democracies Reckon with Former Regimes*, edited by Neil Kritz. 3:369-374. Washington, DC: United States Institute of Peace Studies, 1995.

Czepczyński, Marius. *Cultural Landscapes of Post-Socialist Cities: Representations of Powers and Needs*. Aldershot: Ashgate, 2008.

David, Roman. *Lustration and Transitional Justice: Personnel Systems in the Czech Republic, Hungary, and Poland.* Philadelphia: University of Pennsylvania Press, 2011.

"Decret-Lege 118 din 30 martie 1990 privind acordarea unor drepturi persoanelor persecutate din motive politice de dictatura instaurată cu începere de la 6 martie 1945, precum şi celor deportate în străinătate ori constituite în prizonieri." *Monitorul Oficial al României* 631 (September 23, 2009). Accessed on September 16, 2016. www.cjpolt.ro/DL118.doc.

Deletant, Dennis. "Romania, 1945-1989: Resistance, Protest, and Dissent." In *Revolution and Resistance: Challenges to Communist Rule*, edited by Kevin McDermott and Matthew Stibbe, 81-100. Oxford: Berg, 2006.

—. *Romania under Communist Rule*. Bucharest: Center for Romanian Studies, 1999.

—. *Ceauşescu and the Securitate: Coercion and Dissent in Romania, 1965-1989*. London: M.E. Sharpe, 1995.

DeVault, Marjorie and Liza McCoy. "Institutional Ethnography: Using Interviews to Investigate Ruling Relations." In *Institutional Ethnography as Practice*, edited by Dorothy Smith. 15-44. Lanham: Rowman & Littlefield, 2006.

"Dinescu vrea audierea patriarhului Daniel la CNSAS." *România Liberă*, October 16, 2007. Accessed March 23, 2016. http://www.romanialibera.ro/actualitate/eveniment/dinescu-vrea-audierea-patriarhului-daniel-la-cnsas-108799.

Dobre, Florica. ed. *Membrii CC al PCR 1945–1989. Dicţionar*. Bucharest: Editura Enciclopedică, 2004.

Dobrincu, Dorin. "Miza destainuirii: Accesul la documentele comunismului," *22*, July 3, 2012. Accessed September 16, 2016. http://revista22.ro/16045/.html.

—. "A Brief History of Romanian Arhive Acces Since 1989." *Euxeinos* 3 (2012): 18-25.

—. "Către Corpul de Control din cadrul Ministerului Administraţiei şi Internelor." July 24, 2009, unpublished document available with Dorin Dobrincu.

—. "Neadevăruri despre Arhivele Naţionale," *22*, April 28, 2009. Accessed on September 16, 2016. http://revista22.ro/6005/.html.

Dragomir, Elena. "In Romania, Opinion Polls Show Nostalgia for Communism." Balkananalysis.com, December 27, 2011. Accessed July 10, 2016. http://www.balkanalysis.com/romania/2011/12/27/in-romania-opinion-polls-show-nostalgia-for-communism/.

Durkheim, Emil. *The Elementary Forms of Religious Life*. London: George Allen and Unwin, 1915.

Ecobescu, Nicolae. ed., *Drepturile Omului in Lumea Contemporana. Culegere Selectiva de Documente*. Bucharest: Editura Politica, 1983.

Edelman, Murray. *From Art to Politics. How Artistic Creations Shape Political Conceptions*. Chicago: University of Chicago Press, 1995.

Edensor, Tim. *National Identity, Popular Culture and Everyday Life*. Oxford: Berg, 2002.

—. "National Identity and the Politics of Memory: Remembering Bruce and Wallace in Symbolic Space." *Environment and Planning D* 15:2 (1997): 175-194.

Elster, Jon. ed. *Retribution and Reparation in the Transition to Democracy*. New York: Cambridge University Press, 2006.

—. "Preference Formations in Transitional Justice." In *Preferences and Situations. Points of Intersection between Historical and Rational*

Choice Institutionalism, edited by Ira Katznelson and Barry R. Weingast. 247-278. New York: Russell Sage Foundation, 2005.

Enache, George. *Ortodoxie şi putere politică în România contemporană*. Bucharest: Nemira, 2005.

Enache, George and Adrian Nicolae Petcu. "Biserica Ortodoxă Română şi Securitatea: Note de Lectură," in *Totalitarism şi rezistenţă, teroare şi represiune în România comunistă* (Bucureşti: CNSAS, 2001), 108-137.

Enache, George, Adrian-Nicolae Petcu, Ionuţ-Alexandru Tudorie, and Paul Brusanowski. "Biserica Ortodoxă Română în anii regimului comunist. Observaţii pe marginea capitolului dedicat cultelor din *Raportul final* al Comisiei Prezidenţiale pentru Analiza Dictaturii Comuniste din România." *Studii Teologice* 2 (2009): 7-104.

Engle Merry, Sally. "What Is Legal Culture? An Anthropological Perspective." In *Using Legal Culture*, edited by David Nelken. 52-75. London: Wildy, Simmonds & Hill Publishing, 2012.

Erll, Astrid. "Literature, Film and the Mediality of Cultural Memory." In *Cultural memory studies. An international and interdisciplinary handbook*, edited by Astrid Erll and Ansgar Nunning. 389-398. Berlin: Walter de Gruyter, 2008.

Etkind, Alexander. *Warped Mourning. Stories of the Undead in the Land of the Unburied Cultural Memory in the Present*. Stanford: Stanford University Press, 2013.

Eurobarometer Public Opinion Analysis, various years. Accessed September 15, 2016. http://ec.europa.eu/public_opinion/index_en.htm.

European Elections Database, various years. Accessed September 15, 2016. http://www.nsd.uib.no/european_election_database/country/romania/parties.html.

European Forum for Democracy and Cooperation, various years. Accessed September 15, 2016. http://www.europeanforum.net.

Evans, Martin. "Robert Paxton: The Outsider," *History Today* 51:9 (2001): 26-28.

Fairclough, Norman. *Media Discourse*. London: Edward Arnold, 1995.

Falk, Barbara. *The Dilemmas of Dissidence in East-Central Europe: Citizen Intellectuals and Philosopher Kings*. Budapest: Central European University Press, 2003.

—. "Resistance and Dissent in Central and Eastern Europe, An Emerging Historiography," *East European Politics and Societies,* 25:2 (May 2011) 318-360.

Florian, Alexandru. "The perception of the Holocaust in Historiography an the Romanian Media." In *Local History, Transnational Memory in the*

Romanian Holocaust, edited by Valentin Glajas and Jeanninne Teodorescu. 19-45. New York: Palgrave Macmillan, 2011.

Foote, Kenneth E. and Maoz Azaryahu. "Towards a Geography of Memory: Geographical Dimensions of Public Memory and Commemoration." *Journal of Political and Military Sociology* 35:1 (2007): 125-144.

Foote, Kenneth E., Atilla Tóth and Annet Árvay. "Hungary after 1989: Inscribing a New Past on Place." *Geographical Review* 90:3 (2000): 301-344.

Forest, Benjamin and Juliet Johnson. "Unravelling the Threads of History: Soviet-Era Monuments and Post-Soviet National Identity in Moscow." *Annals of the Association of American Geographers* 92:3 (2002): 524-547.

Forest, Benjamin, Juliet Johnson and Karen Till. "Post-totalitarian National Identity: Public Memory in Germany and Russia." *Social and Cultural Geography* 5:3 (2004): 357-380.

Freckmann, Anke and Thomas Wegerich. *The German Legal System*. London: Sweet and Maxwell, 1999.

Freud, Sigmund. "Analysis Terminable and Interminable." *Standard Edition* 23 (1937): 378-405.

Friedman, Lawrence M. "The Concept of Legal Culture: A Reply." In *Comparing Legal Cultures,* edited by David Nelken. 33-40. Aldershot: Darmouth, 1997.

Frilling, Tuvia, Radu Ioanid and Mihail E. Ionescu. eds. *Final Report*. Iasi: Polirom and International Commission on the Holocaust in Romania, 2005.

Frosh, Stephen. *Psychoanalysis Outside the Clinic: Interventions in Psychosocial Studies*. Basingstoke: Palgrave Macmillan, 2010.

Fulbrook, Mary. *The People's State: East German Society from Hitler to Honecker*. New Haven: Yale University Press, 2005.

Fuller, Lon L. "Positivism and Fidelity to Law – A Replay to Professor Hart." *Harvard Law Review* 71:4 (1958), 630-672.

"Fundația Profesor George Manu." no date. Accessed April 28, 2016. http://www.fgmanu.ro.

"Fundația Sfinții Închisorilor." 2015. Accessed April 28, 2016. http://www.fundatiasfintiiinchisorilor.ro.

Gabriel, Manfred J. "Coming to Terms with the East German Border Guards Cases." *Columbia Journal of Transnational Law* 38:2 (1999): 375-385.

Gaines, Jane M. "Political Mimesis." In *Collecting Visible Evidence*, edited by Jane M. Gaines and Michael Renov. 84-102. Minneapolis: University of Minnesota Press, 1999.

Galasińska, Aleksandra and Dariusz Galasiński. eds. *The Post-Communist Condition: Public and Private Discourses of Transformation*. Amsterdam/Philadelphia, PA: John Benjamins, 2010.

Gallinat, Anselma. "Difficult Stories: Public Discourse and Narrative Identity in Eastern Germany." *Ethnos* 71:3 (2006): 343-366.

"Gasoline." *Martor. The Museum of the Romanian Peasant Anthropology Review* 7 (2002): 75-78.

Geddes, Jennifer. "Religious Rhetoric in Response to Atrocity." In *The Religious in Responses to Mass Atrocity: Interdisciplinary Perspectives*, edited by Thomas Broudholm and Thomas Cushman. 21-27. Cambridge: Cambridge University Press, 2009.

Geiger, Rudolf. "The German Border Guard Cases and International Human Rights." *European Journal of International Law* 9:3 (1998): 540-549.

Georgescu, Vlad. *The Romanians: A History*. London: I. B. Tauris, 1991.

Ghenie, Adrian. "Painting a dictator in the moment before his execution." San Francisco Museum of Modern Art video interview, October 15, 2012. Accessed May 1, 2016. https://www.youtube.com/watch?v=2f8IlnRnL8U.

Gherghina, Sergiu. "Attitudes towards the Communist Past in Five Central and East European Countries." *History of Communism in Europe* I (2010): 167-181.

Gilberg, Trond. *Nationalism and Communism in Romania: The Rise and Fall Ceaușescu's Personal Dictatorship*. Boulder, CO: Westview Press, 1990.

Gillis, John R. "Memory and Identity: The History of a Relationship." In *Commemorations: The Politics of National Identity*, edited by John R. Gillis. 3-25. Princeton: Princeton University Press, 1994.

Giurescu, Constantin C. "Postfață." In *Adevaruri incomde. Decembrie 1989*, edited by ACMRRSRI. 385-388. Bucharest: Semne, 2013.

Gomez-Barris, Macarena. *Where Memory Dwells. Culture and State Violence in Chile*. Berkley, CA: University of California Press, 2009.

Gordon, Bertram M. "The Morphology of the Collaborator: The French Case," *Journal of European Studies* 23:89-90 (1993): 1-25.

Gottlieb, Roger S. "The Concept of Resistance: Jewish Resistance during the Holocaust," *Social Theory and Practice*, 9:1 (1983): 31-49.

Grigore, Monica. "The Aiud Prison Saints. History, Memory and Lived Religion." *Eurostudia* 10:1 (2015): 33-49.

Griswold, Charles. *Forgiveness: A Philosophical Exploration*. New York: Cambridge University Press, 2007.

Grodsky, Brian. *The Costs of Justice: How New Leaders Respond to Previous Rights Abuses*. Notre Dame: University of Notre Dame Press, 2010.

Gron, Arne. "The Limits of Ethics - The Ethics of the Limit." In *The Religious in Responses to Mass Atrocity: Interdisciplinary Perspectives*, edited by Thomas Broudholm and Thomas Cushman. 38-59. Cambridge: Cambridge University Press, 2009.

Raluca Grosescu, "Conversia elitelor comuniste în perioada de tranziție: 1989-2000," in *Mobilitatea elitelor în România secolului XX*, eds. Mihai Dinu Ghorghiu and Mihăiță Lupu (Pitesti: Paralela 45, 2008), 299-338

—. "Fizionomia nomenclaturii." *Anuarul Institutului de Investigare a Crimelor Comunismului* I (2006): 109-140.

Grosescu, Raluca and Raluca Ursachi. "Transitional Criminal Justice in Post-Communist Romania." In *Kilometer Null. Politische Transformation und gesellschaftiche Entwicklungen in Rumanienseit 1989,* edited by Thede Kahl and Larisa Schippel. 405-422. Berlin: Frank & Timme, 2011.

—. *Justitia Penala de Transitie de la Nuremberg la Post-comunismul Romanesc*. Iasi: Polirom, 2009.

Grubsztein, Meir, ed. *Jewish Resistance during the Holocaust: Proceedings of the Conference on Manifestations of Jewish Resistance, Jerusalem, April 7-11, 1968*. Jerusalem: Yad Vashem, 1971.

Grzymala-Busse, Anna. *Rebuilding Leviathan. Party Competition and State Exploitation in Post-communist Democracies*. New York: Cambridge University Press, 2007.

—. *Redeeming the Communist Past: The Regeneration of Communist Parties in East Central Europe*. New York: Cambridge University Press, 2002.

Gussi, Alexandru. "Political Uses of Memory and the State in Post-Communism." *Studia Politica. Romanian Political Science Review* XIII:4 (2013): 721-732.

—. *La Roumanie face à son passé communiste. Mémoires et cultures politiques*. Paris : l'Harmattan, 2011.

—. "The Ex-communists' Policy of Forgetting in Romania after 1990." *Studia Politica. Romanian Political Science Review* IX:2 (2009): 273-290.

—. "L'anticommunisme en Roumanie (1996-2000)." *Studia Politica. Romanian Political Science Review* VII:1 (2007): 117-132.

—. “Construction et usages politiques d’un lieu de mémoire. La Place de l’Université de Bucarest.“ *Studia Politica. Romanian Political Science Review* II:4 (2002): 1058-1091.

Gutmann, Amy and Dennis Thomson. “The Moral Foundations of Truth Commissions.” In *Truth vs. Justice*, edited by Robert Rothberg and Dennis Thompson. 22-44. Princeton, NJ: Princeton University Press, 2000.

Halbwachs, Maurice. *On Collective Memory*. Chicago, IL: Chicago University Press, 1952/1992.

Hall, Derek. “Brand Development, Tourism and National Identity: The Re-imaging of Former Yugoslavia.” *Brand Management* 9:4-5 (2001): 323-334.

—. “Destination Branding, Niche Marketing and National Image Projection in Central and Eastern Europe.” *Journal of Vacation Marketing* 5:3 (1999): 227-237.

Hall, Michael C. *Tourism: Rethinking the Social Science of Mobility*. London: Routledge, 2005.

—. *Tourism and Politics: Policy, Power and Place*. Chichester: Wiley, 1994.

Hamber, Brendon, Liz Ševčenko and Ereshnee Naidu. “Utopian Dreams or Practical Possibilities? The Challenges of Evaluating the Impact of Memorialization in Societies in Transition.” *International Journal of Transitional Justice* 4:3 (2010): 297-420.

Hann, Chris. “Transition, Tradition, and Nostalgia: Postsocialist Transformations in a Comparative Framework.” *Collegium Atropologicum* 36:4 (2012): 1119-1128.

Harré, Rom and Grant Gillett. *The Discursive Mind*. London: Sage, 1994.

Hart, Herbert L.A. “Positivism and the Separation of Law and Morals.” *Harvard Law Review* 71:4 (1958), 593-629.

Havel, Vaclav. “The Power of the Powerless,” October 1978, available at: http://vaclavhavel.cz/showtrans.php?cat=clanky&val=72_aj_clanky.html&typ=HTML, accessed on 13 June 2015.

“Heating.” *Martor. The Museum of the Romanian Peasant Anthropology Review* 7 (2002): 81-82.

Helsinki Watch. “Decommunization in Bulgaria.” *Human Rights Watch* 5:14 (August 1993). Accessed September 14, 2016. https://www.hrw.org/sites/default/files/reports/BULGARIA938.PDF.

Hermet, Guy. *L'hiver de la democratie ou le nouveau regime*. Paris: Armand Colin, 2007.

Hilberg, Raul. *Perpetrators, Victims, Bystanders: The Jewish Catastrophe, 1933-1945*. New York: Aaron Asher Books, 1992.

Hintikka, Kaisamari. *The Romanian Orthodox Church and the World Council of Churches, 1961-1977*. Helsinki: Luther Agricola Society, 2000.

Hirsch, Marianne. *The Generation of Post-Memory*. New York: Columbia University Press, 2012.

—. "The Generation of Post-Memory." *Poetics Today* 29:1 (2008): 103-128.

Hirschfeld, Gerhard and Patrick Marsh, eds. *Collaboration in France: Politics and Culture During the Nazi Occupation 1940-1944*. New York: Berg, 1989.

Horne, Cynthia M. "'Silent Lustration:' Public Disclosures as Informal Lustration Mechanisms in Bulgaria and Romania." *Problems of Post-Communism* 62:3 (2015): 131-144.

—. "Assessing the Impact of Lustration on Trust in Public Institutions and National Government in Central and Eastern Europe." *Comparative Political Studies* 45:4 (2012): 412-446.

—. "Late Lustration Programmes in Romania and Poland: Supporting or Undermining Democratic Transitions?" *Democratization* 16:2 (2009): 344-376.

Horne, Cynthia and Margaret Levi. "Does Lustration Promote Trustworthy Governance? An Exploration of the Experience of Central and Eastern Europe." In *Building a Trustworthy State in Post-Socialist Transition*, edited by János Kornai and Susan Rose-Ackerman. 52-74. New York: Palgrave/Macmillan Press, 2004.

Horne, Donald. *The Great Museum: The Re-presentation of History*. London: Pluto, 1984.

Hossu Longin, Lucia. *Memorialul Durerii: O istorie care nu se invata la scoala* [The Memorial of Pain: A History Not Taught in School], 2nd ed. Bucharest: Humanitas, 2013.

—. *Memorialul Durerii: O istorie care nu se invata la scoala* [The Memorial of Pain: A History Not Taught in School]. Book and 10-DVD set. Bucharest: Humanitas, 2007.

"Hotărîrea Guvernului no. 563/2014 privind organizarea si functionarea Secretariatului de stat pentru recunoaşterea meritelor luptătorilor împotriva regimului comunist instaurat în România în perioada 1945-1989." *Monitorul Oficial* 72 (October 19, 2014). Accessed April 26, 2016. http://lege5.ro/en/Gratuit/gqydgobqge/hotararea-nr-563-2014-privind-organizarea-si-functionarea-secretariatului-de-stat-pentru-recunoasterea-meritelor-luptatorilor-impotriva-regimului-comunist-instaurat-in-romania-in-perioada-1945-1989.

Hristov, Hristo. "The Bulgarian Gulag." No date. Accessed October 11, 2015. http://www.vagabond.bg/politics/item/1390-the-bulgarian-gulag.html.

Hristov, Hristo and Alexander Kashumov. "Justice and Accountability Mechanisms in Bulgaria in the Transition Period (1989-2008)." In *After Oppression. Transitional Justice in Latin America and Eastern Europe*, edited by Vesselin Popovski and Monica Serrano. 273-297. New York: United Nations University Press, 2012.

"Hungary: Constitutional Court Decision on the Statute of Limitations, No. 2086/A/1991/14 (March 5, 1992)." In *Transitional Justice*: *How Emerging Democracies Reckon with Former Regimes*, edited by Neil Kritz. 3: 629-632. Washington, DC: United States Institute of Peace Studies, 1995.

Huntington, Samuel. *The Third Wave: Democratization in the Late Twentieth Century*. London: University of Oklahoma Press, 1991.

Huyssen, Andreas. *Present Pasts, Urban Palimpsests and the Politics of Memory*. Stanford: Stanford University Press, 2003.

Iacob, Bogdan. "Avem nevoie de o pedagogie a memoriei colective a trecutului communist." *Evenimentul Zilei*, September 23, 2010. Accessed May 25, 2016. http://www.evz.ro/bogdan-cristian-iacob-avem-nevoie-de-o-pedagogie-a-memoriei-colective-a-trecutului-comunist-90689.html.

Iancu, Bogdan. "Post-Accession Constitutionalism with a Human Face: Judicial Reform and Lustration in Romania." *European Constitutional Law Review* 6:1 (2010): 28-58.

INSCOP-Adevărul. "Barometrul despre România: Atunci vs. Acum," December 2014. Accessed April 10, 2016. http://www.inscop.ro/wp-content/uploads/2014/12/INSCOP-Dec.2014.-Acum-vs.-Atunci1.pdf.

Iohannis, Klaus. *Pas cu pas*. Bucharest: Curtea Veche, 2015.

Ilie, Ionela. "Nostalgia lui Igu." *Esquire*, December 2007. Accessed July 10, 2016. http://www.esquire.ro/articole/reportaje/nostalgia-lui-igu.htm.

Iliescu, Ion. "Cred in schimbarea in bine a Romaniei." In Ion Iliescu, *Momente de istorie*. 3: 313-331. Bucharest: Editura Enciclopedică, 1996.

—. *Momente de istorie*. Bucharest: Editura Enciclopedică, 1996.

—. "Keynote Speech at the National Salvation Front Conference." *Dimineața*, April 8, 1990.

—. "Discourse at the Romanian Public Radio and Television." *Monitorul Oficial al României*, January 8, 1990.

—. „Mesajul lui Ion Iliescu la Conferinta Nationala a PDSR," *Adevărul*, November 25, 1995.

Imholz, Kathleen. “A Landmark Constitutional Court Decision in Albania.” *East European Constitutional Review* 2:3 (1993): 22-25.

Înalta Curte de Casație și Justiție, Secția de Contencios Administrativ și Fiscal. “Decizia nr. 3678 din 23 iunie 2001: Respinge contestația în anulare formulată de V. D. ca inadmisibilă.” June 23, 2001. Accessed July 8, 2016. http://legeaz.net/spete-contencios-inalta-curte-iccj-2011/decizia-3678-2011.

International Center for Transitional Justice. “What Is Transitional Justice?,” 2016. Accessed September 23, 2016. https://www.ictj.org/about/transitional-justice.

Ioanid, Ioan. *Închisoarea noastră cea de toate zilele*, vol. 1. Bucharest: Humanitas, 1999.

Ioanolide, Ioan. *Deținutul profet*. Bucharest: Bonifaciu, 2009.

Iordachi, Constantin and Balázs Trencsényi. “In Search of a Usable Past: The Question of National Identity in Romanian Studies, 1990-2000.” *East European Politics and Societies* 17:3 (2003): 415-453.

“Jack Frost.” *Martor. The Museum of the Romanian Peasant Anthropology Review* 7 (2002): 93.

Jarausch, Konrad. ed. *Dictatorship as Experience: Towards a Socio-Cultural History of the GDR*. New York: Berghahn Books, 1999.

Jaskovska, Eva and John Moran. “Justice or Politics? Criminal, Civil and Political Adjudication in the Newly Independent Baltic States.” *Journal of Communist Studies and Transition Politics* 22:4 (2006), 485-506.

Jela, Doina. *Drumul Damascului*. Bucharest: Humanitas, 1999.

Jelin, Elisabeth. *Los trabajos de la memoria*. Lima: Instituto de Estudios Peruanos, 2012.

—. “Public Memorialization in Perspective: Truth, Justice and the Memory of Past Repression in the Southern Cone of South America.” *International Journal of Transitional Justice* 1:1 (2007): 138-156.

Johnson, James. “The Arithmetic of Compassion: Rethinking the Politics of Photography.” *British Journal of Political Science* 31:3 (2000): 621-643.

Johnson, Nuala C. “Public Memory.” In *A Companion to Cultural Geography*, edited by James S. Duncan, Nuala C. Johnson and Richard H. Schein. 316-327. Oxford: Blackwell, 2004.

Jones, Sara. “Uneasy Heritage: Remembering Everyday Life in Post-Socialist Memorials and Museums.” In *Encounters with Popular Pasts: Cultural Heritage and Popular Culture*, edited by Mike Robinson and Helaine Silverman. 219-234. Cham: Springer, 2015.

—. "Memory on Film: Testimony and Constructions of Authenticity in Documentaries about the German Democratic Republic." *European Journal of Cultural Studies* 16:2 (2012): 194-210.

Jowitt, Kenneth. *Revolutionary Breakthroughs and National Development: The Case of Romania, 1944-1965*. Berkeley: University of California Press, 1971.

Judt, Tony. "Captive Minds, Then and Now," *The New York Review of Books* (13 July 2010), available at: http://www.nybooks.com/blogs/nyrblog/2010/jul/13/captive-minds-then-and-now, accessed on 11 June 2015.

Kansteiner, Wulf. "Finding Meaning in Memory: A Methodological Critique of Collective Memory Studies." *History & Theory* 41:2 (2002): 179-197.

"Kapitalism – our secret recipe." Medias Central European Film Festival, 2015. Accessed May 1, 2016. http://www.meceff.ro/kapitalism-our-secret-recipe.aspx.

Keightley, Emily and Michael Pickering, "Painful Pasts," in *Research Methods for Memory Studies*, eds. Emily Keightley and Michael Pickering (Edinburgh: Edinburgh University Press, 2013), 151-166.

Kelsen, Hans. *The Communist Theory of Law*. London: Stevens & Sons, 1955.

Kenney, Padraic. *A Carnival of Revolution: Central Europe 1989*. Princeton: Princeton University Press, 2002.

Kideckel, David. "The Unmaking of an East-Central European Working Class." In *Postsocialism: Ideals, Ideologies and Practices in Eurasia*, edited by Chris M. Hann. 114-132. London: Routledge, 2002.

Kinder, Donald R. and Cindy D. Kam. *Us against Them: Ethnocentric Foundations of American Opinion*. Chicago: Chicago University Press, 2009.

King, Ronald and Paul Sum. eds. *Romania Under Băsescu: Aspirations, Achievements, and Frustrations During His First Presidential Term*. Lanham, MD: Rowan & Littlefield, 2011.

Kitschelt, Herbert, Zdenka Mansfeldova, Radoslaw Markowski and Gábor Tóka. *Post-Communist Party Systems: Competition, Representation, and Inter-Party Cooperation*. Cambridge: Cambridge University Press, 1999.

Kitson, Simon. *The Hunt for Nazi Spies: Fighting Espionage in Vichy France*, translated by Catherine Tihanyi. Chicago: University of Chicago Press, 2008.

Kligman, Gail. *The Politics of Duplicity: Controlling Reproduction in Ceauşescu's Romania*. Berkeley, CA: University of California Press, 1998.

Kligman, Gail and Katherine Verdery. *Peasants Under Siege: The Collectivization of Romanian Agriculture, 1949-1962*. Princeton: Princeton University Press, 2011.

Kocka, Jürgen. "Eine durchherrschte Gesselschaft." In *Die Sozialgeschichte der DDR*, edited by Hartmut Kaelble, Jürgen Kocka and Hartmut Zwahr. 547-563. Stuttgart: Klett-Cotta, 1994.

Kokoška, Stanislav. "Resistance, Collaboration, Adaptation: Some Notes on the Research of the Czech Society in the Protectorate," *Czech Journal of Contemporary History* 1 (2013): 54-76.

Kornai, János and Susan Rose-Ackerman. eds. *Building a Trustworthy State in Post-Socialist Transition*. New York: Palgrave/Macmillan Press, 2004.

Kritz, Neil. "Policy Implications of Empirical Research on Transitional Justice." In *Assessing the Impact of Transitional Justice*, edited by Hugo Van der Merwe, Victoria Baxter and Audrey Chapman. 13-22. Washington, D.C.: U.S. Institute of Peace, 2009.

—. *Transitional Justice: How Emerging Democracies Reckon with Former Regimes*, 3 vols. Washington, DC: US Institute of Peace, 1995.

LaCapra, Dominick. *Writing History, Writing Trauma*. Baltimore, MD: Johns Hopkins University Press, 2001.

—. *Representing the Holocaust: History, Theory, Trauma*. Ithaca: Cornell University Press, 1994.

Landsberg, Alison. *Prosthetic Memory. The Transformation of American Remembrance in the Age of Mass Culture*. New York: Columbia University Press, 2004.

Langer, Lawrence. *Holocaust Testimonies: The Ruins of Memory*. New Haven: Yale University Press, 1991.

—. *Versions of Survival: The Holocaust and the Human Spirit*. Albany: State University of New York Press, 1982.

Lanzman, Claude. *Shoah: An Oral History of the Holocaust*. New York: Pantheon Books, 1985.

"Law for Access and Disclosure of the Documents and Announcing Affiliations of Bulgarian Citizens to the State Security and the Intelligence Services of the Bulgarian National Army." December 2006. Accessed August 26, 2016.
http://lex.bg/bg/laws/ldoc/2135540283.

"Law for Banks and Credit of March 4, 1992" cited in Human Rights Watch, "Decommunization in Bulgaria," 5:14 (August 1993): 5, available at: https://www.hrw.org/sites/default/files/reports/BULGARIA938.PDF accessed on October 30, 2016.

"Law for Temporary Introduction of Additional Requirements for Members of the Executive Bodies of the Scientific Organizations and the Higher Certifying Commission of December 9, 1992 (Panev Law)," cited in Human Rights Watch, "Decommunization in Bulgaria," 5:14 (August 1993): 5, available at: https://www.hrw.org/sites/default/files/reports/BULGARIA938.PDF accessed on October 30, 2016.

"Law no. 187 on the Access to the Personal File and the Disclosure of the Securitate as a Political Police," *Monitorul Oficial*, part I, no. 603 (9 December 1999), available at: http://www.cdep.ro/legislatie/eng/vol44eng.pdf, accessed on 5 June 2015.

Lazzara, Michael. *Chile in Transition: The Poetics and Politics of Memory*. Gainesville: University Press of Florida, 2006.

"Legea lustrației privind limitarea temporară a accesului la unele funcții și demnități publice pentru persoanele care au făcut parte din structurile de putere și din aparatul represiv al regimului communist în perioada 6 martie 1945–22 decembrie 1989," May 19, 2010. Accessed April 10, 2016. http://www.cdep.ro/proiecte/2006/200/80/2/pr282_06.pdf.

"Lege nr. 293 din 14 noiembrie 2008 pentru aprobarea Ordonanței de urgență a Guvernului nr. 24/2008 privind accesul la propriul dosar și deconspirarea Securității." *Monitorul Oficial al Romaniei* 800 (November 28, 2008): 1–4. Accessed September 16, 2016. http://www.cnsas.ro/documente/cadru_legal/LEGE%20293_2008.pdf.

"Lege nr. 187 din 7 decembrie 1999 privind accesul la propriul dosar și deconspirarea Securității ca poliție politică." *Monitorul Oficial al Romaniei* 603 (December 9, 1999): 1–5. Accessed May 25, 2016. http://legislatie.resurse-pentru-democratie.org/legea/187-1999.php.

Leśkiewicz, Rafał and Pavel Žáček. eds. *Handbook of the European Network of Official Authorities in Charge of the Secret Police Files*. Prague: The Institute for the Study of Totalitarian Regimes and the Institute of National Remembrance, 2013.

Letki, Natalia. "Lustration and Democratisation in East-Central Europe." *Europe-Asia Studies* 54:4 (2002): 529-552.

Leustean, Lucian N. *Orthodoxy and the Cold War Religion and Political Power in Romania, 1947-65*. Basingstoke: Palgrave Macmillan, 2009.

Levine, Allison J. *Framing the Nation: Documentary Film in Interwar France*. New York: Continuum, 2010.

Lewis, Ben. *Hammer & Tickle: The History of Communism Told Through Communist Jokes*. London: Weidenfeld & Nicholson, 2008.

Liiceanu, Gabriel. "Adsum? Modelul cultural Noica si urgentele istoriei / Noica's Cultural Model and the Emergencies of History," *22* (November 23, 1990), 6-7.

—. "Nesansa mea sau a Luciei Hossu Longin a fost ca am cunoscut-o ca persoana!" [My Bad Luck or That of Lucia Hossu Longin Was that I knew Her as a Person]. *Adevarul*, October 6, 1998.

Light, Duncan. "Romania: National Identity, Tourism Promotion and European Integration." In *Tourism in the New Europe: The Challenges and Opportunities of EU Enlargement*, edited by Derek Hall, Melanie Smith and Barbara Marciszewska. 256-269. Wallingford: CABI.

—. "Street Names in Bucharest, 1990–1997: Exploring the Modern Historical Geographies of Post-Socialist Change." *Journal of Historical Geography* 30:1 (2004): 154-172.

—. "Gazing on Communism: Heritage Tourism and Post-Communist Identities in Germany, Hungary and Romania." *Tourism Geographies: An International Journal of Tourism Space, Place and Environment* 2:2 (2000): 157-176.

—. "Heritage as Informal Education." In *Heritage, Tourism and Society*, edited by David T. Herbert. 117-145. London: Mansell, 1995.

Light, Duncan and Craig Young. "Public Memory, Commemoration and Transitional Justice: Reconfiguring the Past in Public Space." In *Post-Communist Transitional Justice: Lessons from 25 Years of Experience*, edited by Lavinia Stan and Nadya Nedelsky. 233-251. New York: Cambridge University Press, 2015.

—. "Public Space and the Material Legacies of Communism in Bucharest." In *Post-Communist Romania at Twenty-Five: Linking Past, Present and Future*, edited by Lavinia Stan and Diana Vancea. 46-50. Lanham, MD: Lexington Books 2015.

—. "Local and Counter-Memories of Socialism in Post-Socialist Romania." In *Local Memories in a Nationalizing and Globalizing World*, edited by Marnix Beyen and Brecht Deseure. 221-243. Basingstoke: Palgrave, 2015.

—. "Socialist Statuary as Post-Socialist Hybrids: Following the Statues of Dr Petru Groza in Romania." *Journal of Historical Geography* 37:4 (2011): 493-501.

Linz, Juan J. and Alfred Stepan. *Problems of Democratic Transition and Consolidation: Southern Europe, South America, and Post-Communist Europe*. Baltimore: The Johns Hopkins University Press, 1996.

Lipset, Seymour M. *Political Man: The Social Basis of Politics*. New York: Doubleday, 1960.

Littlejohn, David. *Patriotic Traitors: History of Collaboration in German Occupied Europe, 1940-1945*. London: W. Heinemann, 1972.

Livezeanu, Irina. "Romania's Cultural Wars: Intellectual Debates about the Recent Past," *Working Papers Series of the National Council for Eurasian and East European Research* (March 27, 2003). Available at https://www.ucis.pitt.edu/nceeer/2003-816-08-Livezeanu.pdf (accessed on November 4, 2016).

Longoni, Ana. "Crossroads for Activist Art in Argentina." *Third Text* 22:5 (2008): 575-587.

Łoś, Maria. *Communist Ideology, Law and Crime. A Comparative View of the USSR and Poland.* New York: St. Martin's Press, 1988.

Löwenthal, Richard. "Widerstand in totalen Staat," in Richard Löwenthal and Patrik von zur Mühlen, *Widerstand und Verweigerung in Deutschland 1933 bis 1945* (Berlin: Dietz, 1982) 13-14.

Lüdtke, Alf. ed. *The History of Everyday Life: Reconstructing Historical Experiences and Ways of Life*. Princeton: Princeton University Press, 1995.

Lynch, Michael. "Archives in Formation: Privileged Spaces, Popular Archives and Paper Trails." *History of the Human Sciences* 12:2 (1999): 65-87.

Maier, Charles S. *The Unmasterable Past: History, Holocaust, and German National Identify*. Cambridge, MA: Harvard University Press, 1998.

Major, Patrick. *The Death of the KPD: Communism and Anti-Communism in West Germany, 1945-1956*. Oxford: Oxford University Press, 1997.

"Manastirea Recea: Parintele Ioan Iovan." *Lumea credintei* 10, October 2005. Accessed March 26, 2016. http://www.lumeacredintei.com/reviste/lumea-credintei/lumea-credintei-anul-iii-nr-10-27-octombrie-2005/manastirea-recea-parintele-ioan-iovan/.

Männig, Jana. *Bei Oma schmeckt's besser*. Gudensberg; Wartberg Verlag, 2009.

Margalit, Avishai. *The Ethics of Memory*. Cambridge, MA: Harvard University Press, 2002.

Mărgirescu, Eugen. *Moara dracilor. Amintiri din Ĩnchisoarea de la Piteşti.* Alba Iulia: Fronda, 1994.

Mark, James. *The Unfinished Revolution: Making Sense of the Communist Past in Central and Central-Eastern Europe*. New Haven: Yale University Press, 2010.

Markovits, Inga. "Justice in Lüritz." *The American Journal of Comparative Law* 50:4 (2002): 819-874.

Maxfield, Ed. "Romania," in *Encyclopedia of Transitional Justice*, edited by Lavinia Stan and Nadya Nedelsky. 3:398-403. New York: Cambridge University Press, 2013.

Maxim, Virgil. *Imn pentru crucea purtată: abecedar duhovnicesc pentru un frate de cruce*. Bacău: Babel, 2012.

Mayer-Rieckh, Alexander and Pablo de Greiff. eds. *Justice as Prevention: Vetting Public Employees in Transitional Societies*. New York: Social Science Research Council, 2007.

McAdams, James. "Communism on Trial: The East German Past and the German Future." In *Transitional Justice and the Rule of Law in New Democracies,* edited by James McAdams. 239-265. Notre Dame: University of Notre Dame Press, 1997.

McEvoy, Kieran. "Transitional Justice from Below: Towards a Thicker Understanding of Transitional Justice." *Journal of Law and Society* 22:4 (2007): 489-513.

McLean, Fiona. "Museums and the Construction of National Identity: A Review." *International Journal of Heritage Studies* 3:1(1998): 244-252.

"Meat." *Martor. The Museum of the Romanian Peasant Anthropology Review* 7 (2002): 101-104.

Megil, Allan. "History, Memory and Identity." *History of the Human Sciences* 11:3 (1998): 37-62.

"Memorialul Victimelor Comunismului si ale Rezistentei." July 5, 2011. Accessed April 26, 2016. http://sighet.ro/?page_id=557.

Mengel, Ewald and Michela Borzaga. eds. *Trauma, Memory and Narrative in the Contemporary South African Novel*. Amsterdam: Rodopi, 2012.

"Mesajul Președintelui României, 18 December 2006." In *Comisia prezidențială pentru analiza dictaturii communiste din România. Raport Final*, edited by Vladimir Tismăneanu, Dorin Dobrincu and Cristian Vasile. 11-18. Bucharest: Humanitas, 2007.

Metodiev, Momchil. "Bulgaria." In *Encyclopedia of Transitional Justice*, edited by Lavinia Stan and Nadya Nedelsky. 73-79. New York: Cambridge University Press, 2013. New York: Oxford University Press, 1974.

Michman, Dan. "Jewish Resistance during the Holocaust and Its Significance: Theoretical Observations" in *Holocaust Historiography: A Jewish Perspective – Conceptualizations, Terminology, Approaches and Fundamental Issues*, ed. Dan Michman (London: Vallentine Mitchell, 2003), 217-250.

Middleton, David and Steven D. Brown, "Issues in the Socio-Cultural Study of Memory: Making Memory Matter," in *The Cambridge Handbook of Sociocultural Psychology*, eds. Jaan Valsiner and Alberto Rosa (Cambridge: Cambridge University Press, 2007), 661-677.

—. *The Social Psychology of Experience: Studies in Remembering and Forgetting*. London: Sage, 2005.

Milton, Cynthia. ed. *Art from a Fractured Past: Memory and Truth-Telling in Post-Shining Path Peru*. Durham: Duke University Press, 2014.

Minow, Martha. *Between Vengeance and Forgiveness: Facing History after Genocide ad Mass Violence*. Boston: Beacon Press, 1998.

Mioc, Marius. *Revoluţia din Timişoara şi falsificatorii istoriei*. Timişoara: Sedona, 1999.

Misztal, Barbara. "Memory and Democracy." *American Behavioral Scientist* 48:10 (2005): 1320-1338.

Moca, Gheorghe. *Dreptul International*. Bucharest: Editura Politica, 1983.

Modreanu, Cristina. "Cronica de teatru/Dupa 20 de ani de la revolutie - Procesul sotilor Ceausescu vazut ca performance I." *Ziarul de Duminică,* December 16, 2009. Accessed May 1, 2016.
http://www.zf.ro/ziarul-de-duminica/cronica-de-teatru-dupa-20-de-ani-de-la-revolutie-procesul-sotilor-ceausescu-vazut-ca-performance-i-5183980/.

Molloy, Peter. *The Lost World of Communism: An Oral History of Daily Life Behind the Iron Curtain*. London: BBC Books, 2009.

Monson, Robert A. "The West German Statute of Limitations on Murder: A Political, Legal, and Historical Exposition." *American Journal of Comparative Law* 30:4 (1982): 605-625.

Moran, John P. "The Communist Torturers of Eastern Europe: Prosecute and Punish or Forgive and Forget?" *Communist and Post-Communist Studies* 27:1 (1994): 95-109.

Morgan, Nigel and Annette Pritchard. *Tourism, Promotion and Power: Creating Images, Creating Identities*. Chichester: Wiley, 1998.

Morris, James W."Taqīyah," in *Encyclopedia of Religion*, ed. Lindsay Jones (Detroit: Macmillan Reference, 2005), available at:
http://www.encyclopedia.com/environment/encyclopedias-almanacs-transcripts-and-maps/taqiyah, accessed on 11 June 2015.

Mouralis, Guillaume. *Une épuration allemande. La RDA en procès 1949-2004*. Paris: Fayard, 2008.

Mungiu Pippidi, Alina. "Cât de revoluționară a fost revoluția română?" *22*, January 23-29, 2007.

Mutler, Alison. "Feared Romanian Securitate Chief Plesita Dies." *Pittsburgh Post-Gazette*, October 3, 2009. Accessed May 29, 2016. http://www.post-gazette.com/news/obituaries/2009/10/03/Obituary-Nicolae-Plesita-Feared-Romanian-secret-police-chief/stories/200910030131.

Nalepa, Monika. *Skeletons in the Closet: Transitional Justice in Post-Communist Europe*. New York: Cambridge University Press, 2010.

Nedelsky, Nadya. "Divergent Responses to a Common Past: Transitional Justice in the Czech Republic and Slovakia." *Theory and Society* 33:1 (2004), 65-115.

Nelken, David. "Using Legal Culture: Purposes and Problems." In *Using Legal Culture*, edited by David Nelken. 1-51. London: Wildy, Simmonds & Hill Publishing, 2012.

—. "Using the Concept of Legal Culture." *Australian Journal of Legal Philosophy* 29:1 (2004): 1-26.

Nichols, Bill. *Representing Reality: Issues and Concepts in Documentary*. Bloomington, IN: Indiana University Press, 1991.

Nora, Pierre. "Between Memory and History: Les Lieux de Mémoire." *Representations* 26 (Spring 1989): 7-24.

Nussbaum, Martha. *Political Emotions: Why Love Matters for Justice*. Cambridge, MA: Harvard University Press, 2013.

"Octav Bjoza, decorat cu cea mai înaltă distincție a statului." Digi24.ro, December 22, 2014. Accessed March 21, 2016. http://www.digi24.ro/Stiri/Digi24/Special/1989+Anul+care+a+schimbat+lumea/Octav+Bjoza+decorat+Klaus+Iohannis.

O'Donnell, Guillermo and Philippe Schmitter. *Transitions from Authoritarian Rule: Tentative Conclusions about Uncertain Democracies*. Baltimore: The Johns Hopkins University Press, 1986.

Offe, Claus. *Varieties of Transition: The East European and East German Experience*. Cambridge, MA: MIT Press, 1996.

—. "The Politics of Social Policy in East European Transitions." *Social Research* 60:4 (1993): 649-684.

"Official statement of the Group for Social Dialogue," *22*, June 1, 1990.

O'Neall, Kevin and Alexander L. Hinton. eds. *Genocide: Truth, Memory, and Representation*. Durham, NC: Duke University Press, 2009.

Oprea, Marius. *Banalitatea răului. O istorie a Securității în documente*. Iași: Polirom, 2003.

"Ordonanța de urgență a Guvernului României nr. 24 din 5 martie 2008 privind accesul la propriul dosar și deconspirarea Securității (OUG 24/2008)." *Monitorul Oficial al Romaniei* 182 (March 15, 2008): 2–10. Accessed September 16, 2016. http://www.becparlamentare2012.ro/DOCUMENTE/Legislatie/OUG%2024.pdf.

"Ordonanța de urgență a Guvernului României nr. 1 din 6 februarie 2008 pentru asigurarea continuității unor activități ale Consiliului Național pentru Studierea Arhivelor Securității." *Monitorul Oficial al Romaniei* 95 (February 6, 2008): 9–10. Accessed on September 16, 2016. http://www.societateatimisoara.ro/index.php?page=CNSAS.

"Ordonanța de urgență a Guvernului României nr. 16 din 22 februarie 2006 pentru modificarea și completarea Legii nr. 187/1999 privind accesul la propriul dosar și deconspirarea Securității ca poliție politică." *Monitorul Oficial al Romaniei* 182 (February 27, 2006): 1–8. Accessed September 16, 2016. http://www.cnsas.ro/documente/cadru_legal/OUG%2016_2006.pdf.

"Ordonanța de urgență a Guvernului României nr. 149 din 10 noiembrie 2005 privind unele măsuri pentru asigurarea continuității activității Consiliului Național pentru Studierea Arhivelor Securității." *Monitorul Oficial al Romaniei* 1008 (November 14, 2005): 7–8. Accessed September 16, 2016. http://www.cdep.ro/pls/legis/legis_pck.htp_act_text?idt=67748.

Osiel, Mark. *Mass Atrocity, Collective Memory and the Law*. New Brunswick, NJ: Transaction Publishers, 1997.

Oțel Petrescu, Aspazia. *Strigat-am catre tine, Doamne…* Botoşani: Axa, 2012.

Pakier, Malgorzata and Bo Strath. *A European Memory: Contested Histories and Politics of Remembrance*. New York: Bergham Books, 2010.

Palmer, Catherine. "An Ethnography of Englishness: Experiencing Identity through Tourism." *Annals of Tourism Research* 32:1 (2005): 7-27.

Papacioc, Arsenie. *Ne vorbeşte părintele Arsenie*, vol. 1. Făgăraş: Agaton, 2004.

"Părintele Arsenie Boca (1910-1989)." 2016. Accessed April 28, 2016. http://www.arsenieboca.ro.

Pârvu, Justin. "Aiudul, jertfă și sfințenie." In *Din Temnițe spre Sinaxare*, edited by Justinian Chira. 4-7. Galați: Egumenița, 2008.

Patapievici, Horia-Roman. "Revoluția română și anul 1989." *Idei in dialog* 12:63 (December 2009): 45-47.

Pavel, Dan and Iulia Huiu, *Nu putem reuşi decît împreună. O istorie analitică a Convenţiei Democratice, 1989-2000*. Iasi: Polirom, 2003.

Pavelescu, Alina. "Reconcilierea posttotalitară cu trecutul pe tărâmul istoriei publice-relaţia între arhivişti şi istorici în românia." In *Fără termen de prescriptie. Aspecte ale investigării comunismului în Europa*, edited by Sergiu Mustaţă and Igor Caşu. 190-200. Chişinău: Cartier, 2011.

Pavelescu, Şerban. *Stat şi Biserică în reconstrucţia politică a societăţilor postcomuniste din Balcani. Elemente pentru o sociologie politică a ortodoxiei*. Bucharest: Editura Militară, 2013.

Paxton, Robert O. *Vichy France: Old Guard and New Order, 1940-1944* (New York: Knopf, 1972)

Petrescu, Cristina. *From Robin Hood to Don Quixote: Resistance and Dissent in Communist Romania*. Bucharest: Editura Enciclopedică, 2013.

—. "Cum ne-am recuperat trecutul recent. Interpretarea comunismului în sfera publică postcomunistă." In *Mobilitatea elitelor în România secolului XX*, edited by Mihai Dinu Ghorghiu and Mihăiţă Lupu. 339-372. Piteşti: Paralela 45, 2008.

Petrescu, Cristina and Dragoş Petrescu. "The Canon of Remembering Romanian Communism: From Autobiographical Recollections to Collective Representations." In *Remembering Communism: Private and Public Recollections of Lived Experiences in Southeast Europe*, edited by Maria Todorova, Augusta Dimou and Stefan Troebst. 43-70. Budapest: Central European University Press, 2014.

—. "The Piteşti Syndrome: A Romanian Vergangenheitsbewältigung?" In *Postdiktatorische Geschichtskulturen im Süden und Osten Europas: Bestandsaufnahme und Forschungsperspektiven*, edited by Stefan Troebst. 502–618. Göttingen: Wallstein Verlag, 2010.

—. "Mastering vs. Coming to Terms with the Past: A Critical Analysis of Post-Communist Romanian Historiography." In *Narratives Unbound: Historical Studies in Post-Communist Europe*, edited by Sorin Antohi, Balasz Trencsenyi and Peter Apor. 311-408. Budapest: Central European University Press, 2007.

Petrescu, Dragoş. *Entangled Revolutions: The Breakdown of the Communist Regimes in East-Central Europe*. Bucharest: Editura Enciclopedică, 2014.

—. "Peitsche und Zuckerbrot: Erinnerung an die Ceauşescu-Ära in Rumänien." *Osteuropa Zeitschrift* 63:5-6 (2013): 355-366.

—. *Explaining the Romanian Revolution of 1989. Culture, Structure and Contingecy*. Bucharest: Editura Enciclopedică, 2010.

Pettai, Eva-Clarita and Vello Pettai. *Transitional and Retrospective Justice in the Baltic States*. Cambridge: Cambridge University Press, 2014.

Peukert, Detley. *Inside Nazi Germany: Conformity, Opposition, and Racism in Everyday Life*, translated by R. Deveson. New Haven, CT: Yale University Press, 1987.

Philpott, Daniel. "What Religion Brings to the Politics of Transitional Justice." *Journal of International Affairs* 61:1 (2007): 93-109.

Pine, Frances. "Retreat to the Household? Gendered Domains in Postsocialist Poland." In *Postsocialism: Ideals, Ideologies and Practices in Eurasia*, edited by Chris M. Hann. 95-113. London: Routledge, 2002.

Pintilie, Lucian. "După-amiaza unui torționar. Câteva idei fixe după terminarea filmărilor." *22*, September 17, 2013. Accessed May 29, 2016. http://revista22.ro/31225/bucurestiul-cultural-nr-127----dupa--amiaza-unui-tortionar-câteva-idei-fixe-dupa-terminarea-filmarilor.html.

Pippidi, Andrei. *Despre Statui si Morminte: Pentru o Teorie a Istoriei Simbolice* [On Statues and Tombs: Toward a Theory of Symbolic History]. Iasi: Polirom, 2000.

Plămădeală, Cristina. "The Use and Misuse of the Securitate's Files: The Case of Plamadeala." *Eurostudia* 10:1 (2015): 125-139.

Plesu, Andrei. *Obscenitatea publică*. Bucharest: Humanitas, 2004.

"Plugușor." *Martor. The Museum of the Romanian Peasant Anthropology Review* 7 (2002): 122-123.

Polish Constitutional Tribunal. "Judgment of 11th May 2007," May 11, 2007, file Ref. No. K 2/07_LUSTRATION.

Poole, Ross. "Memory, History and the Claims of the Past." *Memory Studies* 1:2 (2008): 149-166.

Popescu, Corneliu-Liviu. "Uzurparea de putere comisă de Curtea Constituţională în cazul cenzurii dispoziţiilor legale privind deconspirarea poliţiei politice comuniste." *Noua Revistă de Drepturile Omului* 4:1 (2008): 3–14.

Preda, Caterina. "Le rôle de la nostalgie dans la mémoire artistique du passé communiste dans la Roumanie contemporaine." *Canadian Slavonic Papers* 57:3-4 (2015): 268-283.

—. "Looking at the past through an artistic lens: art of memorialization," In *History of Communism in Europe. Politics of memory in Post-communist Europe*. 1: 129-148. Bucharest: Zeta Books, 2010.

"Prezentele presedintelui." April 19, 2016. Accessed April 26, 2016. http://afdpr.ro/categorie/prezentele-presedintelui.

Přibáň, Jiří. *Legal Symbolism: On Law, Time and European Identity*. London: Ashgate, 2007.

"Procesul si executia sotilor Ceausescu." Youtube, June 21, 2014. Accessed May 29, 2016. https://www.youtube.com/watch?v=584UW7dTTT4.

Purcărea, Nicolae. *Urlă haita…* Bucharest: Fundaţia Sfinţii Închisorilor, 2012.

Pusca, Anca M. *Post-Communist Aesthetics*. London: Routledge, 2016.

Quermonne, Jean Louis. *L'appareil administratif de l'Etat*. Paris : Seuil, 1991.

"Queue." *Martor. The Museum of the Romanian Peasant Anthropology Review* 7 (2002): 132-138.

Quint, Peter E. "Judging the Past: The Prosecution of East German Border Guards and the GDR Chain of Command." *The Review of Politics* 61:2 (1999): 303-329.

Radbruch, Gustav. "Injustice légale et droit supralégal." *Archives de l'Association Française de Philosophie du Droit* 39:1 (1994): 305-318.

Răduţă, Cristina. "Statuia lui Ion C. Brătianu va fi reconstruită şi amplasată în Piaţa Universităţii." *Adevarul*, January 31, 2014. Accessed February 12, 2016. http://adevarul.ro/news/bucuresti/statuia-ion-c-bratianu-reconstuita-amplasata-piata-universitatii-1_52eb7965c7b855ff56f4bd06/index.html.

Ramirez-Barat, Clara. *Transitional Justice, Culture and Society: Beyond Outreach*. New York: Columbia University Press, 2014.

Rancière, Jacques. *La fable cinématographique*. Paris: Ed. Du Seuil, 2011.

—. *On the Shores of Politics*. London: Verso, 2007.

"Ration." *Martor. The Museum of the Romanian Peasant Anthropology Review* 7 (2002): 140-141.

Renov, Alan. *Theorizing Documentary*. New York: Routledge, 1993.

"Reţeaua informativă a Securităţii din învăţământul teologic la sfârşitul anilor '70 şi începutul anilor '80." *Arhivele totalitarismului* XI, 40–41:3–4 (2003): 47–53.

Ricoeur, Paul. *Memory, History, Forgetting*. Chicago : Chicago University Press, 2004.

Riis, Carsten. *Religion, Politics, and Historiography in Bulgaria*. Boulder: Columbia University Press, 2002.

Rings, Werner. *Life with the Enemy: Collaboration and Resistance in Hitler's Europe, 1939-1945*, translated by J. M. Brownjohn. New York: Doubleday, 1982.

Rogojanu, Dumitru-Cătălin. *Imaginea torționarului comunist reflectată în memorialistica universului concentraționar românesc (1947-1989)*. Târgovişte: Cetatea de Scaun, 2014.

Romanian Attorney General's decision of 5 April 2016 on the reopening of the prosecution in December 1989 events. Document with Alexandru Gussi.

Romanian Constitutional Court. "Decision no. 820/2010." *Monitorul Oficial al Romaniei* 420 (June 23, 2010).

Rose, Jacqueline. *The Last Resistance*. London: Verso, 2007.

Rose-Redwood, Reuban, Derek Alderman and Maoz Azaryahu. "Geographies of Toponymic Inscription: New Directions in Critical Place-Name Studies." *Progress in Human Geography* 34:4 (2010): 453-470.

Rose, Richard. *New Europe Barometer I-XV Trend Dataset, 1991-2007*. [data collection]. *2nd Edition.* UK Data Service. SN: 5241, 2010. Accessed September 15, 2016. http://dx.doi.org/10.5255/UKDA-SN-5241-1.

Rothberg, Michael. *Multidirectional Memory: Remembering the Holocaust in the Age of Decolonization*. Stanford: Stanford University Press, 2009.

—. *Traumatic Realism: The Demand of Holocaust Representation*. Minneapolis: University of Minnesota Press, 2000.

Rouhier-Willoughby, Jeanmarie. "The Gulag Reclaimed as Sacred Space: The Negotiation of Memory at the Holy Spring of Iskitim." *Laboratorium* 7:1 (2015): 51-70.

Rowe, Shawn, James Wertsch and Tatyana Y. Kosyaeva. "Linking Little Narratives to Big Ones: Narrative and Public Memory in History Museums." *Culture & Psychology* 8:1 (2002): 97–113.

Rus, Alin. *Mineriadele. Între manipulare politică și solidaritate muncitorească*. Bucharest: Curtea Veche, 2007.

Rusan, Romulus, ed. *Memorialul Victimelor Comunismului şi al Rezistenței: ghid și activitate.* Bucharest: Academia Civică, 2014.

—. *Chronology and Geography of Communist Repression in Romania*. Bucharest: Civic Academy Foundation, 2007.

Rush, Peter D. and Olivera Simić. eds. *The Arts of Transitional Justice*. New York: Springer, 2014.

Sadurski, Wojciech. *Rights before Courts: A Study of Constitutional Courts in Postcommunist States of Central and Eastern Europe*. Dordrecht: Springer, 2014, 2nd edition.

Sather-Wagstaff, Joy. *Heritage that Hurts: Tourists in the Memoryscapes of September 11*. Walnut Creek: Left Coast Press, 2011.

Satzeger, Helmut. “German Criminal Law and the Rome Statute - A Critical Analysis of the New German Code of Crimes against International Law.” *International Criminal Law Review* 2:3 (2002): 261-282.

Sava, Ionel Nicu. ed. *Album Memorial – Monumente închinate jertfei, suferinței și luptei împotriva comunismului.* Bucharest: Ziua and AFDPR, 2004.

Schultz, Deborah and Alina Serban. “Public Memory and National Identity under Construction: The Trajectory of Monuments in Romania in the Communist and Post-Communist Periods.” *Centropa* 10:1 (2010): 56-66.

“Seminarul Teologie si politica, Cheia, 16–18 octombrie 2003.” *Revista istorică* 5–6 (2004): 231–233.

Serviciul Roman de Informatii. *Cartea albă a Securității. Istorii literare şi artistice (1969-1989).* Bucharest: Presa Românească, 1996.

—. “Evenimentele din decembrie 1989 vazute de SRI.” *Ordinea, Supliment special*, 1994.

Shafir, Michael. “Memory and History in Postcommunism: Preliminary Theoretical Remarks.” *Sfera Politicii* 120-121-122 (2006). Accessed April 28, 2016. http://www.sferapoliticii.ro/sfera/120-121-122/art21-shafir.html.

—. *Romania - Politics, Economics and Society: Political Stagnation and Simulated Change.* London: Frances Pinter, 1985.

Siani-Davies, Peter. "Revoluția în societățile comuniste și postcomuniste." In *Revoluția Română din decembrie 1989. Istorie și memorie*, edited by Bogdan Murgescu. 115-156. Iasi: Polirom, 2007.

—. *The Romanian Revolution of December 1989.* Ithaca, NY: Cornell University Press, 2005.

Simic, Olivera. “Stories We Tell: Documentary Theater, Performance and Justice in Transition.” In *Post-Communist Transitional Justice: Lesson from Twenty-Five Years of Experience*, edited by Lavinia Stan and Nadya Nedelsky. 252-275. New York: Cambridge University Press, 2015.

Simic, Olivera and Zala Volcic. eds. *Transitional Justice and Civil Society in the Balkans*. New York: Springer, 2013.

Sincan, Anca. “Silencing the Archive – A Methodological Insight into the Research for the Study ‘A Day in the Life of an Inspector for Religious Denominatinos’.” *Anuarul Institutului de Cercetari Socio-Umane ‘Gheorghe Sincai’* 15 (2012): 144-155.

—. “Of Middlemen and Intermediaries: Negotiating the State Church Relationship in Communist Romania. The Formative Years” (PhD diss., Central European University, Budapest, 2011).

Skinner, Quentin. *Visions of Politics: Regarding Method*, vol. I. Cambridge: Cambridge University Press, 2002.

Smith, Dorothy E. *Writing the Social: Critique, Theory and Investigations*. Toronto, ON: University of Toronto Press, 2004.

—. “The Social Construction of Documentary Reality.” *Sociological Inquiry* 44:4 (1974): 257-268.

Smith, Laurajane. “The Cultural ‘Work’ of Tourism.” In *The Cultural Moment in Tourism*, edited by Laurajane Smith, Emma Waterton and Steve Watson. 219-229. London: Routledge, 2012.

Stamatescu, Mihai, Raluca Grosescu, Dorin Dobrincu, Andrei Muraru, Liviu Plesa, and Sorin Andreescu. *O istorie a comunismului din România. Manual pentru liceu*. Iasi: Polirom, 2008.

Stan, Apostol. *România, București 1989. Enigmele Revoluției?* Bucharest: Saeculum I.O, 2013.

Stan, Liviu. “Despre canonizarea sfinților în Biserica ortodoxă - noțuni introductive.” *Ortodoxia* 2:2 (1950).

Stan, Lavinia. *Transitional Justice in Post-Communist Romania: The Politics of Memory*. New York: Cambridge University Press, 2013.

—. “Civil Society and Post-Communist Transitional Justice in Romania.” In *Transitional Justice and Civil Society in the Balkans*, edited by Olivera Simić and Zala Volčič. 17-31. London: Springer, 2013.

—. “Reckoning with the Communist Past in Romania: A Scorecard.” *Europe-Asia Studies* 65:1 (2013): 127-146.

—. “Witch-hunt or Moral Rebirth?: Romanian Parlamentary Debates on Lustration.” *East European Politics and Societies* 26:2 (2012): 274-295.

—. ed., *Transitional Justice in Eastern Europe and the Former Soviet Union*. London: Routledge, 2009.

—. “Romania.” In *Transitional Justice in Eastern Europe and the Former Soviet Union*, edited by Lavinia Stan. 128-151. London: Routledge, 2009.

—. “Truth Commissions in Post-Communism: The Overlooked Solution?,” *Open Political Science Journal*, 2 (2009): 1-13

—. “Comisia Tismăneanu: Repere Internaţionale.” *Sfera Politicii* 126-127 (2007): 7-13.

—. “The Vanishing Truth: Politics and Memory in Post-Communist Europe.” *East European Quarterly* 40:4 (2006): 383-408.

—. "The Roof over Our Head: Property Restitution in Romania." *Journal of Communist Studies and Transition Politics* 22:2 (2006): 180-205.

—. "The Politics of Memory in Poland: Lustration, File Access and Court Proceedings." *Studies in Post-Communism Occasional Paper* 10, St. Francis Xavier University, Centre for Post-Communist Studies, 2006.

—. "The Romanian Anticorruption Bill." *Studies in Post-Communism Occasional Paper* 6, St. Francis Xavier University, Centre for Post-Communist Studies, 2004.

—. "Women as Anti-communist Dissidents and Collaborators of the Secret Police," in *Genre and the (Post)Communist Woman. Analyzing Transformations of the Central and Eastern European Female Ideal*, eds. Florentina Andreescu and Michael Shapiro (New York: Routledge, 2014), 80-97.

Stan, Lavinia and Diane Vancea. "Old Wine in New Bottles: The Romanian Elections of 2008." *Problems of Post-Communism* 56:5 (2009): 47-61.

Stan, Lavinia and Lucian Turcescu. *Church, State, and Democracy in Expanding Europe*. New York: Oxford University Press, 2011.

—. *Religion and Politics in Post-Communist Romania*. New York: Oxford University Press, 2007.

—. "Politics, National Symbols and the Romanian National Cathedral." *Europe-Asia Studies* 58:7 (2006): 1119-1139.

—. "The Devil's Confessors: Priests, Communists, Spies, and Informers." *East European Politics and Societies* 19:4 (2005): 655-688.

Stan, Lavinia and Nadya Nedelsky. eds. *Encyclopedia of Transitional Justice*, 3 vols. New York: Cambridge University Press, 2013.

Stănescu, Mircea *Reeducarea în România Comunistă. Aiud, Suceava, Piteşti, Braşov*. Iaşi: Polirom, 2010.

Ştefănescu, Alex. "La o nouă lectură: Cireşarii." *România literară*, March 9, 2003. Accessed April 10, 2016.
http://www.romlit.ro/constantin_chiri.

Ştefănescu, Domniţa. *Cinci ani din istoria României: O cronologie a evenimentelor decembrie 1989–decembrie 1995*. Bucharest: Maşina de Scris, 1995.

Steinhardt, Nicolae. *Jurnalul Fericirii*. Cluj: Dacia, 1991.

Steinke, Ronen. *The Politics of International Criminal Justice. German Perspective from Nuremberg to The Hague*. Oxford: Hart Publishing, 2012.

Stevens, Garth, Norman Duncan and Derek Hook. eds. *Race, Memory and the Apartheid Archive: Towards a Transformative Psychosocial Praxis*. Basingstoke: Palgrave Macmillan, 2013.

Stransky, Zbynek Z. "Museums in Post-Communist Countries." In *Museums and Europe 1992*, edited by Susan Pearce. 174-176. London: Athlone Press, 1992.

Streletz, Kesseler and Krentz v. Germany (2001), App. 34044/96, 35532/97 and 22801/98, Judgement March, 22. Accessed July 30, 2013. file:///C:/Users/raluca/Downloads/CASE%20OF%20STRELETZ,%20 KESSLER%20AND%20KRENZ%20v.%20GERMANY.pdf.

"Supplies." *Martor. The Museum of the Romanian Peasant Anthropology Review* 7 (2002): 164-165.

Svašek, Maruška. ed. *Postsocialism: Politics and Emotions in Central and Eastern Europe*. New York: Berghahn Books, 2006.

Szelenyi, Ivan and Szonja Szelenyi. "Circulation or Reproduction of Elites during Post-Communist Transformation in Russia and Eastern Europe." *Theory & Society* 24:5 (1995): 615-638.

Tanase, Stelian. *Anatomia mistificarii*. Bucharest: Humanitas, 2000.

Tănăsoiu, Cosmina. "Intellectuals and Post-Communist Politics in Romania. An Analysis of Public Discourse, 1990-2000." *East European Politics and Societies* 22:1 (2008): 80-113.

—. "The Tismăneanu Report: Romania Revisits Its Past." *Problems of Post-Communism* 54:4 (2007): 60-69.

Taylor, Diana. *The Archive and the Repertoire: Performing Cultural Memory in the Americas*. Durham: Duke University Press, 2003.

Teitel, Ruti. *Transitional Justice*. New York: Oxford University Press, 2000.

"Tent (in the House)." *Martor. The Museum of the Romanian Peasant Anthropology Review* 7 (2002): 171-172.

"The End of a Political Career." *Radio Romania International*, Bucharest, September 4, 2006. Accessed August 12, 2015. http://www.rri.ro/index.php?lmb=4&art=16856.

The Romanian Constitution of 1952, 1952. Accessed May 9, 2016. http://legislatie.resurse-pentru-democratie.org/constitutie/constitutia-republicii-populare-romane-1952.php.

Till, Karen. *The New Berlin: Memory, Politics, Place*. Minneapolis: University of Minnesota Press, 2005.

—. "Staging the Past: Landscape Designs, Cultural Identity and Erinnerungspolitik at Berlin's Neue Wache." *Ecumene* 6:3 (1999): 251-283.

Tileagă, Cristian. *The Nature of Prejudice: Society, Discrimination and Moral Exclusion*. London: Routledge, 2015.

—. *Political Psychology: Critical Perspectives*. Cambridge: Cambridge University Press, 2013.

—. "Apologia." In *Research Methods for Memory Studies*, edited by Emily Keightley and Michael Pickering. 185-199. Edinburgh: Edinburgh University Press, 2013.

—. "Communism in Retrospect: The Rhetoric of Historical Representation and Writing the Collective Memory of Recent Past." *Memory Studies* 5:4 (2012): 462-478.

—. "(Re)writing Biography: Memory, Identity, and Textually Mediated Reality in Coming to Terms with the Past." *Culture & Psychology* 17:2 (2011): 197-215.

—. "The Social Organization of Representations of History: The Textual Accomplishment of Coming to Terms with the Past." *British Journal of Social Psychology* 48:2 (2009): 337-355.

—. "What Is a 'Revolution'? National Commemoration, Collective Memory, and Managing Authenticity in the Representation of a Political Event." *Discourse and Society* 19:3 (2008): 359-382.

Tismăneanu, Vladimir. "Democracy and Memory: Romania Confronts Its Communist Past." *The Annals of the American Academy of Political and Social Science* 617:1 (2008): 166-180.

—. "Confronting Romania's Past: A Response to Charles King." *Slavic Review* 66:4 (2007): 724-727.

—. *Refuzul de a uita: articole şi comentarii politice (2006-2007)*. Bucharest: Curtea Veche, 2007.

—. *Stalinism for All Seasons: A Political History of Romanian Communism*. Berkeley, CA: University of California Press, 2003.

—. *Fantasies of Salvation. Democracy, Nationalism and Myth in Post-Communist Europe*. Princeton: Princeton University Press, 1998.

Tismaneanu, Vladimir, Dorin Dobrincu and Cristian Vasile. eds. *Comisia Prezidentiala pentru Analiza Dictaturii Comuniste din Romania. Raport Final*. Bucharest: Humanitas, 2007.

Toea, Diana. "Românii, încă nostalgici după Ceaușescu: Explicațiile unui istoric." Ziare.com, December 18, 2014. Accessed April 10, 2016. http://www.ziare.com/nicolae-ceausescu/comunism/romanii-inca-nostalgici-dupa-ceausescu-explicatiile-unui-istoric-1339109.

Todorov, Tzvetan. *In Defense of the Enlightenment*. London: Atlantic Books, 2009.

"Top Liberals Expelled from the Party." HotNews.ro, September 4, 2006.

Transcriptul 'procesului' Nicolae si Elena Ceausescu. Ceausescu.org, December 25, 1989. Accessed May 29, 2016. http://www.ceausescu.org/ceausescu_texts/revolution/trial-ro.htm.

Transparency International. *Corruption Perception Index*, 1995-2015. Accessed September 15, 2016. http://www.transparency.org/research/cpi/overview.

Tudoran, Dorin. *Eu, fiul lor. Dosar de Securitate*. Iasi: Polirom, 2010.

Todorov, Tzvetan. *Hope and Memory: Reflections on the Twentieth Century*. London: Atlantic Books, 2003.

—. *Facing the Extreme: Moral Life in the Concentrations Camps*. New York: Henry Holt, 1996.

Todorova, Maria and Zsuzsa Gille. eds. *Post-communist Nostalgia*. New York: Berghahn Books, 2010.

Turcescu, Lucian and Lavinia Stan. "Church Collaboration and Resistance under Communism Revisited: The Case of Patriarch Justinian Marina (1948–1977)." *Eurostudia. Revue Transatlantique de Recherche sur l'Europe* 10:1 (2015): 75–103.

—. "The Romanian Orthodox Church and Democratisation: Twenty Years Later." *International Journal for the Study of the Christian Church* 10:2 (2010): 144-159.

Turner, Catherine. "Delivering Lasting Peace, Democracy, and Human Rights in Transition: The Role of International Law." *International Journal of Transitional Justice* 2:2 (2008): 126-151.

Tyson, Adam. "Genocide Documentary as Intervention." *Journal of Genocide Research* 17:2 (2015): 177-199.

Union of American Hebrew Congregations. *Spiritual Resistance: Art from Concentration Camps, 1940-1945: A Selection of Drawings and Paintings from the Collection of Kibbutz Lohamei Haghetaot, Israel*. Philadelphia: The Jewish Publication Society of America, 1981.

UN Security Council. "The Rule of Law and Transitional Justice in Conflict and Post-Conflict Societies: Report of the Secretary-General." UN Doc. S/2004/616. New York: United Nations, 2004. Accessed September 24, 2016. http://www.ipu.org/splz-e/unga07/law.pdf.

Ursachi, Raluca and Raluca Grosescu. "Transitional Criminal Justice in Post-Communist Romania" (paper presented at the Crimes of the Communist Regimes conference, Prague, February 24-26, 2010).

Valery-Gross, Nicole. *Binecuvânatată fii închisoare*. Bucharest: Universul, 1997.

Valsiner, Jaan and Rene van der Veer. *The Social Mind: The Construction of an Idea*. Cambridge: Cambridge University Press, 2000.

van Leeuwen, Theo. "Representing Social Action." *Discourse & Society* 6:1 (1995): 81-106.

Van Stokkom, Bas, Neekle Dorn, and Paul van Togeren. *Public Forgiveness in Post-Conflict Contexts*. Cambridge: Intersentia, 2012.

Vasile, Cristian. “CPACCR, Tismăneanu Commission.” In *Encyclopedia of Transitional Justice*, edited by Lavinia Stan and Nadya Nedelsky. 3:366-371. New York: Cambridge University Press, 2013.

—. “The Orthodox Church and the State in Romania: Experiences with Interference and Separation” (paper presented at the Churches and State Authority / Violence in Central and Eastern Europe conference, Berlin, December 7, 2012).

—. “Comisia Prezidenţială pentru Analiza Dictaturii Comuniste şi accesul la arhivele comunismului românesc.” In *Fără termen de prescriptie. Aspecte ale investigării comunismului în Europa*, edited by Sergiu Mustaţă and Igor Caşu. 201-215. Chişinău: Cartier, 2011.

—. “Biserica şi regimul comunist (1944-1948),” In *Istoria românilor*, vol. 9, *România în anii 1940-1947*, edited by Dinu C. Giurescu, and Florin Şperlea. 873-907. Bucharest: Academia Română and Editura Enciclopedică, 2008.

—. *Biserica Ortodoxă Română în primul deceniu communist*. Bucharest: Curtea Veche, 2005.

—. “Autorităţile comuniste şi problema mănăstirilor ortodoxe în anii ’50.” In *Anii 1954-1960: Fluxurile şi Refluxurile Stalinismului*, edited by Romulus Rusan. 179-189. Bucharest: Civic Academy Foundation, 2000.

Vasile, Danion. “Avva Justin Parvu si Sfintii Inchisorilor,” video, Iasi, March 19, 2014. Accessed March 21, 2016. https://www.youtube.com/watch?v=IXrAEwKHXFM.

—. “Criteriile canonizării sfinţilor închisorilor.” In *Din Temniţe spre Sinaxare*, edited by Justinian Chira. 19-25. Galaţi: Egumeniţa, 2008.

Vatulescu, Cristina. *Police Aesthetics: Literature, Film, and the Secret Police in Soviet Times*. Stanford: Stanford University Press, 2010.

Velikonja, Mitja. “Lost in Transition: Nostalgia for Socialism in Post-Socialist Countries.” *East European Politics and Societies* 23:4 (2009): 533-551.

Venice Commission. “Law on the Cleanliness of the Figure of High Functionaries of the Public Administration and Elected Persons of the Republic of Albania, Opinion No 524/2009.” Strasbourg, August 13, 2009.

Verdery, Katherine. *The Political Lives of Dead Bodies: Reburial and Postsocialist Change*. New York: Columbia University Press, 1999.

—. *What Was Socialism and What Comes Next?* Princeton: Princeton University Press, 1996.

—. *National Ideology under Socialism: Identity and Cultural Politics in Ceauşescu's Romania*. Berkeley, CA: University of California Press, 1991.

Veyne, Paul. *Writing History: Essay on Epistemology*, translated by Mina Moore-Rinvolucri. Middletown, Connecticut: Wesleyan University Press, 1984.

Vultur, Smaranda. *Istoria trăită – Istoria povestită: Deportare în* Bărăgan. Timişoara: Amarcord, 1997.

Vyshinsky, Andrei. *The Law of the Soviet State*. Westport, CT: Greenwood Press, 1948.

Warren, Mark. ed., *Democracy and Trust*. New York: Cambridge University Press, 1999.

Waśkiewicz, Andrzej. "The Polish Home Army and the Politics of Memory." *East European Politics and Society* 24:1 (2010): 44-58.

Welsh, Helga. "Beyond the National: Pathways of Diffusion." In *Post-Communist Transitional Justice: Lessons from Twenty-Five Years of Experience*, edited by Lavinia Stan and Nadya Nedelsky. 167-187. New York: Cambridge University Press, 2015.

—. "Dealing with the Communist Past: Central and East European Experiences after 1990." *Europe Asia Studies* 48:3 (1996): 413-428.

Wertsch, James V. "Collective Memory." In *The Cambridge Handbook of Sociocultural Psychology*, edited by Jaan Valsiner and Alberto Rosa. 625-644. Cambridge: Cambridge University Press, 2007.

—. *Voices of Collective Remembering*. Cambridge: Cambridge University Press, 2002.

Wertsch, James and Zurab Karumidze. "Spinning the Past: Russian and Georgian Accounts of the War of August 2008." *Memory Studies* 2:3 (2009): 377-391.

White, Hayden. "Historical Emplotment and the Problem of Truth." In *Probing the Limits of Representation: Nazism and the Final Solution*, edited by Saul Friedlander. Cambridge, MA: Harvard University Press, 1992.

—. *The Content of the Form: Narrative Discourse and Historical Representation*. Baltimore, MA: Johns Hopkins University Press, 1990.

—. *Metahistory: The Historical Imagination in the Nineteenth Century Europe*. Baltimore: The Johns Hopkins University Press, 1973.

Wilke, Cristiane. "Remembering Complexity? Memorials for Nazi Victims in Berlin." *International Journal of Transitional Justice* 7:1 (2013): 136-156.

Williams, Kieran, Aleks Szczerbiak and Brigid Fowler. "Explaining Lustration in Eastern Europe: A Post-communist politics approach." *SEI Working Paper* 62 (2003), University of Sussex. Accessed September 16, 2016. https://www.sussex.ac.uk/webteam/gateway/file.php?name=sei-working-paper-no-62.pdf&site=266.

Witcombe, Andrea. "Using Immersive and Interactive Approaches to Interpreting Traumatic Experiences for Tourists." In *Heritage and Tourism: Place, Encounter, Engagement*, edited by Russell Staiff, Robyn Bushell and Steve Watson. 152-170. London: Routledge, 2013.

Wurmbrandt, Richard. *Torture for Christ*. Bartlesville: Living Sacrifice Book Company, 1998.

Young, Craig and Duncan Light. "Multiple and Contested Geographies of Memory: Remembering the 1989 Romanian 'Revolution'." In *Memories of War, Place and Identity*, edited by Danielle Drozdzewski, Sarah de Nardi and Emma Waterton. 56-73. London: Routledge, 2016.

Young, James. *At Memory's Edge: After-Images of the Holocaust in Contemporary Art and Architecture*. New Haven: Yale University Press, 2000.

Zeruvabel, Eviatar. *Collective Memory and the Social Shape of the Past*. Chicago: Chicago University Press, 2003.

Movies and art works

89, exhibition by Mircea Suciu opened in 2007 at h'art Gallery, Bucharest.

1989 – Anul care a dispărut (1989 – The Year That Disappeared), theater production directed in 2015 by Ana Mărgineanu at Teatrul Mic, Bucharest.

A fost sau nu a fost (12:08 East of Bucharest), artistic movie directed in 2006 by Corneliu Porumboiu.

Amintiri din epoca de aur (Tales from the Golden Age), artistic movie directed in 2009 by Hanno Höfer, Răzvan Mărculescu, Cristian Mungiu, Constantin Popescu, and Ioana Uricaru.

Balanța (The Oak), artistic movie directed in 1992 by Lucian Pintilie.

Binecuvîntată fii inchisoare (Benie sois-tu prison), artistic movie directed in 2002 by Nicolae Mărgineanu.

Ceaușescu, painting produced in 2007 by Adrian Ghenie.

Comedie Roșie (Red Comedy), theater production directed in 2006 by Alexandru Tocilescu at National Theater, Bucharest.

Cum mi-am petrecut sfârșitul lumii (How I Spent the End of World), artistic movie directed in 2006 by Cătălin Mitulescu.

Dupa-amiaza unui tortionar (The Afternoon of a Torturer), artistic movie directed in 2001 by Lucian Pintilie.

Fernando ha vuelto, documentary film directed in 1997 by Silvio Caiozzi.

Kapitalism, reteta noastra secreta (Kapitalism, Our Secret Receipe), documentary movie directed in 2010 by Alexandru Solomon.

Memorialul Durerii, TVR2, 2013. Accessed April 28, 2016. http://tvr2.tvr.ro/emisiuni/memorialul-durerii_4182.html.

Nicolae, painting produced in 2009 by Adrian Ghenie.

Niki Ardelean, colonel in rezerva, artistic movie directed in 2003 by Lucian Pintilie.

Nunta muta (Silent Wedding), artistic movie directed in 2008 by Horatiu Malaele.

Poarta Albă, artistic movie directed in 2014 by Nicolae Mărgineanu.

Posthumous Dialogue with Nicolae Ceaușescu, video by Ion Grigorescu, exhibited at The Museum of Modern Art, New York in 2016.

Razboi pe calea undelor, movie directed in 2007 by Alexandru Solomon.

Schindler's List, artistic movie directed in 1995 by Steven Spielberg.

Study for the boogyman, painting produced in 2010 by Adrian Ghenie .

Three colours, video produced in 2007-2008 by Istvan Laszlo.

Trei zile pana la Craciun, documentary theater produced in 2012 by Radu Gabrea.

Tuns, ras și frezat, short movie directed in 2013 by Bogdan Mureșanu.

Typographic Majuscule, theater play directed in 2013 by Gianina Cărbunariu.

Ultimele ore ale lui Ceaușescu, documentary theater produced in 2009 by Milo Rau and Simone Eisenring.

Understanding History, a series of paintings produced in 2009 by Dragoș Burlacu.

Xmm from Ykm, theater play directed in 2011 by Gianina Cărbunariu.

Internet comments

Adina. Comment # 6. Latrecut.ro, March 31, 2006. Accessed on 27 May 2016. http://www.latrecut.ro/2006/03/cozi.

Alex33. Comment # 18. Latrecut.ro, August 21, 2006. Accessed May 28, 2016. http://www.latrecut.ro/2006/03/za-darc-said/#comments.

Alice. Comments # 11. Latrecut.ro, June 15, 2008. Accessed May 27, 2016. http://www.latrecut.ro/2008/04/noi-in-anul-2000/#comments.

Analuchian. Comment # 16. December 24, 2006. Accessed May 27, 2016. http://www.latrecut.ro/2006/12/generatia-x/#comments.

Anca. Comment # 29. Latrecut.ro, January 7, 2010. Accessed May 27, 2016. http://www.latrecut.ro/2007/12/1980-1989-amintiri-de-atunci/# comments.

Andreika. "1980-1989, amintiri de-atunci." Latrecut.ro, December 27, 2007. Accessed May 28, 2016. http://www.latrecut.ro/2007/12/1980-1989-amintiri-de-atunci/#comments.

Archive for the 'Scoala' Category. Latrecut.ro, 2006-2015. Accessed May 27, 2016. http://www.latrecut.ro/category/scoala.

Babilonul imobiliar. Comment # 11. Latrecut.ro, January 20, 2008. Accessed July 9, 2016. http://www.latrecut.ro/2007/12/1980-1989-amintiri-de-atunci/#comments.

Balqan. Comment # 12. Latrecut.ro, April 12, 2006. Accessed May 28, 2016. http://www.latrecut.ro/2006/03/za-darc-said/#comments.

"Bancuri din perioada de dinainte de 'astia' – Top 10." Latrecut.ro, January 19, 2010. Accessed May 27, 2016. http://www.latrecut.ro/category/social/bancuri/.

Bb. Comment # 12. Latrecut.ro, December 2, 2008. Accessed May 27, 2016. http://www.latrecut.ro/2008/04/inchiderea-programului/#comments.

Calin. Comment # 22. Latrecut.ro, April 13, 2007. Accessed May 27, 2016. http://www.latrecut.ro/2006/03/za-darc-said/#comments.

Ceasuri. Comment # 23. Latrecut.ro, July 31, 2008. Accessed May 27, 2016. http://www.latrecut.ro/2007/12/1980-1989-amintiri-de-atunci/#comments.

Costi. Comment # 15. Latrecut.ro, August 31, 2006. Accessed May 27, 2016. http://www.latrecut.ro/2006/04/manuale-de-citireromana-din-clasele-primare/#comments.

Dan Adrian. Comment # 41. Latrecut.ro, April 22, 2008. Accessed May 27, 2016. http://www.latrecut.ro/2006/12/amintiri/comment-page-1/#comments.

Dienutza. Comment # 29. Latrecut.ro, July 27, 2009. Accessed May 27, 2016. http://www.latrecut.ro/2006/03/za-darc-said/#comments.

Dr. Me. Comment # 4. Latrecut.ro, December 13, 2006. Accessed May 27, 2016. http://www.latrecut.ro/2006/12/generatia-x/#comments.

Eh. Comment # 1. Latrecut.ro, March 7, 2006. Accessed May 27, 2016. http://www.latrecut.ro/2006/03/cozi./.

Flintobert. "Jocuri pierdute." Latrecut.ro, January 4, 2009. Accessed July 9, 2016. http://www.latrecut.ro/2009/01/jocuri-pierdute/#comments.

GayRo. Comment # 16. Latrecut.ro, September 22, 2006. Accessed May 27, 2016. http://www.latrecut.ro/2006/04/manuale-de-citireromana-din-clasele-primare/#comments.

Grim Riper. "Za darc said." Latrecut.ro, March 31, 2006. Accessed May 27, 2016. http://www.latrecut.ro/?s=darc+said.

Hedes Mihai. Comment # 12. Latrecut.ro, December 12, 2006. Accessed May 27, 2016. http://www.latrecut.ro/2006/12/generatia-x/#comments.

Horia Gârbea. "Poveste românească de Crăciun sau Moartea şi învierea lui Moş Crăciun." Latrecut.ro, May 17, 2006. Accessed May 28, 2016. http://www.latrecut.ro/2006/05/poveste-de-craciun/#comments.

Iani. Comment # 10. Latrecut.ro, April 22, 2008. Accessed May 27, 2016. http://www.latrecut.ro/2006/12/amintiri/comment-page-1/#comments.

Ionut. "Amintiri din copilarie." Latrecut.ro, August 3, 2007. Accessed May 27, 2016. http://www.latrecut.ro/2007/08/amintiri-din-copilarie/# comments.

Iuliduli. Comment # 10. Latrecut.ro, January 14, 2008. Accessed May 28, 2016. http://www.latrecut.ro/2007/12/1980-1989-amintiri-de-atunci/# comments.

Laura Nostalgica. "fascinantii ani '80." Latrecut.ro, February 7, 2008. Accessed July 9, 2016. http://www.latrecut.ro/2008/02/fascinantii-ani-80/#comments.

Leu. Comment # 6. Latrecut.ro, January 7, 2008. Accessed May 27, 2016. http://www.latrecut.ro/2007/12/amintirile-mele-la-30-ani/#comments.

Mande. "Cheia de gat." Latrecut.ro, March 4, 2006. Accessed May 27, 2016. http://www.latrecut.ro/2006/03/cheia-de-gat/#comments.

Meda. Comment # 4. Latrecut.ro, December 31, 2007. Accessed July 9, 2016. http://www.latrecut.ro/2007/07/urme-in-zapada-amintiri-de-mic-copil/#comments.

Micutza. Comment # 24. Latrecut.ro, April 25, 2010. Accessed May 27, 2016. http://www.latrecut.ro/2006/04/ciresari-adevarati/#comments.

Ovidiu. Comment # 18. Latrecut.ro, June 8, 2006. Accessed July 9, 2016. http://www.latrecut.ro/2006/05/poveste-de-craciun/#comments.

Pe vremea mea. Comment # 14. Latrecut.ro, September 11, 2006. Accessed May 27, 2016. http://www.latrecut.ro/2006/03/cozi./#comments.

Pirpirel. Comment # 19. Latrecut.ro, February 21, 2010. Accessed July 9, 2016. http://www.latrecut.ro/2006/03/cozi./.

Razvanx. Comment # 17. Latrecut.ro, January 10, 2007. Accessed May 27, 2016. http://www.latrecut.ro/2006/03/cozi./.

Scrintin. "manuale de citire/romana din clasele primare." Latrecut.ro, April 26, 2006. Accessed July 9, 2016.

http://www.latrecut.ro/2006/04/manuale-de-citireromana-din-clasele-primare/#comments.
Sirg. "Noi in anul 2000." Latrecut.ro, April 25, 2008. Accessed May 27, 2016. http://www.latrecut.ro/2008/04/noi-in-anul-2000/#comments.
Sirg. "Inchiderea programului." Latrecut.ro, April 2, 2008. Accessed July 9, 2016. http://www.latrecut.ro/2008/04/inchiderea-programului/#comments.
Sirg. "Cărți de joc educative." Latrecut.ro, October 6, 2006. Accessed July 9, 2016. http://www.latrecut.ro/2007/10/carti-de-joc-educative-muzica/#comments.
Sorin. Comment # 30. Latrecut.ro, January 11, 2010. Accessed May 27, 2016. http://www.latrecut.ro/2007/12/1980-1989-amintiri-de-atunci/#comments.
Zaqk. Comment # 9. Latrecut.ro, February 17, 2011. Accessed May 28, 2016. http://www.latrecut.ro/2009/01/amintiri-din-acei-ani/#comments.

Archival materials

Archives of the Bucharest Military Court of Appeal (ABMCA). File no. 15/P/1999, "Indictment from 8 of April 1993."
Archives of the Bucharest Military Court of Appeal (ABMCA). File no. 15/P/1999, "Indictment from 7 September 2000."
Archives of the Bulgarian Supreme Court of Justice (ABSCJ). "Accusation Act No. 2 / 1994," 1-5.
Archives of the Bulgarian Supreme Court of Justice (ABSCJ). "Decision No. 3/2002 of the Bulgarian Supreme Court of Justice."
Archive of the Institute for the Investigation of Communist Crimes in Romania (AIICCR). "Answer of the Ministry of Justice regarding the Proposal of the Institute for the Investigation of Communist Crimes in Romania with respect to the modification of the Title XI of the Criminal Code 20 April 2008."
Archive of the Institute for the Investigation of Communist Crimes in Romania (AIICCR). "Proposal regarding the modification of the Title XI of the Criminal Code, 22 February 2008."
Archives of the Romanian Information Service (ASRI). Fond Documentar, File 2487.
Archives of the State Secretariat for Religious Denominations (ASSC). Fond Departamentul Cultelor, Note privind episcopii.
Archives of the State Secretariat for Religious Denominations (ASSC). Fond Justinian Marina, File 2.

Central Historical National Archives (ANIC). Fond Preşedinţia Consiliului de Miniştri – Stenograme (1949–1959), File 2/1947.
Central Historical National Archives (ANIC). Fond Direcţia Generală a Poliţiei, File 36/1943.

CNSAS certificates *(adeverința)*

Adeverința 2512 of July 14, 2015.
Adeverința 480 of May 21, 2015.
Adeverința 479 of May 21, 2015.
Adeverința 1390 of March 21, 2013.
Adeverința 1388 of March 21, 2013.
Adeverința 1386 of March 21, 2013.

Websites

"Amintiri din trecut." Last modified no date. Accessed July 10, 2016. https://etimpu.com/.
"Jocuri din copilarie." Last modified July 30, 2015. Accessed July 10, 2016. http://jocurilecopilariei.blogspot.ro.
"Facut in Romania." Lst modified December 8, 2015. Accessed July 10, 2016. https://facutinromania.wordpress.com/.
"Firme vechi." Last modified September 10, 2011. Accessed July 10, 2016. http://firme-vechi.blogspot.ro/.
"LaTrecut. Amintiri naïve din perioada rosie." Last modified February 27, 2015. Accessed on July 10, 2016. http://www.latrecut.ro/.
"Cutezatorii." Last modified September 16, 2016. Accessed July 10, 2016. http://revistacutezatorii.blogspot.ro/.
"Vederi din trecut." Last modified September 20, 2011. Accessed July 10, 2016. http://vederidintrecut.blogspot.ro/.

Interviews

Alexandru Gussi, personal interview with Teodor Mărieș, Bucharest, September 15. 2013.
Alexandru Gussi, personal interview with Dorin Dobrincu, Bucharest, July 10, 2013.
Cynthia Horne, interviews with members of the CNSAS Collegium, Bucharest, Romania, October 2012.

Cynthia Horne, interview with Mircea Stanescu, historian at the National Archives and formerly with the CNSAS, Bucharest, Romania, October 2012.

Cynthia Horne, interviews with Dr. Dragoş Petrescu, Chairman of the Board, CNSAS, Bucharest, Romania, October 12, 2012.

Cynthia Horne, interviews with Chairman Evtim Kostadinov, Dossier Commission, Sofia, Bulgaria, July 12, 2012.

Cynthia Horne, interview with Alexander Stoyanov, Director Research Vitosha, Sofia, Bulgaria, July 5, 2012.

Cynthia Horne, interview with Dimitar Markov, Senior Analyst/Project Director Anti-corruption and Judicial Reform Unit, Center for the Study of Democracy, Sofia, Bulgaria, July 2, 2012.

Raluca Grosescu, interview with Christian Tomuschat, Berlin, April 24, 2014.

Raluca Grosescu, personal correspondence with Oana Axinia, legal representative of Institute for the Investigation of Communist Crimes in Romania 2008-2013, April 18, 2013.

Raluca Grosescu. interview with Adriana Stamatescu, judge at the Romanian Supreme Court of Justice, Bucharest, April 8, 2013.

Raluca Grosescu. interview with Dan Voinea, military prosecutor in 1982-2009, Bucharest, November 20, 2006.

CONTRIBUTORS

Monica Ciobanu is a Professor of Criminal Justice at Plattsburgh State University of New York, USA. Her research focuses on issues of memory, truth, justice, and democratization in post-communism, especially Romania. Her work appeared in *Europe-Asia Studies*, *Comparative Sociology*, *International Journal of Politics, Culture and Society, Nationalities Papers*, and *Problems of Post-Communism.* She had also contributed to several edited volumes including *Post-Communist Transitional Justice: Lessons from 25 Years of Experience* (edited by Lavinia Stan and Nadya Nedelsky, Cambridge University Press, 2015); *Encyclopedia of Transitional Justice* (3 vols, edited by Lavinia Stan and Nadya Nedelsky, Cambridge University Press, 2013); *International Crime and Justice* (edited by Mangai Natarajan, Cambridge University Press, 2011). In 2014-2015 she received the Chancellor's Award for Excellence in Scholarship and Creative Activities granted by State University of New York. She currently serves on the board of the Society for Romanian Studies.

Agata Fijalkowski is a Senior Lecturer in Law at Lancaster University, the United Kingdom. Her main research interest lies in transitional criminal justice in post-dictatorial and post-conflict states, and she has obtained funding for research in Albania, Poland, Romania and Germany. In 2015, she co-edited *Transitional Criminal Justice in Post-Dictatorial and Post-Conflict Societies* for Intersentia's Series on Transitional Justice. She has written on Polish developments in *From Old Times to New Europe* (Ashgate, 2010), Polish resistance fighters in the *Slavic Review* (2014), the maladministration of justice in communist Europe during 1946-1956, and retroactive justice. Her current research project on 'The Power of Images: Photography, Law and Political Trials' of 1946-1956 considers law as a matter of aesthetics and memory, and seeks to contribute to transitional justice and comparative criminal justice from an interdisciplinary viewpoint. Fijalkowski recently wrote on the life and 1946 trial of the Albanian writer and political dissident, Musine Kokalari.

Raluca Grosescu is an Associate Research Fellow in the Department of History, University of Exeter, the United Kingdom, and a former Director with the Institute for the Investigation of Communist Crimes and the Memory of Romanian Exile, an independent transitional justice agency based in Bucharest, Romania. Among her publications are *Les communistes dans l'après-communisme. Trajectoires de conversion politique de la nomenklatura roumaine après 1989* (Michel Houdiard, 2010), *Justitita penala de tranzitie: de la Nuremberg la postcomunismul romanesc* (*Criminal Transitional Justice from Nurenberg to Post-communist Romania*, co-authored with Raluca Ursachi, Polirom, 2009), and *Transitional Criminal Justice in Post-Dictatorial and Post-Conflict Societies* (co-edited with Agata Fijalkowski, Intersentia, 2015). Grosescu has further authored numerous articles and book chapters on transitional justice issues.

Alexandru Gussi holds a PhD and an MA from Sciences Po in Paris, France. He is a Lecturer in the Department of Political Science, University of Bucharest, Romania, and served as an advisor to President Traian Basescu in 2006-2011. His areas of specialization and research interest are Romanian post-communism, the memory of communism, transitional justice, and comparative politics. His recent publications include *La Roumanie face à son passe communiste. Mémoires et cultures politiques* (Paris: L'Harmattan, 2011); and articles in *Studia Politica: Revista Română de Ştiinţe Politice.*

Duncan Light is Professor at Bournemouth University, the United Kingdom. A cultural geographer with research interests in urban space, power, identity and public memory, he has written on Romania's troubled relationship with Bram Stoker's immortal vampire and 'Dracula tourism' that is grounded in an enduring and alluring place myth of Transylvania as the home of vampires and the supernatural. He has also examined the expectations and performances of Dracula tourists visiting a Transylvania that doesn't quite live up to their expectations! More recently he has become interested in the post-communist mobility of corpses, the growing popularity of graves as tourist sites/sights, and the relationships between tourism and national identity in Romania. Light is the editor of *Post-Communist Romania: Coming to Terms with Transition* (2001), and *The Dracula Dilemma: Tourism, Identity and the State in Romania* (2012).

Cristina Petrescu is Associate Professor in the Department of Political Science, University of Bucharest, Romania. She authored *From Robin Hood to Don Quixote: Resistance and Dissent in Communist Romania* (Editura Enciclopedică, 2013), contributed to the *Final Report of the Presidential Commission for the Analysis of the Communist Dictatorship in Romania* (Humanitas, 2007), and co-edited *Nation-Building and Conflicting Identities: Romanian and Hungarian Case Studies* (Regio Books, 2001). She has written on communism and the memory of this recent past in Central and Eastern Europe in books and peer-reviewed journals published in the United States, the United Kingdom, Spain, Germany, Poland and Hungary.

Dragoş Petrescu is Professor in the Department of Political Science, University of Bucharest, Romania, and President of the Board of the National Council for the Study of Securitate Archives. He has authored *Entangled Revolutions: The Breakdown of the Communist Regimes in East-Central Europe* (Editura Enciclopedică, 2014), and *Explaining the Romanian Revolution of 1989: Culture, Structure, and Contingency* (Editura Enciclopedică, 2010). He has contributed to the *Final Report of the Presidential Commission for the Analysis of the Communist Dictatorship in Romania* (Humanitas, 2007), and co-edited *Nation-Building and Contested Identities: Romanian and Hungarian Case Studies* (Regio Books, 2001). He has published on the communist past and transitional justice in Central and Eastern Europe in peer-reviewed journals and volumes in the United States, Great Britain, Germany, Spain, Poland and Hungary.

Delia Popescu is Chair of the Department of Political Science and Director of the Legal Studies Program and the Peace and Global Studies Program at Le Moyne College, the United States. Her areas of interest include Eastern European political theory as it relates to dissidence, resistance, totalitarianism and political ideology, Vaclav Havel's political thought, Romani studies, Roma minority in the European Union, as well as critical discourse analysis. She is the author of *Political Action in Vaclav Havel's Thought: The Responsibility of Resistance* (Lexington Books, 2011).

Caterina Preda is Senior Lecturer in the Department of Political Science, University of Bucharest, Romania. Her research centers on art and politics in the modern dictatorships of Latin America and Eastern Europe, and the art of memorialization in the two regions. She has authored peer-reviewed articles and chapters in volumes published with Routledge and Palgrave. Preda is currently working on a book that compares case studies drawn from the Southern Cone and Central and Eastern Europe from the perspective of the relationship between art and politics.

Lavinia Stan is Chair of the Political Science Department at St. Francis Xavier University, Canada. She has worked mainly on transitional justice, and religion and politics with a focus on Central and Eastern Europe. She is the President of the Society for Romanian Studies, an Associate Editor for the peer-reviewed *Women's Studies International Forum*, and former member of the Scientific Council of the Institute for the Investigation of Communist Crimes and the Memory of Romania Exile (in Bucharest). Her books include *Encyclopedia of Transitional Justice* (3 volumes), *Post-Communist Transitional Justice at 25*, and *Transitional Justice in Post-Communist Romania* (all published with Cambridge University Press in 2013, 2014, and 2015), *Religion and Politics in Post-Communist Romania* and *Church, State and Democracy in Expanding Europe* (both co-authored with Lucian Turcescu, Oxford University Press, 2007 and 2011), as well as *Transitional Justice in Eastern Europe and the Former Soviet Union* (Routledge, 2009).

Cristian Tileagă is Senior Lecturer at Loughborough University, the United Kingdom. He has a general interest in social memory and transitional justice, discourse analysis, political psychology, and inter-disciplinarity. He is the co-author of *Psychology and History: Interdisciplinary Explorations* (Cambridge University Press, 2014), and the author of *Political Psychology: Critical Perspectives* (Cambridge University Press, 2013), and *The Nature of Prejudice: Society, Discrimination and Moral Exclusion* (Routledge, 2015). Tileagă's scholarly articles, which discuss important themes related to memory, have appeared in numerous English-language peer-reviewed scholarly journals.

Lucian Turcescu is Professor and the Graduate Program Director, Department of Theological Studies at Concordia University, Canada. He has done research and published in early Christianity, religion and politics, and ecumenism. He co-authored (with Lavinia Stan) *Church, State, and Democracy in Expanding Europe* and *Religion and Politics in Post-communist Romania* (Oxford University Press, 2011 and 2007); co-edited *The Reception and Interpretation of the Bible in Late Antiquity* (E.J. Brill, 2008); and single-authored *Gregory of Nyssa and the Concept of Divine Persons* (Oxford University Press, 2005). He is an Associate Editor of the *Journal of Ecumenical Studies* and *Theoforum* (formerly *Eglise et Theologie*), Past President of the Canadian Society of Patristic Studies (2004-2008), former member of the Board of Directors, Canadian Corporation for Studies in Religion, and the Corporation's combined program director (1999-2002). His current research project, generously funded by the Social Sciences and Humanities Research Council of Canada, focuses on the relationship of religion and transitional justice in post-communist Romania.

Cristian Vasile is Senior Researcher at the "Nicolae Iorga" History Institute of the Romanian Academy, specializing in the history of Romanian communism, religion and politics, and the politics of remembrance in post-communist Europe. His recent publications include *Viaţa intelectuală şi artistică în primul deceniu al regimului Ceauşescu. 1965–1974* [The Intellectual and Artistic Life in the First Decade of Ceausescu Regime, 1965-74] (Humanitas, 2015), *Politicile culturale comuniste în timpul regimului Gheorghiu-Dej* [The Communist Cultural Policies During the Gheorghiu-Dej Regime] (Humanitas, 2011), as well as peer-reviewed articles and book chapters.

Craig Young is Reader in the Division of Geography and Environmental Management at Manchester Metropolitan University, the United Kingdom. His research interests focus on the cultural geographies and politics of identity in the context of post-socialist transformation, particularly in Central and Eastern Europe. He is the co-editor of *Cosmopolitan Urbanism* (2006) and co-author of a number of papers in journals such as *Nationalities Papers*, *Europe-Asia Studies*, *Transactions of the Institute of British Geographers* on issues of post-socialist identity formation.

INDEX